Modernizing China's Military

A

Philip E. Lilienthal

■   ■   ■

BOOK

The Philip E. Lilienthal imprint
honors special books
in commemoration of a man whose work
at the University of California Press from 1954 to 1979
was marked by dedication to young authors
and to high standards in the field of Asian Studies.
Friends, family, authors, and foundations have together
endowed the Lilienthal Fund, which enables the Press
to publish under this imprint selected books
in a way that reflects the taste and judgment
of a great and beloved editor.

Modernizing China's Military

Progress, Problems, and Prospects

DAVID SHAMBAUGH

University of California Press

BERKELEY   LOS ANGELES   LONDON

University of California Press
Berkeley and Los Angeles, California

University of California Press, Ltd.
London, England

First paperback printing 2004
© 2002 by the Regents of the University of California

Library of Congress Cataloging-in-Publication Data

Shambaugh, David L.
    Modernizing China's military : progress, problems, and prospects /
David Shambaugh.
        p.   cm.
    Includes bibliographical references and index.
    ISBN 0-520-24238-6 (pbk : alk. paper)
        1. China—Armed forces.   2. China—Defenses.   I. Title.
US835.S465   2002
355'.00951'0905—dc21   2002002310

Manufactured in the United States of America

13   12   11   10   09   08   07   06   05   04
10   9   8   7   6   5   4   3   2   1

Dedicated to the memory of Michel C. Oksenberg

Other Books by David Shambaugh

China and Europe, 1949–1995 (1996)
Beautiful Imperialist: China Perceives America, 1972–1990 (1991)
The Making of a Premier: Zhao Ziyang's Provincial Career (1984)

EDITED VOLUMES

Making China Policy: Lessons from the Bush and Clinton Administrations,
   edited by Ramon H. Myers, Michel C. Oksenberg, and David Shambaugh
   (2001)

Is China Unstable? edited by David Shambaugh (2000)

The Modern Chinese State, edited by David Shambaugh (2000)

China's Military Faces the Future, edited by James R. Lilley and David
   Shambaugh (1999)

The China Reader: The Reform Era, edited by Orville Schell and David
   Shambaugh (1999)

Contemporary Taiwan, edited by David Shambaugh (1998)

China's Military in Transition, edited by David Shambaugh and Richard H.
   Yang (1997)

Deng Xiaoping: Portrait of a Chinese Statesman, edited by David Shambaugh (1995)

Greater China: The Next Superpower? edited by David Shambaugh (1995)

Chinese Foreign Policy: Theory and Practice, edited by Thomas W. Robinson and David Shambaugh (1994)

American Studies of Contemporary China, edited by David Shambaugh
   (1993)

Contents

Illustrations

FIGURES

MAPS

TABLES

Acronyms and Abbreviations

AAA   anti-aircraft artillery

AAM   air-to-air missile

ABM   Anti-Ballistic Missile Treaty

ACDA   Arms Control and Disarmament Agency

AMS   Academy of Military Sciences

AOR   area of responsibility

APC   armored personnel carrier

APEC   Asia Pacific Economic Cooperation

ARF   ASEAN Regional Forum

ASEAN Association of Southeast Asian Nations

ASW   anti-submarine warfare

AVIC   Aviation Industries of China

AWAC   airborne warning and control

B-ISDN broadband integrated services digital networks

BWC   Biological Weapons Convention

CASC   China Aerospace Corporation

C^4I command, control, communications, computers, and intelligence

CBM   confidence-building measures

CBSM   confidence-building and security measures

CCP   Chinese Communist Party

CDIC   China's defense-industrial complex

CDSTIC China Defense Science and Technology Information Center

CEP	circular error probability
CGE	central government expenditure
CIISS	China Institute of International Strategic Studies
CINCPAC	U.S. Commander-in-Chief of the Pacific
CIS	Commonwealth of Independent States
CMC	Central Military Commission
CNNC	China National Nuclear Corporation
COIC	China Ordnance Industry Corporation
COSTIND	Commission on Science, Technology, and Industry for National Defense
CSSC	China State Shipbuilding Corporation
CTBT	Comprehensive Test Ban Treaty
CVBG	[aircraft] carrier battle group
DCT	defense consultation talks
DDG	destroyer with guided missiles
DGA	Délégation générale pour l'armament (France)
DIC	Discipline Inspection Commission
DoD	Department of Defense
EASR	*East Asia Strategy Report*
ECM	electronic countermeasures
ELINT	electronic intelligence
EMP	electromagnetic pulse
EU	European Union
EW	electronic warfare
FAO	U.S. Foreign Area Officer Program
FBIS	Foreign Broadcast Information Service
FBIS–CHI	Foreign Broadcast Information Service–China (*Daily Report*)
FFG	guided missile frigate
FISS	Foundation of International Strategic Studies
FMS	foreign military sales
G-7	Group of Seven (the United States, Great Britain, France, Germany, Italy, Canada, and Japan)
GA	group army
GAD	General Armaments Department

GLD	General Logistics Department
GLD/FB	General Logistics Department/Finance Bureau
GMD	Guomindang (Chinese Nationalist Party)
GNP	gross national product
GPD	General Political Department
GPS	global positioning satellite
GRSD	General Rear Services Department
GSD	General Staff Department
GVIO	gross value of industrial output
HEAT	high explosive anti-tank
HE-FRAG	high explosive fragmentation
HqAF	Headquarters Air Force
IBACS	Integrated Battlefield Area Communications System
ICBM	intercontinental-range ballistic missile
IFV	infantry fighting vehicles
IGO	intergovernmental organizations
IISS	International Institute of Strategic Studies
IMF	International Monetary Fund
IRBM	intermediate-range ballistic missile
IT	information technology
IW	information warfare
JCS	Joint Chiefs of Staff
JPRS	Joint Publications Research Service
JSDF	Japan Self-Defense Forces
LACM	land-attack cruise missile
LAD	*Jiefangjun Bao* (Liberation Army Daily)
LOW	launch-on-warning
LSD	landing ship dock
LST	landing ship tank
MBT	main battle tank
MCTL-WST	*Militarily Critical Technologies List–Weapon Systems Technologies*
MIRV	multiple independent reentry vehicles
MMBs	ministries of machine building
MMCA	Maritime Military Consultative Agreement

MND	Ministry of National Defense
MoD	Ministry of Defense
MOST	Ministry of State Science and Technology
MPS	Minister of Public Security
MR	military region
MRAF	Military Region Air Force
MRBM	medium-range ballistic missile
MTO	Military Training Outline
MTCR	Missile Technology Control Regime
NATO	North Atlantic Treaty Organization
NBC	nuclear, biological, and chemical weapons
NCOs	noncommissioned officers
NDL	National Defense Law
NDU	National Defense University
NFU	No First Use
NGO	nongovernmental organizations
NMD	National Missile Defense
NORINCO	Northern Industries Corporation
NPC	National People's Congress
NSC	New Security Concept
OB	order of battle
O & M	operations and maintenance
OSD	Office of the Secretary of Defense
OTH	over-the-horizon
PACOM	U.S. Pacific Command
PAFC	People's Armed Forces Committees
PAP	People's Armed Police
PGMs	precision-guided munitions
PKO	peacekeeping operations
PLA	People's Liberation Army
PLAAF	PLA Air Force
PLAN	PLA Navy
PLANAF	PLA naval air force
PME	professional military education

PPP	purchasing power parity
PRC	People's Republic of China
RDT&E	research, development, testing, and evaluation
RMA	revolution in military affairs
RMB	renminbi (Chinese currency)
ROC	Republic of China
RRUs	rapid reaction units
SAM	surface-to-air missile
SCOSTIND	State Commission of Science, Technology, and Industry for National Defense
SETC	State Economic and Trade Commission
SIGINT	signals intelligence
SIPRI	Stockholm International Peace Research Institute
SLBM	submarine-launched ballistic missile
SNDMC	State National Defense Mobilization Commission
SOE	state-owned enterprise
SPH	self-propelled howitzers
SRBM	short-range ballistic missile
SSM	surface-to-surface missile
SSN	nuclear-powered attack submarine
SSBN	nuclear ballistic missile submarine
TEL	transporter-erector-launcher
TERCOM	terrain contour mapping
TMD	theater missile defense
TO&E	table of organization and equipment
TRA	Taiwan Relations Act
UAV	unmanned aerial vehicles
WMD	weapons of mass destruction
ZBB	zero-based budgeting

Preface and Acknowledgments

This study joins a growing volume of publications on the Chinese military. When I embarked on it, I felt the need to contribute a study that was comprehensive in scope, covering as many aspects of China's contemporary military as possible in one volume, because it had been a decade since the publication of Ellis Joffe's *The Chinese Army after Mao*, the last book to do so.[1] In the midst of my writing, however, four other generally comprehensive and single-authored monographs were published,[2] as well as a number of other edited overview volumes,[3] and a smaller number of sector-specific

1. Ellis Joffe, *The Chinese Army after Mao* (Cambridge, Mass.: Harvard University Press, 1987).

2. Mel Gurtov and Byong-Moo Hwang, *China's Security: The New Roles of the Military* (Boulder, Colo.: Lynne Rienner, 1998); You Ji, *The Armed Forces of China* (New York: I. B. Tauris, 1999); Solomon Karmel, *China and the People's Liberation Army* (New York: St. Martin's Press, 2000); and Srikanth Kondapalli, *China's Military: The PLA in Transition* (New Delhi: Knowledge World Press, 1999).

3. David Shambaugh and Richard H. Yang, eds., *China's Military in Transition* (Oxford: Clarendon Press, 1997); James Lilley and Chuck Downs, eds., *Crisis in the Taiwan Strait* (Washington, D.C.: American Enterprise Institute and National Defense University Press, 1997); James Lilley and David Shambaugh, eds., *China's Military Faces the Future* (Armonk, N.Y., and Washington, D.C.: M. E. Sharpe and AEI Press, 1999); James C. Mulvenon and Richard H. Yang, eds., *The People's Liberation Army in the Information Age* (Santa Monica, Calif.: RAND Corporation 1999); James Mulvenon and Richard H. Yang, eds., *Seeking Truth from Facts: A Retrospective on Chinese Military Studies in the Post-Mao Era* (Santa Monica, Calif.: RAND Corporation, 2000); Larry Wortzel, ed., *The Chinese Armed Forces in the 21st Century* (Carlisle Barracks, Pa.: U.S. Army War College Strategic Studies Institute, 2000); Susan Puska, ed., *The People's Liberation Army after Next* (Carlisle Barracks, Pa.: U.S. Army War College Strategic Studies Institute, 2000); Andrew Scobell, ed., *The Costs of Conflict: The Impact on China of a Future War* (Carlisle Barracks, Pa.: U.S.

studies that have appeared on China's air force, nuclear forces, and naval forces.[4] Although it is comprehensive in scope and primarily intended for the specialist on Chinese military affairs, I have also endeavored to write this study for the reader who is not expert on military matters. In some areas, however, this is not possible, as the technicalities of the subject demand specificity. Finally, I have attempted to produce a study of policy relevance— particularly for the United States. Policy implications are implicit throughout the text, and the concluding chapter offers explicit policy recommendations for the U.S. government's dealings with the People's Liberation Army (PLA).

It is my hope that this volume will help inform the public and professionals alike, not only about the importance and complexities of the PLA, but also about the necessity for the United States and China's neighbors in East and South Asia to coexist with a more powerful Chinese military. That the PLA will grow more powerful is not in question. The intangibles are:

- How quickly the PLA will modernize

- How effectively the PLA can integrate improvements in hardware with the "software" demands of training and command and control

- How the PLA's new power will be put to use

- What underlying strategy and national interests guide China's resource allocation and the use of coercion and force

- How the United States and other nations on China's periphery will adapt and respond to growing Chinese military capability

The policy consequences of China's military modernization for the United States and China's neighbors are multiple and profound, and they truly involve questions of the global balance of power, war, and peace.

I also hope that this study will stimulate others to write both synthetic

---

Army War College Strategic Studies Institute, 2001); Michael E. Brown et al., eds., *The Rise of China* (Cambridge, Mass.: MIT Press, 2000).

4. On the air force, see Kenneth Allen, Glenn Krumel, and Jonathan D. Pollack, *China's Air Force Enters the 21st Century* (Santa Monica, Calif.: RAND Corporation, 1995). On the nuclear forces, see Mark A. Stokes, *China's Strategic Modernization: Implications for the United States* (Carlisle Barracks, Pa.: U.S. Army War College Strategic Studies Institute, 1999); Robert A. Manning, Ronald Montaperto, and Brad Roberts, *China, Nuclear Weapons, and Arms Control: A Preliminary Assessment* (New York: Council on Foreign Relations, 2000); Ming Zhang, *China's Changing Nuclear Posture* (Washington, D.C.: Carnegie Endowment for International Peace,

comprehensive studies and more specialized monographs on different aspects of the PLA. This is a field rich in data and ripe for research—yet lacking in trained investigators. In particular, the PLA studies community needs the infusion of a new generation of analysts and scholars. Although the field has really come of age in recent years,[5] the PLA studies community needs new blood and particularly individuals trained in *both* Chinese language and security/defense studies skills.

This book had a long gestation. Over the course of a decade, it was completed as I suspect many are written—a little bit here and a little bit there. Two complications slowed things down. First, my subject was a moving target, and I constantly needed to update and rewrite based not only on the evolution of the PLA but also on the appearance of new materials or perspectives. Second, I needed to educate myself about a number of complex aspects of this subject matter—particularly technology, weapons, and force structure. Never having had formal training in these areas, and never having served in the military myself, I had to read a great deal and rely on numerous more knowledgeable colleagues to educate me along the way. For someone trained in area studies and political science, it has truly been a learning experience, and I have developed a real appreciation of those engaged in the very specialized fields of strategic and defense studies.

Although the process was lengthy and often tortuous, preparing this study has been immensely rewarding. The more I dug into the subject matter, the more complex and fascinating it became. Not only was it intellectually engaging, but it also opened up to me a whole new community of professional colleagues—many of whom have become true and lasting friends. This was an unforeseen consequence from which I shall continue to benefit for years to come.

Many individuals and institutions helped to bring this book to fruition. Among these, I would first like to single out the late Michel Oksenberg, a

---

1999). On the navy, see Bernard Cole, *The Great Wall at Sea: China's Navy Enters the 21st Century* (Annapolis, Md.: Naval Institute Press, 2001); Srikanth Kondapalli, *China's Naval Power* (New Delhi: Knowledge World Press, 2001).

5. See David Shambaugh, "PLA Studies Today: A Maturing Field," in James Mulvenon and Richard H. Yang, eds., *The People's Liberation Army in the Information Age* (Santa Monica, Calif.: RAND Corporation, 1999); James Mulvenon and Richard H. Yang, eds., *Seeking Truth from Facts: A Retrospective on Chinese Military Studies in the Post-Mao Era* (Santa Monica, Calif.: RAND Corporation, 2001); June Teufel Dreyer, "State of the Field Report: Research on the Chinese Military," *AccessAsia Review* 1, no. 1 (Summer 1997): 5–30.

giant in the field of Chinese studies and an important influence in Sino-American relations until his premature death in February 2001.[6] Over the years I learned a great deal from Mike—in government service, academe, professional settings, and personally. Our careers and lives were intertwined for a quarter of a century, and throughout he provided steady support, wise counsel, friendship, and a good sense of humor. We had many interests in common—from China to bluegrass music and Michigan football. Mike continually pushed his students and colleagues for precision, accuracy, and relevance. His encyclopedic memory and ability to see the big picture and ask the right questions distinguished his from many lesser minds. This particular study never would have been completed without the support he gave for a grant that afforded me a year of sabbatical writing. In large part, I also owe my initial interest in Chinese military affairs, the Chinese policy process, and the study of Sino-American relations to him. For all of this, I admiringly and respectfully dedicate this study to his memory.

Secondly, I thank my colleagues in the field of PLA studies. I have been laboring in this field on and off since the late 1970s, and throughout I have come to enjoy many friendships with fellow students of the "men in green." It is a generally collegial community, even though there are sometimes sharp differences of opinion. At least twice annually, in recent years, we have retreated to remote conference sites to analyze the latest developments and reforms in the Chinese military and to enjoy fraternity. Intellectually, as well as personally, I owe a tremendous debt to these colleagues.

I have also benefited greatly from discussions over the years with members of the U.S. Defense Attaché's office in Beijing, particularly General Michael T. Byrnes, General Karl Eikenberry, and General Neil Sealock, and with Colonel John Corbett and Colonel Mark Stokes on the China Country Desk in the Office of the Secretary of Defense (OSD) at the Pentagon. I was fortunate to have the opportunity of serving during 1999–2000 as a consultant to OSD/China and observing the process of U.S.-China military relations up close. William Perry, Ashton Carter, Joseph Nye, and Robert Blackwill also provided opportunities to interact with a unique group of American officials and Chinese military officers in several different settings through the Harvard-Stanford Preventive Defense Project and the Kennedy School Executive Program for Senior Chinese Military Officers.

I have also richly benefited from readings of the entire manuscript by members of a study group convened by the China Policy Program at George

6. See David Shambaugh, "In Memoriam: Michel C. Oksenberg," *Washington Journal of Modern China* 7, no. 1 (Spring 2001): 111–18.

Washington University. I am indebted to my friend and valued colleague Bates Gill, who organized and chaired the sessions.[7] The careful readings provided by participants, the dialogue, and the critical feedback proved extremely helpful in sharpening my arguments, fine-tuning the manuscript, and saving me from numerous egregious errors. Harlan Jencks and John Frankenstein were kind enough to read selected chapters and to offer many constructive suggestions. Paul Godwin, Allen Whiting, and Ellis Joffe also provided valuable and trenchant suggestions as external peer reviewers for the University of California Press, strengthening the manuscript significantly. At the University of California Press, too, Sheila Levine, the book's sponsoring editor, exhibited professionalism and patience throughout, and the rest of the editorial team were also first-rate.

I have also had the benefit of some superb student research assistants in the Elliott School of International Affairs at George Washington University. Micah Rapoport, Thomas Sisk, Yisuo Tseng, Cynthia Yung, and Li Zheng all slogged through mountains of material and helped to render it more orderly and comprehensible to me. In the process, I hope to have stimulated some of them to pursue careers in the Chinese security field. My trustworthy executive assistant, Deborah Toy, was of enormous help in preparing many of the graphics used in the study—as well as running my professional life and "keeping the world away" during the time I spent writing at home.

No study of this nature could materialize without significant institutional support. The Elliott School and Dean Harry Harding have offered a collegial and stimulating environment for research and teaching. The Sigur Center for Asian Studies in the Elliott School provided intellectual, moral, and logistical support in many ways. I have also benefited from discussions and the collegiality at The Brookings Institution Center for Northeast Asian Policy Studies (CNAPS) and Foreign Policy Studies Program, where I have enjoyed my tenure as a nonresident senior fellow since 1998. Overseas, I have enjoyed the hospitality of several institutions where I have resided and conducted library research for this study: the International Institute of Strategic Studies and Royal Institute of International Affairs in London, England; the Stockholm International Peace Research Institute; the Sinological Institutes at the University of Heidelberg in Germany and the University of Leiden in Holland; the Universities Service Center at the Chinese Univer-

---

7. Members of the study group included Bates Gill, Eric McVadon, John Corbett, Lonnie Henley, James Mulvenon, Dennis Blasko, David Finkelstein, Bud Cole, and Ken Allen.

sity of Hong Kong; and the Institute of International Relations at National Cheng-chi University in Taiwan. This study has also benefited from numerous interviews conducted in PLA institutions, and visits to several military facilities and bases in China, during three trips under the auspices of the China Institute of International Strategic Studies (CIISS). I wish to thank the staff at CIISS, its chairman General Xiong Guangkai, and deputy chairman General (ret.) Chen Kaizeng, for their assistance. Two further research visits under the sponsorship of the Foreign Ministry's China Institute of International Studies (CIIS) also provided further interviews and materials, and I wish to thank President and Ambassador Yang Chengxu for CIIS's hospitality and logistical help. Unfortunately, I cannot publicly credit several colleagues in the PLA who have taken much time to discuss the topics of this study with me and to comment on parts of the manuscript. Perhaps some day the PLA will become confident and transparent enough for such information to be more public and such individuals can be duly credited.

This study also would not have come to fruition without the significant financial support of the Smith Richardson Foundation, which afforded a year of sabbatical research and writing, travel to China, and research assistants. I am most grateful to the foundation's board and Vice President Marin Strmecki. Additional grants from the Chiang Ching-kuo Foundation and Pacific Cultural Foundation also facilitated valuable travel and research in China, Taiwan, Japan, and Hong Kong. Finally, George Washington University Faculty Facilitation Grants provided supplemental support. Ikuko Turner helped to process all of the attendant accounts and paperwork resulting from these grants, for which I am in her debt.

Last, but not least, I owe a special debt of gratitude to my family. My wife Ingrid has supported me in all manner throughout this lengthy project. Our two wonderful boys, Christopher and Alexander, have developed a healthy interest in "Chinese armymen" but have been deprived of a father for significant periods while I was either overseas or sequestered in my study. Now there should be more time for the things that really matter in life. Finally, I wish to acknowledge the support of my late father throughout this project and during his ninety-five years of life. He took a great interest in the progress of this book and never seemed bored when I tried to describe its minutiae. He always admonished me: "Just put other things aside and finish it!" I only wish he had lived to see its completion.

David Shambaugh
Washington, D.C.

A Note on Sources

Multiple sources were used in this study. There was certainly no dearth of materials and data available. If anything, the problem for active research in PLA studies today is to gain effective bibliographic control over the multitude of sources.[1] This volume taps into six basic types of sources.

The first and most extensively used are Chinese-language books and periodicals. Multiple trips to China during the research and writing phases of the project enabled me to acquire more than 300 books and numerous periodicals dealing with the PLA. The books included both specialized monographs *(zhuanti shu)* and more comprehensive almanacs or encyclopedias *(quan shu* or *da cidian)*. As many PLA periodicals are sold only in current issues at bookstores, one must resort to other methods to secure back issues and complete runs. Moreover, the vast majority of PLA periodicals are designated for restricted circulation within the military *(jun nei faxing)* or are not available to foreigners *(neibu faxing)*. Even those whose circulation is not restricted, like the *Guofang Daxue Xuebao* (National Defense Univer-

---

1. For two excellent, relatively comprehensive, and up-to-date bibliographical assessments of materials available on the PLA, see Evan Medeiros, "Undressing the Dragon: Researching the PLA through Open Source Exploitation," and Taylor Fravel, "The Revolution in Research Affairs: Online Sources and the Study of the PLA" (papers presented at the 2001 CAPS/RAND PLA Conference, June 21–24, 2001, Washington, D.C.). I previously undertook more preliminary efforts in my "Appendix: A Bibliographical Essay on New Sources for the Study of China's Foreign Relations and National Security," in Thomas W. Robinson and David Shambaugh, eds., *Chinese Foreign Policy: Theory and Practice* (Oxford: Clarendon Press, 1994); and "PLA Studies: A Maturing Field," in James C. Mulvenon and Richard H. Yang, eds., *The PLA and the Information Age* (Santa Monica, Calif.: RAND Corporation, 2000), pp. 7–21; and "PLA Strategy and Doctrine: Recommendations for Future Research" (paper presented at the conference "Chinese Military Affairs: The State of the Field," October 26–27, 2000, National Defense University, Washington, D.C.).

sity Journal), cannot be subscribed to outside China. Although not always identified as such in this study, a large number of the sources used were restricted-circulation materials. One must also scour magazine stands on street corners and in train stations and airports in China, which frequently carry PLA and military periodicals that are not available by subscription. The same applies to many *jun nei* or *neibu* books.

These books and periodicals represent just the tip of the iceberg of available material on the PLA in China, and they also belie the common belief that there is no military transparency in China. All one has to do is be able to read Chinese and physically gain access to these materials. To be sure, many data remain that are not evident in these books and periodicals, and the PLA does a good job of protecting its secrets, but there is a tremendous amount of information readily available in these publications. Regrettably, foreign government translation services like the U.S. Foreign Broadcast Information Service spend virtually no time and resources translating such books or parts of them. FBIS translation of Chinese military newspapers and journals is little better.

The second set of sources used are secondary analyses of the PLA generally and of its many specialized aspects. The PLA studies field has grown considerably in the past decade in terms of both quantity and quality. While still a relatively small and insular field, the quality of analysis by active scholars and private sector specialists is quite high and improving noticeably over time. This can be judged, for example, not only from the annual volumes of conference proceedings from the two annual meetings on the PLA sponsored by the American Enterprise Institute and its partners (the Strategic Studies Institute of the U.S. Army War College in recent years) and the Council on Advanced Policy Studies in Taiwan and its partners (the RAND Corporation in recent years), but also from the rising number of PLA and China security articles appearing in Western scholarly and policy journals.

Primary data and assessments in leading defense and security publications were a third source used. These included, of course, the many publications of Jane's Information Group,[2] the Greenhill Military Manuals,[3] and

---

2. *Jane's Fighting Ships; Jane's Strategic Systems; Jane's Fighter Aircraft; Jane's Warship Recognition Guide; Jane's Tank Recognition Guide; Jane's Defense Weekly;* and *Jane's Intelligence Review.*

3. Examples include T. J. O'Malley, *Artillery Guns and Rocket Systems* (London: Greenhill Books, 1994); Michael J. H. Taylor, *Close Air Support: Armed Helicopters and Ground Attack Aircraft* (London: Greenhill Books/Lionel Leventhal Ltd, 1996); Alan K. Russell, *Modern Battle Tanks and Support Vehicles* (London: Greenhill Books/Lionel Leventhal Ltd, 1997).

a number of other such specialized volumes. Of course, the annual volumes of *The Military Balance,* published by the International Institute for Strategic Studies in London, and the annual *SIPRI Yearbook,* published by the Stockholm International Peace Research Institute, were invaluable sources. SIPRI also publishes specialized studies on the arms industry and arms trade, which have included volumes and chapters on China. Specialized journals such as the *Asian Defense Reporter* and *Asian Defense Monthly* also sometimes contain useful information on the PLA. In recent years, the U.S. Department of Defense has begun to publish an annual assessment of the PLA, as mandated by Congress, and this too contains valuable information. The *National Defense Report* published biannually since 1992 by Taiwan's Ministry of Defense (Taiwan's Defense White Paper) is also very informative. China's own defense White Papers, of which two have now been published, are of considerably less empirical value, even if they do represent incremental steps forward in PLA transparency.[4] A final set of sources in this category are the annual *Directory of PRC Military Personalities* and the monthly *PLA Activities Report* and *DSTI Monthly Report* published by Serold Hawaii, Inc. The former is an annual catalogue of hundreds of leading PLA personnel and main organizations, while the latter two publications carefully scan the Chinese military media and Hong Kong press and categorize reports by functional subject area in a 30–40 page report every month.

A fourth illuminating source was provided by over fifty interviews conducted with PLA officers. The vast majority of these discussions took place in China, with some in America and Europe. My questions varied depending on the individual's expertise, the chapter I was currently working on, and the topics of current concern. Interpreters were never used, so any mistakes of translation are my own (this disclaimer applies to the translations of most published data used in this study as well). Wherever possible, I have listed the individual's institution and the date of the interview, but in some cases, I have intentionally omitted the institution so as not to identify the individual. In almost all cases, I have refrained from identifying the individual by name, even when permission to do so was granted, so as not to compromise the source or endanger the individual. I also did some interviewing on Taiwan with knowledgeable individuals, but these interviews were much less valuable than anticipated.

Visits I have paid to PLA bases were a fifth source of information. Although these were not terribly illuminating in themselves, inasmuch as each

---

4. David Shambaugh, "Here Is a Welcome Shift by China toward Military Transparency," *International Herald Tribune,* October 24, 2000.

was to a "showcase" unit, I did gain insights into living and training conditions, weaponry, and the soldiers and officers with whom we spoke.

A sixth source of information was the growing number of Internet websites on global military and security affairs, as well as some devoted exclusively to the PLA.[5] Those of the U.S. Department of Defense, National Resources Defense Council, Federation of American Scientists, Center for Nonproliferation Studies of the Monterey Institute of International Studies, Center for Defense Information, and the Commonwealth Institute proved particularly bountiful. Of the small but growing number of PLA-specific websites, by far the best is James Mulvenon's China Security Homepage (http://mehampton/chinasec.html).

Finally, libraries provided another source (but not a category) of data. The University Services Center at the Chinese University of Hong Kong has a fair collection of books on the PLA, but it also holds the widest variety of PLA journals accessible to foreign researchers. The Institute of International Relations Library at National Cheng-chi University in Taiwan has an unparalleled clippings file on the PLA (as well as other subjects) from mainland newspapers and periodicals. To my knowledge, the library of the Sinological Institute at Heidelberg University in Germany has the only complete collection of *Jiefangjun Bao* available outside China. In the United States, the Hoover Institution at Stanford University, the Center for Chinese Studies library at the University of California, Berkeley, and the library at the Fairbank Center for East Asian Research at Harvard University each have significant holdings of books on the PLA, but none of these parallels the newly established China Security Documentation Center at Gelman Library at the George Washington University.

I have drawn on all of these in the course of this study. Of course, information from such a multitude of sources is by no means necessarily consistent or always accurate. Contradictions and misstatements of fact abound. However, I have spent a lot of time cross-checking sources and checking with knowledgeable experts to verify questionable data or assertions, and I therefore hope to have written a book that is as close to being fully accurate as is humanly possible. Any remaining errors of translation, data, or analysis are my own.

5. For excellent surveys of these, see Fravel, "Revolution in Research Affairs," and Kathleen Walsh, "Chinese Military Affairs Online," *Washington Journal of Modern China* 6, no. 2 (Fall 2000): 97–106.

1 Introduction

In early February 1991, China's High Command was stunned to realize just how far behind modern militaries the People's Liberation Army had fallen. The opening days of the Gulf War convinced PLA analysts that they were witnessing a revolution in military affairs (RMA). American stealth bombers penetrated Iraqi airspace undetected to strike their targets in Baghdad and elsewhere with impunity, while the allied naval armada sat comfortably offshore in the Persian Gulf, well outside the range of Iraqi defenses, launching wave after wave of air strikes and cruise missile attacks. The surgical bombing substantially degraded Iraqi air defenses, while electromagnetic warfare attacks blinded command and control networks. Allied information warfare experts spread viruses into Iraqi computers, scrambling software programs and causing confusion.

With its intelligence eyes and ears incapacitated and its air defenses knocked out, Iraq had no effective defenses against carrier-based air strikes or the saturation bombing of the elite Republican Guards by B-52 and B-1 bombers (which flew round-the-clock missions). Once the allied ground invasion began, Iraqi tanks (ironically, many of them of Chinese origin) became easy fodder for the far more advanced allied tanks, which could target them with laser rangefinders and used night vision equipment to illuminate the desert battlefield. In the infantry offensive that followed, allied units (which were linked to each other by means of global positioning systems, or GPS) quickly decimated Iraqi ground forces. Finally, when Saddam Hussein was forced to play his trump card—Scud missiles potentially armed with biological and chemical weapons—American antimissile defenses were able to intercept many of them in flight after calculating trajectory and targeting coordinates and relaying them to Patriot missile battery commanders via satellite within minutes of the Scud launches.

The Gulf War, with its awesome display of firepower, stealth, electronics, computers, and satellites, revealed that warfare had made a quantum leap into a new era. It was a profound shock to the PLA, but it was not the first time that the Chinese brass had been forced to acknowledge their military shortcomings. Twelve years earlier, during China's punitive attack on Vietnam, the PLA found it difficult to carry out a modest cross-border incursion to subdue a few small cities and suffered enormous casualties against smaller, albeit experienced, opposition.[1] The Chinese army had proven incapable of carrying out a coordinated ground assault from three directions. Command and communications were disjointed, and Chinese forces fell victim to their own "friendly fire." Nor did the PLA bring any air power to bear on their adversaries. As a result, battle-hardened Vietnamese troops were the ones who "taught lessons" to the PLA.[2]

The weaponry that the allied forces threw at Iraq, which was generations ahead of what China had encountered on the Vietnam border in 1979, forced China's generals to the harsh realizations that a new, high-technology era of warfare had dawned and that the Chinese military was unprepared to deal with it. The shock of the Gulf War was all the more traumatic because, since the Vietnam fiasco, China's military had begun a fairly comprehensive modernization and reform program. Deng Xiaoping, who chaired the Central Military Commission, Marshall Ye Jianying, and General Yang Shangkun all harshly criticized the PLA's bloated size, disorganization, political factionalism, lax discipline, and combat ineffectiveness.[3] Deng, Ye, Yang, and others accordingly set in motion a series of initiatives intended to truly "modernize" the military (although military modernization came distinctly last in the "Four Modernizations"). Throughout the 1980s, the PLA was restructured to prepare, first, for "people's war under modern conditions," and then for "limited war." The changes reconfigured ground forces,

1. Hanoi claimed that Vietnamese forces had killed or wounded 42,000 Chinese soldiers in three weeks of combat, while Beijing claimed 50,000 Vietnamese dead or wounded, compared with 20,000 on the Chinese side. See King C. Chen, *China's War with Vietnam: Issues, Decisions, Implications* (Stanford, Calif.: Hoover Institution Press, 1987), p. 114.

2. Among the assessments of this conflict, other than ibid., see esp. Harlan Jencks, "China's 'Punitive' War on Vietnam," *Asian Survey* 19, no. 8 (August 1979); Daniel Tretiak, "China's Vietnam War and Its Consequences," *China Quarterly*, no. 80 (December 1979); and Man Kim Lin, *The Sino-Vietnamese War* (Hong Kong: Kingsway International Publications, 1981).

3. See, e.g., Deng Xiaoping, "Zai Junwei Zuotanhui shang de Jianghua" (Speech to the Discussion Meeting of the Central Military Commission), in *Deng Xiaoping Wenxuan, 1975–1982* (Collected Works of Deng Xiaoping, 1975–1982) (Beijing: Renmin Chubanshe; Hong Kong: San Lian Publishers, 1983), pp. 363–67.

consolidated military regions, began combined arms and joint service exercises, undertook a new recruitment drive along with the demobilization of redundant and incompetent personnel, and pursued new weapons procurement programs. The PLA had been implementing reforms for more than a decade when the Gulf War starkly demonstrated that it was still operating in terms of a bygone era of warfare.

THE CATALYSTS FOR REFORM

The Gulf War stimulated deep introspection and analysis in the PLA about the nature of contemporary warfare and the reforms necessary to ready the Chinese armed forces to wage it. In the wake of the Gulf War, PLA strategy was revised to focus on "limited wars under high-technology conditions." Evidence of new defense policy and doctrinal initiatives, structural reforms, altered training regimen, new weapons procurement programs, and other changes became noticeable during 1995–96. These reforms had some continuity with previous programs and reforms undertaken in the late 1980s and early 1990s, but others were entirely new and could be traced to the lessons learned from the Gulf War.

Then, in March 1996, another event jarred the PLA, provoking further reflection, rethinking, and readjustment. The PLA's strategic rocket forces, the Second Artillery, began to practice coercive "missile diplomacy" in the Taiwan Strait—firing M-9 missiles within miles of the entrances to Kaohsiung and Chi'lung harbors—and the United States dispatched two aircraft carrier battle groups, centered on the USS *Independence* and *Nimitz*, to the vicinity.[4] With their deployment, the powerful American task forces displayed the greatest show of strength directed at China since the Sino-American rapprochement of 1971. From positions in the waters east and north of Taiwan, the small armada flew combat exercises and monitored the PLA's own live-fire "exercises" in the Strait. Washington, Beijing, and Taipei all drew different lessons from the U.S. deployment, but for the PLA it meant only one thing: to expect American military involvement should the PLA use force against Taiwan. PLA leaders had long wondered whether they

4. For excellent analyses of this crisis, see Robert S. Ross, "The 1995–1996 Taiwan Strait Confrontation: Coercion, Credibility, and the Use of Force," *International Security* 25, no. 2 (Fall 2000): 87–123; James R. Lilley and Chuck Downs, eds., *Crisis in the Taiwan Strait* (Washington, D.C.: National Defense University Press and AEI Press, 1997); John Garver, *Face Off: China, the United States, and Taiwan's Democratization* (Seattle: University of Washington Press, 1997).

would have to confront the vaunted U.S. military in a Taiwan crisis—now they could assume so.

The 1996 "Taiwan Crisis" added new urgency to China's military modernization and reform program, focusing some of the lessons of the Gulf War. But it also diverted broader efforts to create a more comprehensive force structure and a balanced military modernization program. Since then many elements of PLA planning, training, and procurement have become contingency-driven, dominated by the specter of a military conflict with the United States over Taiwan. Exercises, force deployments, and weapons procurement (particularly from Russia) are preparing the PLA for such a conflict. Hard allocation choices channeled resources into services, programs, and weapons thought necessary to fight not only Taiwan's military but the United States as well.

Resources that might have contributed to a broad-based and systematic military modernization have instead gone into the purchase of expensive Sovremmeny-class destroyers from Russia, built principally to counter Aegis-equipped destroyers and cruisers (which escort aircraft carriers) and the on-board defenses of American carriers, as well into the procurement of Su-27 and Su-30 fighters, Kilo-class submarines, and other equipment intended to plug critical gaps in PLA capabilities against Taiwanese and U.S. forces. China pursued the acquisition of Israel's Phalcon airborne early-warning and control systems—a sale aborted by the Israeli government in July 2000 under considerable pressure from Washington—as a key to controlling the skies in the Taiwan theater. (Chinese pilots currently only have ground control links and no aerial multiple-tracking capability.) PLA marines and ground forces practice beach assaults and amphibious landings in mock invasions of Taiwan or the offshore islands and increasingly train with air and naval units in joint-force exercises. Knowing that Taiwan currently has no effective defenses against short-range ballistic missiles, the PLA is embarked on a major and rapid buildup of these weapons opposite the island (approximately 300 by 2000 and increasing by about 50 per year). Also, the steady program to modernize and deploy more nuclear-capable intercontinental ballistic missiles is in large part driven by the need to have a bona fide second-strike minimum deterrent against the United States.

Just as the PLA was adapting to the new military challenges posed by the Taiwan situation, the third shock of the 1990s struck: the Kosovo crisis and NATO's war against Serbia in 1999. This time the jarring effect on the PLA was of both a political and a military nature.

On the political level, Beijing perceived NATO's actions as illustrating a new propensity on the part of the United States (which China's media always dubbed "U.S.-led NATO") to intervene in regional conflicts, under the pretext of "humanitarian intervention," for the purpose of extending and consolidating American global "hegemony" and domination. During and after the war, the Chinese media (including the military media) unleashed a barrage of invective against the United States unequaled since the Cultural Revolution and the Vietnam War. NATO and American actions forced Chinese analysts to question the core assumptions about international relations and the global strategic landscape that had guided their worldview since the late Deng Xiaoping's 1985 pronouncement, that the threat of war was on the decline, that the global system of power relations was inexorably moving toward multipolarity, and that all countries sought "peace and development."[5] Instead of sinking into relative, if not absolute, decline, as Chinese analysts had predicted just a few years earlier, the unrivaled strength and unipolar power of the United States now seemed to be growing significantly. Furthermore, contrary to the touted thesis of "peace and development," regional conflicts, and the American propensity to intervene in them, were seen as increasing. Moreover, American military deployment around the world remained at high, even expanded, levels. Although Chinese strategic theology predicted, and the Chinese government had officially called for, the abrogation of alliances and withdrawal of forces from foreign soil, Washington had in fact strengthened and broadened its network of global alliances in the aftermath of the Cold War.

Thus the U.S. role in the Balkan war had a profoundly disturbing and dissonant effect on Chinese military and strategic thinkers as well as on national leaders. When the NATO intervention was considered in the context of the 1991 Gulf War and 1996 Taiwan crisis, China perceived itself to be facing a United States bent on global dominance and the permanent separation of Taiwan from China. The possibility of U.S. intervention in China's ethnic troubles in Xinjiang and Tibet as a result of the "Clinton Doctrine" of humanitarian intervention added to Beijing's sense of urgency.[6]

On a military level, too, the Yugoslav campaign jolted PLA analysts, who paid close attention to how NATO prosecuted the war. They set up two 24-hour centers to monitor the military dimensions of the conflict—one in the General Staff Department's intelligence "Watch Center" and the other at

5. For further analysis of the post-Kosovo strategic debate, see David Finkelstein, *China Reconsiders Its National Security: The Great Peace and Development Debate of 1999* (Alexandria, Va.: CNA Corporation, 2000).

6. In fact, this "doctrine" was the pronouncement of British Prime Minister Tony Blair, but the Chinese associate it with President Clinton.

the Academy of Military Sciences.[7] They witnessed tactics, technology, and weaponry similar to those used in the Gulf War eight years earlier, but they also observed a number of new features. Information and electronic warfare appeared to play a more important role in disabling enemy command infrastructure and defenses. Cruise missiles had improved accuracy. NATO suppressed Serbian air defenses in the early stages of the conflict and gained complete command of the skies; aerial bombardment was significantly more intense (in operational tempo, if not in tonnage of ordnance). With the use of in-flight refueling, bombing raids using the newly deployed B-2 strategic bomber were initiated half a world away instead of within theater. One such bombing raid tragically and mistakenly targeted the Chinese Embassy in Belgrade. The bombs themselves were equipped with new satellite and laser guidance systems. Perhaps most important, PLA analysts watched a war prosecuted from great distances—where the Serbs could not see, hear, or reach their attackers. With all of the high-tech weaponry deployed, not a single allied soldier was lost to hostile fire.

The 2001–2 U.S. military campaign against the Taliban regime and al-Qaeda terrorists in Afghanistan was also carefully studied by PLA analysts, although the lessons derived remain unclear at this time. As in the case of the war against the Serbs in Bosnia, PLA analysts were alarmed on both the political and military levels.

Politically, they were quite uncomfortable with the prospect of U.S. and allied military forces deployed in Pakistan and particularly in Central Asian countries on China's northwestern periphery. The prospect of a long-term American military presence in the Central Asian republics is particularly unsettling to Chinese national security planners, as it represents (in their somewhat paranoid view) a major new step in what is perceived as an American strategy of encircling China. From this perspective, only the direct northern frontier, where China borders Russia, is free from a U.S. military presence.

At the outset of the Afghanistan conflict in October 2001, PLA officers at the PLA National Defense University in Beijing warned, mistakenly, that like the British in the nineteenth century and the Soviet Union, the United States would become bogged down in an Afghan quagmire.[8] They warned that this was a different kind of enemy, which could not be subdued by aerial bombing, and doubted whether America was prepared to insert ground troops and risk casualties (arguing that the United States continued to suffer from a "So-

7. Interview with participant, April 13, 1999.
8. Interviews at National Defense University, October 16, 2001.

malia syndrome").[9] If the United States did deploy ground troops, PLA analysts warned, they would be consumed in a quagmire of guerrilla war, which they were not prepared to fight, and U.S. helicopters and aircraft would be shot down by Stinger missiles in possession of the Taliban and al-Qaeda. Similar prognoses had been offered by PLA analysts at the outset of the Gulf War and the Bosnian bombing. They were proven wrong each time, reflecting fundamental misunderstandings of U.S. military strategy and tactics.

Militarily, in Afghanistan, PLA analysts witnessed displays of high-technology warfare similar to those seen in the Gulf War and the Serbian conflict, as well as some new techniques and ordnance. Long-range strategic bombing with extremely sophisticated precision-guided munitions (PGMs) played a key role. During ninety days of bombing, the United States dropped a total of nearly 13,000 bombs on Afghanistan, of which 9,000 were PGMs. The accuracy and lethality of these weapons proved far more advanced than had been witnessed in Iraq or Bosnia. In addition to sustained precision bombing, and early suppression of Afghan defenses, PLA analysts also noted the key role played by real-time allied intelligence. In addition to the kinds of sensors and satellites previously seen, two new elements appeared in Afghanistan that did much to provide instantaneous intelligence: special operations forces on the ground and unmanned aerial drones. Other new factors noted by PLA analysts included AH-64 attack helicopters and A-130 airborne gunships. These and other new capabilities attracted the attention of PLA analysts.[10] As was the case with the Iraq, Taiwan, and Bosnian conflicts, the Afghan war will be intensively studied for some time in the PLA, with alternations in doctrine, tactics, and training subsequently becoming apparent over time.

The lessons the PLA drew from these conflicts are discussed at much greater length in chapters 3 and 7; suffice it to note here that it increased the Chinese leaders' sense of the urgent need for military modernization, and, particularly, of a looming threat from the United States. Funds for the military continued to rise, on average by 15 percent, in fiscal years 1999–2002. Certainly, popular sentiment against the United States peaked following the Chinese embassy bombing, and there were public calls in China for a reordering of modernization priorities with increased emphasis on the military.

9. Ibid.
10. Interview with Academy of Military Sciences senior analyst, March 4, 2002. Also see Tian Xin, "Afghan War Assaults Chinese Military Theory," *Wen Hui Bao*, February 4, 2002, in Foreign Broadcast Information Service *Daily Report–China* (hereafter cited as FBIS–CHI), February 4, 2002.

Throughout the 1990s, the PLA was reading and hearing about the "revolution in military affairs" *(xin junshi geming)* that was evolving in the United States. As if the Chinese military was not humbled enough by the impressive display of firepower and electronic wizardry on display in the 1991, 1996, and 1999 and 2001–2 conflicts, PLA strategists were led to believe that the U.S. military was entering one of those periods of technological advance that come along every few generations, when there is a quantum leap in a family of technologies and operational concepts that push warfare into completely new realms. Such technological advances stimulate concomitant changes in the way forces are structured and deployed, how logistics are managed, and how force is used. Not only was the PLA High Command thus obliged to witness a series of powerful demonstrations of modern military prowess, but it also had to reflect on the prospect that, while it was trying to upgrade its equipment from the 1960s to the 1970s, and its doctrine from the 1980s to the 1990s, the already impressive American military of the late twentieth century was on the verge of a significant leap forward into the twenty-first century.

THE ELEMENTS OF MODERNIZATION

Despite a decade of extensive reform during the 1980s, the Gulf War graphically demonstrated just how far behind modern militaries the PLA had fallen and how much still needed to be done to close the gap. There is little doubt that the Chinese military leadership has now grasped the totality of the problems and challenges it confronts and has begun to implement sweeping reforms across the spectrum of all services and functional areas. Most services and units are experiencing several transformations simultaneously. In fact, a major challenge is that too much is being thrust on the PLA too quickly. Large, complex organizations, especially militaries, are instinctively resistant to change. Many of these reforms are profound and fundamental in their nature, inasmuch as they are intended to change long-standing practices, regimens, and norms. Naturally, many are being resisted. As is the case with reform in other sectors of Chinese society, there is also a tendency to feign compliance with directives while persisting in entrenched practices. Difficulties of assimilation and adjustment are profound in many areas. Yet the PLA needed reform from top to bottom. The incremental reforms of the late 1980s had proven insufficient, and bolder steps were warranted. Now such reform has truly begun. Just as the rest of China is making the transition to modernity, so too now is the military.

ORGANIZATION OF THE STUDY

This book details these reforms and discusses both the progress achieved and the problems associated with implementing them. Five functional chapters (chapters 2–6) seek to integrate diverse subject areas as naturally as possible while still attempting to be comprehensive in the study's coverage. For example, how militaries exercise and train on the battlefield (and indeed perform in real combat) depends on a number of factors, but clearly the operational doctrine of a military is the starting point for determining the structure and deployment of forces, the strategy for deploying them, and their fighting tactics. Chapter 3 thus treats the PLA's defense doctrine along with its military strategy and training regimen. Chapter 4 considers both the organizational dimensions of the PLA's command and control hierarchy and its force structure at lower levels. Chapter 5 discusses both the formal military budget process and the PLA's less formal (and now greatly reduced) commercial involvement. Chapter 6 combines analysis of China's military-industrial system with cataloguing the weapons currently in the PLA inventory.

The book's remaining three chapters provide historical and comparative perspective. Chapter 2 is an assessment of China's civil-military relations, focusing particularly on the post-1989 evolution of the military elite and the impact of the military suppression in Beijing on June 4, 1989, as well as the broader impact of, and lessons learned from, the roles played by militaries in the collapse of other communist party-states. These events affected the civilian and military elite in China profoundly and triggered considerable factional struggle, purges, and courts-martial, as well as promotions of many new officers. During the 1990s, virtually the entire PLA High Command was replaced. Toward the end of the decade, some interesting legal developments suggested that interactions among the military, the Communist Party, and the state (or government) were changing and possibly evolving in a direction similar to that taken in other East Asian and developing nations.

Chapter 7 assesses China's national security environment as seen through the eyes of PLA analysts. While foreign specialists on Chinese security would observe that China's security has never been better, at least in the fifty years since the Communist Party came to power (if not the 160 years since the Opium Wars), PLA analysts do not necessarily see it that way. The evidence presented in chapter 7, drawn from extensive interviews and published PLA materials, indicates that Chinese military analysts believe they live in a dangerous world, with many uncertainties and potential challenges to China's sovereignty and security. The principal threat they identify comes from the United States, while the principal challenge arises from Taiwan. These twin problems are fused together in the PLA mindset, but it is most likely that they would continue to view the United States as a threat to national security irrespective of American support for Taiwan. The chapter details PLA analyses of the nature of the U.S. threat, which is seen as both global in nature and specific to China's peripheral security. It also brings to light previously opaque PLA assessments of the military dimension of the Taiwan problem—assessing Taiwan's defenses and possible strategies for the use of force against the island. The chapter also considers five scenarios in which a war might evolve should conflict erupt. Aside from the United States and Taiwan, PLA analysts also view Japan and India as potential threats to China's security and national interests. While tensions have abated somewhat on the Korean peninsula, PLA analysts still see the Northeast Asian region, too, as unstable and potentially threatening to China's national security. Even Russia is seen by PLA analysts in a less sanguine light than the vaunted Sino-Russian "strategic partnership" and military assistance to China might indicate. The chapter also considers PLA assessments of global strategic trends, multilateral regional security, and China's "New Security Concept."

Chapter 8 attempts to relate the analysis of preceding chapters to the interests of the United States and focuses on its policy implications for Washington's future dealings with the PLA. Specifically, it discusses the strategic implications of the modernization and reforms of the Chinese military for the United States and its Asia-Pacific security allies and partners. After examining past and future military relations between the two countries, it concludes with recommendations as to how future American exchanges with the PLA should be managed.

As befits a study of such a comprehensive nature, this book makes multiple arguments and subarguments. It has, however, one overarching thesis—namely, that although the PLA has embarked on a systematic and extensive modernization program, entailing reforms in all sectors and services, and although there is a comprehensive vision for pursuing that program, a combination of domestic handicaps and foreign constraints severely limits both the pace and the scope of China's military progress.

2 Civil-Military Relations

Compared with other facets of PLA reforms in recent years, civil-military relations have been slow to change and shifts have been less evident. The events of 1989 had a wrenching political effect on the military, brought to a halt some nascent reforms in the armed forces, and strengthened political priorities relative to professional ones for a period of time—but by the mid 1990s, the debates and reforms of the late 1980s were again in evidence. The composition of military elites also changed, as did some of the modalities of civil-military interaction.

Since the mid 1990s, there has been an evident, if subterranean, three-way struggle being played out among the army, party, and government—with the army seeking greater autonomy from the party, the party attempting to strengthen its control of the army, and the government trying to increase its own jurisdictional oversight of the armed forces (while continuing to delineate its sphere of responsibilities as distinct from that of the party). Because of their inherently political and highly sensitive nature, these changes have been only incremental and subliminal. No radical restructuring of party-army relations has been undertaken. To do so would call into question the very legitimacy and sustenance of the Chinese Communist Party (CCP).

Perhaps more than in other domains, the weight of past traditions has also inhibited overt reform in this area. Relations between the civilian leadership and military in China still very much take place in a CCP-PLA (party-army) context, although, as this chapter argues, there are growing signs of bifurcation between these two institutions. Triggered by the broader drive toward professionalization of the armed forces, there have been a number of key changes in the PLA, some probably unintended, which have fundamentally affected the political identity of the military and its relationship to the CCP.

FROM PARTY-ARMY TO CIVIL-MILITARY RELATIONS

Not long ago, analysts of the PLA considered it more appropriate to discuss "party-army relations" rather than the more generic term "civil-military relations," as commonly used elsewhere in the world. This was so because of a number of important historical considerations distinguishing the PLA's relationship to the ruling Chinese Communist Party from its counterparts in other developing and developed countries. It was recognized that militaries in communist political systems are intrinsically different from those in other one-party authoritarian systems, to say nothing of militaries in democratic polities.

In political systems dominated by a communist party, the People's Republic of China included, the military is an instrument of the party. It brings the party to power in violent revolution and uses occasional coercion and force to keep it in power. Its national security mission is a dual one, targeting both internal and external enemies. Such militaries, the PLA included, are institutionally penetrated by the ruling communist party—particularly through a network of political commissars—and most, if not all, officers are party members. At the top of the political system, there is an "interlocking directorate": a high percentage of senior serving military officers are members of the party's Central Committee and Politburo, and many senior party officials will have previously served in the armed forces (trading their uniforms for civilian garb, but maintaining close factional ties with military elites). In such communist militaries, "political work" and ideological indoctrination of the officer corps and the rank and file is prominent and occupies considerable time (net time not spent in training).

In short, in communist militaries, the PLA included, there is an essential symbiosis between the army and the ruling communist party. Sometimes, this symbiosis is reflected in party attempts to assert greater control over the military, while at other times, communist militaries have become more politically assertive vis-à-vis the ruling party. In such systems, because of the essential symbiosis, militaries generally do not engineer coups d'état against their ruling parties (although they may become involved in intraparty factional maneuvering).

Such a model of party-army relations was wholly applicable to China until the second half of the 1990s, but it has been only partially applicable since that time. For a variety of reasons, and judged by a variety of indicators, the relationship between the PLA and the CCP is changing, perhaps fundamentally. To be sure, it is still a party-army in important respects, but a number of the criteria noted above no longer characterize the CCP-PLA relationship. The "interlocking directorate" has been completely broken by generational succession. Not a single senior party leader today has had a single day of military experience, and only two senior PLA officers in the High Command (Generals Chi Haotian and Wang Ruilin) have any significant experience in high-level politics. The party-army elite is clearly becoming bifurcated. Senior PLA officers, from the Central Military Commission (CMC) down to group army commands, are now promoted based on meritocratic and professional criteria, while political consciousness and activism count for very little. The officer corps is thus becoming increasingly professional, in classic Huntingtonian terms. Indeed, recruitment into the PLA is now based predominantly on technical criteria. The military's mission today is almost exclusively external, to protect national security, rather than internal security. The role of ideology is virtually nil, and political work has declined substantially; concomitantly the General Political Department's mission has become more oriented to providing welfare for soldiers and their families than indoctrinating them. Time formerly spent in political study (approximately 30 percent) is now spent in training. This shift is also true of curriculum content in institutions of professional military education (PME), which is now mandatory for all officers above division level. Moreover, PLA units have been ordered to divest themselves of their commercial holdings, so time formerly dedicated to business is now increasingly spent in training. In place of the earlier informality and personalization of command and control, the military is now also subject to a large number of laws and regulations. The State Council and Ministry of Finance now exert much more control over the PLA budgeting process, and, at least on paper (the National Defense Law), the responsibility for military command and oversight lies with the president and the National People's Congress (NPC).

Accordingly, for these reasons, it is now more analytically appropriate to consider civil-military rather than party-army relations in the PRC. The catalyst for these changes has been the professionalization of the armed forces.[1] To be sure, this evolution is ongoing and incomplete. The former model has not, and is not likely to, completely replace the latter. Yet, by a number of criteria, it does seem clear that the PLA is moving away from its traditional communist institutional ethos into a new stage of limited autonomy from the ruling party.

This new stage of civil-military relations in the PRC may also be viewed

1. See, e.g., You Ji, "China: From Revolutionary Tool to Professional Military," in Muthiah Alagappa, ed., *Military Professionalism in Asia: Conceptual and Empirical Perspectives* (Honolulu: East-West Center, 2001), pp. 111–36.

as the intermediate stage in a transition from a party-army to a "national army." China and the PLA are clearly not there yet. Yet there have been, and continue to be, subterranean discussions in China and the PLA about greater state control of the military, a military that serves the nation and not just the ruling party, and a military controlled by civilian rule and governed my legislative oversight. This cuts right to the core of the PLA's identity and the CCP's legitimacy, if not that of the PRC itself, and, as if to put a fine point on the sensitivity of the issue, there have been a series of condemnations of such "bourgeois" concepts in both party and military media from time to time.

Is it feasible to have a national army in a Leninist system? Or can such a military only exist in a democratic system? Given the evidence of economic and educational reforms in China, to take but two issue areas, a hybrid relationship in which a professional national military coexists with a ruling communist party within a framework of state and legislative control is not inconceivable. Yet many of the conditions necessary to proclaim the PLA a "national army" seem anathema to the CCP and its rule. For example, it would require at least a viable Ministry of National Defense (not the hollow shell of the MND at present); a civilian minister of defense; chairmanship of the Central Military Commission by the president; thorough control of the military by the state president, National People's Congress, and State Council; a series of established laws and procedures governing the use of force and mobilization of the military; strong legislative oversight of the armed forces; complete budgetary control over the military by the legislature and no extrabudgetary revenue; and no political content in professional military education. By all these criteria, it is clear that China has a long way to go before the PLA becomes a national army, despite internal discussions and incremental movement in this direction.

To understand how the PLA and the CCP got to this stage, we need to look at the apex of party-army relations and at the policy issues that have been central to civil-military relations in China since the Tiananmen crisis of 1989, as well as at the historical context.

Historical and Comparative Considerations

Understanding the interrelationship among party, state, and army in the PRC today must take account of several long-standing and unique features of civil-military relations in China. Throughout the twentieth century, from the late imperial to the post-Deng era, the Chinese military played an active role in the political and economic life of the nation (even though soldiers, along with merchants, were at the bottom of the Confucian social order). Key late-Qing reformers, such as Li Hongzhang, were military men who believed that the path to "wealth and power" (*fu-qiang*, the cardinal tenet of all subsequent Chinese elites) lay in mastering military technologies and building a strong self-defense capability so as to be able to rebuff foreign encroachment and regain China's unity and lost greatness. Li's policy of "building shipyards and arsenals" and dispatching students to Europe and America to study in defense colleges and scientific institutes bespoke this bias. To be sure, there was heated debate among the Qing elite over the wisdom of this policy. Some argued that it was a distorted path to development, disproportionately emphasizing military modernization over the need for a more comprehensive technological base; others opposed the inherent "Westernization" and cultural contamination implicit in the strategy; and still others believed that the "sources of wealth and power" were less technological and more civic, political, and intellectual in nature. These debates have resonated over the past century, and echoes of them are still present today.

After the republican revolution of 1911, soldiers were prominent in the new government (among them General Yuan Shikai, who became the first president of the republic), and building a modern military remained a high priority. In the constitutional crisis after Yuan's death in 1916, however, the new regime failed to consolidate national power, and China slipped into a prolonged period of territorial division, fratricide, and rule by a succession of military warlords. This bloodthirsty period was halted only when force was met with force during Generalissimo Chiang Kai-shek's 1928 Northern Expedition, which united the country under the civil-military rule of the Nationalist Party and army (Guomindang and Guominjun). The new GMD elite during the "Nanjing decade" (1927–37) contained a large proportion of military officers, secret police, and intelligence operatives— many trained under Chiang at the Whampoa Military Academy and in military and paramilitary institutions in Germany and the Soviet Union. This regime would only become more militarized following the outbreak of the Sino-Japanese War in 1937.[2]

Meanwhile, in communist-controlled areas of China's interior, a similar militarily dominant political regime was also taking shape. The Chinese Red Army was born not only of necessity, out of the need literally to fight for survival against Japanese and GMD forces, but also from the strong Soviet and German influences on the politicization of the military and militariza-

---

2. Hans van de Ven, "The Military in the Republic," *China Quarterly*, no. 150 (June 1997): 352–74.

tion of the party. Throughout the revolutionary period, there was an essential symbiosis between party and army in pursuit of state power.[3] The two have historically been so closely intertwined that the military has played a unique, and often dominant, normative and institutional role in the life of the nation. The Red Army fought the Japanese invaders, defeated the Guomindang, pacified the countryside, and occupied the cities, making the communist victory in 1949 at least as much military as political.[4] "Political power grows out of the barrel of a gun!" Mao Zedong astutely observed, but as early as 1929, he also warned: "Our principle is that the party commands the gun, and the gun must never be allowed to command the party."[5] Mao's edict actually obscured the organic party-army symbiosis—a condition that obtained until the 1980s, when Deng Xiaoping and Yang Shangkun began to implement reforms that had the net effect of incrementally increasing the corporate autonomy and separate identity of the armed forces. As a result of this symbiosis, the military came to the party's aid in suppressing civil unrest at several key junctures after 1949 (not the least of which came during the Cultural Revolution). The CCP may have been born in the Shanghai underground and Jiangxi Soviet, but it had military parentage and was reared on the battlefield. Its formative years were spent at war, and it matured in a society with a strong militarist tradition.

It was precisely because of this symbiotic relationship that the military never balked when instructed to maintain social order, suppress "counter-revolutionaries," arrest the Gang of Four, or perform other internal security duties. In other words, involvement by the army in "political" affairs and domestic security was considered normal and legitimate. This goes a long way toward explaining the PLA's role in the 1989 suppression of pro-democracy demonstrators and other citizens of Beijing, although the questioning by some senior military elites of this action and insubordination in the ranks at the time suggests that the prior symbiosis had begun to give way to greater autonomy of the armed forces. Following the Tiananmen crackdown, there was a renewed attempt by the party (and its constituent organs inside the PLA) to substantially increase control over, and ensure the loyalty of, the

3. David Shambaugh, "The Soldier and the State in China: The Political Work System in the People's Liberation Army," in Brian Hook, ed., *The Individual and the State in China* (Oxford: Clarendon Press, 1997); Harlan Jencks, *From Muskets to Missiles: Politics and Professionalism in the Chinese Army, 1945–1981* (Boulder, Colo.: Westview Press, 1982), chs. 1–3.

4. This assertion does not obviate the important roles played by land reform and nationalism.

5. Mao Zedong, "Problems of War and Strategy," in *Selected Works of Mao Zedong*, vol. 2 (Beijing: Foreign Languages Press, 1975), p. 224.

military; but this lasted only a year or two, and subsequently disparate signs of increased PLA autonomy have been apparent. As discussed below, one sign of this increased autonomy has been the tentative attempt to increase state (i.e., government and legislative) control over the military, as distinct from party control. This does not mean, however, that a new "national army" *(guomin jundui)* or "state army" *(guojia jundui)* era has dawned, or that the long-standing party-army symbiosis is moribund. But recent changes do indicate that the interrelationship of party, army, and state are in flux, and that the demands of "professionalism" are redefining civil-military relations in China in directions more familiar in other modernizing nations.

The Impact of the Past on the Present

The history of Chinese civil-military relations has profound implications for understanding developments after the CCP came to power and in the present period. Scholarly analysis of this issue in recent years has led to a lively debate among PLA specialists, but it has unfortunately been largely restricted to the periphery of Chinese political studies.[6] Ellis Joffe has noted three schools of thought and lines of argument that have emerged in this discourse over time: *symbiosis, party control,* and *professionalism.*[7] Too often analysts have juxtaposed these approaches—whereas, as Joffe astutely notes, they should be viewed as complementary. These are not mutually exclusive categories of analysis. Professionalism has been ongoing since the 1950s and Marshal Peng Dehuai's tenure as minister of defense. Even under Marshal Lin Biao in the 1960s, and contrary to conventional wisdom, the military continued to professionalize and modernize in several dimensions. If there has been a tension, it has been between party control and limited military autonomy. The norm of a symbiotic party-army relationship has been sustained over time, but in different periods over the past fifty years (notably 1959–62, 1971–82, and 1989–92), the CCP has made extra efforts to exert control over the armed forces, and at other junctures, the military has sought to increase its corporate autonomy from the CCP. On several

6. For an effort to begin a discourse between the two scholarly communities, see David Shambaugh, "Building the Party-State in China, 1949–1965: Bringing the Soldiers Back In," in Timothy Cheek and Tony Saich, eds., *New Perspectives on State Socialism in China, 1949–1965* (Armonk, N.Y.: M. E. Sharpe, 1996).

7. Ellis Joffe, "Party-Army Relations in China: Retrospect and Prospect," in David Shambaugh, ed., *China's Military in Transition* (Oxford: Clarendon Press, 1997). This typology mirrors the debates among scholars of civil-military relations in the former Soviet Union. Albeit in a different context, Timothy Colton articulated the symbiosis thesis, Roman Kolkowitz the control thesis, and William Odom the autonomy thesis.

occasions, the military sought to exert its role in high-level party affairs (notably in 1967, 1976, 1989, and to a certain extent in 1996), but it can be plausibly argued that these efforts had more do with certain elites "pulling" the military into politics during periods of social unrest and party weakness.[8] In other periods (1954–59, 1974–75, and 1982–89), the armed forces have sought to increase their autonomy from the party, but this must be carefully distinguished as *limited autonomy*. At no time has the PLA ever sought to fully separate itself from the CCP (or vice versa).

The military has simply sought greater autonomy over affairs it considers to be fully in its corporate domain—training, doctrine, force structure, personnel appointments, military education, and protection of national security. Meanwhile, professionalizing tendencies have been more or less continual, although with a particular emphasis in the late 1950s, mid 1980s, and late 1990s. The PLA has been, in Joffe's apt phrase, a "party-army with professional characteristics."[9] Thus, the army's relationship with the party-state has evolved and fluctuated over time. Harry Harding has astutely noted that this fluctuation correlates with the strength or weakness of the party-state.[10] That is, during periods when the party-state was strong and the society stable, the military tended to act as a corporate bureaucratic lobby. When the party-state was weakened, the military tended to act as a political arbiter between competing factions, to support one faction against another, or to intervene more broadly to stabilize society.

Joffe's characterization remains partially apt today, although since the mid 1990s we may have witnessed increasing military autonomy from the party in general, as well as nascent signs of increased state (i.e., government) control of the armed forces.[11] This trend would suggest a slight variation on his typology: a more linear evolution from symbiosis to control to limited autonomy. This is discussed at greater length above and below; suffice it to note

8. See Ellis Joffe, *The Military and China's New Politics: Trends and Counter-Trends,* CAPS Papers, no. 19 (Taipei: Chinese Council on Advanced Policy Studies, 1997).

9. Ibid. In his landmark study, Harlan Jencks tends to juxtapose the two and argues that "Chinese officers, especially those below corps level, are strongly disinclined toward political involvement." See Jencks, *From Muskets to Missiles,* p. 255.

10. See Harry Harding, "The Role of the Military in Chinese Politics," in Victor Falkenheim, ed., *Citizens and Groups in Contemporary China* (Ann Arbor: University of Michigan Center for Chinese Studies, 1987).

11. Many analysts are dubious that this process is under way, and some—such as Jeremy Paltiel—believe it to be a false dichotomy. "The Chinese armed forces have never faced a choice between loyalty to the state and obedience to the party," Paltiel asserts in "PLA Allegiance on Parade: Civil-Military Relations in Transition," *China Quarterly,* no. 143 (September 1995). Paltiel is correct in this observation,

here that increased state control need not ipso facto imply the zero-sum displacement of the party's relationship with the army. From one perspective, the relationship of the military to the state and party is complementary. That is, the state may be increasing its mechanisms of control and lines of authority over the armed forces, while the party withdraws to a more "elevated" position. During the past decade, for example, with respect to economic management, the CCP has set forth the broader policy direction *(fangzhen)* while the state has formulated the policy line *(luxian)* more concretely and implemented specific policies *(zhengce)*. The issue here is really one of relative autonomy and jurisdictional distinctions between institutional hierarchies and within functional policy spheres (which some political scientists refer to as the "zoning of authority"). As the party has increasingly withdrawn from its former totalistic and monopolistic influence over society and economy, greater scope and relative autonomy have been created for institutional and civic actors in China. The tight symbiosis of party and army was forged early on, and it is necessarily one of the last bonds to be broken in the reform process.

Any consideration of civil-military relations in China as it enters the twenty-first century must proceed from clear cognizance of the past. Over the past century, individual military actors and the military as an institution have played key active roles in the Chinese regime and nation. These have taken a variety of forms, but the military has never been fully isolated from the political arena. Both military and party elites have viewed military involvement in politics, domestic security, society, and even commerce as legitimate. While the political involvement of the Chinese military is distinct from the Western tradition of military corporatism and separation from the political arena (based on the Ottoman, European, and American experiences),[12] it is hardly unique among developing or socialist countries. Many postcolonial and developing nations have experienced sustained military rule and praetorian intervention,[13] while most former communist party-states were based on the "interlocking directorate" of party and military elites and the penetration of the military and security services by party control mech-

---

but I would argue that increasing state authority and control over the armed forces do not ipso facto imply a zero-sum displacement of the party's relationship with the army. They may be seen as complementary.

12. The classic typology is, of course, that of Samuel P. Huntington, *The Soldier and the State: The Theory and Politics of Civil-Military Relations* (Cambridge, Mass.: Harvard University Press, 1957). Also see Morris Janowitz, *The Professional Soldier* (New York: Free Press, 1960).

13. The literature here is extensive. See, e.g., Timothy Colton and Thane Gustafson, eds., *Soldiers and the Soviet State* (Princeton, N.J.: Princeton University Press,

anisms.[14] More recently, scholarly attention has been paid to the military's withdrawal from politics and subordination to civilian control in the process of the transition to democracy across the developing and industrializing world.[15] An interesting literature has also begun to address civil-military relations in the Chinese context of a democratizing Taiwan.[16] Scholars specializing in post-1949 Chinese military politics would do well to tap into all of these studies, as the PLA shares many commonalties with these other cases. As professionalism and corporate identity rise in the PLA, and greater efforts are made to subject the military to state control, comparing other national experiences will be increasingly pertinent to understanding the future evolution of the PLA.

An Evolving Civil-Military Identity

Since June 1989, when the PLA enforced martial law in Beijing,[17] Chinese civil-military relations have evolved through several stages. The order to

---

1990); Abraham F. Lowenthal and Samuel J. Fitch, eds., *Armies and Politics in Latin America* (New York: Holmes & Meier, 1986); Alfred Stepan, *Rethinking Military Politics* (Princeton, N.J.: Princeton University Press, 1988); Viberto Selochan, *The Military, the State, and Development in Asia and the* Pacific (Boulder, Colo.: Westview Press, 1991); Amos Perlmutter, *The Military and Politics in Modern Times* (New Haven, Conn.: Yale University Press, 1977); Eric A. Nordlinger, *Soldiers in Politics* (Englewood Cliffs, N.J.: Prentice-Hall, 1977); Catherine M. Kelleher, ed., *Political-Military Systems* (Beverly Hills, Calif.: Sage Publications, 1974).

14. This subfield has also generated a substantial, if somewhat dated, literature. See, e.g., Dale Herspring and Ivan Volges, eds., *Civil-Military Relations in Communist Systems* (Boulder, Colo.: Westview Press, 1978); Jonathan Adelman, ed., *Communist Armies in Politics* (Boulder, Colo.: Westview Press, 1982); Dale R. Herspring, *Russian Civil-Military Relations* (Bloomington: Indiana University Press, 1996); Kenneth M. Currie, *Soviet Military Politics* (New York: Paragon Press, 1991).

15. See Larry Diamond and Marc F. Plattner, eds., *Civil-Military Relations and Democracy* (Baltimore: Johns Hopkins University Press, 1996).

16. Monte Bullard, *The Soldier and the Citizen: The Role of the Military in Taiwan's Development* (Armonk, N.Y.: M. E. Sharpe, 1997); Cheng Hsiao-shih, *Party-Military Relations in the PRC and Taiwan* (Boulder, Colo.: Westview Press, 1990); Bruce J. Dickson, *Democratization in China and Taiwan: The Adaptability of Leninist Parties* (Oxford: Clarendon Press, 1998); David Shambaugh, "Taiwan's Security: Maintaining Deterrence Amidst Political Accountability," in David Shambaugh, ed., *Contemporary Taiwan* (Oxford: Clarendon Press, 1998); Lu-Hsun Hung, "Observations on Civilian Control of the ROC Armed Forces Following the Passage of Two Laws Concerning National Defense," *Taiwan Defense Affairs* 1, no. 2 (Winter 2000/2001): 7–38; and Chin-chiang Su and Ming-shih Shen, "Taiwan's Political Warfare System and Civil-Military Relations," ibid.: 39–64.

17. Of the many accounts, see Timothy Brook, *Quelling the People: The Military Suppression of the Beijing Democracy Movement* (Oxford: Oxford University

the PLA to clear Tiananmen Square and Beijing of demonstrators in June 1989 presented enormous challenges to the military and strained party-army relations. Some of the consequences—such as a continuing arms embargo and sanctions imposed by the G-7 countries—are still being felt and have significantly hampered PLA modernization (although some of the slack is being taken up by Russia). Other consequences—such as the extreme indoctrination of the rank and file—stalled professionalism and training. Still others—such as factionalism and purges in the officer corps—induced stress among the elite and diverted attention from pressing needs. While PLA intervention rescued the party and may well have saved the PRC as a state, its use in Tiananmen had largely negative consequences for the armed forces.

One area where the military did stand to benefit in the wake of the Tiananmen confrontation was in its budget—which has risen sharply every year since 1989 (see chapter 4). Moreover, both the military and civilian elite learned that they needed the more flexible paramilitary for riot control; thus the People's Armed Police have received significant government attention and resources during the 1990s. While the PAP has become the first line of defense against domestic unrest, special standing orders issued by the Central Military Commission and the (then) three general departments on May 15, 1992, make it clear that the PLA itself still bears responsibility for maintaining social order. The orders do, however, specify a series of nonlethal tactics to be employed before live ammunition is used, which is only to occur in specific situations.[18] The PLA's ultimate responsibility for internal se-

---

Press, 1992); Andrew Scobell, "Why the People's Army Fired on the People: The Chinese Military and Tiananmen," *Armed Forces and Society* 18, no. 2 (Winter 1992): 192–213; Tai Ming Cheung, "The PLA and Its Role between April–June 1989," Ellis Joffe, "The Tiananmen Crisis and the Politics of the PLA," June Teufel Dreyer, "Tiananmen and the PLA," and Gerald Segal and John Phipps, "Why Communist Armies Defend Their Parties," in Richard H. Yang, ed., *China's Military: The PLA 1990/1991* (Kaohsiung: National Sun Yat-sen University, 1991); and Michael T. Byrnes, "The Death of a People's Army," in George Hicks, ed., *The Broken Mirror: China after Tiananmen* (Harrow, U.K.: Longman, 1990).

18. The standing orders stipulate:

If warnings are not obeyed, use batons, tear gas, and other such methods to force protestors to disperse. Remove or capture those who continue to block the way or who wantonly incite or carry out violence. When there is no alternative, use firearms according to regulations to forcibly manage the situation. . . . The army may use live ammunition if its way is blocked, if key installations or the lives of soldiers are endangered, if those rebelling steal weapons or ammunition, or if the army faces arson, murder, explosions, or serious threats to lives or state property. . . . If live ammunition is used,

curity was reiterated in the 1997 National Defense Law (Article 22): "The standing army, when necessary, may assist in maintaining public order in accordance with the law."[19]

The searing effect of the Tiananmen experience on the Chinese Communist leadership and the PLA was compounded by the uprisings later in the year against communist regimes across eastern Europe. Not only did armed forces fail to suppress demonstrators in these countries (attempting what the former East German strongman Erich Honecker ruefully described as the "Chinese solution"), but some actually turned against the ruling party. The Romanian revolution, which resulted in the summary executions of the dictator Nicolae Ceauşescu and his wife, had a particularly traumatic effect on China's leaders. The failed August 1991 coup in the Soviet Union, and the subsequent disintegration of the Soviet state, fueled further concern among the Chinese leaders about potentially disloyal officers and troops. Taken together, these events convinced the Chinese party and military leadership that "control of the gun" needed to be significantly strengthened lest the East European and Soviet experiences be repeated in China. This conviction extended beyond the PLA to the entire public security and paramilitary apparatus. As a result, steps were taken during the next three years to strengthen "political work" in the armed forces and to ensure the military's loyalty to the party.

Ensuring Loyalties

In the immediate aftermath of June 4, the PLA remained on a state of high alert in the capital until martial law was lifted in January 1990.[20] Twenty-two divisions of thirteen different PLA Group Armies drawn from all across China, occupied Beijing.[21] After several days of terrorizing the capital, restor-

---

the army must, under normal circumstances, fire singly and not in bursts. It must not fire wildly, shoot into crowds, or at children and pregnant women.

Quoted by Reuters (based on a leaked copy of the standing orders), *International Herald Tribune*, September 16, 1992.

19. Law of the People's Republic of China on National Defense, British Broadcasting Service Summary of World Broadcasting/Far East (hereafter cited as SWB/FE), March 22, 1997, S2/3.

20. Parts of this section draw upon my "The Soldier and the State in China: The Political Work System in the People's Liberation Army," *China Quarterly*, no. 127 (September 1991): 527–68.

21. As reported in Central Military Commission documents as cited in Andrew Nathan and Perry Link, eds., *The Tiananmen Papers* (New York: Public Affairs, 2001), p. 239.

ing order, and cleaning up, martial law troops began a political offensive, interrogating citizens and conducting propaganda work aimed at educating the populace about the need for "stability," law and order, and suppressing the "counterrevolutionary armed rebellion." Various civilian institutions were physically occupied by PLA forces, which bivouacked on-site for several months. This was especially the case with educational and research institutions whose members were active during the spring demonstrations: the Chinese Academy of Social Sciences, the Commission and Institute of Economic Reform of the State Council, Beijing University, Beijing Normal University, Beijing Aeronautics Institute, and China Politics and Law University (labeled the six "major disaster zones," or *zhong zai qu*, by martial law authorities). Countless individuals in these and other units *(danwei)* were interrogated and arrested. After Deng Xiaoping met with officers of the Martial Law Command on June 9, and praised them for being the "Great Steel Wall" of the Chinese Communist Party,[22] a propaganda blitz was launched to educate citizens about the army's "heroic deeds" and losses of life at the hands of "counterrevolutionary elements" who "sought to overturn state power."[23] As one *Jiefangjun Bao* (Liberation Army Daily) article put it, "Our cadres and soldiers came under attack from all sides. They were insulted, scolded, and beaten up. They had never experienced this in the past."[24] In other media organizations, such as *Renmin Ribao* (People's Daily), Radio Beijing, and Central China Television, PLA personnel were installed as broadcasters, writers, and editors to oversee the campaign. A special exhibition of the suppression was set up at the Military Museum, and the General Political Department dispatched personnel to distribute propaganda leaflets door-to-door in Beijing neighborhoods.

Apart from restoring order in the capital and launching the propaganda counteroffensive, the principal task facing the PLA was to police its own ranks and ferret out recalcitrant troops who had shirked duty or opposed orders during the crackdown. There were numerous reports of commanders who refused to use force, AWOL troops, and even clashing units. In retro-

22. Deng's speech is available in Orville Schell and David Shambaugh, eds., *The China Reader: The Reform Era* (New York: Vintage Press, 1999).

23. For a sample of some of this campaign and internal leadership speeches, see David Shambaugh, ed., *The Making of the Big Lie: Content and Process in the CCP Propaganda System*, special issue of *Chinese Law and Government* 25, no. 5 (Spring 1992); and anon., *Beijing Fengbo Jishi* (Record of the Beijing Storm) (Beijing: Beijing Renmin Chubanshe, 1989).

24. Zang Wenqing, "Continue to Do Ideological and Political Work Well While Carrying Out the Task of Enforcing Martial Law," *Jiefangjun Bao*, September 7, 1989, in FBIS–CHI, September 22, 1989.

spect, it does not seem that the last took place. To this day, however, the extent of the insubordination remains unclear. It is known that the commander of the pivotal 38th Group Army, General Xu Qinxian, disobeyed orders and was stripped of his command, while his troops were ordered into action.[25] On May 20, the day martial law was proclaimed, Marshal Xu Xiangqian and Marshal Nie Rongzhen reportedly published letters in the Shanghai newspaper *Wen Hui Bao* opposing the use of force by the military, and eight generals and admirals signed a one-sentence letter addressed to Deng Xiaoping and the Central Military Commission, stating, "We request that troops not enter the city and that martial law not be carried out in Beijing."[26]

Although the total extent of the insubordination remains uncertain, it is clear that disciplinary action was taken against large numbers of officers and soldiers. The revitalized Discipline Inspection Commission (DIC) organs in the PLA spearheaded the investigations, and the General Political Department's procuracy court-martialed cases. Within three months, it was reported that half of the "leadership groups [i.e., officers] at or above the division level" had been investigated.[27] This investigation discovered that 92 percent of these units had shown "good or relatively good party style and discipline." Those in breach of discipline, including "seven high-ranking cadres," were dealt with "sternly" by the DIC and GPD. Precise figures for courts-martial have never been publicly released, but the GPD's head, General Yang Baibing, who was put in control of the post-Tiananmen vetting in the PLA, allegedly informed the All-Army Political Work Conference in December 1989 that 111 officers had "breached discipline in a serious way," and that 1,400 soldiers "shed their weapons and ran away."[28] Some reports indicate that as many as 3,500 PLA and PAP commanders and commissars were investigated, with the majority being reprimanded rather than charged.[29] The most important of these was General Xu Qinxian, who

25. Nathan and Link, *Tiananmen Papers*, p. 239.

26. Ibid., p. 265. Those who signed the letter were Wang Ping, Ye Fei, Zhang Aiping, Xiao Ke, Yang Dezhi, Chen Zaidao, Song Shilun, and Li Jukui.

27. Luo Yuwen, "Army Investigates High-Ranking and Middle-Ranking Leadership Groups," *Renmin Ribao*, September 16, 1989, in FBIS–CHI, September 21, 1989.

28. See Willy Wo-lap Lam, "Yang Baibing Reveals Army Defiance in Crackdown," *South China Morning Post*, December 28, 1989. The alleged text of Yang's speech, translated and published in the *China Quarterly* does not cite such figures. See Yang Baibing, "Some Questions Concerning Strengthening and Improving the Political Work of the Army under the New Situation," in "Quarterly Chronicle and Documentation," *China Quarterly*, no. 131 (September 1992): 897–907.

29. Harlan Jencks, "Civil-Military Relations in China: Tiananmen and After," *Problems of Communism* 40 (May–June 1991): 22.

feigned illness to avoid commanding his troops. He was subsequently court-martialed and imprisoned.[30]

Over the next year, as the propaganda campaign intensified, widespread personnel changes took place in the upper reaches of the armed forces. Six of the seven military region commanders and commissars were replaced or reshuffled, and there was an even more thorough housecleaning at the military district level.[31] Those who had distinguished themselves or had demonstrated loyalty during the 1989 crackdown were promoted, along with a large number of ideologically pure political commissars. The shakeup was overseen by General Yang Baibing, who sought to build up his network of cronies in the process (an attempt that would come back to haunt him). To some extent, the personnel changes must be seen as part of a routine rotation, but the choice of those promoted indicates political favoritism.

In the propaganda offensive, four principal themes were stressed:

- · Discipline in the ranks

- · Ensuring the "absolute control" of the Communist Party over the PLA

- · Combating the "new enemies," "peaceful evolution" and "bourgeois liberalization"

- · Improving political work at the basic (i.e., company and regimental) level

These four themes were pursued more or less simultaneously over the next three years. Closely related to the investigations and actions taken to improve discipline in the ranks, noted above, was the emphasis placed on ensuring army loyalty to the CCP.

A 1989 National Day editorial in *Jiefangjun Bao* sounded a clarion call that would be heard repeatedly over the coming months, proclaiming the "party's absolute leadership" *(dang de juedui lingdao)* over the army.[32] Why was this necessary? Because "the counterrevolutionary rebellion in Beijing gave us a strong lesson in blood and helped us understand that, as a strong pillar for the people's democratic dictatorship, this army has an unshirkable duty to resolutely suppress the hostile forces and reactionaries who attempt to subvert the party's leadership and state power under certain circum-

---

30. Ibid.
31. Ibid.
32. Commentator, "Uphold the Party's Absolute Leadership, Ensure That Our Army Is Always Politically Up to Standard," *Jiefangjun Bao,* October 1, 1989, in FBIS–CHI, November 16, 1989.

stances, such as a large-scale counterrevolutionary rebellion breaking out at home."[33] Moreover, the editorial stated that the PLA was "an armed group for carrying out the party's political tasks," and accordingly, "the guns should always be firmly held by those loyal to the party." No clearer statement could have been made signaling the role of the PLA as a political army in the service of those who controlled the party, and that this role naturally extended to the maintenance of internal security. Not a word was said in the editorial about defending the nation against external threats to national security, military modernization, training, or other "professional" pursuits. Indeed, maintaining the "absolute leadership of the party" was cited as "*the* most important task in army building," by the new CMC Chairman Jiang Zemin and First Vice-Chairman Yang Shangkun at the enlarged CMC meeting in November 1989.[34]

This facet of the propaganda campaign—taken together with the strengthening of the party committee, discipline inspection, and political commissar systems—clearly indicates a qualitative shift in army-party relations after Tiananmen. Generally speaking, since the seminal 1985 expanded meeting of the Central Military Commission, political work had been downplayed in the PLA in favor of force modernization. After this meeting and until Tiananmen, the armed forces assumed a more distinct corporate and professional identity, more autonomous from party and political dictates. To be sure, this was a *relative* shift: there was little doubt that the party still "commanded the gun," and that political work still played an important role at the unit level. In retrospect, however, one sensed the first cracks in the symbiotic relationship. This shift was not accidental, as several reformist intellectuals closely allied with CCP General Secretary Zhao Ziyang (particularly Yan Jiaqi and Su Shaozhi of the Chinese Academy of Social Sciences) had floated the concept of "separating party and army" *(dang-jun fenkai)* in tandem with the official policy of "separating party and government" *(dang-zheng fenkai)*. The latter was thought necessary to remove party interference in decision making better left to managers at the enterprise level and economists in government, but the idea of separating party and army was far more radical given the sixty-year symbiotic relationship between the two. It was never implemented, although Zhao Ziyang apparently discussed it with members of the Central Military Commission in his capac-

33. Ibid.
34. Commentator, "Take Political Strengthening as the Most Important Task," *Jiefangjun Bao*, November 27, 1989, in FBIS–CHI, December 22, 1989.

ity as first vice-chairman.[35] Yan and Su had read Samuel Huntington's *The Soldier and the State* and, for various reasons, came to the conclusion that the PLA should be depoliticized and put under state control. The purging of Zhao, the Tiananmen action, and the forced exile of Yan and Su made such considerations moot. After the military suppression, several articles in *Jiefangjun Bao* specifically criticized "some people"—which included "Su Shaozhi and his ilk"—who had pursued the "separation of party and army" and sought "the creation of an army on the Western model that did not meddle in politics."[36] One post-Tiananmen article concluded: "The advocacy [by Su Shaozhi et al.] to separate the army from the party is only a component part of their plot to overthrow the Communist Party leadership in favor of the multiparty system."[37] Yang Baibing himself took aim at the concept of a national army in a 1991 *Renmin Ribao* article and subsequently at a specially convened All-Army Political Work Conference.[38]

Another key issue of political work in the armed forces during the first phase of post-Tiananmen indoctrination campaigns was to combat the "new enemies," "peaceful evolution" and "bourgeois liberalization." The spring 1989 demonstrations themselves were said to be manifestations of the infiltration of these new enemies into China. "Peaceful evolution" was described in PLA documents as the unremitting effort of international monopoly capitalism to "wage a smokeless war" inside the ranks of the PLA and "defeat socialism in China without firing a shot!"[39] The campaign against "bourgeois liberalization" in the PLA actually began in 1987 (in the wake of student demonstrations and labor unrest in December 1986), as it did inside the CCP, but it intensified in the wake of Tiananmen. Stress was placed on "purifying the cultural environment in the barracks" and "rectifying unhealthy tendencies." To this end, the GPD dispatched hundreds of investigative work teams to units across the country—which discovered that units in the Guangzhou, Nanjing, and Jinan Military Regions

35. Interview with Su Shaozhi, July 1994. A senior GPD official denied that Zhao himself had advocated this separation, but indicated that a number of his advisors had. Interview, June 21, 1991.
36. See Lin Jiangong, "Refuting the 'Advocacy of Separating the Army from the Party,'" *Jiefangjun Bao*, November 21, 1989, in FBIS–CHI, December 22, 1989.
37. Ibid.
38. As noted by Michael Swaine, *The Military and Political Succession in China* (Santa Monica, Calif.: RAND Corporation, 1992), pp. 162–63.
39. See, e.g., He Yingquan, "'The Wolf Has Come' and 'Where Is the Wolf?'—Calling for Proper Alertness to the Presence of the Enemy," *Jiefangjun Bao*, October 8, 1989, in FBIS–CHI, November 7, 1989.

were particularly decadent.[40] Pornography was found to be rampant in the ranks.

Six months after Tiananmen, with the siege mentality still gripping the party and military leadership, the CMC convened the All-Army Political Work Conference. The conclave convened as Romanian security forces were battling each other around the presidential palace and on the streets of Bucharest. General Yang Baibing presided over and opened the meeting with the rueful reflection that "this disturbance and the recent developing trend and rapid changes in eastern Europe have raised many weighty problems worth pondering for our political work."[41] The conference necessarily concentrated on ideological and disciplinary matters.[42] It promulgated a document entitled "Concerning Strengthening and Improving the Political Work of the Army under the New Situation," which was circulated for study throughout the armed forces. "The complex situation at home and abroad makes it necessary that gun barrels are wielded by truly politically trustworthy people," this document asserted, saying that under conditions of a "reactionary international tendency" the greatest security threat to China now came in the form of "peaceful evolution." All units were instructed to be vigilant against "infiltration" by this new enemy, as "counterrevolutionary forces abroad" were linking up with "antisocialist elements at home to overturn the socialist system."[43] Following the conference, and over the next year, the propaganda blitz intensified, and "political work" was accorded a priority it had not known for many years. Some units had to devote two or three afternoons per week to special study sessions.[44] This took a number of forms: materials in the military media; short-term rotational classes at the regimental level and above; study groups within units; specialized short courses convened at the National Defense University; and a barrage of GPD-dispatched ideological instructors.[45] The in-

40. See, e.g., Chen Xianyi, "Initial Achievements Made in Cleansing the Cultural Environment in Army Barracks," *Jiefangjun Bao*, October 28, 1989, in FBIS–CHI, November 17, 1989.

41. *Jiefangjun Bao* (Liberation Army Daily), ed., *Jiaqiang Renmin Jundui de Zhengzhi Jianshe: Quanjun Zhengzhi Gongzuo Huiyi Jiyao he Youguan Lunwen, Zhushi Tiaomu* (Beijing: Changzheng Chubanshe, 1990), p. 25.

42. See account in Zhang Yutao, ed., *Xin Zhongguo Junshi Dashiji Yao* (Beijing: Junshi Kexue Chubanshe, 1998), p. 511.

43. Quotations from the summary *(jiyao)* of the document, as published in *Jiefangjun Bao*, ed., *Jiaqiang Renmin Jundui de Zhengzhi Jianshe*, p. 25; a full translation appears in *China Quarterly*, no. 131 (September 1992).

44. Interviews with Beijing Military Region officers, spring 1991.

45. This process is detailed in my "The Soldier and the State in China."

doctrination started at the top and progressively worked down to the regimental level.

A parallel effort was made to strengthen the political commissar, discipline inspection, and party committee systems throughout the armed forces. For the first time, party committees were established at the lowest possible level: the company. This undertaking continued throughout the 1990s, and became the centerpiece of Jiang Zemin's so-called "Sixteen Character Guidance" of 1999, "Collective leadership, democratic centralism, individual deliberation, group decision" *(jiti lingdao, minzhu jizhong, gebie yunniang, huiyi jueding)*. The essence of this directive, PLA documents explained, was to strengthen the role of party committees throughout the military.[46]

The atmosphere of intensified indoctrination and concern over the political loyalty of the army continued to dominate the PLA until the end of 1992. But its intensity, and particularly the role of General Yang Baibing, finally produced a political backlash. The CCP's attempts to ensure PLA loyalty had in fact been used by Yang to concentrate power in his own hands (as secretary-general of the CMC and GPD director) and to install a network of senior officers loyal to him throughout the central PLA departments in Beijing, as well as in regional commands. The GPD became his personal fiefdom. The extent, if any, to which his elder half-brother Yang Shangkun had a hand in these personnel appointments or the propaganda campaign is unclear, but he certainly indirectly benefited from them.

In many ways, the Tiananmen crisis interrupted the process of professionalization that Deng had attempted to institute in the wake of the 1979 Vietnam incursion. Many senior commanders were therefore resentful of the renewed emphasis on politicization in the wake of June 4—and many were perhaps privately opposed to the use of the military for domestic security purposes.[47] Many were also suspicious of the motives for the personnel changes during 1990–91, particularly the fact that a large number of officers with GPD backgrounds and those involved in the Tiananmen suppression were promoted. These concerns were repeatedly conveyed to Deng Xiaoping by senior retired and active duty officers from 1990 through 1992 and came to a head on the eve of the Fourteenth Congress of the CCP in September 1992. Several senior officers warned Deng of the Yangs' empire building and called for remedial action. This approach was apparently pre-

46. See, e.g., Fan Yinhua, "'Shiliugezi' fangzhen shi dangwei lingdao gongzuo de jiben zunxun" (The Sixteen Character Guidance Is Adherence to the Party Committee's Work), *Guofang Daxue Xuebao*, no. 1 (January 1999): 65–67.

47. This is an impression I have gained in numerous discussions with PLA officers and others connected with the military since 1989.

cipitated by several actions taken by Yang Baibing prior to the conference: the convening of secret meetings to discuss contingency plans for Deng Xiaoping's death, and the preparation of officer promotion lists and a list of PLA members to be appointed to the Central Committee at the upcoming Congress (both lists were packed with Yang loyalists).

Within days of the Congress, Deng moved against the Yangs. Both were immediately removed from the Central Military Commission. Yang Baibing was stripped of his GPD directorship but was nonetheless promoted to the Politburo at the Congress (although he wielded no influence and disappeared from public view shortly thereafter). Yang Shangkun was permitted to finish out his term as PRC president but had his formal channels of influence in the army curtailed.

Factionalism, or "mountaintopism," as it is often referred to in the PLA, has long been a feature of Chinese military politics. Deng had witnessed much of it and knew that it was a major impediment to the professionalization of the armed forces. Jiang Zemin knew that the Yangs were a significant obstacle to his gaining control of the army and thereby consolidating his own power. So, despite the lifelong Deng-Yang connection, drastic action was taken. The purge of the Yangs was pivotal in Jiang Zemin's attempts to build his own power base in the military and solidify his nominal role as commander in chief. It also set off a long process of personnel changes in the military.

This was an important turning point in post-Tiananmen civil-military relations. It certainly removed tension from the pinnacle of the system. On another level, the PLA's collective political influence remained strong and its input into policymaking increased—PLA representatives garnered a higher percentage of seats (24 percent) on the Central Committee than at any time since the Eleventh Congress in 1977 (including the appointment of Liu Huaqing to the Politburo Standing Committee), senior commanders sat in on Politburo meetings and certain leading groups, and PLA budgets continued to rise at double-digit rates. Three years of intensified assertion of party control over the military had strengthened the CCP's organization *inside* the military. Nonetheless, the pressures for increased military autonomy and corporate professionalism were building (ironically, this was the very trend set in motion by Deng and Yang Shangkun prior to Tiananmen) and would reassert themselves in the following years.

All three principal tendencies that have endured in PRC civil-military relations over time—symbiosis, control, and relative autonomy—were manifest at this juncture in late 1992. One can only agree with Ellis Joffe in describing this as a confusing and contradictory period of "trends and counter-trends."[48] By 1997–98, however, symbiosis had faded, party control had eroded, state/government authority had increased, and relative PLA autonomy had broadened. In hindsight, the mid 1990s may be seen as the true transition period from the old communist order toward a more corporate, professional, autonomous, and accountable military. Other trends, particularly the military's increasing commercial involvement, were also apparent in the mid 1990s—but curtailing the PLA's financial empire by the end of the decade was a further significant step in the direction of increased professionalism.

While the CCP leadership remained nervous about PLA loyalties, both the players and rules of the game changed after 1992. Personnel changes in the senior officer corps and increased attempts by Jiang Zemin to consolidate his authority over the PLA and PAP changed the players. The military took the opportunity to gain more control of its own affairs and to assert itself in certain national security matters (especially concerning Taiwan), while the state (the National People's Congress and State Council) increased oversight of the armed forces, thus changing the rules.

THE PLAYERS IN MILITARY POLITICS

Following the purge of the Yangs, the participants at the top of the military pyramid changed almost in toto. In assessing the High Command, one must distinguish proximate players from peripheral ones. The true circle of proximate players comprises members of the Central Military Commission, while the peripheral players are the seven military region commanders, their political commissars, and the deputy heads of the four general departments. However, unlike in the Maoist era, today there are no independently powerful regional military commanders who rule "independent kingdoms" and wield clout in Beijing's power game from afar. Since the purge of the Yangs, neither are there powerful retired military elders playing influential roles behind the scenes (although the patronage networks of the octogenarian generals Zhang Zhen and Zhang Aiping remain operative). Indeed, one of the accomplishments of the Jiang era has been to narrow the circle of those who possess authority and influence in military affairs and civil-military

48. Ellis Joffe, *The Military and China's New Politics: Trends and Counter-Trends,* CAPS Papers, no. 19 (Taipei: Chinese Council of Advanced Policy Studies, 1997).

relations. This is true not only in the military but even more noticeably in civilian party politics.[49] Today, only Jiang himself has any influence in military matters—and, as I argue below, his authority is constrained. Vice President Hu Jintao (also a member of the Politburo Standing Committee) is the only other civilian party official with any role in military politics, and this only derives from his promotion to the position of vice chairman of the CMC in September 1999. Hu brings no personal experience in the military, has no personal ties to senior military officers, and is widely known not to command respect from the PLA. For this reason, Hu may lack important institutional support in his anticipated succession to Jiang in 2002–3 as general secretary of the CCP, president of the PRC, and CMC chairman.

The lack of civilian influence over the military is a function more of changes in the party elite than in the military. The current lack of military experience among senior party leaders breaks with a long-standing element of party-army relations. The "interlocking directorate" has been broken, and with it a key component of the traditional symbiotic army-party linkage. The importance of this should not be overstated, but it does begin to fundamentally redefine the overall nature of elite politics in China. This redefinition, in turn, creates the opportunity for the armed forces to carve out greater autonomy from the party. Nonetheless, the CMC remains unquestionably a Communist Party organ; the PLA is still the party's army, all officers above the rank of senior colonel are party members, and the CCP still institutionally penetrates the military apparatus. Nonetheless, these important changes in party-army relations will likely have lasting consequences.

Another factor has to do with the continuing professionalization of the officer corps and concomitant promotion of officers with command experience instead of political commissars.[50] This primarily affects the peripheral military elite—that is, the top forty or fifty full, lieutenant, and major generals—although they are not regularly engaged in civil-military affairs.

The proximate military elite—members of the Central Military Commission—are those who participate in civil-military relations on a regular basis.

---

49. See You Ji, "Jiang Zemin's Command of the Military," *China Journal*, no. 45 (January 2001): 131–38; David Shambaugh, "The Dynamics of Elite Politics during the Jiang Era," ibid.: 101–12.

50. For two excellent studies of the professionalizing officer corps, see James C. Mulvenon, *Professionalization of the Senior Chinese Officer Corps: Trends and Implications* (Santa Monica, Calif.: RAND Corporation, 1997); and June Teufel Dreyer, "The New Officer Corps: Implications for the Future," *China Quarterly*, no. 146 (June 1996): 315–35.

TABLE 1 Central Military Commission Members, 2001

Member	Position	Date of Membership
Jiang Zemin	chairman	November 1989
Hu Jintao	vice-chairman	September 1999
Chi Haotian	vice-chairman	September 1995
Zhang Wannian	vice-chairman	September 1995
Cao Gangchuan	member	November 1998
Fu Quanyou	member	October 1992
Guo Boxiong	member	September 1999
Wang Ke	member	September 1995
Wang Ruilin	member	September 1995
Xu Caihou	member	September 1999
Yu Yongbo	member	October 1992

The Central Military Commission today is chaired by CCP General Secretary and President Jiang Zemin and is composed of three vice-chairmen (Hu Jintao, Zhang Wannian, and Chi Haotian), and seven regular members (Fu Quanyou, Yu Yongbo, Wang Ke, Wang Ruilin, Cao Gangchuan, Guo Boxiong, and Xu Caihou). The group is shown in plate 3, following page 224.

THE CENTRAL MILITARY COMMISSION MEMBERSHIP

Jiang Zemin is by far the most important civilian in the civil-military arena.[51] Indeed, aside from Vice President Hu Jintao, one is hard pressed to identify *any* other member of the party or government elite who has any influence or contact with the PLA High Command. Nor should Hu's influence be exaggerated. He has no military experience, although he did serve as the first party secretary of the Tibet and Guizhou military districts during his service there (1985–88). His elevation to the CMC at the Fourth Plenum of the Fifteenth Central Committee in September 1999 was a transparent move to continue the grooming of Jiang's successor by giving him some military responsibility and exposure (see table 1).

51. The organization and functioning of the CMC, the PLA's most senior body, is provided in chapter 4. For further explication of Jiang's relationship with the PLA, see Tai Ming Cheung, "Jiang Zemin at the Helm: His Quest for Power and Paramount Status," *China Strategic Review* 3, no. 1 (Spring 1998): 167–91; and David Shambaugh, "China's Commander-in-Chief: Jiang Zemin and the PLA," in C. Den-

Hu is no better prepared than Jiang was when he was suddenly appointed chairman of the CMC in November 1989. Upon his appointment, Jiang reportedly confessed:

> At the Fourth Plenum, I said that I was not worthy of being elevated to [the position] of general secretary; I did not have the ideological preparation. This decision to promote me to Central Military Commission chairman has also left me without proper ideological preparation. I have not undertaken work in military affairs and have no experience in this regard. I deeply feel the responsibility, but my ability is insufficient [*li de congxin*]. The party has placed a big responsibility on me. I shall certainly assiduously study military affairs, strive to become quickly familiar with the situation in the military, and diligently and quickly carry out the duties [of the position].[52]

Despite his understandable uncertainty, over the course of the past decade Jiang Zemin has done a remarkably good job of cultivating a base of support in the PLA. He has certainly done a better job of winning military support than either of his predecessors, Hu Yaobang and Zhao Ziyang (both of whom drew lukewarm support or opposition from the PLA High Command). Moreover, he weathered the 1995–96 Taiwan crisis, oversaw the removal of the Yangs and a wholesale turnover of the High Command, and felt confident enough to order the armed forces to divest themselves of their commercial holdings in 1998.

In cultivating a base of support in the PLA, Jiang has been careful, persistent, and methodical in his strategy and tactics. He has certainly been attentive since the beginning of his tenure in office—frequently visiting bases and units, cultivating relationships with various high-ranking officers, and staking out palatable positions on issues of key concern to the PLA. His has been a building-block strategy—establishing bases of support among different institutional subconstituencies in the military, but always being mindful of cultivating relations with key allies in the Central Military Commission, central departments, and regional commands. He has hitched his horse to certain individuals, but he has not been afraid to switch positions and abandon some when it was expedient. He has astutely gauged sentiments

---

nison Lane et al., eds., *Chinese Military Modernization* (London: Kegan Paul International; Washington, D.C.: AEI Press, 1996), pp. 209–45. This section draws, in part, on this earlier work.

52. Li Guoqiang et al., *Zhonggong Junfang Jiangling* (High-Ranking Officers of the Chinese Communist Military) (Hong Kong: Wide Angle Press, 1992), p. 6. Author's translation.

in the armed forces and adapted his speeches and activities accordingly—a characteristic that previously earned Jiang the nickname "the weathervane" of the "wind faction" *(feng pai)*. Key elements of Jiang's strategy include: personnel changes, support for military modernization and professionalism, and receptivity to military sentiments in foreign and domestic policy matters.

Since disposing of the Yangs, Jiang Zemin has paid close attention to personnel policy in the armed forces. He has personally promoted more than fifty officers to the rank of full general. It was reported that in the early 1990s, Jiang himself insisted on reviewing the files of any officer recommended for promotion down to the level of division commander.[53] In personnel matters, Jiang has had to rely heavily on the advice and influence of Generals Wang Ruilin, Yu Yongbo, and Zhang Wannian. Jiang's military secretary *(mishu)* on the CMC, Jia Ting'an, has also played an influential role as deputy director of the CMC General Office.

During Jiang's tenure as chairman of the Central Military Commission, a wholesale turnover of personnel has taken place in the CMC itself, in the four general departments (the General Staff, Logistics, Armaments, and Political Departments), in military region and district commands, at the group army level, in elite military academies, and in the paramilitary People's Armed Police. Not since the aftermath of the Lin Biao affair in the early 1970s or the housecleaning after the purge of the "small Gang of Four" in 1981–82 has the PLA experienced such widespread turnover of personnel. There is considerable evidence that Jiang Zemin has overseen and approved this process and has been personally engaged in specific removals and appointments. He has certainly benefited from the turnover, even if he cannot claim true personal loyalty from many of those promoted. Jiang has overseen the promotion of numerous officers he has met during his tours of the military regions, but otherwise there are really only two examples of promotions directly tied to Jiang: General Ba Zhongtan and his successor General You Xigui as head of the Central Guards Bureau. Thus, in one respect, Jiang has appreciated one of the cardinal tenets of being a Leninist leader—control of the *nomenklatura*. Not only is control of personnel central to political survival and power in a communist political system, it is also key to policy implementation, because one has to be able to trust subordinates to carry out dictates and implement policy.

Another key facet of Jiang's strategy regarding the PLA has been to reach out to various constituencies within the armed forces, trying to mobilize as

53. Lu Yushan, "Jiang Zemin Hits Out in All Directions to Consolidate His Strength," *Dangdai* (Hong Kong), July 15, 1994, in FBIS–CHI, August 17, 1994, p. 14.

broad a coalition of support as possible (what might be described as "pork barrel politics with Chinese characteristics"). In various ways and at various times, Jiang has played to and placated the political commissars (General Political Department), the military-industrial complex (General Logistics Department and five defense corporations), the defense science and technology establishment (COSTIND and GAD), the nuclear forces (Second Artillery), the military academies (NDU and AMS), the People's Armed Police, the General Staff Department, and all three services. Jiang has at various times supported all the important themes: politicization of the military and loyalty to the party; professionalization of the armed forces; modernization of equipment, doctrine, and research and development; and protection of state sovereignty and national security interests. He has been a proponent of "army building," a harsh critic of corruption and laxity, a supporter and then an opponent of commercial activities in the PLA, and a proponent of increased military budgets and improved living standards. And, throughout, he has wrapped himself in the garb of Deng Xiaoping's teachings on "army-building in new historical circumstances."

Jiang has been all things to all quarters and has demonstrated in his moves toward the PLA the same political strategy he has demonstrated toward other constituencies in the Chinese political system. He is a consummate politician—playing to, balancing, and placating different constituencies. Chinese politics should be thought of as an endless web of bureaucratic and political constituencies that compete and bargain for position and resources within a vertically organized Leninist system.[54] In this respect, Jiang is a new breed of Chinese politician, not cut from the same cloth as his Leninist or Maoist predecessors (or even his colleagues Li Peng and Zhu Rongji, both of whom show more autocratic tendencies). Rather than command, Jiang conciliates and arbitrates between competing interests, trying to build support among individual components that can be forged into a broad-based coalition. Jiang is not prone to backroom factional maneuvering or strong-arm tactics but is capable of both. He is not beholden to any bureaucratic or geographic base of support (although he has clearly promoted his colleagues from Shanghai). His inclinations are politically conservative, but this serves him well during times of succession indeterminacy. Prior to 1997, Jiang seemed con-

54. See Kenneth Lieberthal and Michel Oksenberg, *Policy Making in China: Leaders, Structures, and Processes* (Princeton, N.J.: Princeton University Press (1988); Kenneth Lieberthal and David M. Lampton, eds., *Bureaucracy, Politics, and Decision-Making in Post-Mao China* (Berkeley and Los Angeles: University of California Press, 1992); and Susan Shirk, *The Political Logic of Economic Reform in China* (Berkeley and Los Angeles: University of California Press, 1993).

templative, plodding, careful, deliberate, and cautious, but subsequently he has become much more assertive in advocating policy (including toward the military). His political style may reveal an important move away from a hierarchical Leninist system to a more constituency- and coalition-based political system (albeit within a single party system)—one more characteristic of other newly industrializing countries and proto-democracies.[55]

The third facet of Jiang's strategy for earning support from the PLA has been greater sensitivity to PLA concerns in foreign and national security affairs. To some extent, he has had no choice, because the military has asserted itself on several issues of concern to it. Also, it is not unnatural for the PLA to express its views on matters of national security—and it has done so with respect to Taiwan, relations with the United States, the U.S.-Japan Revised Defense Guidelines, India's detonation of nuclear devices, and potential U.S. development and deployment of theater missile defenses (TMD). In all these instances, Jiang has been receptive and responsive to military concerns. The closest he has come to being challenged by the PLA came in the wake of the 1995 visit by Taiwan's President Lee Teng-hui to the United States. Jiang was held personally responsible by the PLA brass for the policy "failure" that permitted the visit, and he and Foreign Minister Qian Qichen were forced to make self-criticisms before the Central Military Commission during the second week of July 1995.[56] Qian was held accountable, because he had assured the Politburo Standing Committee that "under no circumstances" would Lee Teng-hui be granted a visa to the United States.[57] Jiang apparently acquiesced at the CMC meeting to PLA demands that a "military option" be activated vis-à-vis Taiwan.[58] Immediately following Jiang's self-criticism, the PLA announced two rounds of ballistic missile tests just off the northern coast of Taiwan, undertook conventional military exercises in the Taiwan Strait, and continued nuclear testing

55. For more on Jiang Zemin's political style, see Bruce Gilley, *Tiger on the Brink: Jiang Zemin and China's New Elite* (Berkeley and Los Angeles: University of California Press, 1998), and Willy Wo-Lap Lam, *The Era of Jiang Zemin* (Singapore: Simon & Schuster, 1998).

56. Interviews with knowledgeable sources in Hong Kong and Beijing, July 1995. One source argued that in Chinese political culture, Jiang's self-criticism was an astute move. This source claimed that Jiang's self-criticism was self-initiated, and thus Jiang was able to earn kudos by voluntarily taking blame. He could thereafter position himself to "get tough" with both Taipei and Washington.

57. U.S. Secretary of State Warren Christopher had personally assured Qian of this, but President Clinton overruled Christopher and the State Department.

58. See Willy Wo-Lap Lam, "Get Tough with Taiwan and U.S., Generals Tell Jiang," *South China Morning Post*, July 17, 1995, p. 4; id., "Jiang Flexes Muscles," ibid., July 26, 1995, p. 4.

in defiance of the international moratorium. On these and other foreign policy issues, Jiang has been sensitive to PLA concerns, but it is of more importance that the military has been forced to defer to civilian management since the mid 1990s. This is another indication that the PLA's policy jurisdiction has been limited strictly to the military realm.

Among PLA members of the CMC, Zhang Wannian is clearly the most important. Although Zhang had unspecified health difficulties in 1997–98 (reportedly a heart condition), he continues to hold the de facto top spot. Zhang emerged as the most senior member of the PLA High Command in 1996–97, a fact underlined by his inclusion as the military representative in the four-member official delegation for the Hong Kong reversion ceremonies (along with President Jiang Zemin, Premier Li Peng, and Foreign Minister Qian Qichen).

Zhang Wannian's background is typical of the new military leadership; he is a soldier's soldier. His age and career bridge the pre- and post-1949 periods and make him typical of the "third generation" of military leadership. A career field officer from the Fourth Field Army system (under Lin Biao), Zhang took part in the final campaign of the civil war. His star really began to rise, however, in the wake of the 1979 Sino-Vietnamese border war. Zhang distinguished himself during the war, particularly when he led the 127th Division in the battle of Liang Shan, an offensive that turned out to be one of the PLA's few tactical accomplishments in the war. He consequently was decorated and received personal praise from Deng Xiaoping. This put Zhang on the fast track for promotion. In 1982, he became deputy commander of the Wuhan MR, and in 1987, he was appointed commander of the Guangzhou MR. There Zhang created the PLA's first rapid reaction unit *(kuaisu fanying budui)* and convened the first joint-service exercises—thus establishing two core components of contemporary PLA doctrine. In 1988, perhaps in recognition of these achievements, Zhang was promoted to the rank of lieutenant general, and in 1990, he was shifted to command the important Jinan MR. It appears that Zhang's transfer out of his southern stronghold had to do with Yang Baibing's machinations to rotate commanders and build up a power base loyal to him and to Yang Shangkun following the crackdown in Beijing. Yang Baibing personally visited Zhang in Guangzhou in May 1990, apparently seeking Zhang's retirement. Yang was sharply rebuffed, and it took an intervention by Deng Xiaoping and Yang Dezhi to transfer him to Jinan, replacing him with a Deng loyalist, Zhu Dunfa.[59]

59. As recounted in "The Resurgence of Fourth Field Army Veterans," *Kaifang* (Hong Kong), November 1992, p. 25.

The Jinan appointment was significant for Zhang for several reasons. First, as a native of Shandong (Longkou City in Yuanhuang County), he now had an opportunity to establish his credentials with the important "Shandong faction" in the PLA—many of whom occupy high positions in the armed forces. Second, after an entire career in southern and central China, it was important for Zhang to command a military region with a different set of missions. The Jinan MR is home to the North Fleet and is central to contingencies regarding Korea, Japan, the United States, and Taiwan. As the Jinan MR contributed several units to the Tiananmen crackdown (at least one regiment of the 20th Group Army, two infantry divisions from the 54th Group Army, and one division of the 67th Group Army), Zhang thus took command at a sensitive time. Prior to June 4, it was rumored that Zhang sided with Zhao Ziyang and refused to commit Guangzhou MR forces to Beijing, but this does not seem to have been the case (airborne rapid-reaction units were dispatched but did not take part in the assault on the city). Third, after he had assumed his new command, in 1992, the Jinan MR was visited by the new CMC chairman, Jiang Zemin. Jiang's tour of Jinan and other MR commands during the previous two years was instrumental in the promotion of new officers to key central-level positions following the purge of the Yang clique, and Zhang Wannian was to be one of the main beneficiaries.[60] He soon found himself transferred to Beijing to head the General Staff Department, a position he held until 1995. Being an outsider to central-level positions, possessing a solid set of previous command credentials, and not having been involved in politics or closely aligned with any particular faction all accrued to Zhang's promotion. To be sure, Zhang's unequivocal support for the June 4 Beijing massacre and ties to Zhang Zhen also aided his meteoric rise to the top spot in the PLA. After joining the Central Military Commission in December 1995, Zhang Wannian increasingly took over Zhang Zhen's portfolio of operations, training, tactics, and doctrine. He has closely identified himself with high-technology weapons and innovative tactics related to limited war, but his public speeches conform closely to standard rhetoric.

General Zhang Wannian is currently the most senior PLA officer, but he is over seventy years old, his health has not been good, and he has been rumored to be taking the blame for PLA corruption. He can thus probably be expected to "retire" in the not too distant future. His influence will still be felt, however, through a number of officers tied to him who have filled im-

---

60. See Shambaugh, "China's Commander-in-Chief: Jiang Zemin and the PLA," p. 218.

portant central and regional military posts in recent years. These include former Beijing MR Commander Li Xinliang, Nanjing MR Commander Liang Guanglie, former Guangzhou MR Commander Tao Bojun, Guangzhou MR Political Commissar Shi Yuxiao, Shenyang MR Commander Qian Guoliang, former Beijing MR Political Commissar Du Tiehuan, former Air Force Commander Liu Shunyao, Naval Commander Shi Yunsheng, People's Armed Police Commander Yang Guoping, NDU Commandant Xing Shizhong, and former Nanjing MR Commander Gu Hui. A number of officers in the Jinan and Guangzhou MRs also were Zhang's subordinates.

The second most important CMC officer is General Chi Haotian. As minister of national defense since 1993, Chi has had extensive foreign travel and interaction with foreign military and civilian leaders—including a visit to the United States in December 1996. He has also played a key role in brokering the PLA's growing ties with the Russian military and defense industrial sector. General Chi is thought to be the closest of all PLA leaders to Jiang Zemin, and he has extensive ties with the military elders Liu Huaqing, Zhang Aiping, Yang Dezhi, You Taizhong, and, formerly, to Deng Xiaoping and Xu Shiyou. Chi proved his political loyalties during crucial junctures—he played a role in coordinating the arrest of the Gang of Four in 1976 and was chief of staff during the June 4 crackdown (with ultimate command of the troops). Following the 1989 massacre, Chi was a staunch public defender of the actions taken, but he also subsequently developed a fierce rivalry with Yang Baibing. His standing has been enhanced since the dismissal of Yang in 1992, and he is a key member of the Shandong faction now dominant in the upper echelons of the PLA.

Chi Haotian has had a distinguished career in the armed forces. He joined the PLA in 1944 and fought in several key battles of the Sino-Japanese and civil wars, including the final phase of the famous Huaihai campaign. He was wounded five times in battle and was decorated as a People's Hero in 1949. He subsequently fought in the Korean War and was again decorated for valor in combat. From 1958 to 1960, Chi studied at the Military Academy in Nanjing under Commandant Zhang Zhen, in the class just before Zhang Wannian (they overlapped by a year). Chi rose to prominence in the Beijing MR in the early 1970s, having been transferred there to serve in a succession of sensitive political commissar posts following the Lin Biao incident in 1971. Throughout the 1970s, he oversaw propaganda in the region, and following the arrest of the Gang of Four, he was appointed deputy editor-in-chief of *Renmin Ribao*. When Deng Xiaoping returned to power and became chief of staff in 1977, Chi was transferred to become his deputy. Inexplicably, Chi dropped from view in 1982, only to reemerge as political commissar of the Jinan MR in 1985. In 1987, he returned to Beijing to become chief of the General Staff.

Chi Haotian is known to be a key advocate of the politicization of the PLA, particularly the subordination of the army to the Communist Party, but he has also been a public advocate of military professionalization and modernization. Given his background as a political commissar and his exposure to foreign militaries as defense minister, Chi is a good complement to the more technical, apolitical, and distinctly less cosmopolitan Zhang Wannian and Fu Quanyou. Chi appears to have few enemies in the PLA (save Yang Baibing), but—aside from Jiang Zemin—neither does he have PLA superiors to whom he is closely tied. His two previous patrons, Marshals Ye Jianying and Nie Rongzhen (both of whom promoted Chi for his role in the arrest of the Gang of Four), have died. His longevity as defense minister seems to be the result of his antipathy for the Yangs, his support for Jiang Zemin, and possibly the support of Zhang Zhen, stemming from their days together in Nanjing.

At present, the third most important member of the new PLA leadership is Fu Quanyou, currently chief of the General Staff and previously head of the General Logistics Department from 1992 to 1995. Fu is another example of the strong professional background and ethos characteristic of many of the new PLA leadership. Another highly decorated veteran of the Korean and 1979 Vietnam conflicts, General Fu has served in a series of ground force commands along China's restive minority-occupied borderlands throughout his career. A native of Shanxi and veteran of the famous First Corps of the First Field Army, Fu has spent most of his career in the Lanzhou MR—which he wound up commanding in 1990. Fu has the distinction of being a "model soldier," based on his command of the legendary "Hard Bone Sixth Company." Fu also fought in the Korean War and engaged in intensive combat with South Korean troops during 1952, when he was noted for his combined use of tanks and artillery. Fu was selected as the top student of his class of 1960 at the Nanjing Military Academy. He also served as Chengdu MR Commander from 1985 to 1990, during which time he enforced martial law in Tibet (perhaps working closely with the rising Party star Hu Jintao). His lifelong ties to Marshal He Long clearly benefited Fu, although he was purged together with He Long during the Cultural Revolution.

Fu's background has also been that of a soldier's soldier—having experience in strategy and tactics, commanding large numbers of troops, combat experience in large-scale battles, and functional expertise working in artillery, armor, infantry, and the engineering corps. His background is ideal for heading the GSD and overseeing the modernization of the PLA under the new doctrinal requirements. As chief of staff, Fu has begun to travel more widely overseas, but he is described by those who have met him as being uncomfortable in meeting with foreigners and discussing global strategic affairs (he frequently reads from a script, though he did not do so when I met him in December 1998).

The fourth most important member of the CMC is Yu Yongbo, currently director of the General Political Department. Yu has served as head of the GPD since November 1992, the longest-held position of any member of the High Command. Throughout this period, Yu has shown his loyalty to Jiang Zemin. In fact, the Jiang-Yu relationship dates to the 1980s, when Jiang was mayor of Shanghai and Yu was director of the political department of Nanjing MR, responsible for liaison with local civilian leaderships. As head of the GPD today, Yu is not only responsible for propaganda and political work in the armed forces but also plays a key role in vetting promotions. In this capacity, Yu has worked closely with General Wang Ruilin. The two men had direct responsibility for ferreting out followers of Yang Baibing following his dismissal in 1992. Yu was once thought to be a member of Yang's faction, but it seems that Yu was all along reporting to Jiang Zemin and Deng Xiaoping about the Yangs' machinations. For his loyalty he has been maintained in this sensitive position despite tremendous turnover elsewhere in the High Command.

Another important member of the PLA leadership is General Wang Ke. Wang owes much of his career rise to the PLA elder Zhang Zhen, who personally trained him in the Fourth Division of the New Fourth Field Army during the civil war. Zhang Zhen subsequently followed and oversaw Wang Ke's advancement. A veteran artillery commander, Wang has been described as a "jack of all guns."[61] He has served most of his career in the northwest—primarily in the Xinjiang Military District of the Lanzhou MR. Wang has thus also enjoyed career-long ties to Fu Quanyou and undoubtedly to the late PLA elder Wang "Big Cannon" Zhen, who oversaw Lanzhou and Xinjiang as his personal military fiefdoms during his lifetime. Wang Ke was also praised by Jiang Zemin during his 1991 tour of Xinjiang, and soon found himself propelled to be commander of the important Shenyang MR (another regional commander with whom Jiang met during his 1991–92 tours who now occupies a top position). Wang Ke is also known to be a leading advocate of reforming tactics in line with the new doctrine of "limited war under high-technology conditions." After the Gulf

61. "Wang Ke, Commander of the Shenyang Military Region," *Inside China Mainland,* March 1994, p. 83.

War, Wang submitted a report on Desert Storm to the CMC, which was reportedly well-received.[62]

Wang Ke thus also perfectly fits the profile of the new Chinese military leadership: he is in his sixties, has a ground force background, combat experience, extensive regional command experience (in more than one region), functional expertise (in artillery), connections to Jiang Zemin and important PLA elders, and an interest in reforming doctrine and tactics appropriate to making the PLA a modern military.

Although relatively new to the CMC (promoted in November 1998), General Cao Gangchuan has rapidly earned the respect and support of Jiang Zemin and other senior members of the CMC. He is a top candidate to succeed Zhang Wannian and Chi Haotian as the leading officer on the CMC, if they retire at the Sixteenth Party Congress.[63]

Two characteristics distinguish Cao Gangchuan's career path: expertise in conventional land armaments and ties to Russia. These two attributes were fused when Cao was promoted to the position of director of the Military Products Trade Office of the CMC in 1990 and consequently became the PLA point man for negotiating weapons purchases and military cooperation with Russia. For the previous five years, Cao had served as deputy director of the Armaments Department of the Headquarters of the General Staff Department, and in November 1992, he was promoted to the position of deputy chief of staff with overall responsibility for PLA equipment and weaponry. Cao succeeded Ding Henggao as director of COSTIND in 1996 and presided over its dismantling. Previously he had expressed great frustration with COSTIND and its failure to produce high-quality weaponry. General Cao was therefore the logical candidate for inaugural director of the General Armaments Department when it was created in 1998 (he may well, in fact, have been responsible for conceptualizing the new body and the revision of COSTIND).

From the time he joined the army at the age of nineteen, Cao was associated with artillery.[64] A native of Henan, he was sent to the Third Artillery Technical School in Zhengzhou. From there, he was selected to attend the Russian training school in Dalian. After two years of Russian, Cao was sent to Moscow's Artillery Engineering Academy, where he studied for six years.

62. Ibid., p. 84.

63. General Cao Gangchuan was born in December 1935 and thus will be nearly sixty-seven at the time of the Congress.

64. Much of this biographical information derives from Jerry Hung, "Cao Gangchuan—Deputy Chief of Staff, People's Liberation Army," *Inside China Mainland*, January 1995, pp. 84–86.

He returned to China in 1963, after the Sino-Soviet split, fluent in Russian and with an extensive knowledge of the Soviet Red Army's artillery development. For much of the next fifteen years, Cao worked in the Ordnance Department of the General Logistics Department, but in 1979, he was sent to the front lines of the Sino-Vietnamese conflict to help coordinate artillery attacks. This experience earned Cao a place in the advanced class of the National Defense University. After a two-year year stint, he embarked on the fast track through the GSD to his appointment as director of the new GAD. He was promoted to full general in March 1998, and shortly thereafter, he became a full member of the CMC.

Another key member of the current CMC is General Wang Ruilin. Wang rose not as a result of any strategic expertise but rather as an administrator. His career has been closely tied to the late Deng Xiaoping. Deng chose Wang to be his personal military secretary *(mishu)* in the early 1960s, and thereafter he became one of Deng's most important confidants and assistants. When Deng was purged during the Cultural Revolution and sent to work in a tractor factory, he was allowed to select and take with him one assistant; Deng chose Wang Ruilin. When Deng chaired the CMC in the 1980s, Wang acted as director of the CMC's General Office, handling all confidential material. In this capacity, Wang is reported to have routinely represented Deng at CMC meetings and in other communications. But Wang's power and influence were not limited to military affairs, because he was also appointed deputy director of the General Office of the Central Committee—the key staff position for the Politburo and high-level party affairs. From the late 1980s on, Wang also served as senior secretary of Deng's personal office (the Deng Ban). In Deng's final years, Wang was thus quite possibly the most important official in China (playing a role similar to that played by Mao Yuanxin and Wang Hairong during Chairman Mao's final days). Wang Ruilin was the conduit between the ailing leader and his family (including his powerful daughters) and the Politburo and other senior leaders, controlling access to Deng and interpreting his wishes and dictates. The Deng Ban was disbanded following the patriarch's death, but Wang Ruilin continued his duties as a CMC member and GPD's deputy director.[65] In 1992, he also became director of the CMC's Discipline Inspection Commission.

Not only did Wang Ruilin handle key staff work and confidential material for Deng for thirty-five years, he also had the sensitive and difficult job of executing Deng's orders in the armed forces. Probably one of the

---

65. "Deng Office Disbanded—Office Site Handed Over," *Ming Bao* (Hong Kong), July 25, 1997, SWB/FE, July 28, 1997, G7.

toughest tasks Deng gave Wang was to weed out and dismantle the Yang Shangkun–Yang Baibing network in 1992–93. As the network was anchored in the General Political Department, which serves as the principal PLA organ for vetting personnel assignments, Wang was installed as deputy director in December 1992 (a position he still holds). In engineering the purge of the Yang network, Wang made himself indispensable to Jiang Zemin and his attempts to cultivate support in the PLA. In fact, as a "talent spotter" experienced in high-level military personnel affairs, it is quite likely that Wang Ruilin has been the guiding hand behind assembling the new PLA leadership and carrying out Deng's wishes to help Jiang Zemin solidify loyalties in the military through promotions and appointments. While Wang possesses no independent power base (despite his background in the Eighth Route Army and membership, by birth, in the Shandong faction), this role and his work for Deng and Jiang have made Wang an important player in civil-military relations.

In September 1999, at the Fourth Plenum of the Fifteenth Central Committee, two new members were added to the CMC: Lieutenant Generals Guo Boxiong and Xu Caihou. It is assumed that each will move into functional positions in one of the four general headquarters in the next few years. At the time of his appointment, General Guo was commander of the Lanzhou Military Region, while General Xu was the political commissar of the Jinan MR. As such, Xu is tipped to replace Yu Yongbo as GPD director, while Bo may succeed Fu Quanyou as chief of the General Staff. They are fifty-seven and fifty-six respectively, making them representative of the "fourth generation" of military leaders.

General Guo rose through the ranks of the Lanzhou MR, serving successively as a squad leader, platoon leader, regimental propaganda cadre, headquarters staff officer, and eventually MR deputy chief of staff. From 1994 to 1997, he was transferred to the Beijing MR, where he had the opportunity to travel abroad with Defense Minister Chi Haotian and domestically with President Jiang Zemin. In 1997, he was sent back to Lanzhou as MR commander. Guo has long-standing career ties to Chief of Staff Fu Quanyou, who was his commander in the 47th Group Army, as well as to former Lanzhou MR commander Wang Ke. Eventually, he is likely to succeed one or both in the PLA leadership.

General Xu Caihou has had a career in PLA political work. He has spent most of his career in the Jilin Military District of the Shenyang MR— although at the time of his promotion to the CMC, he worked in the Jinan MR. In Jilin, Xu held a succession of propaganda and GPD jobs. In November 1992, he was transferred to Beijing, where he became assistant to GPD chief Yu Yongbo but also worked closely with Wang Ruilin. With this backing, Xu is undoubtedly on track to head the GPD following their retirements. In mid 1993, following the purge of Yang Baibing, Xu also became coeditor of *Jiefangjun Bao*. This was a sensitive time, given the need to take control of the GPD apparatus. Xu performed well and was promoted to deputy director of the GPD in July 1994. From 1997 to 1999, he served as political commissar of the Jinan MR.

These are the current proximate players in civil-military relations in China today. The current CMC appears to be relatively faction-free, very professional (rather than political) in its orientation, technically competent, and focused on implementing the various programs associated with "building an elite army with Chinese characteristics." Although it is ostensibly a party organ, this body is the nexus of civil-military relations. Channels of interaction outside the CMC have been radically reduced in recent years. The PLA no longer has a representative on the Politburo Standing Committee, for example, and its representation on this body is presently limited to Zhang Wannian and Chi Haotian. (It will be interesting to see if this changes at the Sixteenth Party Congress, although traditionally there has not necessarily been a military member of the Politburo Standing Committee.)

Other informal channels of PLA influence have also been reduced. As late as the mid 1990s, the Hong Kong media reported that senior military officers personally visited and lobbied Deng Xiaoping and other leaders, sometimes submitted "letters of opinion" and other documents expressing their views in inner-party circles, and sat in on Politburo meetings. At the time, retired PLA elders allegedly weighed in on policy deliberations. Assuming these reports were correct to begin with, this all seems to have stopped, and the channels of civil-military interaction have been restricted to the CMC, even during the 2001 EP-3 spy plane incident with the United States. As a result of these changes and the general bifurcation of army and party elites of the "third generation," noted above, civil-military relations have entered an entirely new and unprecedented period.

The Changing Rules of Civil-Military Relations

The rules of the game in civil-military relations have changed as a result of several developments:

- · The institutional narrowing of the arenas of interaction (to the CMC)
- · The more limited range of issues on which PLA leaders have a legitimate right to voice opinions, and their increasing reluctance to do so
- · Increased professionalism in the senior officer corps and a concomi-

tant decline in the promotion of officers with backgrounds as political commissars

· A PLA desire to concentrate solely on issues of "army building" and a generally noninterventionist approach to nonmilitary issues

· The creation of the PAP and concomitant disengagement of the PLA from internal security functions

· An implicit bargain struck between Jiang Zemin and the PLA High Command that as long as he supports PLA budgets and professional goals, they will defer to his leadership status

The rules of the game have also been changed fundamentally by being codified: recently, for the first time, the military's functions and roles have been outlined in several laws, documents, and regulations. Their promulgation has been instrumental in advancing the twin goals of regularization *(zhengguihua)* and professionalization *(zhiyehua)* of the armed forces. The National People's Congress has passed twelve laws and regulations, including the National Defense Law, Military Service Law, Military Facilities Protection Law, Civil Air Defense Law, Reserve Officers' Law, Hong Kong Special Administrative Region Garrison Law, Military Service Regulations, and Military Officers' Ranks and Regulations.[66] The State Council and CMC have jointly adopted forty-odd administrative laws and regulations, and the CMC has implemented seventy-odd on its own, while individual PLA departments, service arms, and MRs have formulated more than one thousand military rules and regulations.[67] Taken together, the roles and functions of the PLA are now specified as never before.

The National Defense Law (NDL) has significant implications for civil-military relations. Adopted as law by the Fifth Session of the Eighth National People's Congress in March 1997 and authorized by Presidential Decree No. 84, the NDL is important for a number of reasons.[68] The law went through five years of drafting and revision prior to its promulgation. This drafting process took place entirely within military legal circles, coordinated by the Military Legal Office of the CMC.[69] The NDL provides an overall

66. See Thomas A. Bickford, "Regularization and the Chinese People's Liberation Army: An Assessment of Change," *Asian Survey,* May–June 2000, pp. 456–74.

67. *China's National Defense* (Defense White Paper), issued by the Information Office of the State Council, July 1998.

68. For an excellent evaluation, see Samantha Blum, "The National Defense Law of China—the Dragon's Head of Military Law" (unpublished paper, May 2001).

69. Interview with Sr. Col. Zhu Jianye and Sr. Col. Shen Qiuchao of this office, April 1999.

framework for "administering the army according to law" *(yifa zhijun)* and elaborates in some detail various aspects of the armed forces' organization, duties, "construction," and legal responsibilities. It contains specific information about mobilization for war, maintenance of the armed forces during peacetime, leadership of the armed forces, the military-industrial and scientific establishment, military education and training, and many other aspects. These details are set forth in a lengthy document of twelve chapters and seventy articles. Associated publications interpret and spell out in further detail the content and meaning of the law's provisions.[70]

The NDL is particularly striking for one provision: the subordination of the military to the state. In Chinese, the clear connotation of the term for state *(guojia)* is government, as distinct from the party. It collectively refers in practice to the State Council, its constituent ministries and commissions, the president of the PRC, and the NPC. Beginning in the 1980s, there was a conscious and deliberate attempt to more clearly demarcate the jurisdictional responsibilities of the CCP, State Council, and NPC—particularly the policy of "separating party from government" *(dang-zheng fenkai)* in economic policymaking and commercial management. Of course, this general process required the promulgation of numerous laws and regulations—which had the cumulative effect of strengthening the NPC as a fourth institutional pillar of the PRC, along with the party, army, and government. In the process, the NPC gained increased oversight functions. State Council policies, budgets, and appointments became at least nominally subject to legislative review by the NPC. However, the Chinese Communist Party has always insisted that it should police itself and its own membership, and this remains unchanged. Party members in the armed forces are also subject to the CCP's DIC system. The CCP accordingly has its own constitution and its own "election" procedures for its leadership. The party is clearly separated from the state. Its relationship to the armed forces, as noted throughout this chapter, has always been one of symbiosis or control. Certainly, the party has institutionally penetrated the military to ensure this relationship.

However, the 1997 National Defense Law suggests some fundamental shifts in the relationship of the military to the party and state. A number of its articles clearly subordinate the "armed forces" (defined as including the People's Armed Police, militia, and reserves) to the state. The term "state"

70. The most important of these is Xu Jiangrui and Fang Ning, *Guofangfa Gailun* (Survey of the National Defense Law) (Beijing: Junshi Kexue Chubanshe, 1998).

(guojia) is mentioned no fewer than thirty-nine times in the law. The implications of this term and the institutional subordination of the armed forces to state control, are specified in some detail. Only in a single clause is the relationship of the army to the party mentioned (Article 19): "The armed forces of the People's Republic of China are subject to leadership by the Communist Party, and CCP organizations in the armed forces shall conduct activities in accordance with the CCP constitution" (i.e., presumably, with regard to party committees and discipline inspection work). Everywhere else in the NDL, the military's subordination to the state is made abundantly clear. It is affirmed, for example, that:

- (Article 5): "The state shall exercise unified leadership over national defense activities."

- (Article 7): "The Chinese People's Liberation Army and the Chinese People's Armed Police shall carry out activities to support the government."

- (Article 10): "The Standing Committee of the National People's Congress shall decide on the proclamation of a state of war and on general mobilization or partial mobilization in accordance with provisions of the constitution, and shall exercise other functions and powers in national defense as prescribed by the constitution."

- (Article 11): "The President of the People's Republic of China shall proclaim a state of war and issue mobilization orders in pursuance with the decisions of the National People's Congress and its Standing Committee."

- (Article 12): "The State Council shall direct and administer the building of national defense and exercise the following functions and powers" (nine categories of responsibilities, including fiscal appropriation).

- (Article 13): "The Central Military Commission shall direct the armed forces of the country and exercise the following functions and powers" (ten categories).

- (Article 14): "The State Council and Central Military Commission may call coordination meetings according to circumstances to solve problems concerning national defense."

In numerous other articles, the NDL stipulates responsibilities of the state for national defense matters. The absence of mention of the CCP in this important law signals a striking shift in civil-military relations.

This shift was explicated further in the 1998 National Defense White Paper. While the White Paper includes the single clause that "Given the new historical conditions the Chinese army upholds the absolute leadership of the CCP," greater emphasis is placed on the NPC, State Council, and CMC as the institutions controlling the PLA. Thus, for example:

> In accordance with the Constitution, the National Defense Law and other relevant laws, China has established and improved its national defense system. *The state exercises unified leadership over defense-related activities.* The NPC of the PRC is the highest organ of state power. It decides on questions of war and peace, and exercises other defense-related functions and powers provided for in the Constitution. . . . *The State Council directs and administers national defense work,* and the CMC directs and assumes unified command of the nation's armed forces. . . . *The active components of the PLA comprise the state's standing army. . . . The state exercises unified leadership and planned control over defense research and production. The State Council leads and administrates defense research and production, as well as defense expenditure and assets.* The CMC *approves* the military equipment system of the armed forces and military equipment development plans and programs . . . in coordination with the State Council, and manages defense outlays and assets jointly with the State Council. *The state* practices a *state* military supplies order system to guarantee the acquisition of weapons and other war materials. *The state* practices a financial allocations system for defense spending. It decides the size, structure, and location of defense assets and the adjustment and disposal of these assets in accordance with the needs of national defense and economic construction. The State Council and CMC jointly lead mobilization preparation and implementation work.[71] (Emphasis added)

The adoption of the NDL provides evidence that the PLA is being placed increasingly under state control, with the concomitant removal of party controls. To be sure, ambiguities remain. For example, it is unclear whether references to the Central Military Commission mean the state or party CMC (a parallel state CMC, identical in membership to the party CMC, was created in 1985). This may be a moot point given that the membership of these two bodies is currently identical, although the language describing the CMC strongly suggests that its relationship to the armed forces is either one of joint administration with the State Council or merely "line authority" to implement decisions, whereas broad decision-making authority seems to rest ultimately with the State Council, NPC Standing Committee, and president of the republic. But, here, ambiguity exists insofar as Jiang Zemin concur-

71. Ibid., pp. 15–17 (English edition).

rently holds the offices of president, CCP general secretary, and CMC chairman. Only when the president no longer heads the party but nonetheless directs the CMC will we know for sure that the party-army link has been severed. Another sign would be a CMC composed solely of military officers (like the U.S. Joint Chiefs of Staff) under a civilian minister of defense.

While little doubt exists that the Chinese Communist Party and its leadership remain the ultimate source of political power and authority in China, it does seem clear that these steps taken since 1997 are efforts to disentangle the military from party control. While the 1975 and 1978 national constitutions both explicitly subordinated the armed forces to the command of the CCP and its chairman, that is no longer the case. Even much of the ambiguity of the early 1990s is being clarified.[72] Of course, it is difficult to determine whether these reforms are taking root normatively and psychologically in the army, state, and society. Interviews with PLA officers in the late 1990s still suggest substantial ambiguity over the issue of state versus party control; to many it remains a nonissue. When asked whether the armed forces are subordinate to the state or party, some officers look puzzled. "What do you mean?" one responded. "Of course, the PLA is loyal to the party! The party rules the country and the PLA defends it!"[73] For many in the PLA, as this officer's response illustrates, the issue is precisely one of loyalty rather than constitutional control, and many still see the CCP as synonymous with the state and country. If orders came to defend the nation against an external opponent or enforce internal security, few officers or soldiers would question whether the order ultimately came from the CMC, State Council, NPC Standing Committee, PRC president, or CCP general secretary. Although there have clearly been attempts to delineate the authority of the party, army, and state by law, the three still remain essentially fused—with ultimate party control—in the minds of most Chinese citizens. After decades of party control and symbiotic fusion between the three, it is not easy to redefine these interrelationships.

The continued ambiguity is also reflected in PLA publications and materials used by the General Political Department. Authoritative materials published to explain the new National Defense Law tend to emphasize the state's control over the armed forces, while GPD materials tend to take the opposite tack and emphasize party leadership.

---

72. For excellent and learned discussions of the legalities during this period, see Paltiel, "PLA Allegiance on Parade," and "Civil-Military Relations in China: An Obstacle to Constitutionalism?" *Journal of Chinese Law,* September 1995, pp. 35–65.

73. Interview with Academy of Military Sciences officer, September 1998.

The standard textbook used for "political work" in the armed forces, published *after* the promulgation of the National Defense Law, is explicit about the CCP's relationship to the PLA.[74] It states unambiguously:

> The party's absolute leadership over the army is a fundamental feature of army building. . . . The CCP should be our army's only and independent leader and commander. . . . At no time can the CCP share authority over the military with other parties or organizations. . . . If the Communist Party loses its military authority, it will have no status. . . . Our army is an armed group to carry out the party's political tasks.[75]

The GPD volume is also explicit that the PLA is organizationally subordinate to the CCP Central Committee and the *party's* CMC.[76] This runs in direct contradiction to the NDL and line of authority discussed above. Nowhere does the volume make mention of the role of the state president, the NPC, the State Council, or the state more generally. Perhaps most interesting is the extent to which the "bourgeois" notion of state control of the armed forces is sharply criticized:

> Bourgeois liberal elements' advocacy of the military's "non-party-fication" [*jundui feidanghua*] is nonsense. In modern society, there is no army that is not involved in politics, and, essentially, there is no army not controlled by a ruling party. In Western capitalist countries, which practice the multiparty system, armies superficially do not belong to the party but to the state. But, in essence, it is a military that is led by the capitalist class and its ruling agent, the party. . . . Therefore, behind the state there are always capitalist parties that lead and command armies, and carry out capitalist dictatorship. Capitalist parties are never neutral in politics. . . . The basic content of this involvement is to oppress the proletariat and people's revolutions internally and carry out invasion and expansion externally. . . . We must never allow ourselves to copy the Western capitalist countries' model, and never allow the excuse of the state's leadership over the army to deny the party's leadership of the army. Political work in our armed forces should criticize the absurd theory of a "non-party-fied army" and should emphasize and consistently insist on the [party's] absolute leadership of the army and ensure that our army is under the party's absolute leadership forever.[77]

74. National Defense University Party History and Party Building Research Office, ed., *Zhongguo Renmin Jiefangjun Zhengzhi Gongzuoxue* (Beijing: National Defense University Press, 1998).

75. Ibid., pp. 197–98.
76. Ibid., pp. 198–200.
77. Ibid., pp. 203–4.

In contrast, PLA materials used to explain the National Defense Law to troops take a very different approach by emphasizing state control.[78] Unlike the GPD source quoted above, for example, Xu Jiangrui and Fang Ning's 1998 *Guofangfa Gailun* (Survey of the National Defense Law) states unambiguously, "National defense is one of the state's functions, and therefore the leadership and management of national defense is an important expression for state organs to realize their state functions."[79] In 550 pages, this volume explicates the various ways and justifications for state control of the military in China. After saying that the head of state exercises "commanding power over the armed forces," it subsequently states that this "commanding power" is "exercised by the CMC chairman."[80] This is not a problem at present, because Jiang Zemin occupies both positions, but this has not historically always been the case. *Guofangfa Gailun* states clearly that the NPC Standing Committee is the "highest organ of state power" and that the "CMC is subordinate to the highest organ of state power," but then confuses matters by stating that "it is *also* subordinate to the CCP Central Committee."[81] In a telling paragraph (that should not be surprising, but makes a mockery of efforts to separate and strengthen state power), *Guofangfa Gailun* explains: "Insisting on the party's leadership over the army is important in realizing *the party's leadership over the state. . . . For historical reasons, the army is actually led by the party's CMC*" (emphasis added).[82] The volume then goes on to define and justify various mechanisms that have been put into place to increase state supervision over various aspects of military matters.

Discussions in the Chinese military media, such as the army newspaper *Jiefangjun Bao,* also continue to indicate that the debate over party versus state control of the armed forces remains alive. A sharp, unsigned article in April 2001 attacked "Western hostile forces that vigorously advocate the armed forces should be 'separated from the party' [*fei dang hua*], 'depoliticized' [*fei zhengzhi hua*] and 'placed under the state' [*guojia hua*]." The article went on to add that, "This is a corrosive agent that vainly attempts to weaken and do away with the CCP leadership and tries to disintegrate the soul of our armed forces, and is the great enemy of our party, state, and armed forces."[83]

78. Xu and Fang, *Guofangfa Gailun.*
79. Ibid., p. 114.
80. Ibid., pp. 122–23.
81. Ibid., p. 118.
82. Ibid.
83. "Clearly Understanding the Essence of 'Separating the Armed Forces from the Party,' 'Depoliticizing Them,' and 'Placing Them Under the State,'" *Jiefangjun Bao,* April 18, 2001, in FBIS–CHI, April 18, 2001.

Thus, despite efforts to legislate and codify increased state/government authority over the PLA, the essential control by the CCP remains apparent. If anything, there appears to be an ongoing struggle between the party and the state, but the winner is likely to be the military, which displays increased autonomy from both.

Changes in the interrelationship of party, army, and state in contemporary China must also be viewed in the context of emerging patterns of civil-military relations across Asia. With few exceptions (North Korea, Vietnam), civil-military relations in East, Southeast, and South Asia have been fundamentally redefined in recent years in the process of democratization. In a number of countries that have known harsh authoritarian and military rule (South Korea, Taiwan, the Philippines, Indonesia, Thailand, and Bangladesh), the armed forces have been removed from political power and influence, made accountable to sovereign legislatures, and returned to their barracks. Military in mufti have been replaced by democratically elected civilians. In all of these countries, controlling the political power and praetorian tendencies of militaries has been a crucial element in establishing democratic institutions and rule. The trend in Asia follows that of Latin America and Africa. The experiences of these countries, but particularly Taiwan, are suggestive for future civil-military relations in China. The literature on the process of democratic transition in Asia has paid relatively little attention to the civil-military dimension,[84] although it is viewed as an important variable in the comparative literature.[85] More comparative research needs to be done on Asian militaries and civil-military relations.[86] Scholars of the PLA and Chinese politics need to place the recent changes in civil-military relations in the PRC, outlined above, in this broader regional context, while comparativists need to look more closely at the Chinese case. The current state of politics in the PRC certainly does not suggest that a creeping transition to democracy is silently taking place,[87] because the CCP retains its grip on

---

84. See Larry Diamond and Marc F. Plattner, eds., *Democracy in East Asia* (Baltimore: Johns Hopkins University Press, 1998); and Diamond, Plattner, Yun-han Chu, and Hung-mao Tien, eds., *Consolidating the Third Wave Democracies* (Baltimore: Johns Hopkins University Press, 1997).

85. See Larry Diamond and Marc F. Plattner, eds., *Civil-Military Relations and Democracy* (Baltimore: Johns Hopkins University Press, 1996).

86. For a significant effort in this direction see Muthiah Alagappa, ed., *Coercion and Governance: The Declining Role of the Military in Asia* (Stanford, Calif.: Stanford University Press, 2001).

87. For one view to the contrary see Minxin Pei, "'Creeping Democratization' in China," in Diamond, Plattner, Han, and Tien, eds., *Consolidating the Third Wave Democracies*.

power. But, at the same time, we must not mistake the potential significance of the legislative efforts to subordinate the PLA to state control.

The Chinese case must also be placed in the comparative context of former socialist states led by communist parties.[88] Broadly speaking, the experiences of the former Soviet and East European militaries suggest that professionalization and party control are by no means mutually exclusive, but in not a single case were these militaries consciously placed under state control via legislative means. Indeed, in many cases, they fought (unsuccessfully) to save their ruling communist parties.[89] The problem for the Chinese military has never been to subordinate itself to civilian authority, but rather to state control. Also, unlike the former Soviet and East European militaries, the PLA has exhibited a long-standing tension between professionalization and attempts at politicization by the CCP.[90] In both of these respects, the reforms noted in this and subsequent chapters suggest that the Chinese military is moving—or rather being moved—into an entirely new era of civil-military relations and corporate professionalism. One may surmise that the PLA would not shrink from the task of defending China against external enemies—but would it again combat internal enemies that threaten the rule of the Communist Party? This will be the ultimate test of the redefined relationship of the army to the party and state in China.

88. To be sure, there is no small literature in this field. See the sources noted in footnote 14.

89. See Gerald Segal and John Phipps, "Why Communist Armies Defend Their Parties," in Richard H. Yang, ed., *China's Military: The PLA in 1990/91* (Kaohsiung: National Sun Yat-sen University, 1991), pp. 133–44.

90. In the large literature on this subject, see esp. Jencks, *From Muskets to Missiles*.

3 Doctrine and Training

Doctrine is fundamental to all facets of China's military modernization. Doctrine is far more than the abstract study of warfare—it is central to how the PLA is organized and prepares to apply lethal force. Training is the practical application of doctrine. Over the past three decades, reforming doctrine has been a catalyst for a vast range of PLA reforms, professionalization, and modernization—reconfiguring the force structure, personnel recruitment, military education, training regimens, hardware needs, research and development, weapons procurement, and operational strategy. One can clearly see the lessons learned by the PLA from foreign conflicts and the resulting changes in doctrine as applied to military exercises and force structure in PLA battlefield training in recent years.

Not surprisingly, Chinese military strategists do not use key doctrinal concepts and terms in the same way as their Western counterparts; this is cause for considerable confusion both in communicating with the PLA about doctrinal issues and in understanding its thinking about warfare. It is important, therefore, to consider such concepts and terminology in the Chinese context.

Concepts and Definitions

In all militaries, doctrine consists of the basic principles that guide military commanders and their staff in planning and executing the application of military force to achieve specific military objectives.[1] As succinctly described in

---

1. I am indebted to David Finkelstein for this definition and discussions of doctrine in the U.S and Chinese militaries. See Finkelstein's *China's National Military Strategy* (Alexandria, Va.: CNA Corporation, 2000). For further discussion, see Paul H. B. Godwin, "Compensating for Deficiencies: Doctrinal Evolution in the Chinese People's Liberation Army, 1978–1999," in James Mulvenon and Andrew Yang, eds.,

the U.S. Army's principal field training manual (FM-100-5), "Doctrine captures the lessons of past wars, reflects on the nature of war and conflict in its own time, and anticipates intellectual and technological developments in future times."[2] Military doctrine must also be distinguished from military *strategy*, which in Western usage is usually concerned with linking those military objectives to a set of desired political-strategic goals.[3] The U.S. Government, for example, has an explicit and published National Security Strategy, from which a National Military Strategy is derived.[4] Thus, in Western militaries, general warfare doctrine is a set of usually broad precepts used as a guide for tactics in military campaigns. This is usually distinguished as *basic* doctrine and *operational* doctrine respectively.

Western and Chinese military thinkers only partially agree on these definitions and distinctions. As one leading PLA strategic thinker at the elite Academy of Military Sciences (the PLA's leading institution for formulating military doctrine and strategy) succinctly put it: "In our analysis, wars are composed of a series of campaigns which are made up of numerous general operations and specific battles. For the PLA, the strategy of active defense guides us at all four levels [wars, campaigns, operations, and battles]."[5] Thus, for the PLA, a campaign is a series of related military operations aimed at achieving specific objectives on the battlefield. A variety of PLA writings indicate that the campaign is the key level of combat, and that a successful military strategy at this level, which dictates the actual nature and tempo of battlefield operations, can be decisive in war.[6]

In Chinese doctrine, however, the term "strategy" *(zhanlüe)* is *not* used in the Western sense of linking military activities to broad national security objectives in a political-military context. In Chinese strategic thinking,

---

Seeking Truth from Facts: A Retrospective on Chinese Military Studies in the Post-Mao Era (Santa Monica, Calif.: RAND Corporation, 2001).

2. U.S. Army Field Manual (FM) 100–5, *Operations,* June 1993.

3. For a discussion of these in the Chinese context, see, in particular, Wang Wencai, ed., *Zhanluexue* (The Study of Strategy) (Beijing: Guofang Daxue Chubanshe, 1999). This volume is used as the standard textbook on the subject at the PLA NDU.

4. See President William J. Clinton, *A National Security Strategy for a New Century* (Washington, D.C.: White House, 1998); Joint Chiefs of Staff, *National Military Strategy of the United States of America: Shape, Respond, Prepare Now—A Military Strategy for a New Era* (Washington, D.C.: Government Printing Office, 1998).

5. Interview with AMS strategist, November 11, 2000.

6. By far the most thorough discussion of PLA campaign strategy and tactics is Wang Houqing and Zhang Xingye, *Zhanyixue* (The Study of Campaigns) (Beijing: Guofang Daxue Chubanshe, 2000).

politics and military art are much more clearly differentiated than in Western thinking (recall Carl von Clausewitz's maxim that "war is the continuation of politics by other means"). To Chinese military thinkers, strategy is the manner in which military force is applied to achieve the desired outcome of an actual or potential military conflict.[7]

For many years, the PLA's operative military strategy, primarily at the campaign level of warfare, has been known as "active defense" *(jiji fangyü)*. This term has its origins in the Chinese revolutionary war, when Mao proposed a military strategy of "offensive defense or defense through decisive engagements," in which PLA units (then the Red Army) would proactively engage the enemy, exploiting its weak points and attempting to destroy enemy capabilities and will.[8] "Active defense," as elaborated by Mao, takes place within a broader context of "people's war." The Maoist theory of people's war is often regarded as passive warfare of necessity—to "lure the enemy in deep" in order to overcome the enemy's technological superiority by playing to the strengths of geography and the civilian population. But Mao's writings on active defense make clear that people's war also has an offensive and proactive component.

This definition and conceptualization of active defense as a military strategy is thus a core component of broader Chinese military doctrine. It can best be thought of as "operational doctrine" in the Western sense, while people's war and its modern equivalents fit the category of "basic doctrine."

To compound conceptual problems, there is no precise equivalent for "doctrine" in Chinese. The closest appears to be *junshi sixiang*, "military thought," or *junshi fangzhen*, which translates as "military guiding principles." From reading PLA writings employing these two terms, though, one gains the strong impression that both are roughly equivalent to Western "basic doctrine." The PLA also distinguishes "operational principles" *(zuozhan tiaoli)*, which is a level of analysis more refined than military strategy, but not as precise as specific tactics *(zhanshu)*. As the term suggests, operational principles are applicable to large-scale operations within broader campaigns. These operational principles include such concepts as mobility *(jidong)*, attrition *(xiaohaozhan)*, annihilation *(jianmeizhan)*, quick-decision battle *(sujuezhan)*, close or deep defense *(qian zongshen* or *quan zongshen)*, layered defense *(tidui guofang)*, joint operations *(xietong dongzuo* or *lianhe*

---

7. I am indebted to Paul Godwin for this definition.
8. Mao Zedong, "Problems of Strategy in China's Revolutionary War," in *Selected Military Writings of Mao Zedong* (Beijing: Foreign Languages Press, 1972), p. 105.

TABLE 2 Levels of Doctrinal Analysis in the PLA

	PLA	Western Military	Level of Conflict
(Broad)			
Level 1	Military thought *(junshi sixiang)* and military principles *(junshi fangzhen)*	Basic doctrine	Total war *(zongti zhan)* and limited war *(youxian zhanzheng)*
Level 2	Strategic principles *(zhanlüe tiaoli)* and military strategy *(junshi zhanlüe)*	Operational doctrine	Campaigns *(zhanyi)*
Level 3	Operational principles *(zuozhan tiaoli)*	Operations	Theater of operations *(zhanqu)*
Level 4	Tactics *(zhanshu)*	Tactics	Specific battle space *(zhandi* or *zhandou)*
(Specific)			

zuozhan), combined arms operations *(hetong zuozhan)*, preemptive strikes *(xianji zhidi)*, asymmetrical warfare *(buduideng zhanzheng)*, transregional operations *(kuaqu zuozhan)*, offensive operations *(jinggong zuozhan)*, and other general concepts.[9] Finally, Chinese military writings discuss actual fighting tactics at the specific battlefield (battle-space) level.

Although China did publish an official Defense White Paper in 2000,[10] which outlined its assessment of China's national security environment and other subjects, unlike many militaries the PLA unfortunately does not publish a National Military Strategy document explicitly outlining its warfighting doctrine. Yet from reading various publications (many published for teaching senior officers at the National Defense University in Beijing), one can piece together different elements of PLA doctrine. There appear to be four separate levels of doctrinal theory and planning, which are presented in table 2. The parallels with Western doctrine are also given.

9. For a good discussion of both operational principles and battlefield tactics, see Nan Li, "The PLA's Evolving Campaign Doctrine and Strategies," in James Mulvenon and Richard Yang, eds., *The People's Liberation Army in the Information Age* (Santa Monica, Calif.: RAND Corporation, 1999); and Nan Li, "The PLA's Warfighting Doctrine, Strategy, and Tactics, 1985–95: A Chinese Perspective," in David Shambaugh and Richard Yang, eds., *China's Military in Transition* (Oxford: Clarendon Press, 1997).

10. Information Office of the State Council, *China's National Defense in 2000* (Beijing: State Council, 2000).

Threat perception and the national security environment are major determinants of a nation's defense posture (see chapter 7), while technological innovation serves as a supply-side stimulant to or constraint on the types of weapons and communications systems fielded (see chapter 6). It is often presumed that a military doctrine guides technological investments and weapons procurements, but it is often the other way around. All three elements—doctrine, technology, and threat—have interacted to shape the PLA's posture over time, but the causal linkages have changed. For many years, the PLA had no choice but to adhere to the law of technological disadvantage. This was first enunciated by Red Army Marshal Zhu De: "The kind of war to fight depends on what kind of arms we have." This axiom has now been replaced by "Build weapons necessary to fight whatever kind of war."[11] To be sure, the PLA remains technologically inferior to most potential adversaries and must continue to rely on asymmetrical warfare strategies. Despite the exigencies of the Taiwan situation, the Chinese military's overall posture today thus remains largely driven by doctrine.

No matter how dynamic and adaptable doctrine is in a given military, it still takes a long time to translate doctrinal innovation into actual strategy and tactical changes in training and on the battlefield. In the U.S. military, it normally takes seven or eight years for significant doctrinal change to penetrate to the unit level of the armed forces. For the PLA, it is undoubtedly longer. Thus, one should not assume that the promulgation of a new or adapted military doctrine is instantaneously put into practice. This reinforces a more basic point about Western analyses of Chinese military writings, namely, that one should not confuse rhetoric or aspirations with reality.

FROM STRATEGIC RETREAT TO PRECISION STRIKE: THE PLA'S EVOLVING MILITARY DOCTRINE

Over the past seven decades, the PLA doctrine has evolved through roughly four phases: "people's war" (1935–79); "people's war under modern conditions" (1979–85); "limited war" (1985–91); and "limited war under high-technology conditions" (1991 to the present). Thus, the PLA's operative doctrine today is the product of decades of rethinking the nature of contemporary conflict, the potential threats to China, and the adequacy of the PLA force structure.

11. "You shenme wuqi, da shenme zhan"; "Da shenme zhan, zao shenme wuqi."

Many PLA publications point to the landmark Expanded Central Military Commission Conference of May 23–June 6, 1985, as the departure point for contemporary Chinese doctrinal and military reform. In fact, doctrinal rethinking was initiated by Deng Xiaoping a decade earlier, in 1975, when he briefly returned to the position of chief of General Staff after being purged during the Cultural Revolution in 1967. Together with Marshal Ye Jianying, Deng presided over a specially convened Enlarged Meeting of the Central Military Commission, which lasted for three weeks in June–July 1975. It was at this meeting that Deng first publicly criticized the PLA for being "swollen, lax, self-conceited, extravagant, and lazy," and leading military organs for being "weak, lazy, and loose leading bodies."[12] Deng's admonitions led to the decision to begin streamlining the force structure, demobilizing 600,000 servicemen by the early 1980s and consolidating redundant organizations. These reductions came on top of a fairly thorough purge of the upper echelons of the PLA following the Lin Biao affair of 1971.

The 1975 CMC meeting also marked the initial reevaluation of the theory of the "inevitability of war." Although the conferees continued to believe that (world) war was inevitable, Deng for the first time offered the view that it could be "postponed." This "strategic transformation" *(zhanlüe zhuanbian)* had profound implications, because the PLA had been preparing to "fight an early, large, and nuclear war" *(zaoda, dada, dahe zhanzheng)* since 1968–69. This very important doctrinal opening provided the PLA with breathing space to undertake reforms during peacetime and to prepare for other types of wars besides full-scale global nuclear conflicts. It also supported the broader move to comprehensive modernization, whereby human and material resources that were being consumed by the civil defense program could be reallocated more effectively to commercial development. "Peace and development" replaced war preparedness as the basis for China's national security. This assessment also justified a continued strategic tilt toward the United States in order to offset the ongoing Soviet threat. The thesis that "peace and development" was the principal strategic trend of the

---

12. Zhang Yutao, ed., *Xin Zhongguo Junshi Dashijiyao* (Chronicle of New China's Military Affairs) (Beijing: Junshi Kexue Chubanshe, 1998), pp. 289–90; Academy of Military Sciences Military History Research Department, *Zhongguo Renmin Jiefangjun de Qishi Nian* (Seventy Years of the PLA) (Beijing: Junshi Kexue Chubanshe, 1997), pp. 379–81; Deng Xiaoping, "Speech at an Enlarged Meeting of the Military Commission of the Party Central Committee" (July 14, 1975), in *Deng Xiaoping Wenxuan* (Selected Works of Deng Xiaoping), translated in JPRS, *China Report*, October 31, 1983, p. 19.

times, and its corollary that military modernization could proceed at a measured pace, remained sacrosanct until it was challenged in 1999.[13]

"People's War under Modern Conditions": Redefining "Active Defense"

Within a matter of months of launching these modest military (and other) reforms, on the eve of Mao's death, Deng Xiaoping again fell victim to political maneuvering and was purged for the third time in his career.[14] When Deng returned to power in 1977, he again oversaw PLA affairs as chief of staff and vice-chairman of the CMC. At a series of military conferences in 1978–79, Marshals Nie Rongzhen and Xu Xiangqian and General Su Yu all began to gently question the utility of Mao's "people's war" doctrine. As noted in chapter 1, these critiques became much sharper in the wake of the botched war against Vietnam in 1979. At an expanded CMC conclave on March 12, 1980, Deng and the marshals pursued their doctrinal revisionism and stimulated another round of structural adjustments in the armed forces. This time, Deng cut to the core of Mao's "people's war" doctrine by questioning the excessively defensive posture of fighting adversaries deep inside China in a war of attrition. Deng observed in his speech that the maxim "lure the enemy in deep" was no longer appropriate to "people's war under modern conditions."[15] In a deft terminological move, Deng truncated Mao's long-standing dictum of "lure the enemy in deep and actively defend" simply to "active defense." Deng went even further, suggesting that active defense should no longer involve defense-in-depth, but rather frontier defense.

As noted earlier in this chapter, active defense had been a key component of Chinese operational military strategy since the early civil war and anti-Japanese war.[16] At that time, the concept involved tactics of harassing a stronger opponent by turning weakness and passivity to asymmetrical advantage, probing enemy weaknesses and actively exploiting them. Following the Korean War, the concept was revived by Defense Minister Marshal

13. See David Finkelstein, *China Reconsiders Its National Security: The Great Peace and Development Debate of 1999* (Alexandria, Va.: CNA Corporation, 2000).
14. See David Shambaugh, "Deng Xiaoping: The Politician," in id., ed., *Deng Xiaoping: Portrait of a Chinese Statesman* (Oxford: Clarendon Press, 1995).
15. General Su Yu had coined this new term in a speech to the Military Academy in 1979. See the discussion in Ellis Joffe, *The Chinese Army after Mao* (Cambridge, Mass.: Harvard University Press, 1987), ch. 4; Paul H. B. Godwin, "People's War Revised: Military, Doctrine, Strategy, and Operations," in Charles Lovejoy and Bruce Watson, eds., *China's Military Reforms* (Boulder, Colo.: Westview Press, 1986).
16. See Mao, "Problems of Strategy in Revolutionary War."

Peng Dehuai in 1956, but with a very different meaning. One of the key lessons learned by the Chinese from the Korean War was that American and allied forces did not heed their warnings not to approach the Chinese border. Thus Marshal Peng argued that, in the future, "active defense" required a frontier-based deterrent. This argument was similarly applied in 1965, when the American bombing of North Vietnam escalated and serious "strategic debate" commenced in Beijing over whether the Americans would repeat their Korean War thrust to the border, or even invade China. Some, such as Chief of Staff Luo Ruiqing, argued that the best way to forestall such aggression was to position large numbers of forces at the North Vietnamese border as a deterrent. This was done (although Luo lost his job), and for the first time, China deployed forces over the border into Vietnam. Between 1965 and 1973, approximately 320,000 PLA troops served in Vietnam (largely in engineering and anti-aircraft capacities), reaching a maximum of 170,000 in 1967.[17] This definition of "active defense" was revised again by Chairman Mao during the height of the Soviet threat, in favor of the more traditional and passive strategy of people's war in depth. Deng's redefinition of frontier-based "active defense" in 1977 thus actually represented a return to the operative definition of the 1950s and 1960s.

With the new thinking about frontier defense came a new attention to weaponry. One of Deng's more important doctrinal revisions was the increased emphasis on weaponry and technology instead of the human factor in war (thus implicitly undermining a cardinal tenet of Maoist military thought). These redefinitions called for a new guiding phrase *(kouhao)*, and the formula "people's war under modern conditions" was born.[18]

Further doctrinal revisionism came during 1983–85 in a series of speeches by Deng on the international situation.[19] Deng argued that with the U.S. defense buildup during the Reagan administration, the military balance be-

17. Qiang Zhai, *China and the Vietnam Wars, 1950–1975* (Chapel Hill, N.C.: University of North Carolina Press, 2000), p. 135. Also see Chen Jian, "China's Involvement in the Vietnam War, 1964–1969," *China Quarterly*, no. 142 (June 1995): 356–87; and Allen S. Whiting, *Reflections on "Misunderstanding" China*, Asia Papers, no. 13 (Washington, D.C.: Sigur Center for Asian Studies, 2001), p. 7.

18. Actually, it is claimed by PLA scholars that Marshal Ye Jianying first used the phrase in 1958. See Yao Yunzhu, "The Evolution of Military Doctrine of the Chinese PLA from 1985 to 1995," *Korean Journal of Defense Analysis* 7, no. 2 (Winter 1995): 74.

19. For a useful summary of Deng's views on the changing nature of international security and warfare, see Wang Changtan and Cui Haiming, "Deng Xiaoping de Junshi Sixiang Chutan," in Xiang Shiying, ed., *Dangdai Zhongguo Junshi Sixiang Jingyao* (Beijing: Jiefangjun Chubanshe, 1992), pp. 92–135.

tween the superpowers was essentially in equilibrium, and that neither was likely to start a world war. Moreover, Deng believed that the chances of a massive Soviet attack against China were fading, and that détente with Moscow would further reduce the pressure and augment China's national security. Deng also argued that China's military base could only be modernized gradually, with the overall development of the economy and a strong defense scientific and technological establishment. In light of the PLA's questionable performance in its incursion into Vietnam in 1979, Deng repeated his condemnation of it as an unfit force and called for its further restructuring and streamlining.

These strategic views were systematically set forth in his speech "Strategic Changes to the Guiding Principles on National Defense Construction and Army Building" and endorsed at a landmark meeting of the Central Military Commission in May–June 1985. With an "early, major, and nuclear war" no longer deemed imminent, PLA planners began to contemplate a new and different threat environment. At another key CMC expanded meeting in December 1985, Deng Xiaoping told them what to expect: future conflicts were likely to be localized yet intensive. This recognition was further justified by the war then raging between Iran and Iraq. Chinese strategic planners thus began to voice the view that "local war" (jubu zhanzheng) and "limited war" (youxian zhanzheng) had replaced "total war" (zongti zhanzheng) as the prevalent form of international conflict.[20] A huge cottage industry of analyzing limited wars began in the PLA.

Chinese defense analysts characterized local or limited wars as conflicts that were geographically localized, did not spread to regional or global proportions, and usually involved only two combatants. They were often fought for ethnic, religious, or political reasons. They were generally short, although some—such as the Iran-Iraq War—could drag on for several years. The combatants generally deployed massive ground forces and various types of land-attack weapons. Conventional weapons were prominently used, and in some instances (such as the Iran-Iraq case), ballistic missiles

20. For excellent studies of the doctrinal shifts in Chinese defense doctrine during this period, see Ellis Joffe, "People's War under Modern Conditions: A Doctrine for Modern War," *China Quarterly*, no. 112 (December 1987): 555–73; Paul H. B. Godwin, "Changing Concepts of Doctrine, Strategy and Operations in the Chinese People's Liberation Army, 1978–87," *China Quarterly*, no. 112 (December 1987): 578–81; id., "Chinese Military Strategy Revised," *Annals of the American Academy of Political and Social Science*, no. 519 (January 1992): 191–201; id., "Compensating for Deficiencies"; and Yao, "Evolution of Military Doctrine of the Chinese PLA from 1985 to 1995."

and weapons of mass destruction were considered usable. Use of air power was minimal. Some were undertaken by vastly superior nations against small ones (such as the U.S. invasions of Grenada and Panama, the British-Argentine war in the Falklands, or the Soviet invasion of Afghanistan), while others pitted combatants of a more equal capability against each other (e.g., Iran and Iraq). Some were fought over natural resources, many involved boundary disputes, some were fought by client states of major powers, and some were thought to be fought to ensure local or regional "hegemony" or spheres of influence.[21]

The doctrine of people's war under modern conditions also mandated changes in battlefield tactics.[22] Active defense required greater attention to offensive operations, seizing the strategic initiative or even striking first. This replaced the classic Maoist triad of defense, stalemate, and offense: "When the enemy advances, we retreat; when the enemy camps, we harass; when the enemy tires, we attack; when the enemy retreats, we pursue."[23] Doctrinally revisionist thinkers in the PLA pointedly observed that contemporary warfare does not permit the luxury of passively absorbing an attack before launching a counteroffensive, because command nodes and forces in the field may be wiped out before a counterattack can be launched. Similarly, guerrilla warfare and dispersed units of light infantry were thought to be no substitute for highly mobile, integrated joint-force operations. Positional warfare and the establishment of "war zones" *(zhanqu)* were further doctrinal innovations of this period.[24] Although the concept of "war zones" in PLA operations dates to the 1930s, its new incarnation centralized command and control of forces spread over a large-scale regional battle theater.[25] In the new system, military region commanders became the dominant decision-makers in their theater of operations. The new emphasis was on coordination rather than the tradition of autonomous units fighting in a redundant and isolated fashion from each other. This initiative was the precursor to joint-

21. See, e.g., the discussion in Xiao Xianshe, "A Retrospective of Limited War since World War II and Future Prospects," *Zhongguo Minbing,* no. 10 (October 9, 1990), in JPRS-CAR-91–005, January 31, 1991.

22. See the discussion in Huang Dafu et al., *Jubu Zhanzheng Zhong de Zhanshe* (Tactics of Limited War) (Beijing: National Defense University Press, 1989); and Yao, "Evolution of Military Doctrine of the Chinese PLA from 1985 to 1995."

23. Mao, "Problems of Strategy in China's Revolutionary War," p. 111.

24. On the role of positional warfare, see Major General Gao Guozhen and Senior Colonel Ye Zheng, "A Preliminary Study of Sea and Air Blockade Campaign under High-Tech Conditions: Operational Doctrine Must Change over Time," *Zhongguo Junshi Kexue* (Chinese Military Science), November 20, 1996, pp. 85–93.

25. Ibid.

service maneuvers, which were begun a few years later. The PLA also began to experiment with prepositioned combat units, weapons, and logistics supplies—further breaking with the Maoist emphasis on unit-based "self-reliance." Also, in 1984, the PLA began to shrink the size of operational commands, experimenting with brigade- and battalion-level units instead of larger division-sized forces, and developing mobile and rapidly deployable "fist units" *(quantou budui)* on an experimental basis.

Little by little, the mainstays of PLA operations and deployments were being subjected to doctrinal reform. Further realizations would come in the 1990s, following the Gulf War and NATO's intervention in the former Yugoslavia. The 2001–2 allied war against the Taliban and al-Qaeda in Afghanistan was also carefully studied by PLA strategists and produced further revisions in PLA doctrine and training.

Redefining Strategic Frontiers

Commensurate with expanded notions of active defense and people's war under modern conditions came a reexamination of China's "strategic frontiers." This concept delineates the territorial parameters of a nation's *perceived* national security interests—that is, territories to which it would be willing to commit military forces in pursuit of goals that it defines to be in its national interests. These need not coincide with the territorial boundaries of the nation; indeed, they often involve the redefinition and extension of those boundaries. Strategic frontiers sometimes coincide with, but are not identical to, spheres of influence. Global powers such as the United States define their strategic frontiers in truly global terms. Latin America, western and central Europe, the Persian Gulf, Northeast Asia, and outer space all fall within America's perceived strategic frontiers. Japan's extend to the Persian Gulf, and India's to the Strait of Malacca. As embodied in the former Russian Defense Minister Pavel Grachev's "Near Abroad" policy, Russia's include central Europe, the Caucasus and Central Asia, and the Sea of Okhotsk and Kamchatka Peninsula.

China's claimed strategic frontiers now extend beyond its immediate borders into its regional periphery. They have always included Taiwan and countries contiguous to Chinese boundaries (hence the sensitivity to U.S. military actions in Korea and Vietnam). Some have also thought of China's sphere of interests as extending to the whole of Mongolia, into Central Asia, and along the ancient Silk Road. However, concomitant with the post-1977 redefinition of active defense and abandonment of "luring the enemy in deep," China's national security strategists began to define its strategic frontiers in more elastic ways. As one article bluntly emphasized: "Strategic frontiers are far greater than geographic boundaries."[26]

The principal shift was from continental to maritime and national to regional definitions. They also include defined spheres under the sea and in space. A redefinition of China's maritime interests has been cultivated, and Chinese are now told to develop a "conception of sea as territory" *(haiyang guotuguan)*.[27] This was one of the main arguments offered in the popular 1980s television series *River Elegy*, which castigated China's insular and continental mentality in favor of fostering an external, coastal, and maritime outlook. Chinese are now regularly taught in textbooks that their "sovereignty" includes three million square kilometers of ocean and seas,[28] and this is codified in the 1992 Maritime Law adopted by the National People's Congress.

This new perspective has certainly been taken seriously, because China's perceived strategic frontiers are now identified by many PLA and civilian strategists to include China's entire continental shelf, the north Pacific contiguous to Russia and Japan, the Bohai Gulf, the Taiwan Strait, the East China Sea, the South China Sea, and the area westward through the Malacca Strait into the Indian Ocean. Inasmuch as China became a net petroleum importer in the 1990s, some strategists even define its strategic frontiers as encompassing the Persian Gulf.[29] Its claims to vast expanses of ocean and islets in the South China Sea strike many observers as either nonsensical or aggressive, given the sheer distance from continental China and nearness to other Southeast Asian nations, even if China apparently has a strong claim under international law. Chinese strategic maritime frontiers are also described as ultimately extending far into the Pacific Ocean. The concept of three "island chains" grew out of former CMC Vice-Chairman Admiral Liu Huaqing's 1988 instruction to the PLA Navy to establish a long-term development plan. Establishing a blue-water presence in the first island chain, which runs south from Japan past Taiwan to the Philippines, was to be attained by 2010. The second island chain, running south from Sakhalin to the islands of the Southwest Pacific, was the established goal for 2025. The third island chain, extending from the Aleutian Islands in the north to Antarctica in the south, was to be the goal for 2050. The degree to which

26. Xu Guangyu, "Pursuit of Equitable Three-Dimensional Strategic Frontiers," *Jiefangjun Bao*, April 3, 1987, JPRS-CAR-88–016, March 29, 1988.

27. Yao, "Evolution of Military Doctrine of the Chinese PLA from 1985 to 1995."

28. Xu, "Pursuit of Equitable Three-Dimensional Strategic Frontiers."

29. Interview, PLA General Staff Department Second Department (Intelligence), December 8, 1998.

these goals have actually been incorporated into PLAN planning is unclear, but presumably the operational task would be to establish a "sea" or "area denial" capacity in a progressively phased fashion.

These new strategic maritime frontiers are discussed in detail in Ye Shiping's surprisingly candid 1998 volume *Zhongguo Haiquan* (China's Sea Power), which makes clear China's aspirations to be a regional and pan-Pacific naval power by the middle of the twenty-first century.[30] The rationale given for these aspirations is both logical and alarming. On the one hand, Ye notes China's increased needs for energy imports that travel by sea and its dependence on merchandise exports. It is also duly noted that modern powers are sea powers, and, since China aspires to comprehensive national power, it must logically also become a global ocean-going power. Thus, in addition to objective economic justifications, the author offers a more status-oriented rationale. More disturbing, however, are Ye's observations about the need for "living space" *(kongjian)* for China's large population, which is forced to live on a limited arable land mass, and the need for excess Chinese labor to find employment destinations.[31]

China's extension of its sea and space strategic frontiers began in the mid 1980s. In April 1987, an alarming article by Xu Guangyu in *Jiefangjun Bao* (Liberation Army Daily) spoke of the need for "living space," distinguished between "visible space" (controlled territory) and "invisible space" (undersea and space jurisdiction), and called for an expansion of China's ground, sea, and air strategic frontiers.[32] Xu introduced the concept of "national gateways" and argued that, while guarding its existing strategic land frontiers, China should fix its ocean "gateway" at the edge of a three-million-square-kilometer zone and embrace a "high frontier" in space. The concept of strategic frontiers was central to a redefinition of defense doctrine. The concept of expanded active defense, now the underpinning of PLA doctrine, grows directly out of the redefinition of strategic frontiers. To meet challenges to these three "national gateways," it was decided in 1987 to embark on a concerted program to develop flexible modern naval, air, and ground forces. As Xu concluded:

> The "national gateway" concept of active defense that we are accustomed to using must be pushed outward from traditional geographic borders to strategic boundaries. . . . For this purpose, we need to build a three-dimensional menacing force that is able to protect China's legitimate

30. Ye Shiping, *Zhongguo Haiquan* (Beijing: Renmin Ribao Chubanshe, 1998).
31. Ibid., esp. ch. 4.
32. Xu, "Pursuit of Equitable Three-Dimensional Strategic Frontiers."

rights and interests, and is able to operate on a battlefield far removed from China. For example, it would be a force able to move rapidly over great distances, and able to carry out land warfare on a different scale and of different intensity in all-weather conditions, and it would use long-range detection, interception, and strategic defensive and offensive weapons systems for carrying out prompt counterattacks in space, on land and at sea.[33]

The definition of these strategic frontiers continued to evolve during the 1990s, although the degree to which they have actually been incorporated into PLA doctrine and plans is unclear. But the rationale for expansion is there. Since about 1991, Chinese strategists have spoken of the strategic importance of Southeast Asian shipping lanes and the Strait of Malacca for China's foreign trade.[34] Since the late 1980s, China has been concerned that India not become the dominant power in South Asia or the Indian Ocean. The PRC's assertive claims over the Xisha (Paracel) and Nansha (Spratly) island groups in the South China Sea are proof of its inclusion of these territories within its strategic frontiers. As one article put it, "The strategically and economically important Nansha Islands and surrounding waters have a bearing on the basic interest of the Chinese nation. We should adopt a modern concept of the 'strategic ocean' in forming our perspective on these islands."[35]

Limited War under High-Technology Conditions, I: Lessons of the Gulf War

The Gulf War of 1991 had a jarring effect on the PLA. Before Operation Desert Storm, PLA analysts had predicted that U.S. forces would become bogged down in a ground war. This mistaken assessment was based on the PLA's study of the Soviet experience in Afghanistan and on the Iran-Iraq conflict. The PLA's previous concepts of limited wars had all envisaged medium- to low-technology adversaries, and its planners had never imagined the application of the numerous new high technologies developed by the United States and its coalition partners. Nearly every aspect of the campaign reminded the PLA High Command of its deficiencies:[36] electronic war-

33. Ibid.
34. Interviews with member of the PLA General Staff, June 1991.
35. Among many articles, see Shen Changjing, "What We Have Learned from the Spratly Islands," *Jianchuan Zhishi*, no. 2 (February 8, 1988): 4–5, in JPRS-CAR-88–034, 28 June 1988, pp. 12–14.
36. This impression derives from numerous discussions with personnel at the Academy of Military Sciences and National Defense University during the spring of 1991 and subsequently.

fare; precision-guided munitions; stealth technology; precision bombing of military targets with minimized collateral damage; the sheer number of sorties flown, with minimal loss of attack aircraft and life; campaign coordination through airborne command and control systems; the deployment of attack aircraft from half a world away using in-flight refueling; the use of satellites in targeting and intelligence gathering; space-based early warning and surveillance; the use of command centers in the United States to coordinate Patriot anti-missile defenses in Saudi Arabia and Israel; the massive naval flotilla assembled in the Gulf; the airlift and rapid deployment capability; the maintenance of high-tempo operations; the ability of troops to exist in desert conditions; modern logistics; information warfare and the ability to "blind" Iraqi intelligence and defenses; and so on.

The Gulf War precipitated a thorough revision of operational doctrine and training in the PLA. But it also had an important additional effect on basic doctrine, causing the doctrines of people's war under modern conditions, active defense, and limited war to evolve into a new doctrine of "limited war under high-technology conditions" *(gao jishu tiaojian xia de jubu zhanzheng)*. Among the lessons learned by the PLA, perhaps the most important concerned weaponry. Breaking with the cardinal Maoist tenet that man was the most important element in warfare, PLA writings began to evince a new appreciation of the role of weapons and technology.

Inasmuch as the Gulf War was a high-tech war, the Chinese military-industrial complex was ordered to redirect investment into research and development associated with a broad range of advanced weapons and technologies. High priority was subsequently placed on mastering electronic warfare and electronic countermeasures (particularly air and naval countermeasures); improving ballistic missile production and precision-guided munitions (PGMs); building satellites, early warning and command systems, and advanced communication relay stations; investigating laser technologies; developing artificial intelligence and information warfare skills; improving avionics and mastering in-flight refueling; and developing anti–ballistic missile systems.

The new emphasis on research and development was a mixed blessing to the Chinese defense industries. On the one hand, they welcomed the opportunity to improve their research and production capabilities, but on the other, they were not well prepared either technologically or financially. The new doctrinal needs spurred an intensive debate during 1993 over the advantages of buying arms from abroad versus producing them indigenously (echoing debates dating back to the late Qing dynasty). The armed services, mainly the navy and air force, apparently argued for substantial purchases of off-the-shelf systems from Moscow, while the Commission on Science, Technology, and Industry for National Defense (COSTIND) argued for upgrading China's military-industrial base—with the help of Russian scientists and technicians—while not becoming overly dependent on foreign suppliers. While it was decided that certain systems would be purchased to plug pressing gaps (particularly in air defense and fighters), COSTIND's position prevailed. The COSTIND logic was bolstered by experience with the Russians during the 1950s and the Americans during the late 1980s, as well as the inhibiting foreign currency expenditure necessary. The strong legacy and ethos of "self-reliance" *(zili gengshen)* was also a factor. Perhaps most constraining of all was the fact that, even if China had sought to buy abroad, all Western avenues were closed following the 1989 debacle and subsequent sanctions.

The PLA had no option but to turn to Moscow. China's defense industries were in no position to meet the needs of the new high-tech doctrine or to fill the military's most pressing needs. Over the course of the decade, Moscow would transfer fighters, submarines, destroyers, helicopters, antiaircraft missiles, transport aircraft, aircraft engines, and other equipment to the PLA. These sales amounted to approximately U.S.$6 billion in total during 1992–98, on average about $750 million per annum.[37] Russian technicians also undertook to assist Chinese defense industries in a wide range of production.

Thus, the PLA intensively studied and quickly began to assimilate doctrinal lessons learned from the Gulf War into reform of the force structure. The Gulf War stimulated scores of symposia in the PLA to discuss its details and implications, as well as numerous publications in the PLA newspaper *Jiefangjun Bao*, military journals, and books. Military publishing houses in China began turning out large quantities of books on high-technology warfare.[38]

The PLA's goal is clearly to develop a multifaceted, technologically modern force structure capable of pursuing multiple missions in a regional context

37. See Richard F. Grimmett, *Conventional Arms Transfers to Developing Nations, 1992–1999*, Congressional Research Service Report to Congress, August 2000.

38. See, e.g., Jiang Wenming, "Study and Anticipate the Enemy Beforehand—Series on High-Tech War Has Been Published," *Jiefangjun Bao*, December 6, 1993, p. 3, in FBIS–CHI, December 21, 1993. Some of the selections in Michael's Pillsbury's edited volume *Chinese Views of Future Warfare* also illustrate these lessons. See Michael Pillsbury, ed., *Chinese Views of Future Warfare* (Washington, D.C.: National Defense University Press, 1997). By the late 1990s, nearly 300 volumes had been published on high-tech war.

(there does not appear to be any attempt to project power at greater distances, far from China). "Flexible response" is probably the most apt description of the PLA's evolving doctrine. That is, the PLA seeks to develop the capabilities to meet a range of contingencies—including a conventional land invasion; strategic or tactical nuclear attack; the use of chemical or biological weapons; air-to-air engagement over land and sea; coastal and deepwater naval battles; and peripheral deployment of forces. The PLA is developing and upgrading its entire force structure to contend with this range of contingencies.

One leading analyst of the Gulf War and its implications for the PLA is Major General Wang Zhenxi of the Academy of Military Sciences (AMS), where he directed the Foreign Military Studies Division in the wake of the Gulf War and was responsible for a number of briefing papers for military leaders. In a 1998 interview following his retirement, General Wang explained to me some of the principal lessons learned:

> The Gulf War taught us the great challenges we faced. Iraq's command and control systems were paralyzed. Therefore, the first lesson we learned was the importance of electronic warfare as a central ingredient of modern warfare, and the need for strong electronic countermeasures. Second, we learned the importance of integrated command and control, particularly the important role played by AWACs and satellites. Third, we learned about the transparency of battlespace and the need to hide and camouflage weapons and equipment. Not only do they have to be well hidden, they also need to be well fortified. Iraq hid its tanks underground and fortified many of its bunkers. Night-vision equipment is also important. We need to make our battle space less transparent to potential enemies. We also need to learn how to upgrade the survivability of our weapons, logistics stocks, and command and control units. We also need to counter rapid reaction units and protect against precision-guided munitions. We are accustomed to close combat, but not stand-off weapons. We also need our own PGMs. We are conducting research in this area, but have not yet developed such systems. These were the principal lessons we learned from the Gulf War and our principal weaknesses.[39]

Another lesson learned by the PLA was the importance of real-time intelligence and overhead reconnaissance, which allowed coalition forces to seize and keep the initiative in the Gulf War. Intercepts of civilian and military com-

39. Major General Wang Zhenxi, interview with the author, December 8, 1998, Beijing.

munications and the ability to track every Iraqi military movement and Scud missile launch were critical to coordinating the strategic bombing campaign and ground force attacks. The PLA also noted the ability of coalition forces to "blind" Iraq's own intelligence and reconnaissance, anti-aircraft defenses, and communications facilities.[40] The extensive use of satellites and space-based sensors, coordinated from North America, but with downlinks to forces in the field, exposed the PLA's critical weaknesses in these areas. Use of communication and real-time intelligence networks in the field was a critical element of the allied forces' success. As one *Jiefangjun Bao* commentator noted, "In the Gulf War the United States deployed three defense communications satellites, established 128 defense satellite communication terminals, and built an ultra-high frequency network *before* the assembling of allied troops."[41]

The interoperability of forces employing the AirLand Battle doctrine further proved to the PLA that its inability to conduct truly joint operations, especially at high operational tempo, was a critical tactical problem. Even after the 1980s reforms that created group armies, the PLA began to realize that its force structure was still dominated by the ground forces and too large. It simply did not possess flexible brigade-based units that could work in tandem with a range of air assets and real-time intelligence and total battle-space awareness under all-weather and day/night conditions. The Gulf War convinced PLA analysts that high-tech warfare involved joint-service operations carried out across an invisible geographical spectrum of "battle space" *(zhanjian).* As Chief of Staff Fu Quanyou himself noted, "Future high-tech warfare will be five-dimensional warfare involving land, sea and air forces, as well as space and electronic technologies."[42]

The extensive use of standoff precision-guided weapons that can be fired at great distances, but with high accuracy and tremendous lethality, also left a profound impression. As one *Jiefangjun Bao* article later noted, "The large numbers of smart and long-range weapons [have] changed the form of combat. . . . Future combat will be fought by highly intelligent personnel operating technical weapons from a distance without coming into contact with

40. "Gulf War Reconnaissance Lessons," *Xiandai Bingqi* (Modern Weaponry), no. 9 (September 1991): 30–34, in JPRS-CAR-91–071, pp. 43–47.

41. Teng Renshun, "Network Distribution: Nerve Center of the Information Battlefield," *Jiefangjun Bao,* November 24, 1998, in FBIS–CHI, December 10, 1998.

42. Fu Quanyou, "Make Active Explorations, Deepen Reform, Advance Military Work in an All-Round Way," *Qiushi,* March 16, 1998, in FBIS–CHI, April 3, 1998. Also see Academy of Military Sciences, *Shijie Junshi Nianjian 1997* (World Military Yearbook) (Beijing: AMS Press, 1998), pp. 239–41.

the opposition."[43] The ability to carry a war deep into enemy territory without ever coming close to territorial borders must have caused a few PLA strategists to think hard about the efficacy of even a frontier-based "active defense."

The Gulf War thus had a profound impact on PLA doctrinal thinking about the nature of warfare and defense stimulating comprehensive, far-reaching, fundamental reconsiderations and revisions. In the PLA's seventy-year history, only the Korean War produced such a thoroughgoing reassessment. Many cherished, long-standing beliefs and practices were challenged, and many new vistas were opened up to PLA strategists. As a result, the Central Military Commission shifted its military modernization priorities "from quantitative to qualitative and from manpower-intensive to technology-intensive mode in army building. . . . Under modern conditions, high technology has become the basic factor and new area of growth in the combat effectiveness of the armed forces. It has also become the basic criterion for judging the level of modernization of the armed forces."[44]

Limited War under High-Technology Conditions, II: The Revolution in Military Affairs

Just as the PLA was digesting all of the complex lessons from the Gulf War, U.S. military journals and officials began discussing a new "revolution in military affairs" (RMA). PLA analysts were quick to pick up on the new term (*xin junshi geming* in Chinese), translate U.S. writings on the subject, and convene many meetings to discuss this key new development in warfare.[45] The PLA National Defense University's Scientific Research Department sponsored a major conference on the subject for senior officers in early 1998,[46] while the Academy of Military Sciences (the PLA's leading research organ) commissioned a special issue of its journal on the RMA.[47]

---

43. Yang Xuhua, "Reunderstanding Modernization of the Armed Forces," *Jiefangjun Bao*, August 18, 1998, in FBIS–CHI, September 14, 1998.

44. Ibid.

45. For a good survey of PLA attention to the RMA, see You Ji, "The Revolution in Military Affairs and the Evolution of China's Strategic Thinking," *Contemporary Southeast Asia* 21, no. 3 (December 1999): 344–64; and Michael Pillsbury, ed., *Chinese Views of Future Warfare* (Washington, D.C.: National Defense University Press, 1997).

46. See Zhang Hui, "Xin Junshi Geming Wenti Yanjiu Xinlun" (New Theories in Research on the RMA), *Guofang Daxue Xuebao*, no. 2–3 (1998): 66–69.

47. *Zhongguo Junshi Kexue*, no. 1, 1996 (Spring). These articles were republished in Gao Chunxiang, ed., *Xin Junshi Geming Lun* (Theories of the New Military Revolution) (Beijing: Junshi Kexue Chubanshe, 1996).

Contemporary discussions of a revolution in military affairs began in American strategic studies circles in the mid 1990s and in the Pentagon's Office of Net Assessment (headed by the iconoclastic strategic thinker Andrew Marshall). While the current RMA is considered to include multiple aspects, the baseline is the application of information technology to the battlefield and contemporary warfare. Cyberspace is now a crucial zone of conflict, and today's RMA is primarily associated with the new theater of information warfare (IW) made possible by the military exploitation of satellites, computers, and variety of data links. As the word "revolution" implies, the new breakthroughs are considered fundamental and revolutionary, rather than incremental, like the advent of the tank and armored infantry, the aircraft and strategic bombing, and the submarine and subsurface stealth previously.[48]

The use of information and intelligence has always been a critical element of strategic advantage in warfare, as was noted by Sun Zi, Cao Cao, and other ancient Chinese strategists. To possess timely and accurate intelligence, to communicate promptly and securely with one's own forces, and to deceive and confuse the enemy with misleading information while concealing one's own information advantages and communications channels have always been important in warfare.

Computers and satellites have thrust warfare into an entirely new information age.[49] They are important not only to communications and intelligence collection but also as guidance systems for "smart weapons": air-dropped laser- and satellite-guided bombs; precision-guided air-, sea-, and ground-launched cruise missiles; ballistic missiles and anti–ballistic missile defenses.[50] Satellites and computers have also transformed air and ground warfare. The information age has revolutionized the physical domain of combat, for the first time providing modern militaries with the hope of achieving "total battlespace awareness."

The lessons of the Gulf War were reinforced by NATO's 1999 operations

48. The term was actually first coined in connection with historical debates over the sweeping changes in warfare that occurred during the sixteenth and seventeenth centuries, as the leading British strategist Lawrence Freedman notes in *The Revolution in Strategic Affairs,* Adelphi Paper no. 318 (London: IISS, 1998), p. 7; also see Geoffrey Parker, *The Military Revolution: Military Innovation and the Rise of the West, 1500–1800* (Cambridge: Cambridge University Press, 1996).

49. Among the many useful explications of the RMA, see William E. Odom, *America's Military Revolution: Strategy and Structure after the Cold War* (Washington, D.C.: American University Press, 1993).

50. See Frank Barnaby, *The Automated Battlefield* (London: Sidgwick & Jackson; New York: Free Press, 1986); and "Select Enemy: Delete," *Economist,* March 8, 1997.

in the former Yugoslavia.[51] Senior Colonel Wang Baocun, an expert in IW and the RMA at the Academy of Military Sciences, penned an extensive analysis of the IW reconnaissance and jamming systems employed by NATO.[52] Wang noted in particular the extensive use of satellites and reconnaissance aircraft (RC-135 and U-2), as well as SIGINT interception. Wang observed that NATO electronic warfare (EW) planes emitted powerful electromagnetic pulses to jam and confuse Serbian communications. He also distinguished in his article between offensive and defensive IW and noted that Serbia was quite good at the latter—that is, hiding its C^4I (command, control, communications, computers, and intelligence) sites in caves, underground, alongside roads, and in large population centers. He also noted the vulnerabilities of the Serb MiG-29s, which lacked sophisticated counter-EW avionics.

PLA writings on the RMA tend to focus on IW and command and control systems, rather than a broader spectrum of weaponry and technological advancement, although Wang Baocun has authored a more comprehensive assessment of the strategies, weapons, and technologies involved in the RMA.[53] Michael Pillsbury of the U.S. Department of Defense's Office of Net Assessment has extensively surveyed PLA writings on the RMA and found that some writers look at a broader range of cutting-edge battlefield technologies, such as laser weapons, ultra-high frequency weapons, ultrasonic-wave weapons, stealth weapons, mirror-beam weapons, electromagnetic weapons, plasma weapons, and robotic and nanotechnology weapons.[54] Pillsbury also includes PLA writers who address a wide range of smart weapons and other military technologies used in the Gulf War, labeling them the "RMA School," which he distinguishes from the "People's War" and "Local War" schools of PLA analysts. But these are not necessarily doctrinal debates.

Information Warfare

Clearly, the PLA has grasped the importance of IW in contemporary warfare. "The transition from mechanized warfare to information warfare is an

51. See, e.g., Song Youwen et al., *Gao Jixu Tiaojian Xia de Xinxi Zhan* (Information Warfare under High Technology Conditions) (Beijing: Junshi Kexue Chubanshe, 1993).

52. Wang Baocun, "Information Warfare and the Kosovo Conflict," *Jiefangjun Bao*, May 25, 1999, in FBIS–CHI, June 23, 1999.

53. Wang Baocun, *Shijie Xin Junshi Geming* (The Global Revolution in Military Affairs) (Beijing: Jiefangjun Chubanshe, 2000). For another more thorough and systematic treatment, see Gao, ed., *Xin Junshi Geming Lun*.

54. Michael Pillsbury, "China and the Revolution in Military Affairs" (unpublished paper). Also see Pillsbury, ed., *Chinese Views of Future Warfare*.

epoch-making revolution in military history. It is a fundamental historical change," one *Jiefangjun Bao* article observed.[55] Another noted that:

> Information has climbed into the ranks of the key elements of combat strength, and has opened up a new theater of invisible contention. . . . Information tactics have penetrated into all types of armament and equipment, combat tactics, and command—combining them in the form of a network, with the result that in future warfare the traditional race to control the air and the sea will become contention for control of information. The struggle between gaining and countering the gaining of information, jamming and counter-jamming, and destroying information systems and countering such destruction will become the major form of warfare.[56]

In the words of Wang Baocun, "In military affairs, knowledge is being elevated as the key ingredient of combat power, while materials and energy in the form of firepower and mechanized power will be downgraded to a secondary position. The quality of an army is no longer determined by its size but by the presence of knowledge-intensive qualified personnel and smart weapons and high-tech equipment."[57] Three other authors writing in *Jiefangjun Bao* go further to define the urgency of mastering IW as an offensive military capability:

> It is essential to have an all-conquering offensive technology and to develop software and technology for [Inter]net offensives, so as to be able to launch attacks and countermeasures on the [Inter]net—including information-paralyzing software and information deception software. Some of these are like bombs—they are electronic bombs that saturate the enemy's cyberspace. Some are like painting—they are electronic scrawls which appear and disappear on the enemy's pages in chaotic fashion. Some are like phantoms and electronic flying saucers which come and go on the [Inter]net and disrupt the enemy's systems.[58]

More specifically, PLA writings on the offensive use of IW tend to divide into "hard" and "soft" IW. The former, learned from the Gulf War, empha-

---

55. Chen Qingrong, "Five Major Technologies Supporting Information Warfare," *Jiefangjun Bao*, December 1, 1998, in FBIS–CHI, December 25, 1998.

56. Zhang Panxiong and Chen Yonghui, "New Trends in Future Warfare," *Jiefangjun Bao*, December 15, 1998, in FBIS–CHI, January 10, 1999.

57. Zhang Guoyu, "Symposium on Challenge of the Knowledge Revolution for the Military," *Jiefangjun Bao*, January 5, 1999, in FBIS–CHI, January 27, 1999. Also see Wang, *Shijie Xin Junshi Geming*.

58. Leng Bingling, Wang Yulin, and Zhao Wenxiang, "Bringing Internet Warfare into the Military System Is of Equal Significance with Land, Sea and Air Power," *Jiefangjun Bao*, November 11, 1999, in FBIS–CHI, November 17, 1999.

sizes knocking out the enemy's C⁴I military infrastructure (or "nodes") and disrupting communications and logistics in order to reduce its ability to defend and respond. The latter emphasizes offensive use of computer viruses, space-based lasers, and electromagnetic warfare to confuse and paralyze an enemy's communications systems on the ground, in the air, and at sea. One writer even speaks of "developing some 'secret weapon' that could plunge the hegemonists' [i.e., the United States's] entire electronic financial system into chaos."[59] Taken together, hard and soft IW can provide the attacker with information dominance *(zhixin xiquan)* and the opportunity to follow up with more conventional weapons of attack.

Most PLA writings on IW are oriented not so much toward the offensive use of IW as toward creating and establishing a digitized and information-based command and control system. Most of these writings are merely translations or descriptions of U.S. or NATO C⁴I gleaned from Western publications, combined with sections on how the PLA should develop IW in order to fight potential "hegemonic" enemies (i.e., the United States). Some analyses often selectively lift verbatim text from U.S. military operational guides such as *Information Operations* (FM-100–6) and the Joint Chiefs of Staff's *Joint Doctrine for Command and Control Warfare Operations,* and *Joint Vision 2010.*[60] Others comb a variety of Western publications to introduce PLA readers to the broad spectrum of uses of information technology in modern militaries.[61] Protection of intellectual property rights is not a priority in PLA writings on IW! Only a few PLA writings on IW indicate independent analysis. One such case is a series of articles compiled by the editorial board of *Junshi Xueshu* (Military Art, a restricted-circulation journal published by the Academy of Military Sciences).[62] This volume contains multiple analyses of how to apply IW in every service, at different levels of the force structure, in offensive and defensive operations, and in command and control. On balance, however, one must conclude (as has the RAND Corporation analyst James Mulvenon, after a careful read-

59. Huang Dongjia, "Xinxi Zhanzheng he Zhongguo Junshi Xiandaihua," (Information Warfare and Chinese Military Modernization), *Xiandai Junshi,* no. 240 (January 1997).

60. See, e.g., Shen Weiguang, *Xin Zhan Zhenglun* (Debates on New Warfare) (Beijing: Renmin Chubanshe, 1997).

61. See, e.g., Li Xianyao and Zhou Bisong et al., *Xinxi Zhanzheng* (Information Warfare) (Beijing: Jiefangjun Chubanshe, 1998).

62. *Junshi Xueshu* Bianjibu, ed., *Wo Jun Xinxizhan Wenti Yanjiu* (Research on Issues in Our Army's Information Warfare) (Beijing: Guofang Daxue Chubanshe, 1999).

ing of many PLA IW texts), that the PLA has not developed an *independent* IW strategy.[63]

One must still ask, though, whether these internal writings and discussions are actually being developed and implemented in the PLA. While certain elements of the PLA force structure are being digitized and linked together in computer networks, troops are now being trained in IW, and offensive IW viruses are being developed, on balance, IW in the PLA still exists much more in the realm of theory than in practice. This is also the opinion of one leading PLA IW expert, who, in an interview, was actually quite pessimistic about the PLA's ability to adapt and adopt IW technologies, complaining, "The PLA must mechanize before it can informationize!"[64] This said, the recognition placed on the importance of IW and EW, and the courses taught in PLA staff colleges, do indicate that resources and training are now increasingly being devoted to these key dimensions. In late 1998, it was reported that the Beijing Military Region had established the "first military information superhighway," linking together by computer all group armies, military districts, garrison commands, and air force units in the MR into a single "central operations center."[65] According to the report, this was the first time PLA units had all been networked together within a single MR and thus acquired the ability to share "comprehensive processing and fast transmission of graphics, characters, audio data, and data encryption" in a series of exercises.

To be sure, establishing a computer network is not the same thing as undertaking offensive information warfare, and establishing a computer network at MR headquarters is far different from employing one at the tactical battlefield level, but it nonetheless does suggest a new level of computerization capability for the PLA. There apparently are plans to set up a national IW simulation training center at the Shijiazhuang Army Staff Academy.[66] In 1998, the PLA Communications Command Academy established degree programs in "IW command and control science" and "IW technological science,"[67] and in 1999, a PLA Information Engineering University was estab-

---

63. James Mulvenon, "The PLA and Information Warfare," in id. and Richard H. Yang, eds., *The PLA in the Information Age* (Santa Monica, Calif.: RAND Corporation, 1999).

64. Interview with AMS IW expert, Beijing, October 23, 1998.

65. Chen Hui, "Military Information Superhighway Established," Xinhua Domestic Service, October 26, 1998, in FBIS–CHI, November 2, 1998.

66. *PLA Activities Report* (February 1997), p. 23, citing a February 14, 1997, *Zhongguo Guofang Bao* article.

67. *DSTI Monthly Report* (June 1998), p. 25, citing a June 22, 1998, *Jiefangjun Bao* article.

lished in Zhengzhou.[68] A careful study by U.S. Air Force Colonel Mark Stokes suggests that quite a lot of investment is being devoted to developing space and ground-based IW systems,[69] some in support of building a national signals intelligence (SIGINT) complex.[70] PLA intelligence operates an extensive network of land-based SIGINT monitoring sites, while the PLA Navy operates at least ten ELINT ships, and the PLA Air Force maintains a handful of EY-8 turboprop reconnaissance aircraft.[71] Certainly, the sheer volume of PLA publications is an indication of the importance attached to understanding the RMA and mastering IW. One survey of these indicates PLA writings in all six areas of IW as defined by the U.S. Joint Chiefs of Staff: psychological operations, denial and deception, electronic warfare, computer network attack, physical destruction of information systems, and computer network defense.[72] An official 1998 U.S. Department of Defense report noted that, "In recent years, the PLA has shown an exceptional interest in information warfare and has begun programs to develop IW capabilities at the strategic, operational, and tactical levels, as part of its overall military modernization effort. The PLA's interest in IW is reflected particularly in the number of articles which appear frequently in military publications and in the use of IW-related scenarios in exercises and wargames."[73]

While the Academy of Military Sciences in Beijing is the institutional locus of such research, many other staff colleges and units are also actively involved in RMA-related research. In 1998, the PLA's Communication Command Academy established a graduate training program on IW, and it has compiled and published a series of textbooks in the field. The Academy graduates classes of approximately 150 IW specialists per year, who will command

68. Xinhua, "PLA Information Engineering University Set Up," July 2, 1999, in FBIS–CHI, July 6, 1999. The university combined together the former PLA Zhengzhou Information Engineering College, the PLA Electronic Technology College, and the PLA Topography College. The new university, one of five comprehensive PLA universities, has a total of 10,000 students and faculty, and 32 graduate-level research centers.

69. See Mark A. Stokes, *China's Strategic Modernization: Implications for the United States* (Carlisle Barracks, Pa.: U.S. Army War College Strategic Studies Institute, 1999), esp. ch. 2.

70. See Desmond Ball, "Signals Intelligence in China," *Jane's Intelligence Review* 7, no. 8 (1989): 365–70.

71. Robert Karniol, "China's SIGINT Capabilities Exposed," *Jane's Defense Weekly*, Internet edition, April 6, 2001.

72. Kate Farris, "Chinese Views of Information Warfare" (unpublished paper).

73. *Future Military Capabilities and Strategy of the People's Republic of China*, Report to Congress Submitted by the Secretary of Defense Pursuant to Section 1226 of the FY98 National Defense Authorization Act, July 9, 1998, p. 6.

"digitized combat units" and promulgate knowledge about IW throughout the armed forces.[74] The Third Department (responsible for signals intelligence) and Fourth Department (responsible for electronic warfare and communications) of the PLA General Staff Department are involved in coordinating and disseminating such research, and, together with the General Staff's Information Engineering Academy and COSTIND's Institute of System Engineering, are developing a servicewide computerized C⁴I infrastructure. A PLA-wide Society for the Study of Future Warfare has been established, a special working group of IW specialists from different units convenes quarterly around the country, while *Jiefangjun Bao* gives an annual prize (the "Tongchuang Cup") for the best article on high-tech warfare, and special IW symposia are frequently convened.[75]

In addition to IW, some PLA authors write about other forms of unconventional warfare. Most noteworthy here is *Chao Xian Zhan* (Unrestricted Warfare), a book by two officers in the PLA Air Force, which attracted much media attention in the United States at the time of its publication in 1999 and was translated by the U.S. government's Foreign Broadcast Information Service.[76] The book was controversial because it advocated unconventional methods of attack *on the United States,* including terrorist attacks on and sabotage of U.S. civilian and military targets, cyber attacks on Wall Street and major financial institutions, computer attacks on major government and media sites, psychological propaganda operations, and other unorthodox tactics. While the book borders on fiction, it is indicative of thinking about asymmetric warfare in the PLA today. PLA strategists are convinced that they must fight the United States in ways that negate comparative American advantages while exploiting relative weaknesses.

Progress and Impediments to IW and the RMA in China

The PLA is attempting to bring information technology to its forces by creating integrated, secure, and digitized command and control networks, simulation training and computerized war-gaming, intelligence collection, com-

---

74. "PLA Trains Information Warfare Specialists," *Keji Ribao,* April 27, 1999, in FBIS–CHI, May 27, 1999.

75. Li Pengqing and Zhang Zhanjun, "Explore Information Warfare Theories with PLA Characteristics—*Junshi Xueshu* Magazine Holds Symposium," *Jiefangjun Bao,* November 24, 1998, in FBIS–CHI, December 15, 1998.

76. Qiao Liang and Wang Xiangsui, *Chao Xian Zhan: Dui Quanqiuhua Shidai Zhanzheng yu Zhanfa de Xiangding* (Unrestricted Warfare: Judgment of War and Methods of War in the Era of Globalization) (Beijing: PLA Literature and Arts Publishing House, 1999). For an interesting review, see Ming Zhang, "War without Rules," *Bulletin of Atomic Scientists,* November–December 1999, pp. 16–18.

puter attacks and other offensive IW operations, general telecommunications, and classroom teaching. Fiber-optic cable is now predominantly used in military communications. Several of China's seven military regions now have secure intranet communications systems. In addition, China's urban civilian society is increasingly wired to broadband telecommunications and the Internet. For these reasons and others, Wang Baocun and the RAND Corporation specialist James Mulvenon have concluded in a joint assessment that China is in the nascent phase of the RMA, although the PLA leadership may not be aware of the fact.[77]

Despite this nascent progress and the importance attached to IW and related technologies, there are various impediments to the PLA developing, acquiring, and assimilating these and other RMA-era technologies into its force structure. Some are cultural, some political, some organizational, some technological, and some generational.

To begin with, information is a controlled commodity in China. The Communist Party and its propaganda apparatus have done a good job of restricting information flows from outside into China and keeping a close eye on the dissemination of some kinds of information within the country. Freedom of the press and information has never been a CCP hallmark. Generally speaking, technical information, particularly in the scientific and military sectors, is disseminated on a "need to know" basis. The general bifurcation of civilian and military information in China is a further impediment. For the PLA to join the RMA requires a more fundamental loosening of information flow within Chinese society and between the civilian and military sectors.

Several cultural factors also inhibit discovery and assimilation of the RMA: rigid social and professional hierarchies that discourage flexibility; a conservatism in thought and behavioral norms that inhibit innovation; a preference for the status quo and fear of change (fostering risk aversion); pressures for conformity to the collective, with disincentives to individualism; authoritarianism; a preference for "self-reliance" over interdependence; and other inhibiting factors.[78]

Technological impediments also constitute significant constraints.[79] The

77. Wang Baocun and James Mulvenon, "China and the RMA," *Korean Journal of Defense Analysis* 12, no. 2 (Winter 2000): 275–304.

78. Several of these are noted in Bates Gill's study *China and the Revolution in Military Affairs: Assessing Economic and Socio-Cultural Factors* (Carlisle, Pa.: U.S. Army War College Strategic Studies Institute, 1996).

79. See Lonnie Henley, *China's Capacity for Achieving a Revolution in Military Affairs* (Carlisle, Pa.: U.S. Army War College Strategic Studies Institute, 1996).

Australian defense expert Paul Dibb writes that China may be able to achieve "a range of hybrid RMAs based on indigenous R&D combined with imported combat systems and sensors and locally designed precision weapons," although he, too, is deeply skeptical of China's technological ability to innovate, design, build, and deploy in areas involving advanced information technology (IT).[80] Certainly the development of China's telecommunications industry and the introduction of advanced foreign technology will also be key variables.[81] Work in remote sensing, laser technology, satellites, and advanced electronics and guidance systems will have an important effect.

Additional impediments to the PLA's pursuit of IW and the RMA are the age and orientation of the senior High Command. As noted, the background of the senior PLA elite is an extremely insular one; they have had long experience in the ground forces and very little exposure to high technology. They themselves do not know how to type, much less use a computer. According to one leading RMA expert in the PLA, when a group of such specialists briefed senior members of the Central Military Commission on the RMA and information warfare, the CMC generals appeared completely befuddled by many of the concepts and technologies discussed in the briefing.[82] It is difficult to oversee the technological transformation of the armed forces if the military leadership itself is ignorant of such technologies and remains instinctively cautious about them.

Limited War under High-Technology Conditions, III: The Lessons of the Yugoslav War

If the NATO attacks on the former Yugoslavia in 1999 reinforced old lessons from the Gulf War, they also offered some new ones. According to one PLA officer, NATO's military tactics in the Balkans produced a "major debate" in the PLA.[83]

First, as noted in chapter 1, Chinese analysts focused on the broad strategic significance of the Yugoslav war. Both civilian and military analysts in China perceived the Kosovo crisis and use of force by NATO against Yugoslav/Serbian targets and military forces, first and foremost as an important new bid by the United States to extend its global "hegemony." Interviews with

80. Paul Dibb, "The Revolution in Military Affairs and Asian Security," *Survival*, Winter 1997–98, p. 107.

81. See Thomas Bickford and James Mulvenon, "The PLA and the Telecommunications Industry in China," in Mulvenon and Yang, eds., *People's Liberation Army in the Information Age*.

82. Interview with AMS participant, April 26, 1999.

83. Interview with Academy of Military Sciences officer, May 1999.

strategic analysts in China at the outset of the war revealed the perception that this was a blatant attempt by the United States, under the guise of NATO, to seize control of southeastern Europe and thereby control the continent.[84] Nothing was said or recognized about NATO's rationale for intervention in Yugoslavia—to end Serbian ethnic cleansing, genocide, and the refugee crisis—nor did the Chinese media report these factors. For the Chinese, this was imperialistic and hegemonic expansion pure and simple. The eastward expansion of NATO in the preceding years, incorporating several central European nations into the alliance or Partnership for Peace framework, had presaged this strategic thrust into the Balkans. Having defeated the Soviet Union and won the Cold War, Chinese analysts reasoned, America was turning its hegemonic aspirations to central and eastern Europe. Chinese analysts also perceived the United States to be expanding its sphere of strategic interest and military power into Central, South, and East Asia. Intervention in the Balkans would also give the United States a toehold for further expansion into the Middle East, enabling it to contain Russia on the southern flank.[85] Having achieved dominance over Europe, China's military analysts predicted, the United States would target Asia next in its attempts to establish global hegemony *(xian Ou, hou Ya)*. Chinese analysts further dismissed the involvement of other NATO members in the conflict, instead portraying only U.S. involvement or that of "U.S.-led NATO." The fact that there was unanimous NATO involvement, and that several countries with which China had good relations were involved, was conveniently overlooked in Chinese analyses. PLA analysts also postulated that NATO was experiencing an "identity crisis" in the wake of the Cold War, arguing that without the Soviet Union, the alliance's raison d'être had disappeared.[86] The United States, these analysts argued, was trying to reinvent NATO's mission by "globalizing" it (to intervene outside Europe, if necessary), sidestepping the authority of the United Nations, and justifying the use of military force under the guise of "humanitarian intervention." The Kosovo intervention was portrayed as a "dress rehearsal" for this new NATO strategy and "plot for global dominance" by the United States.[87]

84. Numerous interviews in Shanghai and Beijing, April 1999.

85. Ibid.

86. "FRY Crisis Shows Need to Strengthen PLA: Discussion of the Kosovo Crisis among PLA Experts and Scholars," *Jiefangjun Bao,* April 13, 1999, in FBIS–CHI, April 28, 1999.

87. Ibid., views of Liu Mingde of the China Institute of International Strategic Studies.

Such geopolitical simplicity on the part of China's strategic analysts is striking. But the Yugoslav war obviously struck a nerve, given China's fears of U.S. and Japanese intervention in a similar crisis over Taiwan. Also, the PRC's own history of ethnic and religious unrest in Tibet and Xinjiang may have made Beijing extra sensitive. The Yugoslav war clearly created a sense of urgency in China's military and strategic circles, with many warning that previous Chinese predictions that "peace and development" were the dominant trends of the times had been wrong, and that war with the United States was imminent.

PLA analysts also paid close attention to the military dimensions of the Yugoslav war and NATO's strategy, tactics, and weapons, noting tactics and firepower similar to those employed in the 1991 Gulf War and the 1998 Operation Desert Fox,[88] such as:

· Initial attacks against Yugoslavia's command and control infrastructure

· Extensive electronic jamming of both military and public communications

· Remote targeting by long-range cruise missiles, launched from sea and air

· Achievement of "information dominance," making extensive use of space-based sensors and satellites[89]

· Air strikes launched from as far away as North America, utilizing inflight refueling

PLA analysts were also particularly impressed by the success of the aerial bombardment campaign in Yugoslavia. "Kosovo is the first time in history that a war was won with air power only," observed Senior Colonel Yao Yunzhu of the Academy of Military Sciences,[90] noting the ominous implications for China and the PLA:

The dominance of the air battlefield illustrated by the Yugoslav war has great implications for China. The PLA is mainly a traditional ground force. It has to adjust its force structure, command and control system,

88. Zhang Zhaozhong, "Rethinking 'Desert Fox,'" *Jiefangjun Bao*, January 11, 1999, in FBIS–CHI, January 19, 1999.

89. See, in particular, Wang Baocun, "Information Warfare in the Kosovo Conflict."

90. Yao Yunzhu, "Chinese PLA's Thinking on the Yugoslav War" (unpublished paper, May 1999), p. 4.

doctrinal development, and training and education, as well as weapons acquisition, in accordance with this fundamental change in warfare. For example, the PLA would have to change its air defense concepts. Both survivable and effective air defense capabilities are essential to win a war. Such air defense capabilities include passive and active means to counter enemy strikes.[91]

Chinese military analysts also took note of several new weapon systems that were deployed, such as precision munitions that used a variety of active homing and guidance devices. GBU-28/B "smart" gravity bombs—three of which, launched from B-2 strategic bombers, mistakenly hit the Chinese embassy in Belgrade—were among these. Also on display were satellite-guided, TV-guided, and GPS-guided bombs, delivering 1,000–2,500-pound warheads with incredible accuracy (a circular error probability of a few meters). They also noted the use, for the first time, of electromagnetic pulse (EMP) bombs that could sabotage electronic equipment, missile target seekers, computer networks, and data transmission lines.[92]

The extensive use of cruise missiles and other PGMs from ranges outside Yugoslav point defenses reminded PLA analysts that war could be prosecuted from great distances. The realization that the Chinese military might one day find itself in a position where it could not even see, much less defend against, distant attacking adversaries apparently caused great consternation in the PLA High Command. It prompted the PLA to undertake a review of strategic air defenses and offensive counterweapons capable of destroying enemy targets at a distance.[93] As one PLA analyst noted, "In the future, we will be faced mostly with an enemy who uses advanced smart weapons and long-range precision guided weapons."[94] The AMS expert Wang Baocun noted that NATO was able to "decapitate" more than sixty Serbian command and control targets in just the first day of the war with using more than a hundred Tomahawk missiles and eighty air-launched PGMs.[95]

PLA analysts were also surprised by NATO's sustained strategic bomb-

91. Ibid., p. 5.
92. Wang Zudian, "The Offense and Defense of High-Technology Armaments," *Liaowang*, May 24, 1999, in FBIS–CHI, May 27, 1999.
93. James Kynge, "Chinese Army Calls for Strategic Review," *Financial Times*, May 5, 1999.
94. Jia Weidong, "Asymmetrical Warfare and Our Defense," *Jiefangjun Bao*, April 17, 1999, in FBIS–CHI, May 24, 1999.
95. Wang, "Information Warfare in the Kosovo Conflict."

ing campaign. After destroying Serbian C⁴I nodes, NATO bombers waged a prolonged strategic campaign against a wide range of targets. In seventy days of sustained bombing, the air campaign included 33,000 sorties flown, delivering approximately 14,000 bombs and cruise missile ordnance.[96] Many involved planes based far away and utilized more than three hundred in-flight refueling tankers (more than thirty of which were deployed in Italy alone). The B-2 stealth strategic bomber, for example, traveled 20,000 kilometers roundtrip from the United States on each sortie. Many planes flew 2,500 kilometers from bases in England and northern Europe. The operational tempo of these sorties also impressed Chinese analysts, as most aircraft flew daily missions and some attack fighters flew several sorties per day.

PLA analysts applied these lessons to China's own defenses. Many noted the importance of air defenses to protect against aerial bombing. But two analysts from the Academy of Military Sciences noted that Yugoslavia had been successful in hiding its anti-aircraft defenses, scattering them in mountain caves and along highways, and activating their radar intermittently. This made it difficult, the AMS analysts Yao Yunzhu and Wang Baocun concluded, for NATO planes to attack the SAM sites.[97] They also noted the need for China to harden and better defend its C⁴I centers. Senior Colonel Yao of the AMS also noted that NATO attackers had difficulty in locating Yugoslav ground forces, which were physically scattered, made good use of mountains, forests, and villages, moved at night, and camouflaged their equipment well. Wang Baocun noted that Serb forces concealed their tanks, APCs, artillery, and other equipment in forests, caves, and other locations difficult to identify from the air and used corrugated iron and other methods to deceive heat-seeking missiles and PGMs. Attacks on such forces, moreover, required low-flying ground-attack aircraft, which were more vulnerable to interdiction.

As a result of the Yugoslav War, and particularly as a result of the lessons derived from the PLA's study of the air war, a new program known as the "three attacks and three defenses" *(san da san fang)* was initiated throughout the military beginning in late 1999. The "three attacks" are attacking stealth aircraft, cruise missiles, and armed helicopters. The "three defenses"

96. "NATO Campaign Showcased Use of Air Power," *Wall Street Journal,* June 2, 1999.
97. Yao Yunzhu in "FRY Crisis Shows Need to Strengthen PLA"; Wang, "Information Warfare in the Kosovo Conflict."

are defending against enemy reconnaissance and surveillance, precision strikes, and electronic interference.[98] Since 2000, units in various military regions have reported that they have integrated the new strategy into their training regimen.

In general, PLA analysts took consolation in the Serbian fortitude against NATO's firepower and were heartened to realize that it would be much easier for China to absorb such punishment. The expanse of China would definitely play to PRC advantage in the face of sustained air and over-the-horizon cruise missile attacks, because strategic targets in China are far more dispersed. They are also better hidden and hardened. China's anti-aircraft, anti-stealth, and electronic countermeasure capabilities are also probably better than Yugoslavia's. Given the necessary staging areas in northeast Asia and the western Pacific, the PLA Navy (PLAN) could disrupt operations. In a conflict contingency, such as one involving Taiwan, China would not face a broad coalition of countries, much less an integrated and experienced military command structure like NATO's. Although NATO prosecuted the Yugoslav conflict on its own, in the end, the UN Security Council (on which China has a permanent seat) came to play a role in brokering the peace.

On the other hand, with regard to China's own potential coercion of Taiwan, the Yugoslav conflict could not have been encouraging. Inasmuch as the PLA would have to rely heavily on ballistic and cruise missile attacks to "soften up" the island for a follow-on invasion force, the example of Yugoslavia absorbing an enormous pounding from the air without capitulating does not augur well for PLA planners, given a determined Taiwanese population. The stigma of bombing civilian populations would also not have been lost on China. Moreover, Taiwan undoubtedly has also learned to harden its C[4]I nodes and other potential targets.

These are some of the lessons that the 1999 war in the former Yugoslavia taught the PLA. Throughout the 1990s—from the Gulf War to NATO's intervention in the Balkans—PLA doctrine thus evolved a great deal, largely as a result of close scrutiny of foreign conflicts. The Gulf War was a watershed for the PLA, because it was previously believed that "local wars" were waged essentially with ground forces and conventional munitions. After Desert Storm, the PLA came to the stark and disturbing revelation that mod-

98. See, e.g., Chen Hui, "Chinese Military Conducts Training to Fight High-Tech Wars," Xinhua Hong Kong Service, August 11, 2000, in FBIS–CHI, August 11, 2000. I am also grateful to Mark Stokes and Tai Ming Cheung for drawing this campaign to my attention.

ern warfare could be waged from a great distance and utilize a variety of high-technology weaponry and information-based command and control systems. It also realized the importance of "jointness" and integrated interservice coordination on the battlefield, because army, navy, and air force must now pursue mutually reinforcing missions. Furthermore, mobility *(biandong)*, surprise *(turanxing)*, and preemptive attacks *(sujuexing)* were now seen to be important ingredients in modern war.[99] A military that struck first and incapacitated the enemy before it could respond, without engaging forces, would have a good chance of victory. If ground forces had to be committed to combat, the enemy's command, control, and logistics systems should be disrupted or destroyed first.

Limited War under High-Technology Conditions, IV: What Role for Weapons of Mass Destruction?

Although focusing on the PLA's attempts to come to grips with high-tech warfare, the preceding discussion has concentrated on conventional warfare and weapons. We also, however, need to assess PLA doctrine and planning with regard to nuclear, biological, and chemical (NBC) weapons of mass destruction (WMD). There are few subjects in Chinese military affairs about which less is known than how the PLA actually plans for the use of NBC weapons in combat, either offensively or defensively.[100] We do know that, during the 1990s, China acceded to international covenants prohibiting such WMD.

With respect to chemical weapons, the PLA has for many years maintained an Anti-Chemical [weapons] Corps (Fang Hua Bing), which in the mid 1980s was incorporated into the General Staff Department's Special Arms Department (Te Bing Bu). In addition, since at least the mid 1980s, PLA exercises have simulated enemy use of chemical weapons. China is also known to have maintained chemical weapons stockpiles as recently as the late 1980s.[101] During Japan's invasion in the 1930s–1940s, China was attacked with chemical weapons, large and dispersed quantities of which the Japanese left buried in Chinese soil (destruction of these remains a bone of

99. See also Nan, "PLA's Evolving Warfighting Doctrine."

100. The most thorough and up-to-date source on Chinese WMD is National Intelligence Council and Federal Research Division, Library of Congress, *China and Weapons of Mass Destruction: Implications for the United States* (Washington, D.C., 2000).

101. See Eric Croddy, "Chinese Chemical and Biological Warfare (CBW) Capabilities," in ibid., p. 66. This is by far the most detailed and knowledgeable assessment on the subject published.

contention between the two governments). Japan likewise subjected Chinese people to horrendous biological "experiments" during World War II. China has conducted research into, or maintained stockpiles of, biological weapons in the past, but there is no evidence that such programs continue today.[102] However, China became an early member of the Convention on the Prohibition of the Development, Production, and Stockpiling of Bacteriological (Biological) and Toxic Weapons and Their Destruction (known as the Biological Weapons Convention, or BWC). Officially, China has long advocated the prohibition of chemical weapons and the destruction of stockpiles worldwide. China was an initial signatory of the Chemical Weapons Convention in 1993, ratified it in 1996, and deposited the instruments of ratification in 1997. Since that time, it is presumed that China has destroyed its own chemical weapons stockpiles.

Nuclear weapons and doctrine are another matter. China detonated an atomic bomb on October 16, 1964, and has subsequently developed a full panoply of delivery systems (although it has yet to deploy MIRV warheads on its missiles). These are detailed in chapter 6, but some discussion of China's nuclear doctrine is appropriate here.

China's official nuclear doctrine is straightforward and long-standing: no first use (NFU). China has also supported nuclear-free zones and has been an unstinting advocate of the prohibition and destruction of all nuclear weapons stockpiles, the withdrawal of nuclear weapons from foreign countries and territories, and universal nuclear disarmament. China has consistently taken the "high ground" on global nuclear disarmament but has itself been unwilling to enter into negotiations to reduce its own stockpiles until the other declared nuclear powers reduce their inventories to China's levels first.

Doctrinally, Chinese strategists have exhibited ambivalence about nuclear weapons. Mao used to refer to them (and the United States) as "paper tigers," but he also warned that they should be "despised strategically, but respected tactically." On the other hand, Mao certainly viewed China's nuclear weapons as carriers of international status as well as deterrents.

Soon after the Soviet detonation of a hydrogen bomb in 1953, Mao and his colleagues tried hard to gain sample atomic and hydrogen weapons from their ally. In August 1957, Nikita Khrushchev reneged on a secret agreement and refused to supply such samples. Sino-Soviet relations never recovered, eventually rupturing fully in 1962. After the political fallout,

102. Ibid.

China's nuclear scientists embarked on a crash development program of their own nuclear weapons[103] and ballistic missiles.[104]

Following the detonation of an atomic bomb in October 1964, China faced an increasingly worrying two-front threat from the Soviet Union and United States. China had the bomb but not a nuclear doctrine. By virtue of necessity, China's strategists formulated the doctrine of "minimum deterrence," whereby Chinese nuclear forces could be assured of absorbing an initial first strike while still being able to retaliate with intercontinental missiles into the Soviet heartland or against American targets in East Asia or the North Pacific (after 1980, China achieved the capability to hit the continental United States with ICBMs). This minimum deterrent doctrine was a "countervalue" one, because China's weapons did not have the accuracy to represent a true counterforce threat against Soviet or U.S. nuclear installations.

Although China's nuclear strategists and arsenal bear the stamp of this nuclear doctrine even today, in recent years there has been some evidence of debate and change. Alastair I. Johnston's research has indicated that some Chinese nuclear strategists advocate moving from *minimum deterrence* toward *limited deterrence (youxian weishe)*.[105] This doctrinal evolution represents a shift from an ability to inflict damage on an aggressor to being able to wage a nuclear war, albeit minimally. As Johnston observes, such thinking represents a significant departure in nuclear doctrine, as it constitutes a war-fighting doctrine *(shizhan nengli)*, based on the premise that credible deterrence depends on a bona fide ability to fight a nuclear war. This represents a more diversified targeting doctrine, which includes both countervalue and counterforce targets. It also envisions use of tactical nuclear weapons in a battlefield environment—either airbursts or fired from artillery. Since the mid 1980s, PLA forces training in north China (Hua Bei) have simulated such conditions.

From this perspective, minimum and limited deterrence are not mutually exclusive nuclear doctrines, but rather can be complementary at different

103. See John Wilson Lewis, *China Builds the Bomb* (Stanford, Calif.: Stanford University Press, 1988).

104. For a thorough chronicle of the ballistic missile program, see Xue Guo'an and Xiao Tianliang, eds., *Yi Tian: Gongheguo Daodan Hewuqi Fazhan Jishi* (Beijing: Xiyuan Chubanshe, 1999).

105. See Alastair I. Johnston, "Prospects for Chinese Nuclear Force Modernization: Limited Deterrence versus Multilateral Arms Control," in Shambaugh and Yang, eds., *China's Military in Transition;* id., "China's New 'Old Thinking': The Concept of Limited Deterrence," *International Security* 20, no. 3 (Winter 1995).

levels of conflict. As Bates Gill, James Mulvenon, and Mark Stokes have observed in their study of China's nuclear forces, minimal deterrence is the likely operative doctrine at the strategic intercontinental level, while a limited deterrent—which envisions offensive limited nuclear war-fighting—is likely operational at a regional, intermediate-range, theater level. Continuing "down" the spectrum of conflict, they further observe that China's conventionally armed short-range ballistic missiles are likely configured in an offensive, preemptive, counterforce, war-fighting posture.[106] They posit that configuration of China's nuclear and ballistic missile forces at these three levels, taken together, provides China with "credible deterrence."

Thus, at least at some levels, the PLA's Second Artillery most likely operates on the presumption of offensive nuclear war-fighting, albeit always couched in terms of a "nuclear counterattack campaign" *(he fanji zhanyi)*. Some internal PLA training manuals explicitly discuss such "nuclear counterattacks." These are of concern. One internal manual used for training commanders at the National Defense University, entitled *Zhanyixue* (The Study of Military Campaigns), includes an unusual, explicit, and lengthy description of the conditions under which the PLA Second Artillery would launch intercontinental nuclear counterattacks.[107] This manual emphasizes the use of land-based ICBMs but also stresses the importance of mobile missiles—assuming, perhaps, that fixed launchers in silos would be taken out by a nuclear adversary. "In order to enhance the battlefield survivability of our strategic missile forces under nuclear conditions, the combat locations of the Second Artillery strategic forces were built according to strategic directives of the highest order," it states. "Its combat positions are scattered extensively in the nation's strategic depth and therefore the [nuclear counterattack] campaign distribution is also highly dispersed. Such a campaign distribution is instrumental to stealth and survival."[108] The manual also emphasizes extremely tight command and control "from the country's highest body of decision-making."[109] It specifies extreme secrecy in giving, receiving, and protecting launch codes, while giving "[nuclear] campaign commanders" of the Second Artillery discretion in selecting specific target sites following

106. Bates Gill, James Mulvenon, and Mark Stokes, "The Chinese Second Artillery Corps: Transition to Credible Deterrence" (paper presented at the CAPS/RAND Conference "The PLA as Organization," Warrenton, Virginia, August 2000).

107. See, e.g., the discussion in Wang Houqing and Zhang Xingye, eds., *Zhanyixue* (The Study of Military Campaigns) (Beijing: Guofang Daxue Chubanshe, 2000), pp. 369–74.

108. Ibid., p. 370.

109. Ibid.

a launch order from the "supreme command."[110] We know from other internal PLA sources that the Standing Committee of the Politburo of the Central Committee holds ultimate authority to order the launch of nuclear weapons and missiles, but these sources are not clear as to whether such an order would be issued directly to missile units or transmitted to them via the chain of command of the Central Military Commission to the Second Artillery, and then in turn to specific missile brigades (see discussion in chapter 4). The manual also anticipates the extreme disruption of China's nuclear installations: "Because the strategic missile forces of the Second Artillery will be the key target of a nuclear strike by the enemy, the Second Artillery units have to conduct combat action under extremely difficult conditions. The personnel, facilities, equipment, weapons, and command and control system of Second Artillery missile troops, and the roads and bridges within the war zone, will suffer severe casualties and damage."[111] It also implies a launch-on-warning (LOW) doctrine, "The nuclear counterattack campaign of the Second Artillery will be conducted after the enemy launched a nuclear strike against us first."[112] Finally, while the manual anticipates a nuclear counterforce strike against China's missile assets, it envisions a combined counterforce/countervalue counterattack that "can swiftly destroy the enemy's important strategic targets of political, economic and military centers."[113]

In sum, this important PLA manual offers unique insights into internal PLA plans for the conduct of nuclear warfare. It is clear that the PLA anticipates fighting a nuclear conflict *if attacked first,* but it is inaccurate to assert that the PLA has a first-strike strategy. The PLA's strategic nuclear doctrine is one of deterrence in the first instance, maintaining a retaliatory second-strike capability, and entering into intercontinental nuclear combat only if deterrence fails and China is attacked.

The lack of foreign interaction with China's nuclear strategists and nuclear weapons establishment, and the general lack of Chinese transparency on such matters, often leads to guesswork, inference, and worse-case assumptions by foreign observers. China's nuclear doctrine, nuclear forces, and ballistic missile establishment are clearly all undergoing dynamic changes, but the motivations and end goals catalyzing these changes are much less obvious.[114]

110. Ibid., pp. 365–66.
111. Ibid., p. 370.
112. Ibid.
113. Ibid.
114. For further discussion, see Robert A. Manning, Ronald Montaperto, and Brad Roberts, *China, Nuclear Weapons, and Arms Control: A Preliminary Assess-*

APPLYING DOCTRINE ON THE BATTLEFIELD:
TRENDS IN PLA TRAINING

Theoretical doctrine is one thing, but operational training and experience in modern combat is quite another. The PLA can study modern warfare techniques ad nauseam, but it is of little utility unless the lessons can be assimilated into the force structure and applied on the battlefield. What we know of PLA training suggests that much more innovation has occurred theoretically in the Academy of Military Sciences and other research organs than has actually taken place in units on the ground. In any military, it takes a long time to assimilate and operationalize new doctrinal innovations, especially if they call for wholesale overhaul of existing tactics and practices (as has been the case with the PLA over the past decade). Training—especially live-fire exercises—is also expensive; the PLA literally cannot afford regular exercises that burn up fuel, cause wear on engines and other equipment, and reduce munitions stockpiles.[115] One PLA journal article claims that firing a single shell from a tank costs over 10,000 renminbi (approximately U.S.$1,200).[116] As a result of these strictures, resources and live-fire training are concentrated in the top tier category 1 (jialei budui) and rapid reaction units, while category 2 and category 3 units (yilei and binglei budui) have more meager ammunition stockpiles and poorer and less equipment, are maintained at a lower level of readiness, and are generally composed of less educated and capable troops.

Partial substitutes for training are computerized war games and simulator training for pilots, tanks operators, and so on. Accordingly, a real effort has been made over the past decade to provide simulators to all category 1 and category 2 units across service lines. China's Second Aeronautic Institute produces simulators for the air force, the Armored Force Engineering Institute produces them for tank and mechanized units, and the navy uses a series of factories to produce a wide range of surface, subsurface, and naval air simulators.[117] Nonetheless, sand-table exercises and simulators are no

ment (New York: Council on Foreign Relations, 2000); Ming Zhang, China's Changing Nuclear Posture (Washington, D.C.: Carnegie Endowment for International Peace, 1999).

115. A visit to an artillery brigade in the Beijing Military Region in December 1998 revealed that the unit only fired fifty rounds of live ammunition per gun per year!

116. Li Xiangjun, "Zhongguo Zuixin Junbei Da Gongkai," Zhongguo Kua Shijie Jun Qing, no. 66 (September 1998): 70.

117. Ibid.

substitute for actual field exercises. A National Training Center has been established in eastern Anhui Province in the Nanjing Military Region, where more experimental exercises are conducted, but the PLA needs to increase its experimentation and evaluation of exercises, such as the U.S. military carries out at Fort Irwin in California.[118] In the wake of the Yugoslav war, the PLA established a "surface-to-air missile simulated battlefield" in the Gobi Desert, where air force SAM units are trained to deal with "aerial bombardment, cruise missiles, stealth aircraft, anti-radiation heat-seeking missiles, and other high-tech weapons."[119] Increasingly, actual battlefield exercises now also pit red and blue team opposing forces against each other. (In China, the red force is always the PLA and the blue force the enemy.) Although they have been standard in most Western militaries for half a century, the PLA only began such adversarial force-on-force exercises in 1985,[120] and not outside of north China until a decade later (in 1998, for example, the military media reported mechanized group army confrontation exercises in the Shenyang MR and joint-force exercises in the "Fujian battle zone" of the Nanjing MR).[121] The PLA's confrontational training remains too infrequent, small-scale, and oversimplified to significantly improve readiness.

Until the mid 1990s, the PLA tended to exercise only in the spring and summer, during daylight, and generally in good weather conditions. As the Donghai No. 5 exercises carried out in the Taiwan Strait in 1996 illustrated, bad weather is still a major problem for PLA units—especially operating offshore. This showcase exercise had to be suspended for three days due to rain, high winds, and choppy seas. More recently, training has been expanded to take place in every season and under conditions of poor weather and darkness.

Training has also increased in scope and frequency. Hundreds of division-, brigade-, and regiment-level exercises are reported in the military media each year. Research by Dennis Blasko, Philip Klapakis, and John Corbett also indicates an average of fifteen to twenty exercises at the group army or fleet

118. I am indebted to Paul Godwin for this insight.
119. *DSTI Monthly Report* (November 1999), p. 17, citing a November 7, 1999, *Wen Hui Bao* (Hong Kong) article.
120. Chen Hui, "New Military Training Developments Noted," Xinhua, April 8, 1998, in FBIS–CHI, April 23, 1998.
121. Ren Yanjun and Zhang Jianjun, "General Staff Department Holds All-Army High-Tech Training Reform Exercises," *Jiefangjun Bao*, October 2, 1998, in FBIS–CHI, October 29, 1998; Zhou Zongfan, "Zhongguo Qingbing Zhilu" (The Road to Building Crack Troops), *Junshi Wenzhai*, no. 16–17 (1998): 25.

level per annum.[122] But when considered in the context of the size and dispersion of the PLA, this averages merely two major exercises per MR per year!

Effective training requires evaluation according to set standards. Until a few years ago, there had never been any standards for evaluating training performance, but in March 1997, the PLA adopted what are called "stipulations on grading military training assessment." According to the new standards, all forces at and below the division level are graded annually according to several criteria.[123] By the end of 1998, it was reported that 91.5 percent of troops had been assessed as "up to standard," while 30 percent of units were rated "first class."[124]

Moreover, military proficiency demands familiarity and repeated drill. One argument in favor of shifting from conscription to an all-volunteer force is precisely to increase familiarity within and between units through high retention rates. Conscript armies do not generally enjoy the same esprit de corps. This problem has always hampered the PLA. Until 1998, because of the annual conscription and demobilization cycles, between one-quarter and one-third of the force in most units was always new. In 1998, the three-year basic conscription was shortened to two years. This change made the situation worse, because up to half of each unit turned over annually. In addition, since 1989, freshmen in many universities have had to undergo some form of military training; in 1994, for example, this included 155,000 students from 143 universities, or 40 percent of all freshmen.[125] Time training university students is time not spent training soldiers.

Standardization of training regimens has also been a problem—and, again, it is becoming worse instead of better as the PLA attempts to introduce multiple changes simultaneously in line with the new doctrine of "limited war under high-technology conditions." In 1990, the General Staff Department issued a comprehensive new set of guidelines for military training (*Junshi Xunlian Dagang*), which was updated and revised annually until a

122. Dennis J. Blasko, Philip T. Klapakis, and John F. Corbett Jr., "Training Tomorrow's PLA: A Mixed Bag of Tricks," in Shambaugh and Yang, eds., *China's Military in Transition*, p. 252.

123. Xiao Yuhong and Ren Yanjun, "Practice of a Graded Military Training Assessment Introduced in the Whole Army," *Jiefangjun Bao*, May 21, 1997, in SWB/FE, April 25, 1997.

124. Ma Xiaochun and Zhao Xiujuan, "The PLA's Training Reform Achievements," Xinhua, December 8, 1998, in FBIS–CHI, December 14, 1998.

125. Xinhua, January 14, 1995, in FBIS–CHI, January 17, 1995.

new set was promulgated at the end of 1995.[126] These, in turn, were revised and reissued in January 1999.[127] This latest batch of training guidelines, considered by the PLA to be the fourth comprehensive set *(quanmian tixi)* issued since 1987, is said to stress joint over combined-arms campaigns *(lianhe zhanyi* instead of *hetong zuozhan).*[128] Following promulgation, the guidelines are then transferred down through the GSD system of every military region, which then tasks certain group armies (corps), divisions, and brigades with carrying out specific simulated, real, and live-fire drills and exercises. Despite the systematic dissemination, it should not be assumed that all units receive the MTO, much less implement it. A review of training in the Chengdu MR in 1997 revealed "failure to standardize, poor training quality due to poor organization, an inability to integrate high-tech study and application, and inadequate training support."[129]

PLA forces have encountered many other problems in training. Anecdotes of such problems are occasionally reported in the military media: falsified training forms, random altering of training plans and shortening of training times, absentee personnel, and misuse of military vehicles and equipment for commercial purposes. Some naval units are accused of conducting night training at dusk and submarine training on the surface rather than submerged.[130] Mechanized units and truck corps in Yunnan are accused of refusing to train on rainy days.[131] Aside from fudging training requirements, there are numerous reports of units unable to use new high-technology equipment. The Baoding-based 38th Group Army, a mobile mechanized unit, revealed that it could not operate its new laser, infrared, electronic, and optical range-finding equipment, while another Beijing MR regiment had to hire outside experts for technical support during an exercise, because it was afraid of damaging new computerized equipment.[132] The officers of an engineering regiment of the 64th Group Army were found unable to operate radar, thermal imagery, spectrum night-vision, and other surveillance equip-

126. Ibid; and Ma Xiaochun and Zhao Xiujuan, "The PLA's Training Reform Achievements," Xinhua, December 8, 1998, in FBIS–CHI, December 14, 1998.

127. Ma Xiaochun, "PLA Plans Training Tasks for 1999," Xinhua, January 6, 1999, in FBIS–CHI, January 7, 1999.

128. Interviews with Academy of Military Sciences personnel, April 1999.

129. *PLA Activities Report,* September 1997, p. 9, citing *Zhanqi Bao* (the Chengdu MR newspaper), July 5, 1997.

130. *PLA Activities Report,* April 1997, p. 8, citing *Renmin Haijun,* March 25, 1997.

131. Ibid., January 1998, p. 18, citing *Zhanqi Bao,* December 2, 1997.

132. Ibid., citing *Jiefangjun Bao,* April 22 and 28, 1997.

ment during training.[133] In a remarkable admission from the Lanzhou MR, during one exercise, the battlefield TV surveillance system went blind, the unmanned aircraft reconnaissance system was out of control, interference from local radio stations prevented accurate readings in the radar reconnaissance systems, and high-tension power lines interfered with sound-activated reconnaissance systems.[134] PLAAF and naval air force planes and helicopters have been known to crash during training, although this is usually not reported. Officially, the mishap rate for the naval air force in 1997 was 0.215 incidents per 10,000 hours of flight time.[135] It is thought that the PLAAF has lost at least two of its highly prized Sukhoi-27s, and it restricts the training time and degree of difficulty for these aircraft. Apparently, fuel is also restricted, so as to prevent pilots from defecting across the strait to Taiwan.

Getting to Grips with the Modern Battlefield: Mobility and Jointness

Evidence that the PLA's study of modern warfare was being implemented on the battlefield first emerged in the late 1980s. A series of exercises in 1988 in the Lanzhou, Shenyang, Beijing, and Guangzhou military regions indicated that the PLA was experimenting with joint-force operations and developing rapid reaction units *(kuaisu fanying budui).*[136] The exercises in the north were postulated against a potential land invasion and paratroop drop, while the Guangzhou exercises simulated both land border and coastal maritime conflicts. The PLA's first marine rapid reaction "fist" brigade, based on Hainan Island, participated in the Guangzi-15 exercises—seizing small islands in the South China Sea.[137]

All of the 1988 MR exercises involved air, ground, naval, and special operation units, but subsequent press commentary and interviews revealed real lack of coordination among participating units. Command and control lines of communication still ran through each service up to the MR commander— the effect being that units exercised with considerable autonomy from one

133. Ibid., September 1997, p. 17, citing *Jiefangjun Bao*, September 2, 1997.

134. Ibid., August 1998, pp. 7–8, citing *Renmin Jundui* (the Lanzhou MR newspaper), July 28, 1998.

135. Ibid., January 1998, p. 14, citing *Renmin Haijun*, December 4, 1997.

136. For another analysis of these exercises, see Paul H. B. Godwin, "Chinese Defense Policy and Military Strategy in the 1990s," in Joint Economic Committee of the U.S. Congress, *China's Economic Dilemmas in the 1990s: The Problems of Reform, Modernization, and Interdependence* (Armonk, N.Y.: M. E. Sharpe, 1992), pp. 648–63.

137. At the time, only about 15,000 troops were designated as "fist units"—today perhaps one-tenth of the total force structure are such units.

another, rather than in true joint fashion. In particular, there was little evidence of close air support for ground operations (a problem that severely impaired the PLA in its 1979 punitive attack on Vietnam). The lack of real "jointness" continued to plague the PLA over the next decade. It is an old habit that dies hard. As three U.S. Department of Defense officials pithily observed in 1997, "It still appears that the PLA considers an exercise to be joint when forces from different services merely arrive in the same area at the same time and then conduct exercise scenarios separate from each other."[138] The 1988 exercises also revealed the lack of integrated logistics. Again, this was a problem inherited from the old Maoist emphasis on unit-based "self-reliance." Another interesting feature of the 1988 exercises, particularly the Yanhang-88 exercises carried out by Beijing MR units on the North China Plain, was the simulated use of chemical and battlefield tactical nuclear weapons. Presumably, such use was by "the enemy" (i.e., the USSR) rather than by PLA units, but this is not clear from reports.

The doctrinal revisions stimulated by the Gulf War first became evident in training during 1993–95. The most significant training reform was the increase in joint and combined-arms exercises.[139] A majority of reported exercises during this period involved some combination of different ground force units (armor, infantry, anti-chemical, heliborne, etc.), as well as multiservice joint exercises. Many involved both. Army helicopters were involved in a large-scale operation with ground forces for the first time in the "93-West" exercises in the Lanzhou MR in 1993. But PLA ground forces still severely lack helicopter transport, not to speak of a fleet of capable helicopter gunships or attack helicopters. In 1991–92, the PLA acquired twenty-eight Mi-17 transport helicopters from Russia, which joined twenty-five older Mi-6 and Mi-8s. The Mi-17s were apparently used in a confrontational red force/blue force exercise in the Lanzhou MR in 1998.[140] Most of the twenty-four Sikorsky Blackhawk helicopters sold to the PLA by the United States in the 1980s have been grounded for a decade because of a lack of spare parts (victims of the post-1989 arms embargo). Also in 1993, pilotless drones were used for the first time in Nanjing MR exercises.

---

138. Blasko, Klapakis, and Corbett, "Training Tomorrow's PLA," p. 253.

139. Much of this information is drawn from ibid., and the sources cited therein. For a PLA assessment, see Han Weiguo, "Wo Jun Lianhe Zhanshe Xianzhuang Tedian he Fazhan Qushi Yuce" (Forecasting the Characteristics, Status, and Future Trends of Our Army's Joint Campaigns), *Guofang Daxue Xuebao*, May 1999, pp. 50–51.

140. "Zhonguo Lujun Hangkongbing Da Xieyi" (A Large Overview of the Chinese Army's Airborne Troops), *Junshi Wenzhai*, no. 16–17 (1998): 28.

Moving to a heliborne force will be critical to improving the PLA's mobility and rapid-deployment capabilities, as well its ability to undertake a variety of combined-arms and joint-force operations. This recognition exists among officers in the Strategy Department of the Academy of Military Sciences, the institution charged with formulating PLA war-fighting doctrine, strategy, and tactics.[141] In fact, helicopters were introduced into several military regions in the mid 1980s—although their missions were limited to search and rescue and VIP transport, with only minimal tactical airlift and no real air assault capacity.[142] In 1988, the first army aviation regiments (Lujun Hangkongbing) were established in a number of group armies, with the expressed missions of tactical airlift, air assault, anti-tank, and special operations. Today, the Lu Hang, as it is known, operates a total of approximately 220 helicopters of different types.[143] Many of these are obsolescent and being retired; perhaps only 100 semimodern helicopters are capable of tactical airlift and air assault (the Sikorsky S-70C2 Blackhawks, and the Mi-8 and Mi-17s). While the Lu Hang is developing these units and increasingly using them in exercises, it is apparent that the PLA's helicopter capabilities remain limited to transport roles and close air support for ground operations. It is nowhere near developing a "force-insertion" strike capacity, even at the level achieved by the U.S. Army in the Vietnam War. If the PLA seeks to achieve true rapid reaction and force-projection capabilities, it must pay much greater attention to developing heliborne forces. Theoretically, this should not be too difficult for China's domestic defense industries to achieve, because helicopters are considerably easier to build than fighter aircraft (although the same problems of avionics will likely plague both).

Beginning in 1994, units of the Nanjing MR began again (after a twenty-year hiatus) to undertake exercises in and north of the Taiwan Strait, involving mock amphibious landings and combined air-ground-naval operations. In 1995 and 1996, these so-called East Sea (Donghai) exercises increased dramatically in scale, involving live firing from ships, tanks, and bombers. Even more notably, in both years the PLA's Second Artillery introduced a new element into the mix: short-range ballistic missiles (DF-15). In 1995, five of these were targeted into impact zones north of Taiwan, and in 1996, four

---

141. Interview, AMS Strategy Department, April 1999.

142. See Luke G. S. Colton, "Bamboo Blades: The Rise of China's Army Aviation," *Rotor and Wing,* January 2000, pp. 42–47.

143. Luke S. G. Colton, "'Blue Sword and Iron Fist of the Air': The Rise of Army Aviation in the Chinese Military" (unpublished paper, December 1999).

DF-15s "bracketed" the Taiwan harbors of Kaohsiung and Jeelung. While the PLA never had any intention of attacking Taiwan or the offshore islands, China did seek to send a clear political message that it was prepared to use force to prevent the island from asserting its independence. In response to the 1996 exercises and missile firings, the United States deployed two aircraft carrier battle groups (centered on the USS *Independence* and *Nimitz*) to operate for two weeks east of Taiwan. They were deployed to deter any risky PLA actions and as a reminder to China that use of PLA force against Taiwan might have "grave consequences."[144] The PLA's show of naval force, and amphibious landings on Pingtan and other small islands off the Zhejiang coast, was one of the most complex and largest exercises undertaken by the PLA since the war with Vietnam in 1979. The full panoply of new equipment acquired from Russia was utilized in the 1996 exercises. The PLA Air Force used its new Su-27 "Flanker" multirole fighters in a live exercise for the first time (in both air-to-air interception and ground-attack roles), while Mi-17 helicopters, Il-76 transports, SA-10 SAMs, and Kilo class submarines were also deployed.

PLA exercises since 1996 indicate serious attempts to apply the lessons learned from the Gulf War and studying "limited wars under high-technology conditions."

Post-1996 Training Trends

Since the 1996 Taiwan Strait exercises, PLA training has become more diversified. A variety of exercises have been reported in the military media. The emphasis on smaller exercises is consistent with organizational and doctrinal changes that have emphasized brigade- rather than division-sized units. PLA units have also engaged in a number of more specialized maneuvers. Occasionally, the PLA undertakes large-scale drills.

For the PLA Navy, a new training threshold was reached in April 1998 when surface combatants (including the Luhu-class destroyer *Qingdao*) trained near the Philippines, away from Chinese coastal and contiguous waters. These exercises included the first airborne supply operation at sea, simulated anti-ship missile attacks, helicopter takeoff and landing, fire-damage control, deep-ocean combat, and night training.[145] Another threshold was

---

144. For further analysis, see John Garver, *Face Off: China, the United States, and Taiwan's Democratization* (Seattle: University of Washington Press, 1997); and James R. Lilley and Chuck Downs, *Crisis in the Taiwan Strait* (Washington, D.C.: National Defense University Press, 1997).

145. *PLA Activities Report*, May 1998, p. 11, citing *Renmin Haijun*, April 23, 1998.

crossed in June 1999 exercises in the Yellow Sea, where surface combatants and naval tactical air units trained under conditions of intense electronic warfare.[146] Submarine and anti–submarine warfare exercises also increased after 1998. Increasingly, PLAN submarines are also training in blue water, away from the coast.[147] During 1999, Western military intelligence reported that PLAN submarines from the East Sea Fleet and South Sea Fleet were undertaking much longer sea patrols—forty-five days for diesel-electric and sixty days for nuclear-powered subs—and were doing so around the eastern coast of Taiwan for the first time; previously only North Sea Fleet submarines had conducted such patrols.[148] Much of this submarine training also now employs "confrontational training" sub-versus-sub techniques.[149] A new (presumably Song class) submarine was also reported to have engaged in "deep-sea mine laying and torpedo attack" simulation.[150]

There have been many reports of amphibious landing drills, presumably in preparation for Taiwan-type contingencies. Naturally, the Nanjing MR has undertaken the majority of these, including exercises involving large-scale transport of tanks, APCs, trucks, and other vehicles needed for a major landing.[151] The Nanjing MR has also accelerated its formation and training of rapid reaction units and has increasingly exercised them in offshore maneuvers.[152] In August 1997, joint forces undertook the largest mock amphibious landing in the history of the Jinan MR.[153] Units of the Guangzhou MR simulated an assault on Hainan island by reportedly landing 10,000 troops and over 1,000 vehicles, while another marine assault in the South China Sea utilized new hovercraft.[154] The largest such exercise came in June 2001, when air, ground, naval, and marine forces from several military regions carried out the "Liberation No. 1" exercises on and around Dongshan

146. Ibid., July 1999, p. 9, citing *Renmin Haijun,* June 17, 1999.

147. See, e.g., ibid., July 1998, p. 14, citing *Renmin Haijun,* June 11, 1998.

148. John Pomfret, "In Beijing's Moves, a Strategy on Taiwan," *Washington Post,* April 6, 2001. Also see *PLA Activities Report,* November 1999, p. 11, citing *Jiefangjun Bao,* November 7, 1999.

149. *PLA Activities Report,* June 1998, p. 14, citing *Renmin Haijun,* May 28, 1998.

150. Ibid., March 1997, p. 9, citing *Jiefangjun Bao,* March 10, 1998.

151. Ibid., September 1997, p. 15, citing *Renmin Qianxian* (the Nanjing MR newspaper), July 8, 1997.

152. Ibid., October 1997, p. 14, citing *Kongjun Bao* (the Air Force newspaper), September 4, 1997.

153. Ibid., p. 8, citing *Jiefangjun Bao,* October 13, 1997.

154. Ibid., January 1997, p. 4, citing *Jiefangjun Bao,* January 15, 1997; ibid., April 1998, p. 12, citing *Renmin Haijun,* March 14, 1998.

Island, southwest of Taiwan.[155] This small island has been the scene of similar exercises in the past and is used to simulate large amphibious landings, backed by air and naval bombardment. The forces involved came from the Nanjing and Guangzhou military regions, the East Sea Fleet, and air force and Second Artillery units in the Nanjing MR. The exercises involved at least four group armies (the 1st, 31st, and 42d armies, and the 15th Airborne Army), Su-27 fighters, DF-15 missile units, a variety of frigates and destroyers (including the Sovremmeny class), submarines, and a large number of amphibious craft.[156]

It is also apparent that the PLA assimilated the lessons of the 1999 Yugoslav war quickly and began to implement them promptly in simulated and actual battlefield exercises. Thereafter, most MRs reoriented their training regimen to exercise against a "strong high-tech enemy."[157] The newspaper of the Beijing MR reported an increase in training to defend against stealth aircraft, cruise missiles, electronic warfare, and helicopter gunships.[158] Units in the Jinan MR are reported to have trained against electromagnetic pulse bombs and electronic interference and to have learned the importance of hiding tanks and camouflaging equipment from the Serbian experience.[159] Numerous PLA media reports indicate that all MRs stepped-up anti–air raid operations, counter-IW, and anti-EW training. Several MRs reported exercises to shoot down incoming cruise missiles with artillery and "new model missiles."[160] Much more war-gaming and exercise simulation is being done online, and many large cities are undertaking civilian air raid drills. Clearly, the Yugoslav war convinced the PLA of the need to focus more specifically and urgently on the possibility of a multifaceted attack by the U.S. military against mainland China.

Other reports emphasize exercises under a variety of difficult climatic, weather, or nighttime conditions. Chengdu MR units train at high altitude in Tibet; Lanzhou MR units train in extremely hot weather on the Qinghai plateau, Taklimakan desert, and Tianshan mountains; Beijing MR units con-

---

155. See Erik Eckholm, "China Prepares Big Exercise near Island Facing Taiwan," *New York Times*, June 1, 2001; John Pomfret, "China Prepares for Drills near Taiwan," *International Herald Tribune*, June 2–3, 2001.

156. "Big Military Exercise Directed against Taiwan in Fuzhou Theater," *Wen Hui Bao* (Hong Kong), June 1, 2001.

157. See, e.g., *PLA Activities Report*, November 1999.

158. *PLA Activities Report*, July 1999, p. 5, citing *Zhanyou Bao*, June 17, 1999.

159. Ibid., July 1999, p. 6, citing *Qianwei Bao*, June 16, 1999.

160. See, e.g., ibid., January 2000, citing *Jiefangjun Bao* report of such exercises in the Jinan MR, January 12, 2000.

duct exercises in the Gobi desert; and Shenyang MR forces train in severe winter conditions. Coastal MR troops are said to train in stormy conditions. Many air force reports cite units training at night and in all-weather conditions. Amphibious exercises have also increased since the 1996 and 1999 tensions over Taiwan. In September 1999 and June 2001, the Guangzhou and Nanjing MRs undertook large-scale amphibious and joint-force landing exercises, meant to simulate an attack on Taiwan or the offshore islands.[161] The former Nanjing MR commander Chen Bingde was quoted as saying that his "area command can mobilize more than 100,000 civilian ships for military use if necessary to meet the needs of large-scale sea crossings and landing operations."[162] If this were possible, there would certainly be no element of surprise involved, because Taiwan and U.S. intelligence would quickly pick up on such a mobilization.

Another trend is training against specialized conventional and nonconventional weapons, particularly anti-tank and anti-chemical exercises. However, unlike the late-1980s Huabei exercises, there have been no reports of maneuvers simulating battlefield tactical nuclear weapons. One of the anti-tank exercises in the Guangzhou MR specifically simulated repelling an invasion force of American tanks,[163] but otherwise the "enemy" force is usually not so specifically identified. Several reports noted training against cruise missile attacks, using anti-aircraft fire and shoulder-fired missiles![164] Various cities, particularly Shanghai and Beijing, have improved their anti-aircraft capabilities and have undertaken a number of air defense drills.[165] An increasing number of reports in the military media mention electronic warfare training, particularly tactics for countering electromagnetic interference. The Beijing MR seems to be way ahead of other regions in this area, but EW and counter-EW and ECM (electronic countermeasures) are obviously top priorities for the PLA.[166]

Training of special forces units *(tezhong zuozhan budui)* has also picked up. These come in a variety of forms: from relatively small sabotage and unconventional commando warfare teams to medium-sized anti-terrorist

161. "PLA Holds Landing Exercises," *China Daily*, September 11, 1999, pp. 1–2.
162. Ibid.
163. *PLA Activities Report*, October 1997, p. 6, citing *Zhanshi Bao* (the Guangzhou MR newspaper), September 9, 1997.
164. Ibid., September 1998, p. 4, citing *Zhanyou Bao* (the Beijing MR newspaper), August 11, 1998.
165. See, e.g., ibid., June 1997, p. 7, citing *Jiefangjun Bao*, June 10, 1997.
166. See, e.g., Zhang Kunping et al., "Beijing Junqu Dianzizhan Shibing Yanxi" (Beijing Military Region Carries Out Electronic Warfare Maneuvers), *Shijie Junshi Huakan*, no. 10 (October 2000): 18–19.

units and battalion-sized heliborne special forces units. Most reports of such units come from the Beijing, Shenyang, Jinan, Nanjing, and Guangzhou MRs. Special ops forces are said to be equipped with GPS locating systems, airfoil parachutes (offering much better drift and control capability), new 5.8 mm sniping rifles, special "Kafra" synthetic helmets fitted with night vision headsets, and light bulletproof vests.[167] Some sources report exercises where commando units penetrate into enemy territory to recapture hostages or seize enemy commanders,[168] and in one exercise, over 100 heliborne paratroopers "penetrated" 500 kilometers into "enemy" territory to destroy and incapacitate C⁴I nodes. This particular exercise, in the Beijing MR, was said to have successfully knocked out the enemy's anti-aircraft batteries, radar early warning, and command and control complexes, as well as airfield control towers![169] In the Jinan MR, other special forces units have practiced parachuting behind enemy lines to sabotage electronic warfare and anti-aircraft missile batteries and seize enemy air bases.[170]

Despite training innovations, exercises still are largely confined within military regions. This is a definite impediment to establishing truly joint operations. The PLA lacks a more "theater"-based organizational structure, as well as a real national training center. Although a new "combined arms tactical training center" was opened in June 1999, the PLA still lacks a facility for comprehensive and innovative joint-force training. The new combined arms training center is reportedly specifically geared to creating "battlefield environments of future warfare," where three-dimensional opposing-force exercises are carried out over large areas.[171]

MELDING DOCTRINE AND TRAINING: A SUMMARY

The foregoing analysis indicates a substantial evolution, and thoroughgoing revision, of PLA war-fighting doctrine, strategy, tactics, and training in recent years, showing in particular that Chinese military analysts have a good grasp of contemporary military affairs. They know all the buzzwords and concepts and write a substantial amount on the subject. In the past few years,

167. Zhou Linwu, "Zhongguo Tezhong Budui" (China's Special Forces Units), *Junshi Wenzhai*, no. 10 (1997): 3.

168. See e.g., *PLA Activities Report*, August 1997, p. 9, citing *Qianjin Bao* (the Shenyang MR newspaper), June 4, 1997.

169. Ibid., July 1998, p. 8, citing *Zhanyou Bao*, June 20, 1998.

170. Ibid., December 1999, pp. 8–9, citing, respectively, *Zhongguo Guofang Bao*, December 3, 1999, and *Jiefangjun Bao*, December 15, 1999.

171. *PLA Activities Bulletin*, June 1999, p. 10, citing *Jiefangjun Bao*, June 3, 1999.

this awareness has spread from a handful of military research institutes into the force structure more generally. Not only are young officers at and below the group army level now contributing treatises on IW, joint, and combined-arms operations, the RMA, and so forth, but the PLA General Staff Department has also included many contemporary operational concepts in its quadrennial and annual military training outlines (MTO). Furthermore, as we have seen in this chapter, implementation of some of these concepts—particularly "jointness," combined-arms operations, electronic warfare, automated command and control, and, to a lesser extent, IW—is being practiced in exercises. There *is* a sea change taking place, not only in the realm of theory but also in actual training.

Recognizing this progress, the PLA's attempts to master a doctrine of "limited war under high-technology conditions" still suffer from numerous insufficiencies and impediments. Many of these have been noted throughout this chapter:

- An overall organizational command structure and deployment of forces that is ill-suited to joint operations

- Interservice incompatibilities, which also impede jointness

- Relative lack of air- and sealift capacity

- Limited amphibious capability

- Lack of all-weather air force capability

- A minimal number of blue-water-capable surface warships and submarines

- Low counter-EW and minimal offensive EW capability

- Only nascent IW capability

- A fragmented logistics supply system

- No ballistic missile defense and substantial vulnerability (particularly in C^4I) to standoff precision-guided munitions

- A varied ability to assimilate and use new technology and equipment

- A lack of resources that inhibits live-fire training exercises

Moreover, the PLA simply lacks much of the equipment and technology needed to implement the new high-tech doctrine (see chapter 6). It is one thing to develop rapid reaction units, but if there is inadequate air- and sealift capacity to transport such forces, they cannot be rapidly deployed. Unless air dominance can be achieved in a given theater of operations, ground forces are vulnerable to being pulverized with impunity from the air—and the PLAAF has neither the fighter-interceptors nor the trained pilots to attain such aerial dominance. Further, it has a *total lack* of airborne command and control platforms to coordinate a complex air campaign and of sufficient numbers of in-flight tankers to refuel fighters while they loiter.

In sum, there remains a large gap between the theory and aspirations of the PLA's new doctrine of fighting "limited wars under high-technology conditions" and its actual capabilities. PLA leaders and analysts are also clearly and painfully aware of their military's limitations. Nonetheless, a vision of where the PLA wants to go is the first step toward getting there. Modest progress is being made, and when one realizes the PLA's advances over the past three decades, the qualitative change is impressive. However, modern warfare is highly complex, requires extremely well-educated soldiers to operate highly sophisticated weapons and equipment, is based on real-time intelligence and battle assessment, and necessitates a flexible force structure to operationalize doctrine in a wide variety of geographic and combat environments. Moreover, the RMA is driving new military innovations much faster than the PLA can adapt and assimilate the preceding generation of technology, weapons, and management. Although it may appear that the PLA is closing the gap with modern militaries, the opposite is actually the case.

4 Command, Control, and Force Structure

Institutional structure and lines of authority are fundamental to the function of any large and complex organization. This is particularly true of militaries. Hierarchy and official channels of command and control are crucial to the predictable functioning of armed forces in peacetime and wartime. Unlike more modern Western militaries, which devolve a fairly high degree of unit and individual autonomy in combat situations, Leninist militaries are given minimal leeway for independent interpretation of orders. Professionalism, which is central to the efficient performance of a military,[1] depends in large part on predictability—which, in turn, is the result of both repetitive training and a set of organizational relationships that instills normative and behavioral standards in the individual officer and soldier. Such military professionalism is the basis of strong collective institutional corporatism as well as service- and unit-based esprit de corps. Understanding the organization, disposition, and deployments of a military also reveals much about the conflicts and contingencies it is prepared for.

Military organization also reflects the cultural particularities of a nation. There is no standard template for organizing militaries—although in modern times the Prussian, British, American, and Soviet models have been copied by many around the world. Some, such as the Japanese military prior to World War II, evolved organically from its own distinct militarist class (Samurai) and cultural (Bushido) traditions. No doubt, the Chinese military today exhibits proclivities and organizational behavior that are unique

---

1. See Samuel Huntington, *The Soldier and the State: The Theory and Politics of Civil-Military Relations* (Cambridge, Mass.: Harvard University Press, 1957), and Morris Janowitz, *The Professional Soldier* (New York: Free Press, 1960).

to China and shared by Chinese civilian bureaucratic ministries and organs,[2] but in the modern Chinese military, two foreign models have been particularly important in organizing the armed forces: the German and Soviet models. During the war against the Japanese, General Joseph Stilwell endured a frustrating few years as military adviser to Generalissimo Chiang Kai-shek, and the Chinese Nationalist (Guominjun) forces also drew on the American military model and, following their retreat to Taiwan, adopted many aspects of U.S. force structure.[3] But the German and Soviet military models were predominant before 1949.[4] After the Communists took power and the Red Army became the PLA, the Soviet organizational influence grew substantially. Soviet military advisers were assigned to various levels of the armed forces, and the Soviet military model was extensively copied (as in other spheres).

Although some streamlining and downsizing has taken place since the mid 1980s, the organizational structure of the PLA today remains essentially that of the Soviet model imported during the 1950s: a Central Military Commission, general departments (with, notably, Communist Party dominance and a political commissar system), military regions and districts, and configuration of services.[5] While there are those in the Chinese High Command today who are convinced that this organizational structure is ill-suited to contemporary warfare and who argue in favor of adopting an American-style joint staff and war theater system,[6] creating a separate service for the army (currently the ground forces are basically commanded by the General Staff Department), and elevating the missile forces (Second Artillery) to the status of a full service, the PLA has yet to fundamentally alter

2. There is a large literature on Chinese bureaucracy. See, e.g., Kenneth Lieberthal and Michel Oksenberg, *Policy Making in China* (Princeton, N.J.: Princeton University Press, 1988), and David M. Lampton, ed., *Policy Implementation in the People's Republic of China* (Berkeley and Los Angeles: University of California Press, 1987).

3. See Barbara Tuchman, *Stilwell and the American Experience in China, 1911–1945* (New York: Macmillan, 1970).

4. See William Kirby, *Germany and Republican China* (Princeton, N.J.: Princeton University Press, 1984), and C. Martin Wilbur and Julie Lien-ying How, *Missionaries of Revolution: Soviet Advisors and Nationalist China* (Cambridge, Mass.: Harvard University Press, 1989).

5. For an earlier assessment, see Harvey W. Nelsen, *The Chinese Military System: An Organizational Study of the People's Liberation Army* (Boulder, Colo.: Westview Press, 1977).

6. See "Mainland to Abolish Seven Military Regions and Three General Departments, PLA Structure to be Reorganized in Light of U.S. Military Structure in Effort to 'Slash Local Power,'" *Singdao Ribao* (Hong Kong), February 20, 1998, in BBC SWB/FE, February 21, 1998.

the cloned Soviet system. This said, the PLA leadership and research organs have systematically reexamined its force structure and lines of command and control and have made a number of important, if incremental, changes to both in recent years. The impetus for this reexamination and reorganization seems to have begun with the creation of a "Military System Reform Leading Group" in the Central Military Commission, which was established in February 1982.[7] In July–September of that year, the CMC convened a lengthy discussion meeting *(zuotanhui)* on military system reform, which set in motion a series of changes (largely to the ground forces and MR commands).[8] In 1985, an important expanded meeting *(kuoda huiyi)* of the CMC took significant further decisions and steps to reform PLA organization, as embodied in the Program on Military System Reform, Reduction, and Retrenchment (Junshi Tizhi Gaige Jingjian Zhengbian Fang'an).[9]

In this chapter I examine this system and the organizational changes undertaken since the early 1980s in considerable detail. Every effort has been made to be as comprehensive and accurate as possible, although the status of some subdepartments simply remains uncertain. Chinese-language sources, many published by the PLA, have been extensively tapped and have proven very illuminating. Most of these sources are filled with historical detail about the evolution of these organizations, but for the purposes of this chapter I have chosen to discuss only recent history as it has influenced the contemporary structure of various organs. These published Chinese sources have been supplemented by interviews with knowledgeable PLA personnel. Finally, I have drawn upon U.S. Department of Defense publications[10] and some useful studies undertaken by Western analysts.[11] When sources conflict, I have generally opted to use the Chinese source as definitive.

The overall organizational structure of the PLA is depicted in figure 1. In addition to those organs directly attached to the Central Military Commission, it reveals a three-tiered command structure of four general departments (also known as the *si zong silingbu,* or "four general headquarters"), three services, Second Artillery, and the People's Armed Police, and the geographic commands of the seven military regions and military districts.

7. Academy of Military Sciences History Research Department, ed., *Zhongguo Renmin Jiefangjun de Qishinian* (Beijing: Junshi Kexue Chubanshe, 1997), p. 624.

8. Ibid., p. 622.

9. Ibid., p. 623.

10. The most useful of these is the annual *Directory of PRC Military Personalities* published by Serold Hawaii Inc., Honolulu.

11. Of particular use were the papers presented at the CAPS/RAND Conference "The PLA as Organization," Warrenton, Virginia, August 2000.

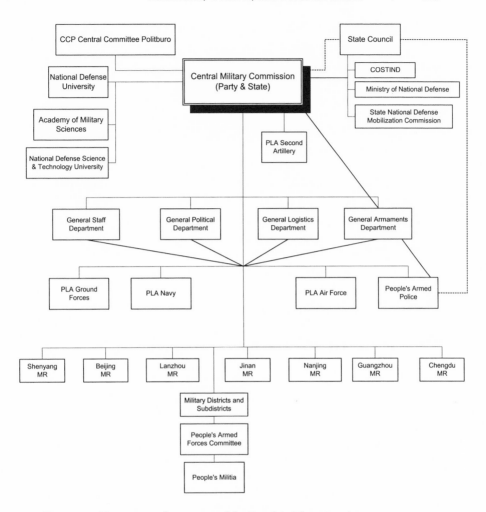

Figure 1.   The command structure of the People's Liberation Army.

From figure 1, it should be clear that the most important line of command authority runs from the CMC to the four general headquarters and, in turn, to each of the services and military regions. The CMC itself has other subordinate organs, as depicted in figure 2.

At the pinnacle of the Chinese military sit the twin Central Military Commissions—one is an organ of the CCP and the other ostensibly beholden to the National People's Congress (i.e., the state). Command authority and all decision-making power to deploy China's armed forces resides with the CMC—although one authoritative and *neibu* PLA source states that, "Prac-

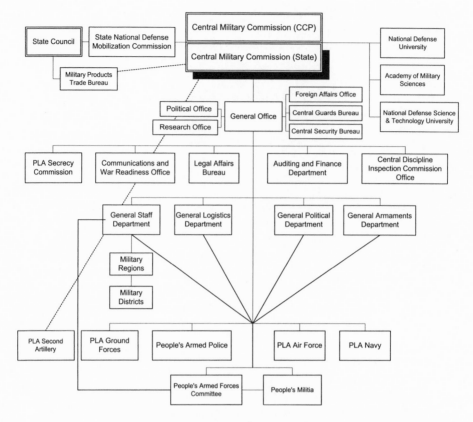

Figure 2.   The Central Military Commission. *Sources: Directory of PRC Military Personalities* (Honolulu: Serold Hawaii Inc., various years); Academy of Military Sciences, ed., *Shijie Junshi Nianjian* (Beijing: Junshi Kexue Chubanshe, various years); Yao Yanjin et al., eds., *Junshi Zuzhi Tizhi Yanjiu* (Beijing: Guofang Daxue Chubanshe, *junnei faxing,* 1997); interviews.

tically speaking *[shiji shang]*, major questions concerning war, armed force, and national defense building are decided by the Central Committee Politburo. Therefore, in reality, the highest-level decision-making authority is the Central Committee Politburo [Zhongyang Zhengzhi Ju]."[12]

The party CMC has a long history, dating back to October 1925. It was reorganized numerous times during the Civil and Anti-Japanese Wars, but has retained the name Zhongyang Junshi Weiyuanhui (CMC) and the ad-

12. Yao Yanjin et al., eds., *Junshi Zuzhi Tizhi Yanjiu* (Beijing: Guofang Daxue Chubanshe, 1997), p. 371.

ministrative level of a Central Committee commission (which ranks higher than Central Committee departments such as the Organization, Propaganda, United Front Work, and Investigation departments) since March 1930.[13] In September 1949, the armed forces were reorganized and centralized into the People's Liberation Army and the People's Public Security Forces (Renmin Gong'an Budui), and a Central People's Government Revolutionary Military Affairs Commission (Zhongyang Zhengfu Geming Junshi Weiyuanhui) was established.[14] After the PRC was proclaimed on October 1, a CMC was created inside the party *(dang nei)*.[15] In September 1954, at the First Session of the First National People's Congress, a new constitution was promulgated and a new National Defense Commission (Guofang Weiyuanhui) was created under the Central Government, but it is described as having been intended "as a consultative *[zixunxing]* body, not as an armed forces leadership organ."[16] At the same time, the Central Committee decided to create a new Central Military Commission under the CCP, which would have complete leadership *(quan lingdao)* of the PLA and other armed forces, and a new Ministry of National Defense under the State Council. This dual arrangement of having state and party military commissions existed on paper until January 1975, when the fourth session of the NPC decided to formally abolish the post of president of the PRC and the National Defense Commission—although, in fact, both had ceased to function after the Cultural Revolution broke out in 1966. President Liu Shaoqi, chairman of the National Defense Commission, was purged and died in a solitary cell in a Kaifeng prison in 1969.

During the Cultural Revolution, like those of almost all central-level organs, the CMC's membership and responsibilities were disrupted. However, it continued to meet on several occasions, and when it met, the CMC generally sought to insulate the military from the Red Guards and the political radicalism rampant at the time. For example, the CMC convened an expanded session at the Jingxi Hotel in February 1967.[17] This meeting produced an "eight-point circular" (known as the *Ba Tiao*) aimed at strengthening command and control over geographically based military units, protecting

13. See Lei Yuanshen, "Zhongyang Junwei Biandong" (The Evolution of the Central Military Commission), *Zhonggong Dangshi Ziliao* 34 (1990): 219; Pu Xingzu, *Zhonghua Renmin Gongheguo Zhengzhi Zhidu* (Shanghai: Renmin Chubanshe, 1999), pp. 557–58.

14. Pu, *Zhonghua Renmin Gongheguo Zhengzhi Zhidu.*

15. Ibid.

16. Ibid., p. 559.

17. Academy of Military Sciences History Department, ed., *Zhongguo Renmin Jiefangjun de Qishinian,* p. 556.

weapons stocks from raiding by Red Guards, protecting secret documents and archives, and regularizing the PLA's training regimen.[18]

Throughout this period, major military decisions were made in ad hoc meetings of Chairman Mao, Defense Minister Lin Biao (prior to his death in September 1971), and several senior PLA marshals who had been fortunate enough not to be purged (notably Ye Jianying, Xu Xiangqian, and Chen Yi).[19] Mao relied heavily on these elder marshals during this time, particularly as tensions with the Soviet Union mounted. In fact, the Chairman assigned the triumvirate of Chen Yi, Ye Jianying, and Xu Xiangqian to assess China's national security environment in the aftermath of the 1968 Soviet invasion of Czechoslovakia. The marshals convinced Mao that the situation was extremely threatening, that war with Moscow was imminent (and would likely include nuclear conflict), and that China needed a dramatic opening to the United States to offset the Soviet threat.[20]

Although the CMC was moribund during these years, the six subordinate units of the CMC all continued to function to varying degrees, and in effect substituted for the CMC by running the PLA. The General Staff Department continued to operate thirteen departments and to direct forces in the field.[21] Its General Office was merged with the General Office of the CMC.[22] However, the General Political Department was in political chaos and underwent a sweeping purge (see below), while the General Logistics Department, National Defense Science and Technology Commission, and National Defense Industries Office maintained a modicum of production and research (see chapter 6).[23] The Academy of Military Sciences, however, was severely disrupted and essentially ceased to function *(tingzhi)*.[24]

After the worst of the Cultural Revolution chaos and the opening to the United States, Deng Xiaoping and the marshals set about rebuilding the PLA in 1974–75. One of the first steps was to reconstitute the CMC, which was in disarray after the death of Lin Biao, following an alleged coup d'état attempt, and the purge of his followers in the upper echelons of the PLA. The CMC was gutted and radically reduced in size (see below). It took several

18. Ibid., p. 557.

19. See Li Ke and Hao Shengzhang, *"Wenhua Da Geming" zhong de Renmin Jiefangjun* (Beijing: Zhonggong Dangshi Ziliao Chubanshe, 1990).

20. Interview with Chen Yi's son Chen Xiaolu, March 1990. This account has been subsequently confirmed by Chinese historians.

21. Li and Hao, *"Wenhua Da Geming" zhong de Renmin Jiefangjun*, pp. 351–52.

22. Ibid., p. 353.

23. Ibid., pp. 351–52.

24. Academy of Military Sciences History Department, ed., *Zhongguo Renmin Jiefangjun de Qishinian*, p. 560.

years to weed out the "Lin Biao counterrevolutionary clique" in the CMC, general headquarters, and services (especially the air force and navy),[25] but once it was done, the new CMC met in February 1975.[26] Ye Jianying and Deng Xiaoping were put in charge of overseeing the daily work of the CMC. The revamped CMC convened a work conference from June 24 to July 15, 1975, which took a series of decisions on the restructuring of the PLA and China's international security environment (see chapter 6). Even when Deng was purged again in 1976, the revamped CMC continued to function under the leadership of Marshal Ye Jianying.[27]

When Deng returned to the stage in 1977, he worked to regain control over the military. By 1982, he had usurped Hua Guofeng's role as chairman of the CMC and reinstalled himself as chief of General Staff. A state CMC was reestablished at the fifth session of the Fifth NPC in December 1982, and it was enshrined in a new national constitution (a revised parallel CCP constitution reaffirmed the party CMC). The restoration of a separate CMC under the government was seen as an important manifestation of the new policy of "separating party from government" *(dang-zheng fenkai)*, as advocated by the reformist Premier Zhao Ziyang and the CCP's General Secretary Hu Yaobang.[28] Certainly, Deng Xiaoping supported the initiative at the time. But after Zhao was purged in 1989, he was criticized for having tried to usurp party authority over the military by (re)creating a state CMC (discussed in chapter 2), while in fact the move proved purely cosmetic, as the state CMC existed only on paper. The membership of the two bodies was identical, the state CMC never met separately, and it had no separate powers other than ostensibly being responsible to the president of the republic and the chairman of the Standing Committee of the National People's Congress. The two bodies were the same—described by Chinese as "one overlapping body and one organization" *(yitao banzi, yige jigou)* or "two signs, one organization" *(liangge paizi, tong yige jigou)*—and the party CMC is the one with real power and authority. Other Chinese sources claim that the existence of two CMCs is no contradiction *(liang zhe bing bu maodun)* but is meant to illustrate that the "party and state have united leadership and organizational assurance towards national military power," and that "the party and government are not separated, but that the party leads the

25. For a description of this process, see ibid, pp. 564–68.

26. Ibid., p. 569.

27. For an excellent study of this period, see Cheng Zhongyuan et al., *1976–1981 Nian de Zhongguo* (Beijing: Zhongyang Wenzhai Chubanshe, 1998).

28. Academy of Military Sciences History Research Department, *Zhongguo Renmin Jiefangjun de Qishinian*, p. 622.

government."[29] It is clear, however, that the state CMC is a hollow body with no autonomous power. The PLA remains a party army.

While membership on the two CMCs is identical, the process of selecting members has changed in recent years as part of the process of regularizing and standardizing PLA procedures. In earlier years, the CMC was a large organ that included a wide variety of senior military commanders and leaders. As such, it fluctuated greatly in size and composition. From 1949 to 1954, it had no fewer than twenty-eight members; it shrank to twelve in 1954, grew again to twenty-one in 1959, contracted to only four in 1966, and then ballooned to forty-nine in 1969 and eighty-one in 1977![30] To be sure, during much of this time, an "inner cabinet" of the CMC existed, consisting of Mao and perhaps a half dozen senior military leaders, who met and made key decisions—although it was by no means unknown for Mao to convene a full or expanded *(kuoda)* CMC meeting when warranted.[31] After 1982, when Deng Xiaoping regained authority over the PLA, the CMC shrank considerably and instituted an ex officio system of membership. Under the new system, the heads of the (then) three general departments and the minister of defense automatically served on the CMC. In addition, there was a chairman (Deng), several vice-chairmen (usually three but unspecified), and a secretary-general. After 1992 and the purge of Yang Baibing, the position of secretary-general was eliminated.

Since 1989, the president of the PRC, Jiang Zemin, has served simultaneously as chairman of both CMCs. The constitution of the PRC states that the chairman of the *state* CMC shall be elected by the National People's Congress and is responsible to the NPC and its Standing Committee, but that, once elected, the CMC chairman chooses the other CMC members (subject to NPC approval).[32] Jiang's dual position as party leader and state

29. Li Shouchu, ed., *Zhongguo Zhengfu Zhidu* (Beijing: Zhongyang Minzu Daxue Chubanshe, 1997), p. 297.

30. Numbers compiled by author from Jiang Jianhua et al., eds., *Zhonghua Renmin Gongheguo Ziliao Shouce* (Beijing: Shehui Kexue Wenzhai Chubanshe, 1999), pp. 303–4. For membership listings, see also Academy of Military Sciences, ed., *Zhongguo Renmin Jiefangjun Zuzhi Yange he Geji Lingdao Chengyuan Minglu* (Beijing: Junshi Kexue Chubanshe, 1987), and Liao Gailong, ed., *Dangdai Zhongguo Zhengzhi Dashidian, 1949–1990* (Changchun: Jilin Wenhua Lishi Chubanshe, 1991).

31. For a detailed listing of these expanded CMC meetings, see Hou Shudong et al., eds., *Guofang Jiaoyu Da Cidian* (Beijing: Junshi Kexue Chubanshe, 1992), pp. 96–97.

32. Academy of Military Sciences, ed., *Shijie Junshi Nianjian 2000* (Beijing: Junshi Kexue Chubanshe, 2000), p. 130.

president blurs any distinction between the two CMCs, but it does provide some validity to the concept of having two separate military commissions. Theoretically, the membership of the two bodies could diverge, especially if the state president were different from the CCP secretary-general. Such a situation could come to pass if Jiang remained as president while relinquishing his party leadership position to Hu Jintao at the Sixteenth Party Congress in 2002. In 1999, after several attempts to install him on the CMC, the vice president of the PRC (Hu Jintao) was added as first vice-chairman (a position resurrected from the 1980s, when Zhao Ziyang held it), becoming only the second civilian member of the commission. Hu has no background in military matters whatsoever,[33] and commands little respect from the military brass, but the appointment was mandated by protocol. However, the premier of the State Council, Zhu Rongji, is not a member of either CMC. In terms of actual power and decision-making authority, the two senior vice chairmen and serving officers—Zhang Wannian and Chi Haotian today—enjoy overall authority within the CMC (see chapter 2). No doubt, Jiang Zemin and, certainly, Hu Jintao defer to the judgment of these men on most matters. It is not clear if Generals Zhang and Chi divide the responsibilities of overseeing different elements of defense policy and the military establishment,[34] as did their predecessors, Generals Liu Huaqing and Zhang Zhen: Liu oversaw weapons production, defense industries, and military diplomacy, while Zhang was in charge of doctrine, training, deployments, and military education.[35] The other members of the CMC constitute an informal executive committee, with functional responsibilities for their respective bailiwicks (not unlike the "leading small group" system in civilian policymaking).[36] It remains permissible to include members of the CMC who command military regions or have other portfolios (such as Wang Ruilin, Guo Boxiong, and Xu Caihou today), but the enlarged and packed CMCs ended with the Maoist era.

33. See my "China's Commander-in-Chief: Jiang Zemin and the PLA," in C. Dennison Lane et al., eds., *Chinese Military Modernization* (London: Kegan Paul International; Washington, D.C.: AEI Press, 1996), pp. 209–45.

34. One Hong Kong source asserts that Chi is merely responsible for military diplomacy in his capacity as minister of defense, while Zhang has authority over all military matters. "Beijing Holds Enlarged Meeting of Central Military Commission: Zhang Wannian Pursues New Ideas for Developing Weapons," *Guang Jiao Jing* (Wide Angle), December 16, 1997, translated in BBC SWB/FE, December 30, 1997.

35. Interview with aide to General Liu Huaqing, June 1993.

36. See Michael Swaine, *The Role of the Chinese Military in National Security Policymaking,* rev. ed. (Santa Monica, Calif.: RAND Corporation, 1998), pp. 43–44.

The CMC usually convenes in full session about half a dozen times per year, always following a party plenum or congress, always in December to approve the proposed military budget for forwarding to the State Council, and whenever else a meeting is warranted. These meetings usually last several days and have taken place in the Jingxi Hotel (a military guest house owned by the General Political Department in central Beijing), the Zhongnanhai, or the Great Hall of the People. Today, however, the CMC convenes in the Ministry of Defense building, where the CMC's offices occupy the top two floors. It is unclear how the meetings are actually run and whether decisions are made by vote or consensus. Participants include CMC members, but others can be invited: sometimes CMC meetings receive special briefings on specific situations, such as Taiwan. Usually, one or two "decision" documents are promulgated after a full CMC meeting, but the content of these is likely prepared and agreed on in advance. The agenda itself is likely shaped by subordinates in the CMC General Office. Contrary to numerous reports in the Hong Kong media, it is highly unlikely that CMC meetings consider "petitions" put forward by dissatisfied generals or become forums for table-pounding military bluster against Taiwan, the United States, Japan, or other potential foes. The PLA analyst Tai Ming Cheung distinguishes several other types of CMC meetings (although these are not confirmed by other sources):

- A weekly work conference *(gongzuo hui)* that meets every Thursday to discuss routine administrative and staffing matters. Presumably, this is attended by members of the General Office staff.

- Irregular "brainstorming" meetings *(peng-tou hui)* for informal discussion of pressing issues, which are usually attended by CMC military members and other senior PLA officers.

- Discussion meetings *(zuotan hui)*, which last for several days, often after a Party plenum, for detailed discussion of major defense and national security issues.

- Plenary meetings *(quanti hui)*, usually at the end of every calendar year to assess the past year's work and finalize the next year's budget and annual plan.

- Enlarged meetings *(kuoda hui)* convened on special occasions and including several hundred military leaders.[37]

37. Tai Ming Cheung, "The Influence of the Gun: China's Central Military Commission and Its Relationship with the Military, Party, and State Decision-Making

What are the duties and functions of the CMC? According to published Chinese sources, the CMC:

- Establishes unified command over the nation's armed forces

- Decides military strategy and the war-fighting principles for the armed forces

- Leads and manages PLA building, formulates regulations, and plans and organizes deployments

- Implements resolutions of the National People's Congress and its Standing Committee

- Formulates military regulations according to the Constitution and law, and disseminates decisions and orders

- Determines PLA structure and personnel and oversees the general departments and military regions, as well as other organs under the military regions

- Appoints and removes, cultivates, investigates, rewards, and punishes armed forces personnel according to military law and regulations

- Oversees and approves the armed forces' weapons equipment system and weapons equipment development orders and development plan, and, in coordination with the State Council, leads and manages national defense science and technology research and production

- Jointly with the State Council organizes and manages the military budget and national defense investment[38]

The CMC exercises administrative control and oversight over the four general headquarters (the General Staff, Logistics, Political, and Equipment departments). This is ostensibly done via the statutory membership on the CMC of each department director, but apparently there are representatives of each serving in the General Office of the CMC who serve as liaisons. The CMC also exercises direct command authority over the seven military regions and services, although in practice this is done via the General Staff Department (particularly to the ground forces). The CMC also has admin-

System," in David M. Lampton, ed., *The Making of Chinese Foreign and Security Policy in the Era of Reform* (Stanford, Calif.: Stanford University Press, 2001).

38. Academy of Military Sciences, ed., *Shijie Junshi Nianjian 2000*, p. 130; and Pu, *Zhonghua Renmin Gongheguo Zhengzhi Zhidu*, p. 560.

istrative responsibility for the armed forces' two principal institutions of professional military education (PME), the National Defense University and Academy of Military Sciences (whose organization is described below and shown in figures 15 and 16). It is significant that, according to an internal Chinese military source, the Second Artillery (strategic and tactical missile forces) is "under the CMC's direct leadership, exercising vertical command" ("Di Er Pao Bing zai Zhongyang Jun Wei zhijie lingdao xia, shixing chuizhi zhihui"), although operationally command and control most likely runs via the General Staff Department.[39]

The CMC also has command authority over the unit that offers security protection to all Central Committee members and leading military officials—the Central Security Bureau (Zhongyang Bao'an Ju), which is more commonly known as the Central Guards Bureau (Zhongyang Jingwei Ju).[40] For many years this elite guard unit was known simply as the 8341 Regiment. The number had no military significance, but rather came from the serial number on a rifle that Mao Zedong purchased during the 1927 Autumn Harvest Uprising. Mao kept the rifle throughout the Long March and in the Yanan base area. He was very proud of it, enjoyed cleaning it, and accordingly decided to name his personal guard detachment in Yanan by the number—and henceforth the 8341 Regiment assumed a lore of its own.[41] While the CMC has direct command over this unit and the CMC General Office oversees it on a daily basis,[42] the Beijing Military District Garrison of the Beijing Military Region and the Security Bureau of the PLA General Staff Department apparently share some command authority and provide funds, equipment, training, and barracks for the elite guards.[43] It is apparent, though, that the General Staff maintains a separate guard unit solely for top military leaders, while the Central Guards Bureau protects civilian leaders. The Ministry of Public Security, Ministry of State Security, and People's Armed Police (PAP) also maintain their own elite guard units, but it is unclear how

---

39. Yao et al., eds., *Junshi Zuzhi Tizhi Yanjiu*, p. 372.

40. See Wei Li, "The Security Service for Chinese Central Leaders," *China Quarterly*, , no. 143 (September 1995): 814–27.

41. "Shuo Bu Wan Dao Bu Pu de Shenmi Fuhao: '8341' Cong Qiyong Dao Xiaoshi Zhimi" (The Endless Story of the Mysterious Symbol: '8341' and the Mystery from Its Inception to Its Disappearance), *Huaxia*, no. 70 (June 1997): 31–35; and "Zhongnanhai de Di Yizhi Jingwei Budui" (The Zhongnanhai's First Central Guard Unit), ibid.: 12–17.

42. Interview with former Chinese military intelligence official, August 5, 2000.

43. Ibid. and Wei, "Security Service for Chinese Central Leaders." The aforementioned interview source described the General Staff's command as *yewu zhidao* (professional guidance) instead of *lingdao guanxi* (leadership relations).

their jurisdiction is distinguished from the Central Guards (probably for local and visiting overseas officials). Each senior leader receives two types of security protection—from one to six bodyguards, who are responsible for the leader's personal security, as well as various daily logistical matters (arranging meals, medical care, clothing, transport, and other personal needs),[44] and a larger military/security detachment, ranging in size from a squad *(ban)* to a company *(lian)* to secure an area during the leader's visit.[45]

The internal organization of the CMC is not entirely clear—and is, in fact, a state secret. It is known, however, that the CMC contains at least five key organs. The most important is the General Office (Zhong Ban), which serves as the nerve center for all CMC communications, documents, and coordination of meetings and conveyance of orders and directives to other subordinate organs. It was formerly housed in the Sanzuomen complex just north of the Forbidden City in central Beijing, within a short distance of the Zhongnanhai leadership compound (to which it was reportedly connected via underground tunnel), but it moved, along with the CMC, to the top floors of the new, palatial Ministry of Defense compound in western Beijing when it opened in 2000. The General Office is known to have a director (Lieutenant General Tan Yuexin since January 2000) and a number of deputy directors. The General Office also contains a number of administrative secretaries *(mishu)*, although each CMC member has his own personal *mishu* as well (Jiang Zemin's is Major General Jia Ting'an).[46] According to one source, the General Office has a total staff of between 200 and 300.[47] The General Office also has a subordinate Political Office (Zheng Ban), Research Office (Ke Yan Ban), and Foreign Affairs Office (Wai Ban),[48] and oversees the aforemen-

44. These include massages and sexual favors. Chairman Mao, Ye Jianying, and other senior leaders are known to have used the guard units to procure modern-day concubines, "nurses," etc. See, in particular, Li Zhisui (with the assistance of Anne Thurston), *The Private Life of Chairman Mao* (New York: Random House, 1994).

45. Wei, "Security Service for Chinese Central Leaders," p. 817.

46. Jia Ting'an has served as Jiang's *mishu* for more than twenty years since Jiang was minister of electronics. He became his chief military secretary in the early 1990s and subsequently became director of the Jiang Zemin Office (Jiang Ban). He is thought to often represent Jiang at CMC meetings. In the summer of 2000, however, Jia was reported to have been removed from his position and come under investigation for an alleged connection to the nation's largest smuggling and official corruption case to date, in which a Xiamen-based company (Yuanhua) with close ties to senior central-level leaders smuggled autos and a variety of other products worth nearly U.S.$10 billion in Fujian. See BBC Monitoring, "Hong Kong Source Reports Removal of Jiang Zemin Aide Suspected of Corruption," August 14, 2000.

47. Tai, "Influence of the Gun."

48. Personnel in the Wai Ban have name cards that list both organs.

tioned Central Security Bureau and Central Guards Bureau. In past years, particularly in the late 1980s, when General Li Jijun was director, the General Office was a source of innovative ideas and reform initiatives—although it seems to have reverted to a more bureaucratic role in the 1990s.

The CMC also has at least five separate first-level departments *(yi ji bu)*, although they do not all bear the administrative title of "department." While information is not abundant about the functioning of these organs, some data are available.

The PLA Secrecy Commission (Baomi Weiyuanhui) is, as its name suggests, the body in charge of classifying and maintaining all classified military documents. As such it controls the Central Military Archives (Zhongyang Jundui Dang'an Guan), and maintains an extensive system of subordinate offices throughout the PLA, down to the company level.

The Communications War and Readiness Office is the central command and control organ for disseminating orders and commanding forces in both peacetime and wartime. This office thus liaises directly with the General Staff Department, military region commands, and the Second Artillery. It is most likely that early warning, air defense, and other critical signals intelligence is channeled from the PLA's growing number of transmitters and sensors into this office.[49] The PLA is embarked on a comprehensive upgrading of its communications systems for command and control. According to the U.S. Department of Defense, the PLA now possesses a completely automated command and control system and is developing a new type of integrated battlefield area communications system (IBACS) that includes speech signal processing and broadband integrated services digital networks (B-ISDN).[50]

The CMC also has a Legal Affairs Bureau (responsible for drafting military laws and regulations, and probably overseeing the military judicial system), an Auditing and Finance Department (responsible for formulating the defense budget and liaising with the Ministry of Finance and State Council, as well as the General Logistics Department financial system), a Military Products Trade Bureau (set up in 1989 to oversee both the import and export of weapons and other military equipment), and a Central Discipline Inspection Commission (CDIC) office. The CDIC is a subsystem of the Communist Party within the military and has the principal function of moni-

49. For a list of these command and control facilities, see www.fas.org/nuke/guide/china/facility/c3i.html (August 17, 2001).

50. *Selected Military Capabilities of the People's Republic of China,* Report from the Secretary of Defense to Congress Pursuant to Section 1305 of the FY97 National Defense Authorization Act, p. 5.

toring the performance of party members and policing them for malfeasance, corruption, and other breaches of party discipline and regulations. Since the CDIC was established within party committees *(dangwei)* in the PLA in September 1978 on the order of the CMC,[51] it has been jointly administered by the CDIC of the Central Committee and the CMC, together with the General Political Department.

The CMC also has responsibility for the people's armed forces committees *(renmin wuzhuang weiyuanhui)*, and jointly administers (with the State Council) the State National Defense Mobilization Commission (Guojia Guofang Dongyuan Weiyuanhui). People's Armed Forces Committees (PAFCs) exist within party committees at the levels of province, autonomous region, centrally administered cities, county, and township levels.[52] They were previously known as people's armed forces departments *(renmin wuzhuang bu)*. Their duty is to disseminate national defense information and CMC directives to the civilian population, and to "resolve any problems concerning the militia" (see sections on the People's Armed Police and militia below).[53] They apparently also have some responsibility for PLA recruiting. The PAFCs are supposed to liaise closely with military region and district commands and came under the formal command of the PLA by CMC order on April 1, 1996.[54] Previously, PAFCs were under the administrative control of local government. Thereafter, PAFC officers began wearing PLA uniforms, whereas previously their uniforms were similar but distinct.[55] The PAFCs have existed since at least the Great Leap Forward and became important for providing local security during the Cultural Revolution.[56]

The State National Defense Mobilization Commission (SNDMC) has other responsibilities for civil defense and exists down to the municipal level (presumably it parallels the PACs). It is under the "joint leadership" *(shuangzhong lingdao)* of the CMC and State Council and is described as having at

51. The order was *Guanyu Tuan Yishang Geji Dangwei Chengli Jilu Jiancha Weiyuanhui Zhidao* (Order Concerning the Establishment of the Discipline Inspection Commission in Party Committees at the Regimental Level and Above), in Academy of Military Sciences Military History Research Department, ed., *Zhongguo Dabaike Quanshu: Zhongguo Renmin Jiefangjun Zhengzhi Gongzuo Fence* (Beijing: Junshi Kexue Chubanshe, 1987), p. 37.

52. Academy of Military Sciences, ed., *Shijie Junshi Nianjian 1999* (Beijing: Junshi Kexueyuan Chubanshe, 1999), p. 102.

53. Ibid.

54. Pu, *Zhonghua Renmin Gongheguo Zhengzhi Zhidu*, p. 566.

55. I am indebted to Dennis Blasko for this observation.

56. See Harlan W. Jencks, *From Muskets to Missiles: Politics and Professionalism in the Chinese Army, 1945–1981* (Boulder, Colo.: Westview Press, 1982), esp. pp. 167–69. They were then known as People's Armed Departments.

least four constituent offices: the State People's Armed Mobilization Office (Guojia Renmin Wuzhuang Dongyuan Bangongshi), the State Economic Mobilization Office (Guojia Jingji Dongyuan Bangongshi), the State People's Anti-Air [Defense] Office (Guojia Renmin Fankong Bangongshi), and the State Transportation War Preparedness Office (Guojia Jiaotong Zhanbei Bangongshi).[57]

Both of these organs (the PAFCs and the SNDMC) are no doubt survivors from the 1960s and 1970s, when China anticipated war with the Soviet Union, and would only become active in time of war and invasion.

Clearly, however, the most important set of command relationships for the CMC are those with the four general headquarters (departments) of the PLA. These are not only the principal conduits through which the CMC commands the services and military regions but also large and powerful organizations in their own right. They are described below, after first brief consideration of the Ministry of National Defense.

THE MINISTRY OF NATIONAL DEFENSE

The Ministry of National Defense was created at the First National People's Congress in September 1954.[58] Although it enjoyed some prestige and power during the 1950s under Defense Minister Peng Dehuai,[59] the MND has been a relatively hollow shell of an organization ever since. Administratively, it is under the State Council, but it has few resources and personnel and plays no active role in the command and control structure of the PLA. As figure 3 indicates, its principal function is to carry out foreign military exchanges.

Receiving visiting defense ministers and military delegations has occupied a larger amount of time in recent years, and the PLA has significantly increased the dispatch of its own delegations overseas in recent years.[60] This military diplomacy takes a number of forms, including delegations, ship visits, exchange of students, and so on. To carry out this range of activities, the

57. Liu Zhaoxiang, ed., *Zhongguo Junshi Zhidushi: Junshi Zuzhi Tizhi Bianzhi Juan* (Zhengzhou: Dajia Chubanshe, 1997), p. 545.

58. Pu, *Zhongguo Renmin Gongheguo Zhengzhi Zhidu*, p. 303.

59. See Jencks, *From Muskets to Missiles*, p. 139.

60. For an excellent and comprehensive study of the PLA's "diplomacy," see Ken Allen and Eric McVadon, *China's Foreign Military Relations* (Washington, D.C.: Henry L. Stimson Center, 1999).

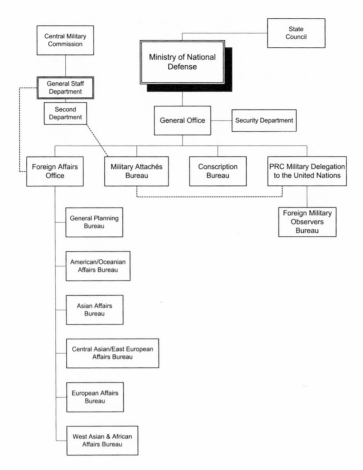

Figure 3. The Ministry of National Defense. *Source: Directory of PRC Military Personalities, 2000* (Honolulu: Serold Hawaii Inc., 2001).

Foreign Affairs Office is the MND's largest department. It is subdivided into five regional bureaus and a general planning bureau to coordinate scheduling and other logistical matters. As noted above, the foreign affairs offices of the MND, CMC, and GSD are one and the same. The MND also apparently has a military attaché bureau, which is logical given that one of the responsibilities of PLA attachés overseas is to arrange foreign military exchanges, but there should be no misunderstanding about the MND having principal authority over its military attachés abroad. The attaché offices, their personnel, and funding all come directly from the Second Department of the General Staff Department (GSD), because their principal job overseas is to collect intelligence (see below).

Another foreign activity that falls to the MND is participation in UN peacekeeping operations (PKO). The PLA has only once dispatched forces to participate in a UN PKO (when it sent an engineering battalion to Kampuchea in the early 1990s), but it has sent numerous military observers to other countries (principally Africa and the Middle East). This participation is overseen by the same office that administers the PRC military delegation to the United Nations in New York (although this office and many of its attachés are intelligence officers of the GSD Second Department).

Finally, the MND has a conscription bureau. To what it extent it becomes involved in PLA conscription is uncertain, but it probably cedes all or most responsibility for recruitment to the Military Affairs and Mobilization departments of the GSD.

Technically, according to the 1982 Constitution, the minister of national defense is appointed by the premier of the State Council and his appointment must be ratified by the Standing Committee of the National People's Congress, although these decisions are usually taken at CCP Central Committee plenary sessions.[61] Since 1954 there have been only eight ministers of defense: Peng Dehaui, Lin Biao, Ye Jianying, Xu Xiangqian, Geng Biao, Zhang Aiping, Qin Jiwei, and, currently, Chi Haotian.

THE FOUR GENERAL HEADQUARTERS

As noted above, the general headquarters (or departments) system originated in the early 1950s and was largely borrowed from the Soviet military system at the time, although it also reflected some elements of the Red Army as it developed during the civil war. In the winter of 1949–50, three "general headquarters" *(san zong silingbu)* were set up under the People's Revolutionary Military Affairs Commission: the General Staff, the General Political Department, and the General Rear Services Department (GRSD).[62] From this time until 1958, the general headquarters grew and fluctuated in number and responsibility.

In September 1950, after the outbreak of the Korean War (but before

---

61. Liu, ed., *Zhongguo Junshi Zhidushi,* p. 544.
62. Ibid., p. 545. Other historical information in this paragraph derives from this source.

China's entry), a General Cadre Management Department was established with five subunits under it. In November 1954 a fifth general department was established, the General Military Ordnance Department (Zong Junxie Bu) with ten subdepartments. In April 1955, the General Staff Department underwent a significant reorganization and expansion, adding eight first-level subdepartments and three second-level bureaus. At the same time, a sixth autonomous department was created: the Training General Investigation Department (Xunlian Zong Cha Bu). In June 1955, a seventh general department was established: the Armed Forces Supervision Department (Wuzhuang Liliang Jiancha Bu), and this spawned offspring in all three services and the GRSD's logistics finance system (Houfang Houqin Caiwu Jiancha Xitong). In August 1955, this latter organ was elevated to full department status and put under direct administrative control of the newly created CMC (becoming the Central Military Commission General Financial Department), with at least seven identified subbureaus. Thus, by the end of 1955, a total of eight separate general departments existed under the CMC. In January 1957, however, the CMC took the decision to shrink the PLA by one-third and streamline its organizational structure. This resulted in a return to the three general headquarters system, with the five redundant departments being reabsorbed back into the original three over a period of a year. By July 1958, an expanded CMC meeting proclaimed the reorganization successful, and in 1960, it renamed the GRSD the General Logistics Department. Until the April 1998 establishment of a fourth general department, the General Armaments Department, this tripartite system comprised the principal organizational construct for the PLA (although numerous reorganizations took place within each general department).

The General Staff Department

The GSD is the largest and most important of the four general headquarters. Like the other three, the GSD exists as an organ under the CMC. It has a large organization and staff in Beijing, but it also permeates the entire organizational structure of the PLA. All the service arms, military regions, military districts, and People's Armed Police have a "headquarters department" *(silingbu)* within them at every level, which is the institutional locus of the GSD's chain of command. This GSD headquarters system has been reorganized and strengthened since the promulgation of new "PLA Headquarters Regulations" *(Jiefangjun Zong Silingbu Tiaoling)* in 1997. These regulations and a subsequently published internal PLA handbook clearly delineate the structure and functions of the GSD vertically down to the military subdistrict level.[63] The regulations are unambiguous about the GSD's overall command authority and responsibilities within the PLA:

> The Headquarters is an organization from which senior officers direct operations. It is the command center of the army and the leading organ for military work. Its basic function is to support senior officers in making decisions and to ensure that they are executed. . . . The Headquarters at various levels in the PLA are an organic whole and are the "nerves" that control the action of units. The Headquarters is the only organ in the PLA that has command authority.[64]

This would suggest that, at least in wartime, commanding officers in the field have authority over political commissars.

Thus, the GSD is not only the largest and most important of the four general headquarters, but almost all of the GSD's nine main subdepartments are mirrored and replicated down through the services and geographic divisions of the PLA (see figure 4).

The GSD has undergone a series of expansions and contractions since its inception. By 1958, it had ten first-level departments, fourteen second-level subdepartments, and two bureaus.[65] In September 1982, another major reorganization took place, in which three previously separate units of the PLA ground forces were amalgamated into the GSD. The Artillery Corps (Qiang Pao Bing), Armored Corps (Zhuangjia Bing), Anti-Chemical Corps (Fang Hua Bing), and the Engineering Corps (Gongcheng Bing) were absorbed into the newly created Service Arms Department.[66] This reform was in line with the first attempts to create combined-arms and joint operations in the PLA. These previously horizontally related units *(yewu budui)* now operated together at the military region level and were commanded on a direct line from the new GSD Service Arms Department. At the same time, in 1982, the decision was taken to establish a Fourth Department of the GSD, specifically for electronic warfare and counterelectronic warfare.[67] The Fourth Department may also share some electronic

---

63. See Wang An, *Jundui Siling yu Guanli* (Beijing: Junshi Kexue Chubanshe, 1992).

64. Expert Group for Revising Regulations of Headquarters, Campaign and Tactics Research Department, Academy of Military Sciences, "Distinct Characteristics, Strategic Advantage: On the Main Characteristics of the 'Chinese PLA Headquarters Regulations,'" *Jiefangjun Bao*, February 4, 1997, in BBC SWB/FE, April 25, 1997.

65. Liu, ed., *Zhongguo Junshi Zhidu Shi*, p. 546.

66. Ibid.

67. Academy of Military Sciences History Research Department, ed., *Zhongguo Renmin Jiefangjun Qishinian*, p. 622.

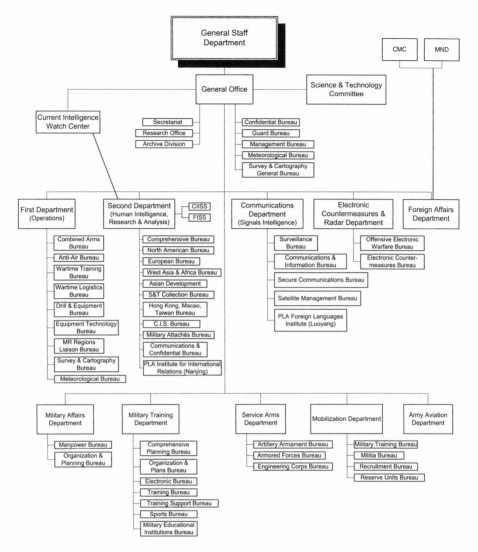

Figure 4. The General Staff Department. *Sources: Directory of PRC Military Personalities, 2000* (Honolulu: Serold Hawaii Inc., 2001); Zhang Wannian, ed., *Dangdai Shijie Junshi yu Zhongguo Guofang* (Beijing: Junshi Kexue Chubanshe, 1999); Academy of Military Sciences, ed., *Shijie Junshi Nianjian 2000* (Beijing: Junshi Kexue Chubanshe, 2000);Yao Yanjin et al., eds., *Junshi Zuzhi Tizhi Yanjiu* (Beijing: Guofang Daxue Chubanshe, 1997); David Finkelstein, "The General Staff Department of the Chinese People's Liberation Army: Organization, Roles, Missions" (paper presented at the 2000 CAPS/RAND Conference "The PLA as Organization"); interviews.

intelligence (ELINT) functions with the Third Department.[68] Then, in 1987, the Army Air Corps was elevated to a full second-level bureau *(er ji ju)*.[69] Around 1997, the Meteorological Bureau and the Survey and Cartography Bureau were folded into the First Department as second-level units. In 1998, the GSD Equipment Department (Junxie Bu) was absorbed by the newly created General Armaments Department (GAD). During the 1990s, the Confidential Department (Jiyao Bu) was moved from being a first-level department to a constituent unit of the General Office of the GSD, while the Foreign Affairs Bureau was bureaucratically upgraded to be the Foreign Affairs Office. A separate Science and Technology Committee was also established.

This leaves the GSD today with a total of nine first-level departments *(yi ji bu):* the First Department (Operations, or Zuozhan Bu), the Second Department (known as the Er Bu or Qingbao Bu and responsible for human intelligence collection and multisource analysis), the Communications Department (Tongxin Bu, also known as the Third Department, or San Bu, and responsible for signals intelligence),[70] the Electronic Countermeasures and Radar Department (Dianzi Duikang Leida Bu, also known as the Fourth Department), the Military Affairs Department (Jun Wu Bu), the Military Training Department (Jun Xun Bu), the Service Arms Department (Bingzhong Bu), the Army Aviation Department (Lujun Hangkong Bu), and the Foreign Affairs Department (Waishi Bu). The GSD has five second-level bureaus, the Confidential Bureau (Jiyao Ju), the Guard Bureau (Jingwei Ju), the Meteorological Bureau (Qixiang Ju), the Management Bureau (Guanli Ju), and the Survey and Cartography Bureau (Cehui Zongju). The internal organization and subdepartments of these GSD departments are detailed, to the best of my knowledge and drawing on a number of oral and published Chinese sources, in figure 4. In a comprehensive study of the GSD, David

68. For more on the Third and Fourth Departments, see Desmond Ball, "Signals Intelligence in China," *Jane's Intelligence Review* 7, no. 8 (1991): 365–70.

69. Ibid., p. 623.

70. There is a discrepancy between Chinese and U.S. sources on the name and responsibility of this department. Without variance, authoritative PLA published sources refer to this department as the Tongxin Bu, or Communications Department, and list it in protocol order immediately following the Second Department. U.S. Defense Department sources identify two separate departments for Communications and a Third (Intelligence) Department. See *Directory of PRC Military Personalities, 2000* (Honolulu: Serold Hawaii Inc., 2001), p. 18; Zhang Wannian, ed., *Dangdai Shijie Junshi yu Zhongguo Guofang* (Beijing: Junshi Kexue Chubanshe, 2000), p. 309; Academy of Military Sciences, ed., *Shijie Junshi Nianjian 2000*, p. 130; Yao et al., eds., *Zhongguo Zuzhi Tizhi Yanjiu*, p. 373.

Finkelstein expands in some detail on the probable responsibilities of these subdepartments.[71] As his study and figure 4 show, there is much that remains uncertain about GSD suborganization. Very few PLA sources explicate the internal organization and work of the GSD.[72]

In addition to these subdepartments, the General Office of GSD Headquarters in Beijing manages a series of smaller, albeit important, offices. The Science and Technology Committee is presumably linked to the GAD and military-industrial establishment, and is probably involved in conveying the needs of the services to weapons and equipment producers. The Secretariat Division (Mishu Chu) is the general office for the chief and deputy chiefs of General Staff. There is also known to be an Archive Office for the cataloging and storage of documents—which, of course, works closely with the Confidential Bureau. Finally, there is a small Research Office (Zhong Ban Yanjiu Shi), which does research on international defense and security affairs, directly for the chief and deputy chiefs of General Staff.[73] This office enjoys close ties to the Second Department (human intelligence and research) and its affiliated China Institute of International Strategic Studies (CIISS) and the Foundation of International Strategic Studies (FISS)—the PLA's principal open think tanks.

Of the two, the CIISS is the larger, better funded, and more accessible to foreigners. It is staffed by a combination of researchers of colonel and senior colonel rank and retired military attachés. CIISS researchers write reports that circulate to the General Staff and throughout the PLA senior hierarchy, as well as publishing the open journal *Guoji Zhanlüe Yanjiu* (International Strategic Studies). The FISS is a smaller operation run by a group of younger intelligence and international security specialists.[74]

The General Political Department

The GPD is one of the oldest organizations within the PLA.[75] Inasmuch as the Chinese military and Communist Party have had a symbiotic relation-

71. David Finkelstein, "The General Staff Department of the Chinese People's Liberation Army: Organization, Roles, Missions" (paper presented at the 2000 CAPS/RAND Conference "The PLA as Organization").

72. One that does so in some detail is the internally circulated *(junnei faxing)* volume edited by Ma Jinsheng, *Canmou Junguan Zhanshi Yewu Zhinan,* 2d ed. (Beijing: Junshi Kexue Chubanshe, 1998).

73. Interview with a member of this office, October 1999.

74. For more on CIISS and FISS, see Bates Gill and James Mulvenon, "Military Think Tanks," *China Quarterly,* forthcoming (September 2002).

75. For an excellent and thorough authorized history of the GPD through 1989, see National Defense University Party History and Party Building Political Work

ship since their inception in the 1920s,[76] and the PLA today remains a party-army (see chapter 2), "political work" *(zhengzhi gongzuo)* has always had a central place in the armed forces.[77] The GPD is one of the primary organizational devices for inculcating and indoctrinating the troops with the party's ethos and propaganda—but it is not the only device for doing so, nor is ideological work by any means the GPD's sole function.

As noted above, there is also a separate system (CDIC), under the CMC and Central Committee, to monitor and police the behavior of party members in the military.[78] As all officers above the rank of colonel are party members,[79] this is an important means by which the party exercises control over the army. In addition, Chinese sources on political work in the military distinguish a separate party committee system *(dangwei zhidu)*, extending from the CMC itself down to the company level.[80] Party cells *(xiaozu)* exist even at the platoon and squad levels.[81] This is a separate chain of command from the CDIC and GPD systems, although foreign analyses rarely distinguish them. The strengthening of party committees, and extension of them down to the company level, has been a high priority since the Tiananmen uprising of 1989. The failure of some troops to follow orders and suppress the demonstrations proved very unnerving to the CCP and PLA leadership—a fear compounded when many communist militaries did not rescue their collapsing ruling parties in eastern Europe and the Soviet Union. One of the principal lessons learned by the Chinese Communist leadership from the collapse of other communist regimes was the vital importance of main-

---

Research Office, ed., *Zhongguo Renmin Jiefangjun Zhengzhi Gongzuo Shi* (Beijing: Guofang Daxue Chubanshe, 1989).

76. For a fuller description of this relationship, see my "The Building of the Party-State in China, 1949–1965: Bringing the Soldier Back In," in Timothy Cheek and Tony Saich, eds., *New Perspectives on State Socialism in China, 1949–1965* (Armonk, N.Y.: M. E. Sharpe, 1996).

77. For one historical description of the GPD and political work in the PLA, see my "The Soldier and the State in China: The Political Work System in the People's Liberation Army," in Brian Hook, ed., *The Individual and the State in China* (Oxford: Clarendon Press, 1997) (originally published in *China Quarterly*, no. 127 [September 1991]: 527–68). Also see Nan Li, "Changing Functions of the Party and Political Work Systems in the PLA and Civil-Military Relations in China," *Armed Forces and Society* 19, no. 3 (Spring 1993): 393–409.

78. Pu, *Zhonghua Renmin Gongheguo Zhengzhi Zhidu*, p. 568.

79. Interview with knowledgeable Academy of Military Sciences officer, October 23, 2000.

80. Ibid.; Zhang Shuitao, *Dangdai Zhongguo Zhengzhi Zhidu* (Beijing: Gaodeng Jiaoyu Chubanshe, 1990), pp. 213–14.

81. Pu, *Zhonghua Renmin Gongheguo Zhengzhi Zhidu*, p. 568.

taining control over the armed forces—described in the PLA as "maintaining the absolute leadership of the party" *(zhichi dang de juedui lingdao)*—and the preparedness of the military to use effective force against the civilian population if necessary.[82] As a result, after 1989, the entire PLA endured a barrage of indoctrination the likes of which it had not experienced for many years, spearheaded by GPD Director and CMC Secretary-General Yang Baibing.[83] After Yang's downfall in 1992, however, another indoctrination campaign began under the aegis of General Wang Ruilin. It was aimed at rooting out the factionalism that the Yang clique had engendered, as well as building new allegiance to Jiang Zemin.[84] As a number of internal sources indicate, battling corruption in the ranks, along with building political loyalty, was a principal theme of political work in the military throughout the 1990s.[85]

The party committee system is the organ primarily responsible for "ideological" indoctrination in the PLA. Chinese sources on the political work system in the PLA clearly distinguish between the political commissar system *(zhengzhi weiyuan zhidu)* and what is described euphemistically as the "system of political organs" *(zhengzhi jiguan zhidu)*.

Political commissars have existed in the PLA since the earliest days of the Red Army, although their roles have evolved over time. Originally, they were intended to win the allegiance of the local population and carry out land reform, as well as to gather intelligence about Nationalist and Japanese forces. After 1949, following the Soviet model, their principal function was to maintain morale and indoctrinate the rank and file (during the Korean War, they also worked to "reeducate" prisoners of war). Under the Soviet system, a "unified command system" *(tongyi zhihui zhidu)* was es-

82. A total of 110 officers "breached discipline in a serious way," 1,400 soldiers "shed their weapons and ran away," and 21 senior offices were court-martialed. Willy Wo-lap Lam, "Yang Baibing Reveals Army Defiance in Crackdown," *South China Morning Post,* December 28, 1989.

83. For a detailed account of this process, see Shambaugh, "Soldier and the State in China."

84. See, e.g., the document promulgated by the CMC after the Fourteenth Party Congress: *Zhonggong Zhongyang Guanyu Jiaqiang Dangde Jianshe Jige Zhongda Wenti de Jueding* (Decision of the Central Committee Central Military Commission Concerning Several Big Problems in Accelerating Party Building), in National Defense University Party History and Party Building Political Work Teaching Office, ed., *Xin Shiqi Jundui Dangde Jianshe Yanjiu* (Beijing: Guofang Daxue Chubanshe, 1997, *junnei faxing*), pp. 1–18.

85. Among many, see ibid. and Academy of Military Sciences, ed., *Zhengzhi Gongzuo de Xin Shijian Xin Tanqin—Gaige Kaifang 20 Nian Jundui Zhengzhi Gongzuo Jingyan Huibian* (Beijing: Junshi Kexue Chubanshe, 1998).

tablished, under which—in theory—field commanders *(zhihuiyuan)* and political commissars *(zhengzhi weiyuan)* would jointly make decisions. During the Korean War and subsequently, this system did not function well and caused a great deal of tension between the two.[86] Today, the function of political commissar *(zhengwei)* exists at the regiment *(tuan)* level and above, but it is known as a political instructor *(jiaodaoyuan)* at the battalion level, political director *(zhidaoyuan)* at the company *(lian)* level, and simply as a political worker *(zhengzhi gongzuoyuan)* at the platoon and squad levels. According to a 1990 source, the commissar at all levels holds status equal to the military commander or senior officer, but, more important, both are "directly subordinate" to the "leading cadre of the party committee."[87] No doubt this assessment had something to do with the tightening of political control in the armed forces after Tiananmen, as it is clear from a number of sources today that the commander enjoys precedence in war and peacetime.

Thus the political commissar's role is principally to supplement the role of the Party committees and secretaries in carrying out ideological work, maintaining morale and discipline, and disseminating the Party's line *(luxian)* in the military. Organizationally, the commissar's work fits within the Organization Department of the GPD. At lower-level units, however, the political commissar and the entirety of other GPD functions are all contained within the "Political Department" (Zhengzhi Bu) at that level. Figure 5 illustrates the table of organization and functional responsibilities of the seven subdepartments within the GPD today.[88]

As the figure shows, the GPD is a fairly large organization. Some of its responsibilities are concerned with political propaganda work broadly defined, as carried out primarily by the Propaganda Department (Xuanchuan Bu). This department also oversees multimedia, publishing, and arts func-

---

86. See Jencks, *From Muskets to Missiles*. For other excellent historical studies of the political work system in the PLA, see Ellis Joffe, *Party and Army: Professionalism and Political Control in the Chinese Officer Corps, 1949–1964* (Cambridge, Mass.: Harvard University Press, 1965); Monte Bullard, *China's Political-Military Evolution: The Party and the Military in the PRC, 1960–1984* (Boulder, Colo.: Westview Press, 1985); Cheng Hsiao-shih, *Party-Military Relations in the PRC and Taiwan: Paradoxes of Control* (Boulder, Colo.: Westview Press, 1990); Jane Price, *Cadres, Commanders, and Commissars* (Boulder, Colo.: Westview Press, 1976).

87. Sun Weiben, ed., *Zhongguo Gongchangdang Dangwu Gongzuo Da Zidian* (Beijing: Zhongguo Zhanwang Chubanshe, 1989), p. 328.

88. Zhang Wannian, ed., *Dangdai Shijie Junshi yu Zhongguo Guofang*, p. 309; Academy of Military Sciences, ed., *Shijie Junshi Nianjian 2000*, p. 130; *Directory of PRC Military Personalities, 2000*, pp. 22–24.

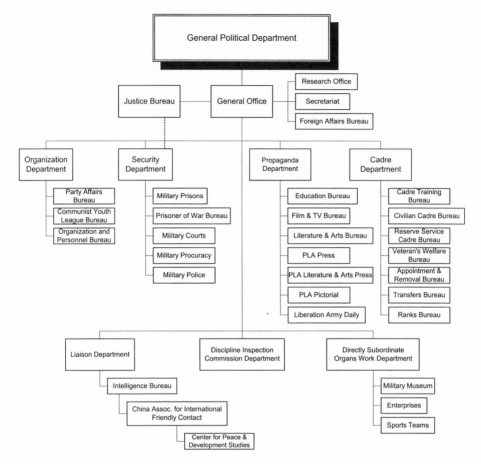

Figure 5. The General Political Department. *Sources:* Zhang Wannian, ed., *Dang-dai Shijie Junshi yu Zhongguo Guofang* (Beijing: Junshi Kexue Chubanshe, 1999); Academy of Military Sciences, ed., *Shijie Junshi Nianjian 2000* (Beijing: Junshi Kexue Chubanshe, 2000); *Directory of PRC Military Personalities, 2000* (Honolulu: Serold Hawaii Inc., 2001).

tions (previously managed by the Cultural Department before it was merged with the Propaganda Department in 1999).

But the GPD performs many other roles and functions beyond propaganda. The Organization Department (Zuzhi Bu) is responsible for coordination with party committees, for running the Communist Youth League (Gong Qing Tuan) program in PLA-administered schools for dependents, and—most important—for managing personnel appointments and files for officers throughout the PLA. It is the GPD that has always maintained the responsibility and records (dossier) for officers, and ultimately must approve all promotions and reassignments. This highly sensitive and important role gives the GPD real power. The Cadre Department (Ganbu Bu) performs this function for large number of civilian employees in the armed forces (known as *wenzhi ganbu*), as well as being in charge of personnel in the reserves and, notably, looking after retired officers' pensions and perquisites. The Security Department (Baowei Bu) administers military prisons and detention centers, manages the military police system, and is in charge of prisoners of war. It oversees the military court *(junshi fating)* and military procuracy *(jianchayuan)* systems. The Liaison Department (Lianluo Bu) is the GPD's intelligence arm. Its size and activities are not well understood, but it does manage a quasi-open organization that conducts work on international security: the Association for International Friendly Contact, formed in the early 1980s as a front for inviting and meeting with select foreigners in China, as well as sending active-duty intelligence collectors abroad under various kinds of cover. The association also administers the Center for Peace and Development, a small but effective think tank specializing in international security. Both operate out of the same small compound in northern Beijing. The center has a tiny permanent staff and acts more as an association *(xiehui)* that draws together senior active-duty and retired PLA and GPD officers. It also publishes a high-quality journal on international security affairs, *Heping yu Fazhan* (Peace and Development). Finally, the GPD also has a separate Discipline Inspection Commission Department (Jilu Jiancha Bu),[89] as well as a department entitled the Directly Subordinate Organs Work Department (Zhishu Jiguan Gongzuo Bu). It is thought that this latter department administers the Military Museum in Beijing and similar organs throughout the country, as well as several enterprises that produce goods directly for the GPD. The CDIC carries out party discipline work at the lower levels of the PLA (company level and below) on behalf of the CDIC, which is statutory organ of both the Communist Party Central Committee and the Central Military Commission.

The General Logistics Department

Inasmuch as no military can operate without logistics—weapons, ammunition and ordnance, food, medicine, clothing, and transportation—the GLD (formerly the General Rear Services Department) necessarily dates back to

89. Liu, ed., *Zhongguo Junshi Zhidu Shi*, p. 547.

the early days of the Red Army. In the days of the Anti-Japanese and Civil wars, the Chinese Communist forces had to depend on a combination of captured weapons and supplies from their adversaries, extreme frugality, and the material support of the local population. It was not until 1950, however, that the Chinese Communist military established its first unified logistics system. This was necessitated by the Korean War, which exposed the PLA's weaknesses in transport and supply. Chinese units suffered shortages of everything during that grueling war.

After the Korean War, logistics became more regularized and systematized under the GRSD. In 1960, the GLD was officially established under the command of the CMC. At that time, the GLD had a Headquarters Department, Political Department, Finance Department, Military Supplies Department, Health Department, Ordnance Department, Military Transport Department, Vehicles and Vessels Department, Oil and Lubricants Department, Materials Department, Barracks Construction Department, Production Management Department, and an Auditing Bureau.[90] Since that time, the GLD has undergone a series of reorganizations—although it has never really received either political or financial priority (nor has the GLD traditionally been on the career path of upwardly mobile PLA officers). In 1969, at the height of the Cultural Revolution, the GLD was drastically reduced in size through mergers of a number of departments: the Finance, Military Supplies, Materials, and Oil and Lubricants Departments were consolidated into a single Supplies Department (Gongying Bu), while the Ordnance, Military Transport, and Equipment Planning Department (which had been created in 1964), were merged into a single Equipment Department (Zhuangbei Bu). Also created were the Enterprises Department (Qiye Bu) and Management Bureau, for a total of eight departments and two bureaus.[91] The years 1972 and 1975 brought additional minor reorganizations, and apparently considerable "interference from Jiang Qing's counterrevolutionary clique," according to an official GLD history.[92]

After the overthrow of the Gang of Four in October 1976, the entire PLA was reorganized in 1977 on the basis of the CMC's *Guanyu Jundui Bianzhi Tizhi de Tiaozhe Fang'an* (Program Concerning the Military Organizational System).[93] For the GLD, this meant a redivision of many of the departments

---

90. Ibid., p. 548.
91. Tong Chao, ed., *Zhongguo Junshi Zhidu Shi: Houqin Zhidu Juan* (Beijing: Dajia Chubanshe, 1997), p. 446. Much of this section derives form this source.
92. Ibid.
93. Ibid., p. 447.

that had previously been amalgamated. The Finance and Materials Department was once again divided into separate Finance, Materials, and Oil and Lubricants Departments; the Ordnance and Amphibious Department was split into two; the Transport Department changed its name to the Military Transportation Department (Junshi Jiaotong Bu), the Barracks Department became the Basic Construction and Barracks Department, and the Military Supplies Department split off a separate Factory Management Department (Gongchang Guanli Bu), which later morphed into the Military Supplies Production Department and then the Production Management Department. Thus, at least on paper, the GLD had grown exponentially as a result of the 1977 reforms.

Then, in June 1981, the CMC decided that further reorganization was required. Apparently, the "leftist" residue of the Gang of Four was well-entrenched in the GLD, and the CMC decided that a special party standing committee *(dangwei changwei)* should be formed at the apex of the GLD, specifically to "increase party leadership over the GLD."[94] This change was accompanied by a further reorganization, in which the Ordnance Department was moved over to the General Staff Department. At the same time, the CMC leadership determined that greater administrative control needed to be established over the entire military transport system and rail network following the Cultural Revolution chaos. Accordingly, the CMC established the Transport Strategy Leading Group (Jiaotong Zhanlüe Xiaozu), and located its office inside the GLD Military Transport Bureau.[95] Other leading groups were established in other GLD departments in an attempt to make them more efficient and politically correct. These groups began to work out detailed plans *(liuhua)* for reforming their respective sectors—and, in 1983, an experimental "test point" unit *(shi dian budui)* was established in the Jinan Military Region, where the new reforms would be tried out.[96] These reforms were to integrate new market mechanisms into logistical work, and these were codified in another CMC directive in 1985—the *Jundui Tizhi Gaige, Jingjian, Zhengbian Fang'an* (Program to Reform, Reduce, and Reorganize the Military System).[97]

In 1988, the GLD was shaken up yet again. This time, the GLD itself issued more than 3,000 directives, and the CMC promulgated 160 concerning logis-

94. Ibid.
95. Ibid., p. 448.
96. Ibid.
97. Ibid., p. 449.

tics reform alone. Another 99 directives were issued in 1989.[98] Their purpose was intended to, once and for all, "completely straighten out" *(quanmian qingli)* the anomalies affecting the GLD. Apparently, a combination of the economic inefficiencies and political interference had left the GLD a mess and ill-suited to supporting the broader reforms and transformation of the PLA envisioned by the CMC.

Judging from the number of reorganizations and new regulations affecting the GLD during the 1990s, the problems have continued—although many changes came after the Gulf War and were tied to the broader doctrinal revision and reorganization of services in accordance with the doctrine of "limited war under high-technology conditions" (see chapter 3). In particular, the GLD has in recent years attempted to standardize its supplies and replace the traditional system of geographically fixed supply depots and unit-based self-sufficiency, associated with positional "front" warfare, with a more flexible and mobile logistics supply system that can support combined arms and joint-force operations.[99]

Of utmost priority has been to build an integrated logistics supply network in which different service arms can draw upon common stockpiles of certain equipment, supplies, and services. By 1993, it was claimed that all of the PLA's "large units" had established "material supply coordination centers" stocked with key "large quantity" materials and centrally monitored by the GLD. Any shortfalls were quickly identified and were to be rectified through purchases from the civilian sector.[100] Previously, PLA services have suffered from excessive and extreme compartmentalization, with each maintaining redundant sets of logistical supplies. The current reforms under GLD Director Wang Ke are aimed at integrating, unifying, and standardizing the system. General Wang's patron and predecessor General Fu Quanyou (now chief of General Staff) himself established the priority of "creating a unified system for overall logistics and for combat equipment,

---

98. Ibid., p. 455.

99. For excellent assessments of these attempts, see Lonnie Henley, "Mobile Warfare and the Total PLA: Logistics Reform and Standardization in the 1999 'Joint Campaign Program'" (paper presented at the American Enterprise Institute and U.S. Army War College Conference on the People's Liberation Army, September 1999); and Tai Ming Cheung, "Reforming the Dragon's Tail: Chinese Military Logistics in the Era of High-Technology Warfare and Market Economics," in James R. Lilley and David Shambaugh, eds., *China's Military Faces the Future* (Washington, D.C.: AEI Press; Armonk, N.Y.: M. E. Sharpe, 1999), pp. 228–46.

100. Zhang Dongbo and Li Songqing, "PLA Logistics Reforms Materials Supply Systems," Xinhua, December 9, 1993, in FBIS–CHI, December 15, 1993.

as well as a coordinated development between the two."[101] Besides being standardized and made physically available to different service arms operating in a joint combat environment, supplies also need to be automated and tracked by computer. A 1998 visit by a high-level GLD delegation to the headquarters and central tracking depot of Federal Express in Memphis, Tennessee, may have been instructive. After returning to China, Wang Ke announced a new ten-year logistics reform program entitled the "All-Army Joint Logistics Implementation Plan," which was part of the broader PLA Joint Campaign Program (1998 Combat Order No. 13).[102] Wang claimed that it would build upon experiments already undertaken in the Shenyang, Jinan, and Guangzhou MRs, and would focus on joint-service logistics operations.[103] One of the first important developments to arise out of this new initiative was to merge the individual services' logistics departments at the MR level into a single Joint Logistics Department (Lianqin Bu). Under the new system, described as a "network-style zoned supply system," the services are surrendering hospitals, medical supply and maintenance units, fuel stocks and distribution networks, general supply warehouses, vehicle supply and maintenance units, and some general transportation units to the control of the new JLD in each MR.[104]

Reforming the PLA logistics system has also required "outsourcing" of various supplies and services to the civilian population.[105] This was necessitated not only by design, as it was to be more cost-effective (as transport costs would theoretically be saved), but also by necessity. Beginning in the early 1990s, the State Council began to reduce the list of commodities that would be procured by the government and military and made available to the GLD at heavily subsidized prices. By 1994, the list of such commodities had fallen from 256 to 71, of which only 27 were guaranteed.[106] This requirement has put a great strain on GLD and unit finances, as the cost of

101. Fu Quanyou, "Future Logistics Modernization," in Michael Pillsbury, ed., *Chinese Views of Future Warfare* (Washington, D.C.: National Defense University Press, 1997), p. 120, as quoted in Tai Ming Cheung, ibid, p. 230.

102. Henley, "Mobile Warfare and the Total PLA."

103. Wang Ke, "Adapt to the Market Economy, Adapt to Future Combat," *Qiushi*, no. 23 (December 1, 1998), in FBIS–CHI, December 8, 1998.

104. Henley, "Mobile Warfare and the Total PLA."

105. This necessity began to be recognized in PLA writings in 1992. See, e.g., Wang Tailan, "Shehuizhuyi Shichang Jingji yu Jundui Houqin Baozhang," *Junshi Jingji Yanjiu*, November 1992, pp. 4–6. The author was Nanjing MR Logistics chief at the time.

106. "PLA Logistics Department Rationalizes Supply," *Zhongguo Tongxunshe*, October 15, 1994, in FBIS–CHI, October 18, 1994.

goods in the private sector is higher and supplies fluctuate (especially in the case of specialized materials like metals, minerals, oils, etc.). In 1996, the GLD attempted to reinstitute a more centralized procurement system for staple goods and commodities, but it appears to have been only partially successful. Private sector warehouses also charged more for storage, thus further taxing units'coffers.[107] To compensate for their lack of funds to purchase goods and services in the private sector, PLA units have ended up bartering their assets—particularly manpower and transport. This has resulted in military units becoming more deeply involved in local commercial activities (often illegal), loss of training time, and additional wear and tear on equipment.

Overall, the logistics system in the PLA remains in transition, with many redundancies and anomalies still to be straightened out. Shortages and inefficiencies can be expected to persist, while the new demands of high-tech warfare will further strain the system. No doubt further experiments and reorganizations can also be expected. The current GLD structure is shown in figure 6. Today, the GLD consists of nine department level sub-units, at least three bureau-level units, and at least three important storage depots around the country.[108] The departments are: Headquarters (Siling Bu), Political (Zhengzhi Bu), Finance (Caiwu Bu), Auditing (Shenji Bu), Military Supplies (Junxu Bu), Health (Weisheng Bu), Oil and Lubricants (Youliao Bu), Capital Construction and Barracks (Jijian Yingfang Bu), and Military Transport and Conveyance (Junjiao Yunshu Bu). Although the Ordnance Department and Military Supplies Production Department were both listed as department-level organs of the GLD in 1997,[109] they were merged into the new General Armaments Department in 1998. The bureau-level organs are the General Engineering Unit (Gongcheng Zongdui), Military Mines (Junkuang Ju), All-Army Land Management Bureau (Quanjun Tudi Guanli Ju), and Production Management Bureau (Shengchan Guanli Ju). The storage depots are the Wuhan Rear Base (Wuhan Houfang Jidi), the Nenjiang Base (Nenjiang Jidi), and the Qinghai-Tibet Army Depot (Qinghai-Xizang Budui).

This structure still leaves the GLD with a sprawling organizational empire

107. Beijing Radio, "PLA Improves Logistics Operations," in FBIS–CHI, December 11, 1998.

108. See Li, *Zhongguo Zhengfu Zhidu*, p. 299; *Directory of PRC Military Personalities, 1999* (Honolulu: Serold Hawaii Inc., 1999); Colonel Susan Puska, "The PLA General Logistics Department" (paper presented at the 2000 CAPS/RAND Conference "The PLA as Organization").

109. Li, *Zhongguo Zhengfu Zhidu*.

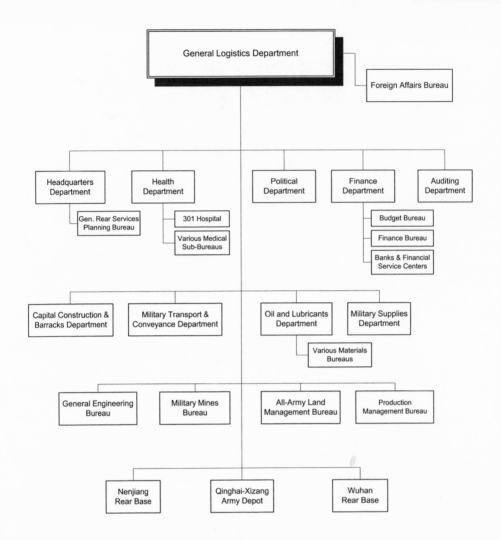

Figure 6. The General Logistics Department. *Sources:* Zhang Wannian, ed., *Dangdai Shijie Junshi yu Zhongguo Guofang* (Beijing: Junshi Kexue Chubanshe, 1999); Academy of Military Sciences, ed., *Shijie Junshi Nianjian 2000* (Beijing: Junshi Kexue Chubanshe, 2000); *Directory of PRC Military Personalities, 2000* (Honolulu: Serold Hawaii Inc., 2001). On allocation of military expenditure, see table 5.

and wide variety of functions. One particular anomaly appears to be the GLD's continuing responsibility for the military budget and finance. No doubt this is an important bureaucratic advantage that the GLD is reluctant to give up, but it would make much more sense to establish an autonomous budgeting system under the CMC (see chapter 5). Reform of the entire GLD will continue to be critical, though, as the PLA tries to adapt its entire force structure into more mobile units and joint forces. GLD Director Wang Ke himself recently claimed that "logistics reform has entered a crucial stage . . . and that logistics departments at all levels must make preparations for warfare."[110] Given the nature of the system outlined above, this will be easier said than done.

The General Armaments Department

The General Armaments Department (Zong Zhuangbei Bu) was established only on April 3, 1998, in a sweeping initiative to reorganize and rationalize the structure and production of the defense industrial complex (see chapter 6). The creation of the GAD was accompanied by a parallel reconfiguration of the Commission on Science, Technology, and Industry for National Defense (COSTIND), which was administratively placed under the State Council and renamed State COSTIND (Guojia Guofang Kewei). The GAD is intended as a superagency, modeled explicitly on the French Délégation générale pour l'armement (DGA), to manage weapons research and production and the military-industrial complex in a centralized fashion. Its creation comes after a long and tortuous history of similar reorganizations of the military-industrial complex and oversight bodies intended to overcome obsolescence and distortions in production costs (see chapter 6). Since it is still rather new, the GAD is still getting itself organized and trying to establish the parameters of its administrative purview and the defense industrial installations that it controls. In particular, it has yet to create a clear division of labor with the "new" SCOSTIND. Harlan Jencks has detailed these redundancies and turf battles in one of the few in-depth Western assessments of the GAD to date.

A visit to the GAD's administrative offices soon after its creation was enlightening as to the basic organizational structure and missions of the GAD.[111] Subsequently, Chinese sources have filled in details left out in the

---

110. Xinhua News Service, "PLA's Wang Ke Urges Logistics Departments to Prepare Well for War, Avoid Extravagance," August 19, 2000, in FBIS–CHI, August 19, 2000.

111. Interview at GAD, December 11, 1998.

briefing at GAD headquarters.[112] Based on these few sources, the apparent structure of the GAD is illustrated in figure 7.

The GAD consists of eight first-level departments, although one authoritative Chinese source also lists an Equipment Technology Cooperation Department (Zhuangbei Jishu Hezuo Bu).[113] These departments are the Headquarters Department (Siling Bu), Political Department (Zhengzhi Bu), Logistics Department (Houqin Bu), Comprehensive Planning Department (Zonghe Jihua Bu), General Purpose Armament Support Department (Tongyong Zhuangbei Baozhang Bu), Service Arms Armaments Department (Jun Bingzhong Zhuangbei Bu), Ground Forces Armaments Research and Order Department (Lujun Zhuangbei Keyan Dinghuo Bu), and Electronics and Information Base Department (Dianzi Xinxi Jichu Bu).

We do not know in any detail the responsibilities of these various departments, although some are clear. The Headquarters Department is the GSD's representative organ in the GAD (as other PLA units), while the Political and Logistics Departments carry out staff functions in these areas and liaise with the GPD and GLD. The Comprehensive Planning Department is responsible for budgetary affairs.[114] The General Purpose Armaments Support Department apparently provides technical support for equipment commonly used throughout the PLA (presumably nonlethal equipment).

The Service Arms Armaments Department is the heart of the GAD. It was formed from the former Special Arms Department (Te Bing Bu) and Equipment Departments of the GSD,[115] and the Ordnance Department and Military Supplies Production Department of the GLD—all of which were merged into the GAD in 1998. It oversees the development of specialized weaponry and equipment for the services, primarily for the air force, navy, and Second Artillery.[116]

As its name implies, the Ground Forces Armaments Research and Order Department supervises equipment research and production for the army, although it may play a role in arranging purchases from foreign countries. The Electronics and Information Base Department is no doubt responsible

112. See Academy of Military Sciences, ed., *Shijie Junshi Nianjian 1999* (Beijing: Jiefangjun Chubanshe, 1999), p. 102; id., *Shijie Junshi Nianjian 2000*, p. 130; Zhang, ed., *Dangdai Shijie Junshi yu Zhongguo Guofang*, pp. 309–10; *Directory of PRC Military Personalities, 2000*, pp. 28–31.

113. Academy of Military Sciences, ed., *Shijie Junshi Nianjian 1999* and *2000*.

114. Interview at GAD, December 11, 1998.

115. Interview with former director of GSD Special Arms Department, December 8, 1998.

116. Harlan Jencks, "The General Armament Department" (paper presented at the 2000 CAPS/RAND Conference "The PLA as Organization").

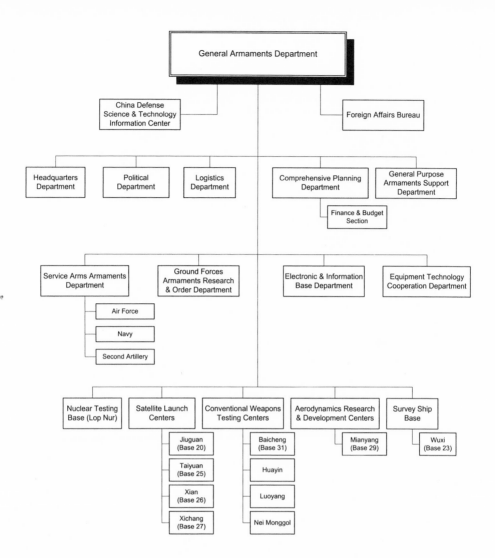

Figure 7.   The General Armaments Department. *Sources:* Zhang Wannian, ed., *Dangdai Shijie Junshi yu Zhongguo Guofang* (Beijing: Junshi Kexue Chubanshe, 1999); Academy of Military Sciences, ed., *Shijie Junshi Nianjian 2000* (Beijing: Junshi Kexue Chubanshe, 2000); *Directory of PRC Military Personalities, 2000* (Honolulu: Serold Hawaii Inc., 2001).

for developing technologies and weapons in electronic, counterelectronic, and information warfare for the Fourth Department of the GSD and other services in the PLA.

Beneath these departments lies a sprawling network of factories, nuclear and conventional weapons test facilities, missile launch centers, research institutes, and bases (see figure 7). Notable among these are the Lop Nur nuclear testing range and Mianyang nuclear weapons production facility; the four main satellite launching centers at Xichang, Xian, Taiyuan, and Jiuguan; and the Chinese Academy of Engineering Physics, or Ninth Academy.[117] The GAD has also absorbed the China Defense Science and Technology Information Center (CDSTIC) from the former COSTIND.

As Harlan Jencks concludes in his study, the GAD certainly remains an organization in transition. It will continue to experience growing pains and institutional jurisdictional conflict for some time to come. Worse yet, as noted in chapter 6, the GAD sits on top of a sprawling military-industrial establishment that has been reorganized repeatedly over the past fifty years in an effort to modernize and make efficient a system that simply seems incapable of it. There is no guarantee that the GAD will succeed where its predecessors have failed.

THE MILITARY REGIONS

The PRC is currently divided into seven large military regions *(da jun qu)*, or MRs, and the Hong Kong and Zhuhai-Macao Special Administrative Regions Garrison Commands. This geographical configuration applies largely to all service arms, although the navy has its own fleet headquarters and the Second Artillery has separate lines of command and control to the CMC and GSD. Within each MR are military districts *(jun qu)* and special garrison headquarters *(weishu qu* or *jingbei qu)* corresponding to provinces or centrally administered municipalities (Beijing, Tianjin, Shanghai, Chongqing) and special administrative regions (Hong Kong and Zhuhai-Macao), beneath which are military subdistricts *(jun fen qu).* (See figure 8 and map 1.)

The number of MRs has fluctuated over time. From 1949 to 1950, there were two; from 1950 to 1954, six; from 1955 to 1956, twelve; from 1956 to 1967, thirteen; from 1967 to 1969, twelve; and from 1969 to 1985, eleven. In 1985, they were consolidated to the present seven. Over this period, the

117. It seems apparent that CAEP has been radically restructured and consolidated in the process of transfer to the GAD. See Jencks, ibid.

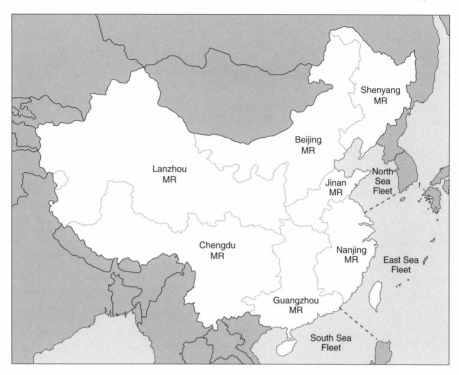

Map 1. China's military regions and fleets. Adapted from U.S. Defense Intelligence Agency map.

number of subordinate levels of command varied from one to three (from province to county to township levels).[118] Today, there are four levels: the military region *(da jun qu)*; the military district at the provincial level *(sheng jun qu)*; the military subdistrict *(jun fen qu)*, which roughly corresponds to the county; and garrisons at the municipal *(weishu qu)* or local *(jingbei qu)* level. These levels are functional not only for the military, but also for the civil defense People's Armed Forces Committees (see above) and People's Armed Police and militia (see below).[119] Additionally, the military organs of local party committees *(difang dangwei junshi jiguan)* assist in organizing militia, reserves, and wartime mobilization.[120]

In addition, specialized "theaters of operation" *(zhanqu)* are coterminous

118. Pu, *Zhonghua Renmin Gongheguo Zhengzhi Zhidu*, pp. 555–56.
119. Ibid., p. 565.
120. Ibid.

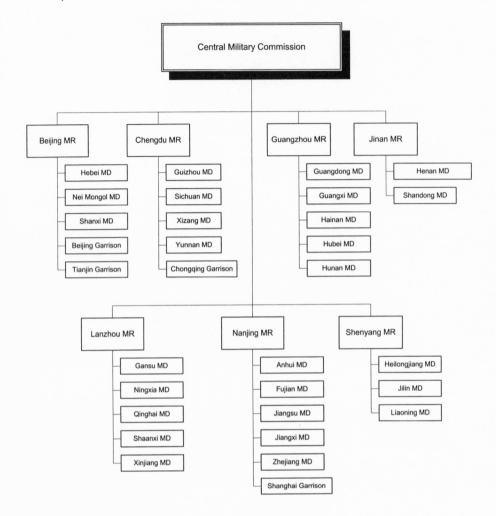

Figure 8.   China's military regions and districts.

with MRs and exist in both wartime and peacetime. (This term is often confused with "war zone," although the Chinese characters for *zhan* are different.) Under such conditions, the command system becomes even more concentrated in the authority of the headquarters commander of the theater *(zhanqu silingyuan)*, usually coterminous with the MR commander.[121]

121. Lei Yuanshen, Zhuang Jinbao, and Hong Yongfeng, eds., *Lu Jun Junzhixue* (Beijing: Junshi Kexue Chubanshe, 1997), p. 184.

An MR commander is usually a lieutenant general. The 1997 Order on PLA Internal Command *(Zhongguo Renmin Jiefangjun Neiwu Siling)* and other PLA materials are quite explicit that, in a war zone, the air force and navy are subordinate to the GSD commander.

Within each MR, each of the four general headquarters (GSD, GPD, GLD, GAD) has parallel departments that are directly linked to their parent organizations in Beijing, and through them directly to the CMC. The Headquarters Department (Siling Bu) is the GSD at the MR level and is explicitly charged with "directly leading *[zhihui lingdao]* and organizing *[zuzhi]* all ground force, naval, and air force operations *[zuozhan]* and movements *[xingdong]*, all construction, training, political work, logistics, militia, reserves, mobilization, people's air defense and airport construction, and so on."[122] There is little doubt that, at this operational level, the Headquarters Department enjoys command authority over the other departments and services. The MR commander *(silingyuan)* and chief of staff *(canmou zhang)* invariably come from the ground forces.[123] Each MR commander has ground and air forces under his command. The ground forces consist of several group armies (see below), independent units (usually of brigade strength), reserve units, and some local forces.

THE ARMED SERVICES

The most notable fact about the physical deployment of Chinese military forces and major conventional weapons platforms is that they have not changed demonstrably since the end of the Cold War. There have been marginal additions in weapons systems and technologies to the PLA's naval and air forces, considerable changes in doctrine and tactics, and some internal organizational changes in the command and control structure of the ground forces, but there has been no appreciable change in force deployments. Thus, China's altered national security environment (see chapter 7) has *not* resulted in the redeployment from one theater (and potential threat) to another. Forces remain essentially as they were deployed in the mid-1980s in the northern sector and since the mid-1970s in the southeastern and southwestern sectors. There has been a substantial demobilization of service personnel since the mid-1980s (approximately 1.1 million between 1985 and 1996, and an additional 500,000 from 1996 to

---

122. Ibid.
123. Ibid., and p. 189.

2000).[124] This large-scale force reduction has resulted in part from the decline in the land-based threat formerly posed by the Soviet Union, but the demobilization has supported the regime's desire to create a real internal paramilitary security force out of the People's Armed Police (into which many demobilized personnel have been moved),[125] as well as the desire to streamline the PLA's bloated force structure and to make it a more effective fighting force. The last significant redeployment of PLA ground forces came in the wake of the Sino-American rapprochement in the early 1970s, when forces were drawn down opposite Taiwan and redeployed to the Soviet and (later) Vietnamese frontiers.

The force reductions of the late 1980s and late 1990s were efforts to streamline and upgrade the readiness of forces, rather than to redeploy them. The numerical reductions were paralleled by organizational changes. In the first round, the CMC decided at a special meeting in July 1985 that thirty-six ground force corps-level units *(junji)* were to be reorganized or disbanded, including twelve ground force field headquarters and at least one MR Air Force Headquarters.[126] The remaining ground forces were reconfigured into twenty-four group army *(jituan jun)* commands,[127] but again there was no significant redeployment between military regions (MR). In 1985, the PLA's eleven MRs were amalgamated into seven. During the late 1980s and early 1990s, many border defense divisions in the Heilongjiang Military District along the Russian border were reduced or eliminated—probably as a good-faith gesture in support of the Sino-Russian border talks. Then, in the late 1990s, three additional group armies were demobilized in Beijing, Shenyang, and Jinan military regions (fourteen PLA divisions nationwide were transferred to the PAP). These were superfluous units and made little difference in the PLA's order of battle. Aside from these minor changes and the aforementioned withdrawal of units 100 kilometers all along the frontier, consistent with the 1996 and 1997 accords, there has been little change

124. The best study of this subject is Yitzhak Shichor, "Demobilization: The Dialectics of PLA Troop Reduction," in David Shambaugh and Richard H. Yang, eds., *China's Military in Transition* (Oxford: Oxford University Press, 1997), pp. 72–95.

125. The best study of the People's Armed Police published to date is Dennis J. Blasko and John F. Corbett, "No More Tiananmens: The People's Armed Police and Stability, 1997," *China Strategic Review,* Spring 1998, pp. 80–103. Also see Murray Scot Tanner, "The Institutional Lessons of Disaster: Reorganizing the People's Armed Police after Tiananmen" (paper presented at the 2000 CAPS/RAND Conference "The PLA as Organization").

126. Academy of Military Sciences History Research Department, ed., *Zhongguo Renmin Jiefangjun de Qishinian*, p. 624.

127. Ibid.

in China's force structure and deployments in the Sino-Russian theater since the amelioration of tensions and formation of a "strategic partnership." The 23d Group Army remains garrisoned at Harbin, the 16th Group Army near Changchun, with two group armies (39th, 40th) in the Liaoning Military District (at Liaoyang and Jinzhou). The Beijing MR, and its subordinate Hebei and Shanxi military districts, still possess the heaviest concentration of ground forces in China. Five GAs are garrisoned in this region (the 24th, 27th, 38th, 63d, and 65th). They continue to be deployed along traditional invasion routes from the north. The Jinan MR, with responsibility for the Shandong peninsula and Henan province, is home to three GAs (the 20th, 26th, and 54th). The Nanjing MR, with responsibility for defending the southeastern coastline from north of Shanghai to the southern perimeter of Taiwan, contains three GAs (the 1st, 12th, and 31st). The Guangzhou, Chengdu, and Lanzhou MRs each contain two GAs. The deployment of the PLA's Group Armies today is shown in table 3.[128]

Chinese ground forces remain predominantly and heavily concentrated around the capital and Bohai Gulf regions. To reiterate, there has been no appreciable change in this garrisoning pattern for many years, and certainly not since the end of the Cold War and the declining threat from the former Soviet Union/Russia. Ground forces are still deployed along the major approaches from the north to the capital. Elsewhere in north China, they are garrisoned near strategic rail junctions and provincial population centers. These deployments are still congruent with a defensive "people's war" orientation, rather than the more recent peripherally oriented, limited war doctrine. In the south, no increase in forces opposite Taiwan or in southern China concomitant with the increased tensions in these theaters in recent years has been noted, although there *has* been a significant buildup in weaponry—particularly short and medium-range ballistic missiles—in the Nanjing MR since the early 1990s. The ground forces deployed near Taiwan have been there since the early 1970s and are far from adequate for an amphibious operation across the Strait. Although the necessary units could be moved fairly rapidly by rail and air into the Taiwan theater, those on the spot remain far short of what would be necessary to mount an invasion of the island.

128. This table is derived from Dennis Blasko, "PLA Ground Forces" (paper presented at the 2000 CAPS/RAND Conference "The PLA as Organization"); and Robert Karniol, "Modernizing PLA Ground Forces" (paper presented at Jane's Information Group Conference on "China's Military Modernization: Strategic and Regional Implications," Rosslyn, Virginia, May 2000). Blasko's paper breaks down each Group Army into its constituent units in considerable detail. Also see *Directory of PRC Military Personalities,* various years.

TABLE 3 PLA Main Ground Force Deployments in 2000

Military Region	Military District	City	Est. Strength
Beijing			410,000
24th GA	Hebei	Chengde	
27th GA	Hebei	Shijiazhuang	
38th Mechanized GA	Hebei	Baoding	
63d GA	Shanxi	Taiyuan	
65th GA	Hebei	Zhangjiakou	
Beijing Garrison	Beijing	Beijing	
Tianjin Garrison	Tianjin	Tianjin	
Shenyang			300,000
16th GA	Jilin	Changchun	
23d GA	Heilongjiang	Harbin	
39th Mechanized GA	Liaoning	Liaoyang	
40th GA	Liaoning	Jinzhou	
Lanzhou			220,000
21st GA	Shaanxi	Baoji	
47th GA	Shaanxi	Lintong	
Jinan			240,000
20th GA	Henan	Kaifeng	
26th GA	Shandong	Laiyang	
54th GA	Henan	Xinxiang	
Chengdu			180,000
13th GA	Sichuan	Chongqing	
14th GA	Yunnan	Kunming	
Chongqing Garrison	Chongqing	Chongqing	
Guangzhou			180,000
41st GA	Guangxi	Liuzhou	
42d GA	Guangdong	Huizhou	
15th Airborne Corps	Hubei	Wuhan	
Hong Kong Garrison	H.K. SAR	Hong Kong	
Zhuhai-Macao Garrison	Zhuhai-Macao SAR	Macao	
Nanjing			300,000
1st GA	Zhejiang	Huzhou	
12th GA	Jiangsu	Xuzhou	
31st GA	Fujian	Xiamen	
Shanghai Garrison	Shanghai	Shanghai	

One must conclude, therefore, that PLA ground forces are not deployed for the purposes of power projection, but rather in defensive positions:

· to cover principal border regions and avenues of approach into eastern China

· to defend the capital

· to defend population and industrial centers

· near key internal lines of communication and transport (particularly rail networks)

· in optimal locations for maintaining internal security

Furthermore, given the increased expenditure on the PLA during the 1990s in upgrading barracks, bases, and quality of life for its personnel, it seems unlikely that major redeployments are in the offing. This does not preclude further troop reductions or reorganizations in the future. Further cuts in the least well-equipped and combat-ready ground forces can be expected. Some units may be disbanded outright, while others may be moved over to the People's Armed Police, as occurred in 1996–97 with the transfer of fourteen PLA divisions nationwide. These were so-called category 2 and 3 forces *(yilei* and *binglei budui)*. For the most part, these forces changed uniforms and missions but not locale. There was minimal regarrisoning or redeployment. Given the top-heavy force structure in north China and the reduced threat in that theater, further cuts will likely come out of the Beijing, Jinan, and Shenyang MRs. The most recent phase of downsizing and streamlining (1997–2000) was intended to reduce the ground forces by 19 percent, the air force by 11 percent, and the navy by 11.6 percent.[129] In addition, the PLA intended to cut the number of conscripts from 82 percent of its total force to less than 65 percent by 2000, and reduced the length of service to two years for all services.[130]

Air and naval deployments have also exhibited little change in recent years. While some new platforms have come onstream and there has been incremental upgrading of armaments, there has been no appreciable redeployment of air or naval forces. China's three naval fleets retain essentially the same complement that they had a decade ago, and their basing

129. Interview, CIISS, December 6, 1998. Similar figures are provided in Information Office of the State Council, "White Paper: China's National Defense," July 27, 1998.

130. "Army Seeks Mobility in Force Cuts," *Jane's Defense Weekly*, December 16, 1998, p. 24.

modes are unchanged (see below). The air force is based in a more diversified fashion than either the ground or naval forces, with a particular concentration of air bases within a 500 nautical-mile radius of Taiwan in the Nanjing and Guangzhou MRs (see chapter 7). Approximately 1,600 of the PLAAF's inventory of 2,748 fighter-interceptors are based in this area.[131] Given the PLAAF's inability to undertake in-flight refueling, this may be an indication of the importance attached to air power in Taiwan contingencies.

Organizationally, each of the services in the PLA has a slightly different structural configuration. This is reflected in the following sections.

THE GROUND FORCES

The ground forces *(lu jun)* have always been the heart and soul of the PLA. Despite considerable reductions and reorganizations in recent years, they remain the dominant service in terms of manpower, resources, doctrine, and prestige. Numerically, they constitute the vast bulk of PLA personnel—approximately 1.6 million out of a total of 2.31 million in 2001.[132] The ground forces of the PLA are configured in three ways: by readiness; by size of unit; and by type of unit.

Units that are at or near full strength and are capable of deploying without additional manpower, equipment, or training are designated category 1 *(jialei* or *jiaxing)* forces and may constitute 30 to 35 percent of total PLA ground forces. Category 2 *(yilei)* units are at 60 to 80 percent readiness and require more ramp-up time before deployment. Today, these probably make up the majority (60 to 65 percent) of units. Prior to the late 1990s, there were also category 3 units *(binglei)* which were far from ready, but some of these units were absorbed into category 2 units, and the majority were disbanded in 1996–97. In fact, the fourteen divisions that were transferred into the PAP at that time were category 3 units. During the 500,000-man reduction in the PLA between 1996 and 2000, three entire group army headquarters were eliminated, leaving a total of twenty-one as of 2000 (further reductions may take place).

In addition, PLA ground forces are configured into eight different sizes

131. International Institute of Strategic Studies, *The Military Balance 1998/99* (Oxford: Oxford University Press, 1998); and Council on Advanced Policy Studies (Taipei), PLA Data Bank (1996).

132. International Institute of Strategic Studies, *The Military Balance 2000/2001* (Oxford: Oxford University Press, 2001), p. 188.

and levels of deployments: group army *(jituan jun)*, division/brigade *(shi/lu)*, regiment *(tuan)*, battalion *(ying)*, company *(lian)*, platoon *(pai)*, and squad *(ban)*. These functional levels are depicted in figure 9 and exist *within* the geographic levels of military region, military district, military subdistrict, and special garrison headquarters.

Functionally, the ground forces are configured into ten separate functional branches *(bingzhong)*, including infantry units *(bu bing)*; armored units *(zhuangjia bing)*; artillery units *(pao bing)*; anti-air units *(fang kong bing)*, anti-chemical units *(fang hua bing)*; electronic countermeasure forces *(dianzi duikang bing)*; communications units *(tongxin bing)*; engineering units *(gongcheng bing)*; cartography *(cehui bing)*; and army aviation *(lujun hangkongbing)*.[133] Infantry units are subdivided into mountain troops *(shandi bubing)*, motorized infantry troops *(motuohua bing)*, and mechanized troops *(jixiehua bing)*. Artillery units include surface artillery troops *(dimian paobing)*, anti-air troops *(gaoshe paobing)*, and surface-to-air missile troops *(dikong daodan bing)*. Armored units include tank units *(tanke budui)*, armored personnel carrier units *(zhuangjia bubing budui)*, anti-artillery units *(fanpao budui)*, anti-tank missile units *(fan tanke daodan budui)*, anti-air units *(fankong budui)*, and anti-chemical units *(fanhua budui)*. Anti-air units include a variety of high and low altitude surface-air units. Some armored units also include amphibious tank units *(shuilu tanke budui)*. Engineering units include pontoon units *(zhouqiao budui)*, construction units *(jianzhu budui)*, engineering protection units *(gongcheng weihu budui)*, camouflage units *(weizhuang budui)*, field operations units *(yezhan budui)*, and amphibious construction units *(shui gongcheng budui)*. Communications units include field *(yezhan)*, fixed *(guding taizhan)*, engineering *(tongxin gongcheng)*, and army postal support *(junyou houwu)* forces.

The total strength of group armies varies (ranging between 40,000 and 90,000 troops), their force structure is configured differently, and they have different complements of weaponry. Only two or three are thought to be fully mechanized, whereas the majority are a combination of some tank or motorized brigades together with infantry, artillery, and anti-chemical units. Group armies are normally configured with two or three infantry divisions, one tank division and/or brigade, one artillery division or brigade, an anti-aircraft brigade, a communications regiment, an engineering regiment, and

133. Zhang, ed., *Dangdai Shijie Junshi yu Zhongguo Guofang*, pp. 310–11; Li, *Zhongguo Zhengfu Zhidu*, pp. 305–6; Academy of Military Sciences, ed., *Shijie Junshi Nianjian 1999*, p. 104. The following breakdown of ground force subunits is derived from these sources. For a detailed breakdown of each group army's combat strength, see Blasko, "PLA Ground Forces."

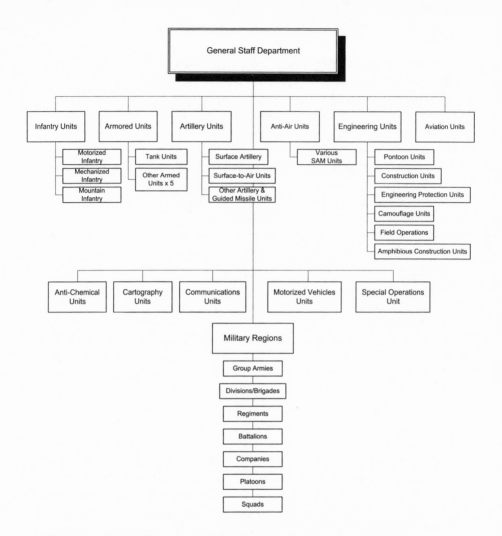

Figure 9.   Command structure of the PLA Ground Forces. *Sources:* Zhang Wannian, ed., *Dangdai Shijie Junshi yu Zhongguo Guofang* (Beijing: Junshi Kexue Chubanshe, 1999); Academy of Military Sciences, ed., *Shijie Junshi Nianjian 2000* (Beijing: Junshi Kexue Chubanshe, 2000); *Directory of PRC Military Personalities, 2000* (Honolulu: Serold Hawaii Inc., 2001).

logistical support units.[134] Each group army is commanded by a major general *(junzhang)*.[135] Some group armies have special operations units *(tezhong zuozhan budui)*, and a few have heliborne units and airlift capacity. In their attempt to become more mobile and rapidly deployable, since the mid 1990s, the group armies have been downsizing some divisions to brigade strength. In 1996, the International Institute of Strategic Studies (IISS) estimated that group armies were almost completely made up of division-strength units (90), but by 2000 it estimated that the number of divisions had been reduced to 59 (44 infantry, 10 tank, and 5 artillery divisions), while the number of brigades had grown from 7 to an estimated 45 (13 infantry, 20 artillery, and 20 tank).[136] In an official report to Congress in 2000, the U.S. Department of Defense estimated that PLA ground forces possessed "some 40 maneuver divisions and approximately 40 maneuver brigades."[137] A "maneuver" unit is considered to be a mobile infantry or armored unit. The idea of emphasizing brigade-sized units is not only to increase flexibility and mobility but also to improve combined arms. Also, some division-designated units were actually under strength. Brigade-strength units normally consist of about 1,000 to 2,500 troops, depending on the type of brigade. A visit to the Sixth Artillery Brigade of the Beijing Military Region in Ping'gu in December 1998 revealed unit manpower of 1,700 enlisted men, 220 noncommissioned officers, and 340 officers.[138] The brigade consisted of five battalions and a variety of field artillery (both towed and self-propelled).

Not every group army yet possesses a rapid reaction unit *(kuaisu fanying budui)*, or RRU, although this is the eventual goal. At present, each military region has at least one unit of division and/or brigade strength designated as an RRU. Currently, the PLA is estimated to have three RRUs capable of being deployed anywhere in the nation within forty-eight hours, with each MR possessing at least one RRU capable of deploying within that region in equal time.[139] This amounts to a maximum of 35,000 personnel, but is more

134. International Institute of Strategic Studies, *The Military Balance 1999/2000* (Oxford: Oxford University Press, 1999), p. 186.

135. Blasko, "PLA Ground Forces."

136. International Institute of Strategic Studies, *Military Balance 1999/2000*, p. 186. Id., *The Military Balance 2001/2002* (Oxford: Oxford University Press, 2001), gives almost identical numbers, suggesting that the readjustments of divisions relative to brigades had largely been completed by 2000.

137. U.S. Department of Defense, Report to Congress Pursuant to the F Y 2000 National Defense Authorization Act, June 2000, as cited in Blasko, "PLA Ground Forces."

138. Author's notes and Blasko, "PLA Ground Forces."

139. International Institute of Strategic Studies, *Military Balance 2001/2002*, p. 188, estimates three RRUs capable of deploying nationally, and nine more with

likely half this number.[140] Since group armies lack airlift capability, and the PLA air force has only very limited airlift assets, the RRUs almost always deploy by road and rail. As they acquire more helicopters, their rapid reaction capacity will grow. Presently, there are only about 130 transport helicopters active in the entire PLA—about half of which are Russian-built Mi-17, Mi-6, and Mi-8s, while the other half are Chinese Z-9s.[141] Most of the 24 Sikorsky Blackhawk helicopters sold by the United States to the PLA in the 1980s are thought to be no longer functional, owing to a lack of spare parts as a result of the post-1989 sanctions. Increasing ground force aviation units *(lujun hangkongbing budui)* is a priority for the PLA in the coming years. The PLAAF's 15th Airborne Corps, based at Wuhan, is one of the best RRUs in the nation, and the 124th Division of the 42d Group Army in the Guangzhou MR and the 162d Division of the 54th Group Army in Jinan MR are also of high standard.

PLA ground forces have thus undergone, and continue to undergo, substantial aggregate downsizing (over 1.5 million personnel in fifteen years), reorganization to emphasize smaller and more mobile units, have increased emphasis on combined arms and joint operations, and are trying to integrate electronic and information technologies into their training. Considering the size and disposition of the ground forces fifteen years ago, the changes are considerable—even if their physical deployment has not changed much over time. For a military that has always been dominated by ground forces and possesses a distinct continental approach to defense, these have been difficult changes to make and adjust to. Yet they are necessary if the PLA is truly going to be able to fight "limited wars under high-technology conditions."

THE PLA AIR FORCE

The PLAAF is a separate service *(junzhong)*, but is very much secondary to the ground forces.[142] The PLAAF's commander is equivalent in rank only

---

MR deployment capability, while the U.S. Defense Department estimates a total of fourteen. See U.S. Department of Defense, *Report to Congress Pursuant to the FY 2000 National Defense Authorization Act.*

140. Karniol, "Modernizing PLA Ground Forces."

141. See Luke G. S. Colton, "Bamboo Blades: The Rise of China's Army Aviation," *Rotor and Wing,* January 2000, pp. 42–47.

142. I am most grateful to Ken Allen for his extensive input into this section.

to the commander of a military region, rather than to the chief of the General Staff (who commands the ground forces).

Analysis of the background for the PLAAF's commanders and deputy commanders provides some insights into the evolution of the PLAAF's role within the PLA. Since 1949, the PLAAF has had nine commanders, ten political commissars, and thirty-two deputy commanders, including four commanders during the past ten years.[143] Prior to the early 1980s, all of the PLAAF's leaders were ground force officers who moved into air force command positions in mid-career. In 1985, Wang Hai became the first aviator to be selected as the commander. Since then, all of the PLAAF's commanders have been career aviators.[144] When ranks were reinstituted in 1988, Wang Hai, who had already held the position for three years, was sixty years old. In recent years, the PLAAF has made a concerted effort to appoint younger leaders.

Although the PLAAF has succeeded in reducing the age of its leadership, as a result it no longer has any leaders with combat experience.[145] When Wang Hai was commander (1985–92), three of the four PLAAF headquarters deputy commanders, three of the military region air force (MRAF) commanders, and two deputy MRAF commanders were Korean War veterans. By the early 1990s, almost all of these officers had retired. The experience today's leaders bring with them comes primarily from the Vietnam War of the 1960s, where the PLAAF's main involvement was its anti-aircraft artillery troops stationed inside Vietnam and Laos, plus a handful of air engagements along the border.

143. The PLAAF's nine commanders since 1949 have been: Liu Yalou (October 1949–May 1965), Wu Faxian (May 1965–September 1971), no commander (September 1971–May 1973), Ma Ning (May 1973–April 1977), Zhang Tingfa (April 1977–July 1985), Wang Hai (July 1985–November 1992), Cao Shuangming (November 1992–November 1994), Yu Zhenwu (November 1994–December 1996), Liu Shunyao (December 1996–February 2002); Qiao Qingchen (February 2002–present).

144. When ranks were restored in October 1988, the PLAAF was allotted one three-star position, which went to the commander, Wang Hai. An analysis of PLAAF leader biographies (Zhu Rongchang) reveals that at least thirty-two officers received the rank of lieutenant general, nineteen of whom were sixty years old or older. The total number included the political commissar and all of the deputy commanders and commissars. As for the MRAFs, seven commanders and four political commissars became lieutenant generals (the remaining three political commissars were promoted in 1990). There were also several MRAF deputy commanders and political commissars who received this rank. Many of the lieutenant generals retired within a couple of years and the position reverted to a major general billet.

145. Although the PLAAF has some input into the selection of its leaders, the senior army leadership is responsible for promoting the top PLAAF officers.

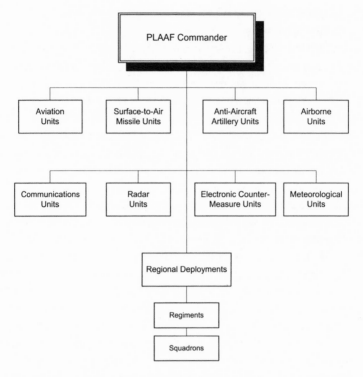

Figure 10.   Command structure of the PLA Air Force. *Source:* Zhang
Wannian, ed., *Dangdai Shijie Junshi yu Zhongguo Guofang* (Beijing:
Junshi Kexue Chubanshe, 1999).

The PLAAF today has about 420,000 personnel in all, as compared with
1.6 million in the ground forces.[146] Its extensive inventory of aircraft and
surface-to-air missiles (SAMs) is largely antiquated (see chapter 6), despite
recent acquisitions of new Russian-built Su-27 and Su-30 fighters, Il-76
transports, and S-300 SAMs. Although airpower and the air force have
definitely received increased priority in doctrinal and financial terms in recent years, the PLAAF remains an obsolescent force.

The PLAAF is divided into eight operational branches *(bingzhong):* aviation units *(hangkong bing);* surface-to-air missile units *(dikong daodan
bing);* anti-aircraft artillery units *(gaoshe pao bing),* or AAA; airborne units
(kongjiang bing); radar units *(leida bing);* communications units *(tongxin*

146. International Institute of Strategic Studies, *Military Balance 2001/2002,*
pp. 189–90.

bing); electronic countermeasure units *(dianzi duikang bing)*; and meteorological units *(qixiang bing)*.

According to a 1999 U.S. Department of Defense report, the PLAAF's combat aircraft are currently organized into some thirty air divisions, plus about 150 transport aircraft organized in two air divisions, compared to the total of fifty air divisions that existed in the late 1980s.[147] In 2000, the PLAAF consisted of thirty-three divisions, including twenty-seven fighter, four bomber, and two transport divisions.[148] Over 1,000 older aircraft have been decommissioned over the past decade, and the remaining 2,000 F-6s (the last of which was produced in 1979) should be retired within the next few years.

A typical PLAAF air division *(shi)* consists of three regiments *(tuan)*, each of which is assigned from 25 to 32 aircraft, but may actually have more or fewer. Each division has two or three airfields, with one or two regiments per airfield. The regiment is the basic organization for training and operations. Each regiment has three flying groups *(dadui)* and one aircraft maintenance group. Each flying group is further divided into three squadrons *(zhongdui)*, with one or two assigned to each aircraft. Although the pilots are assigned to squadrons, each with three to five pilots, the aircraft are assigned to the regiment as a whole, not just to the squadrons. Each pilot, however, normally only flies one to three planes, so that they become familiar with each aircraft's handling capabilities. In the 1980s, age limits of 43 to 45 were established for PLAAF fighter and ground-attack pilots; 47 to 50 for helicopter pilots; 48 to 50 for bomber pilots; and 55 for transport pilots.

Since 1985, the PLAAF has experimented with various organizational structures for its AAA, SAM, and airborne branches. Prior to that time, SAM and AAA units were structured as separate organizations. In most cases, they were organized into divisions, with their subordinate regiments. In other cases, the regiment or brigade was the highest-level structure. In 1985, the PLAAF began restructuring some of the regiments into combined brigades, with the goal of eventually combining as many SAM and AAA units as possible. The process involved turning over most of the AAA to the ground forces, while merging some of the remaining AAA regiments and SAM regiments into combined brigades. By the end of the 1980s, all of the SAM and

147. *The Security Situation in the Taiwan Strait*, Report submitted by Secretary of Defense William Cohen to the U.S. Senate as directed by the FY 1999 Appropriations Bill, February 17, 1999.

148. Robert Sae-Liu, "PLAAF Fixed-Wing Fleet Cut in Major Restructuring," *Jane's Defense Weekly*, June 14, 2000, 41. The article says that the PLAAF has sixteen active air defense (AAA/SAM) divisions.

AAA divisions had apparently been abolished, but some individual SAM and AAA regiments and brigades still existed. By the end of the 1990s, however, the PLAAF had reinstituted the division level, at least for SAMs, and had apparently increased some, if not all, of the combined brigades to a combined division level. This change probably reflects the PLAAF's acquisition of the S-300 surface-to-air missile batteries from Russia, plus the recognition that the combined brigades may not be the best solution to accomplishing the air defense mission.

The organization of airborne forces has also come full circle. These began in the early 1950s as a single brigade and then expanded to become a division. In 1961, the CMC redesignated the PLA's 15th Army as the PLAAF 15th Airborne Army and subordinated the original airborne division to this new organization. By the mid 1970s, this unit had three airborne divisions. Sometime after 1984, the three divisions were reduced to brigades, but they were enlarged again to divisions in 1993, each with about 10,000 troops.

During the 1980s and early 1990s, the basic radar unit was the regiment, but some radar brigades have been noted over the past few years. This indicates that the number of radar units in each military region has grown considerably, thus necessitating higher-level headquarters to maintain proper control.

The PLAAF's combat units, including its surface-to-air missile and antiaircraft artillery air defense units, are directly subordinate to one of four headquarters: Headquarters Air Force in Beijing; one of the seven military region air force Headquarters (Shenyang, Beijing, Lanzhou, Nanjing, Guangzhou, Jinan, and Chengdu); one of five air corps (1st/Changchun, 7th/Nanning, 8th/Fuzhou, 9th/Wulumuqi, and 10th/Datong); or one of six bases that are equivalent to an air corps (Dalian, Tangshan, Xian, Shanghai, Wuhan, and Lhasa). Since each MR covers from two to five provinces, the air corps and bases are located in provinces other than the MRAF headquarters province. The number of aviation and air defense units each headquarters controls depends upon the units located in its area of responsibility.[149]

Today, the administrative structure of the PLAAF consists of four major departments (headquarters, political, logistics, and equipment), reflecting the organizational structure of the four general departments (general staff, political, logistics, and armament). This structure is mirrored through the administrative and operational chain of command from Headquarters Air Force

149. Kenneth W. Allen, "PLA Air Force Organization" (paper presented at the 2000 CAPS/RAND Conference "The PLA as Organization").

(HqAF), through the seven military region air forces, five air corps, and six bases, all the way down to the lowest operational units. Besides the administrative elements, the PLAAF consists of the five branches, plus various communications, logistics, and maintenance support elements, repair facilities, hospitals, schools, and research institutes. This command structure is represented in figure 10. In peacetime, PLAAF bases and troops come under the command authority of the PLA General Staff via the MR commanders, and this authority is strengthened in wartime.

The PLA Navy

The PLA Navy (PLAN) is headquartered in Beijing and consists of three fleet commands, each of which consists of seven to ten coastal defense zones (which include coastal artillery and missile batteries).[150] Functionally, the PLAN is configured into five types of units: naval ship units *(jianting budui)*, submarine units *(qianting budui)*, naval aviation units *(haijun hangkong-bing)*, coastal defense units *(anfang bing)*, and marine units *(haijun luzhan dui)*. The small naval air force (PLANAF) has detachments in all three fleet commands, and two marine brigades *(haijun luzhan dui)*, consisting of rapidly deployable infantry, artillery, armor, and reconnaissance *(zhencha bing)* units, are based in the South Sea Fleet.

The North Sea Fleet is headquartered at Qingdao in Shandong Province, with an area of responsibility (AOR) from the Yalu River, on the border between China and North Korea, down to Lianyu Harbor in Jiangsu Province. This area encompasses the Beijing, Shenyang, and Jinan MRs and includes responsibility for the Bohai Gulf and Yellow Sea. In addition to Qingdao, principal bases for the North Sea Fleet are located at Lushun, Xiaopingdao, Dalian, Huludao, Weihai, Chengshan, Qingshan, Lianyungang, Lingshanwei, Dahushan, Yushan, Yuchi, and other facilities.

The East Sea Fleet headquarters are at Ningbo, near Shanghai. Its AOR stretches from the southern half of the Yellow Sea in the north down to Dongshan in Fujian Province. This includes the entire East China Sea and the sensitive Taiwan Strait, and parallels the Nanjing MR. In addition to Ningbo, principal bases include Shanghai, Dinghai, Zhoushan, Hangzhou, Fuzhou, Wusong, Wenzhou, Xiamen, Xinxiang, and Xiangshan.

The South Sea Fleet headquarters are at Zhanjiang in Guangdong Province, and its AOR includes the entire South China Sea (including the disputed Paracel and Spratly island groups), the Beibu Gulf near Vietnam

150. Li, *Zhongguo Zhengfu Zhidu,* p. 307.

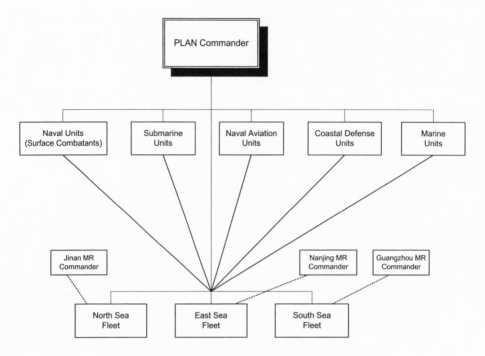

Figure 11. Command structure of the PLA Navy. *Source:* Zhang Wannian, ed., *Dangdai Shijie Junshi yu Zhongguo Guofang* (Beijing: Junshi Kexue Chubanshe, 1999).

and Hainan Island, and the remainder of the Guangzhou Military Region. Other bases include Hong Kong, Shantou, Guangzhou, Haikou, Humen, Beihai, Ping'tan, Sanzhou, Dong'guan, Yulin (Hainan), Lingshui, and other coastal facilities. Both PLAN marine brigades (approximately 7,000 men) are attached to the South Sea Fleet, are trained for various amphibious operations, and are supported by amphibious tanks and APCs, howitzers, and multiple rocket launchers.

Each fleet possesses surface, subsurface (submarine), and naval air units. Each fleet is assigned three divisions of the PLANAF (a division usually includes eight aircraft).[151] The surface combatants are distributed fairly

151. Bernard D. Cole, "The Organization of the People's Liberation Army Navy" (paper presented at the 2000 CAPS/RAND Conference "The PLA as Organization"). This section draws heavily on Professor Cole's paper and insights, for

equally to all three fleets, including the most recent additions of destroyers of the Luhu, Luhai, and Sovremenny classes (see chapter 6). PLAN scholar Professor Bernard Cole of the U.S. National War College has identified six or seven flotillas of submarines in the three fleets:

- · North Sea Fleet: 2d, 12th, 62d (including all six nuclear-powered submarines)
- · East Sea Fleet: 22d and 42d (including all four Kilo-class submarines)
- · South Sea Fleet: 32d and maybe one other flotilla

Each fleet also has a complement of frigates, coastal patrol craft, mine warfare vessels, amphibious assault ships, and various transport and support vessels. Each fleet commander serves as a deputy commander of the relevant military region(s), as does his PLAAF counterpart, and has a dual responsibility to PLAN Headquarters in Beijing and the MR commander (a GSD ground force commander). In wartime, this chain of command is strengthened, and the PLAN commanders in MRs and theaters of operation *(zhanqu)* are firmly subordinated to the GSD ground force commander.[152] This is, of course, not a system conducive to combat agility and freedom of maneuver, and its inflexibility could prove deleterious in time of war.

The PLAN is relatively small. The IISS lists a total of 250,000 personnel,[153] although a recent study by the U.S. Naval attaché in China lists a total of 268,000, including 28,000 coastal defense troops, 25,000 naval air personnel, and 7,000 marines.[154] The PLAN is certainly a growing and increasingly important service, because the PLA emphasizes littoral defense and limited peripheral war. Its equipment is being modernized more quickly than that of other services, and its budget has increased more rapidly in recent years than those of the ground forces or the PLAAF (although the Second Artillery's has risen the fastest).[155] Because of China's growing regional

---

which the author is grateful. More recently, Cole has published the definitive study of the PLAN: *The Great Wall at Sea: China's Navy Enters the Twenty-First Century* (Annapolis, Md.: Naval Institute Press, 2001). See also Srikanta Kondapali, *China's Naval Power* (New Delhi: Institute for Defense Studies and Analyses, 2001).

152. Lei et al., eds., *Lujun Junzhixue.*

153. International Institute of Strategic Studies, *Military Balance 2001/2002,* p. 188.

154. Brad Kaplan, "China's Navy Today," *Navy League of the United States,* Internet edition, June 2001.

155. Interview, Academy of Military Sciences, May 20, 2000.

security interests, as well as Taiwan contingencies, the PLAN's importance and resources are likely to continue to increase.

The Second Artillery

The PLA took the decision to build a strategic missile force,[156] and the first surface-to-surface missile battalion, in December 1957.[157] After March 1960, some military regions began to form similar battalions *(ying)*, and in 1964 they were all elevated to regiment *(tuan)* status.[158] But the Second Artillery was not formally established until the Central Committee and Central Military Commission approved it on June 6, 1966, just as the Cultural Revolution was getting under way.[159] At the meeting, seeking to distinguish it from the PLA's existing Artillery Corps, Premier Zhou Enlai dubbed the new force the "Second Artillery" (Di Er Pao Bing). It was thereby decided that the CMC's Strategic Missile Force Organ (Zhongyang Junwei Zhanlüe Daodan Budui Jiguan), which had commanded these forces since their inception in 1957, should be combined together with the CMC's Artillery Leadership Organ (Paobing Lingdao Jiguan) and the Ministry of Public Security Leadership Organ to form a new Surface-to-Surface Strategic Missile Force Leadership Organ (Didi Zhanlüe Daodan Budui Lingdao Jiguan).[160]

From the beginning, the Second Artillery has maintained the PLA's arsenal of both conventional and nuclear-armed missiles. In 1968, Second Artillery regiments were divided into short-range *(jincheng)*, intermediate-range *(zhongcheng)*, long-range *(yuancheng)*, and intercontinental *(zhouji)* units—although the Er Pao would not successfully test an ICBM until 1980.[161] After the division, the strategic missile forces *(zhanlüe daodan budui)* were further separated administratively.

Organizationally, the Second Artillery does not enjoy the full status of a service *(junzhong)* of the PLA, like the air force or navy. Rather, since its creation, the Second Artillery has been only a service arm *(bingzhong)* and is a half rank lower bureaucratically than the other services, although its

---

156. There are some indications that this decision was taken October 1956. Citing Chinese sources, see Bates Gill, James Mulvenon, and Mark Stokes, "The Chinese Second Artillery Corps: Transition to Credible Deterrence" (paper presented at the 2000 CAPS/RAND Conference "The PLA as Organization").

157. Yao et al., eds., *Junshi Zuzhi Tizhi Yanjiu,* p. 395.

158. Ibid.

159. Liu, ed., *Zhongguo Junshi Zhidu Shi,* p. 555; *Zhongguo Renmin Jiefangjun de Qishinian,* p. 575.

160. *Zhongguo Renmin Jiefangjun de Qishinian.*

161. Yao et al., eds., *Junshi Zuzhi Tizhi Yanjiu,* p. 395.

command chain is directly linked to the CMC via the GSD.[162] From its inception, internal PLA sources assert that it has been under the direct centralized command and control of the CMC.[163] Orders most likely pass from the CMC to the Er Pao via the GSD. It is not certain exactly how the communication to launch missiles is conveyed via the GSD, but it is believed that there are also separate and secure communication lines from the CMC to Second Artillery Headquarters and thence to all launch brigades. It is also understood that a launch brigade must receive separate communications from the CMC and GSD before a launch is authorized. Second Artillery Headquarters also oversee warhead and missile storage facilities, maintenance units, and special transportation services for moving missiles and warheads.[164]

The Second Artillery's internal organization, aside from the Headquarters Department, is shown in figure 12.

There are four first-level departments and ten second-level departments in the Second Artillery.[165] First-level departments have subunits that parallel the internal structure of the four general headquarters and are to be found in the other services.[166] The internal organization of the second-level departments is not clear, and only a single internal PLA published source has detailed the bureaus themselves.[167]

The Second Artillery's ballistic missile arsenal is dispersed across China.[168] The Second Artillery headquarters complex at Qinghe (on the road to the Badaling section of the Great Wall on the northwest outskirts of Beijing near

162. Gill, Mulvenon, and Stokes, "Chinese Second Artillery Corps."

163. Yao et al., eds., *Junshi Zuzhi Tizhi Yanjiu*, p. 372; Pu, *Zhonghua Renmin Gongheguo Zhengzhi Zhidu*, 563.

164. Gill, Mulvenon, and Stokes, "Chinese Second Artillery Corps."

165. Sources for first-level departments include Liu, ed., *Junshi Zuzhi Tizhi Bianzhi Juan*, p. 556. The sole source for second-level departments is Yao et al., eds., *Junshi Zuzhi Tizhi Yanjiu*, p. 396.

166. For a breakout of these, see Gill, Mulvenon, and Stokes, "Chinese Second Artillery Corps."

167. Yao et al., eds., *Junshi Zuzhi Tizhi Yanjiu*, p. 396.

168. Data in this section are derived from the *Directory of PRC Military Personalities, 2000*; Mark A. Stokes, *China's Strategic Modernization: Implications for U.S. National Security* (Carlisle Barracks, Pa.: U.S. Army War College Strategic Studies Institute, 1999); Gill, Mulvenon, and Stokes, "Chinese Second Artillery Corps"; William M. Arkin, Robert S. Norris, and Joshua Handler, *Taking Stock: Worldwide Nuclear Deployments 1998* (Washington, D.C.: National Resources Defense Council Nuclear Program, 1998), app. H, p. 89; Federation of American Scientists, "China—Missile Facilities," at www.fas.org/nuke/guide/china/facility/missile.html (August 17, 2001).

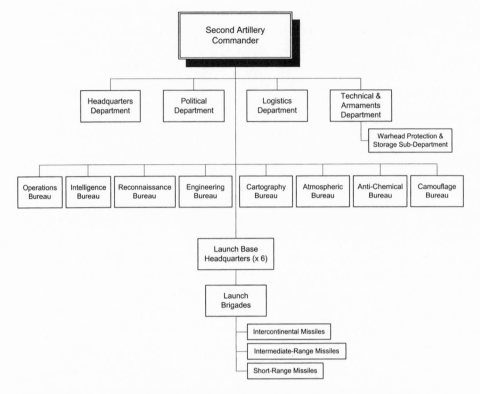

Figure 12.   Command structure of the PLA Second Artillery. *Source:* Zhang Wannian, ed., *Dangdai Shijie Junshi yu Zhongguo Guofang* (Beijing: Junshi Kexue Chubanshe, 1999).

Nankou and Changping) oversees six launch bases, each of corps level *(junji)* size. These are headquartered (launch sites vary) at:

- Shenyang, Liaoning Province (Base No. 51). Five launch brigades: Hancheng (806 Brigade); Dalian (810 Brigade); Jinchang (816 Brigade); Tonghua (818 Brigade); and one mobile brigade. Equipped with DF-3A (CSS-2) and DF-21 (CSS-5) IRBMs, with range to cover the Korean peninsula, Japan and Okinawa, and the Russian Far East.

- Huangshan (Tunxi), Anhui Province (Base No. 52). Four brigades: Shitai, Anhui (807 Brigade); Qimen, Jiangxi (811 Brigade); Leping, Jiangxi (815 Brigade); Yingtan, Jiangxi (817 Brigade). Equipped with DF-15 (CSS-6) and DF-3A (CSS-2) SRBMs and IRBMs, with range to cover the Taiwan theater.

· Kunming, Yunnan Province (Base No. 53). Two brigades in Yunnan: Jianshui (802 Brigade) and Chuxiong (808 Brigade). Equipped with DF-3A (CSS-2) and DF-21 (CSS-5) IRBMs, with range to cover South and Southeast Asia.

· Luoyang, Henan Province (Base No. 54). Three brigades in Henan: Lingbao (801 Brigade); Luanchuan (804 Brigade); Yiyang (813 Brigade). Possibly a fourth brigade at Sundian. Equipped with DF-4 (CSS-3) DF-5 (CSS-4) ICBMs, with range to cover Russia, Europe and North America.

· Huaihua, Hunan Province (Base No. 55). Three brigades in Hunan: Jingzhou (803 Brigade); Tongdao (805 Brigade); Huitong (814 Brigade). Equipped with DF-3A (CSS-2), DF-4 (CSS-3) ICBMs, with range to cover Europe, Russia, and North America.

· Xining, Qinghai Province (Base No. 56). Three brigades: Datong, Qinghai (809 Brigade); Wulan, Qinghai (812 Brigade); Hancheng, Shaanxi (806 Brigade). Possibly three other brigades at Da Qaidam, Xiao Qaidam, and Liujihou. Equipped with DF-3A (CSS-2) and DF-4 (CSS-3) ICBMs, with range to cover Central Asia, India, and Russia.

In addition, the Second Artillery maintains test ranges at Jiuquan, Taiyuan, Wuzhai, Xichang, Baoji, and Lop Nur, several stockpile storage facilities, and a number of colleges (including the Missile Forces Academy at Xi'an). The PLA also apparently maintains a crisis command center in a mountain at Xishan in the military district of western Beijing, which includes command, control, and early-warning equipment. The Chinese leadership also has command bunkers at Hohhot in Inner Mongolia and Yuquan Mountain in the Xishan range just west of Beijing, where they could retreat in the case of nuclear attack.[169] The Second Artillery works closely with the sprawling research and development network under the First, Second, Third, Fourth, Fifth, and Ninth Academies. The First Academy is responsible for surface-to-surface missiles and carrier rocket development, the Second Academy for surface-to-air missiles, the Third Academy for coastal defense missiles, the Fourth Academy for solid-propellant rockets, the Fifth Academy for satellites, and the Ninth Academy for tactical air defense and carrier rockets.

The Second Artillery is clearly a favored force of the PLA, and can be expected to grow in resources, personnel (currently approximately 100,000),

---

169. Federation of American Scientists, "China: Command and Control Facilities," at www.fas.org/nuke/guide/china/facility/c3i.html (August 17, 2001).

and weaponry.[170] As it does so, it will continue to evolve organizationally. Perhaps its command and control procedures, as well as launch procedures and stockpile storage, would also change if and when the Second Artillery engaged in dialogue with other established nuclear powers. During the 1990s, for example, the U.S. government attempted to initiate a "strategic dialogue" between the U.S. Strategic Command (STRATCOM) and the Second Artillery, but the effort was rebuffed by the Chinese government.

THE PEOPLE'S ARMED POLICE, MILITIA, AND RESERVES

China maintains a very large paramilitary force. This includes three principal components: the People's Armed Police (Renmin wuzhuang jingcha budui), the People's Militia (Renmin minbing), and PLA Reserve Corps (Yubei budui).

The People's Armed Police

Although the People's Armed Police was officially established on June 19, 1982, its constituent units have histories stretching back to 1949.[171] In September 1949, on the eve of the founding of the People's Republic, a number of paramilitary organs were merged into the newly established PLA Public Security Corps (Jiefangjun gong'an budui), which was placed under the command of General Luo Ruiqing as minister of public security (MPS).[172] The subsequent history of public security forces and paramilitary police is convoluted, with control alternating between the MPS and the PLA.[173] The PAP was formed in 1982 by the merging of a disparate set of military, para-

170. See Stokes, *China's Strategic Modernization*.

171. The most detailed history of the People's Armed Police and the public security and military organs that were amalgamated to form it can be found in the official (internal circulation) history compiled by the MPS. See Zhongguo Renmin Gong'an Shi Gaobian yu Xiaozu, *Zhongguo Renmin Gong'an Shi Gao* (Beijing: Jingguan Jiaoyu Chubanshe, 1996), esp. pp. 413–16.

172. Luo went on to become chief of the General Staff before being purged in 1965.

173. This history is well traced in Tai Ming Cheung, "Guarding China's Domestic Front Line: The People's Armed Police and China's Stability," *China Quarterly*, June 1996, pp. 525–47; and Tanner, "Institutional Lessons of Disaster." See also Blasko and Corbett, "No More Tiananmens"; James Mulvenon, "The Sword and the Shield: Military Control of the People's Armed Police, 1995–1997" (paper presented at the Association for Asian Studies 1997 Annual Meeting); Hugh Ivory, "The Chinese People's Armed Police: Pillar of the People's Democratic Dictatorship," *Washington Journal of Modern China* 4, no. 1 (Fall–Winter 1997): 43–61; Erik Eckholm, "A Secretive Army Grows to Maintain Order in China," *New York Times*, March 28, 1999.

military, and public security forces. Initially, these consisted of border defense *(bianfang)*, internal guard *(difang neiwei)*, transportation *(jiaotong)*, and railway *(tiedao)* units of the PLA,[174] but in 1985, MPS units responsible for water and electricity defense (hydropower), fire fighting, mines, and gold protection were also merged into the new PAP.[175] From an initial force of approximately 400,000, these additions increased PAP numbers to 600,000 by 1988.[176] In the 1990s, a large number of demobilized PLA forces (including the fourteen divisions transferred wholesale in late 1996) swelled the PAP to about 900,000. The addition of Special Police units and new recruits has brought PAP totals today to approximately 1.5 million.[177] Of these, the IISS estimates that approximately 800,000 are responsible for internal security and 100,000 are deployed in border defense and customs roles, while 69,000 work in communications, special operations, guard units, and other specialized functions.[178]

The principal functions of the PAP today are to perform routine border controls and to maintain internal security and quell civil disturbances. PAP units have been deployed numerous times in recent years—against angry farmers, unemployed workers, miners, and separatist groups. In 1989, they were deployed against students and demonstrators in and around Tiananmen Square in Beijing—but failed utterly to control the crowds (hence the PLA was brought in). Since then, the PAP has been revamped, rearmed, retrained, and refurbished. Whether it is capable of quelling a large-scale urban disturbance, like that of 1989, remains an open question—but the Chinese leadership certainly intends the PAP to be prepared to do so and to shoulder the burden of internal security on a national basis. Some designated PAP units have also been established and trained for a variety of special operations (such as responding to hijackings and terrorist threats).

The PAP is under the dual command and control of the State Council and CMC and is considered a constituent element of the armed forces.[179] In Chinese official nomenclature, there is an important distinction between the military *(jundui)* and the armed forces *(wuzhuang budui):* the former is the

---

174. Zhongguo Renmin Gong'an Shi Gaobian yu Xiaozu, *Zhongguo Renmin Gong'an Shi Gao*, p. 414.

175. "Zhongguo Wujing Budui," *Huaxia*, no. 70 (1998): 9–11.

176. Liu Xiaohua, "Armed Police Force: China's One Million Special Armed Troops," *Guang Jiao Jing* (Hong Kong), April 16, 1998, in FBIS–CHI, May 14, 1998.

177. International Institute of Strategic Studies, *Military Balance, 2001/2002*, p. 191. This estimate is 400,000–500,000 higher than others.

178. Ibid.

179. This is specified in Article 22 of the 1997 National Defense Law.

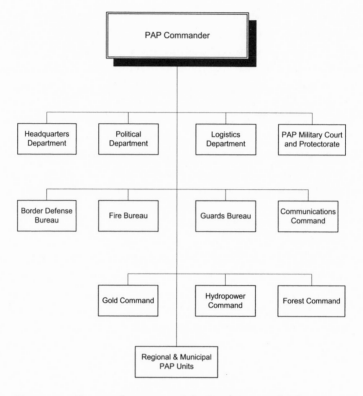

Figure 13. Command structure of the People's Armed Police.

more restrictive term, referring only to the PLA, while the latter encompasses both the PLA and the PAP. Chinese documents often make this distinction but also regularly note that both are under the command authority of the Central Military Commission. After its formal establishment in 1982, the aforementioned units that were merged into the new PAP were removed from the command authority of the Ministry of Public Security. The role of the State Council in managing the PAP is uncertain and probably pro forma (aside from budgetary allocations). An internal Chinese military source simply indicates that the State Council manages the PAP on a "daily basis," while the CMC is specifically in charge of the PAP's personnel, cadre management, orders, training, and political work.[180]

PAP troops are organized into five hierarchical levels: central head-

180. Yao et al., eds., *Junshi Zuzhi Tizhi Yanjiu*, p. 379.

quarters *(zong bu)*, general corps *(zong dui)*, detachment *(zhi dui)*, brigade/battalion *(da dui)*, and company *(zhong dui)*.[181] As in the PLA, each unit has a commander and political commissar. Geographically, the PAP is deployed at province, county, and city or township levels, as well as in the four centrally administered cities of Beijing, Shanghai, Tianjin, and Chongqing (PAP forces in these cities are known to be the best-equipped). Generally speaking, main corps and general corps units are deployed at the level of province or centrally administered city, while a PAP detachment is deployed at the level of prefecture or municipality, a brigade/battalion at the county level, and a company at the township level. There are 31 provinces, 345 prefectures or municipalities, and 2,845 counties in China—and the militia is organized at every level.

The People's Militia

The people's militia *(minbing)* has a long history in modern Chinese history, playing a critical role in local public security and defense when either there was no central military or China was ravaged by competing warlords or paramilitary armies.[182] The Chinese Communists have always seen the local militia as an essential part of the "people's war" strategy of drowning any invader in a sea of humanity. This was particularly the case during the 1960s and 1970s, when China faced possible invasion from the Soviet Union and the population was mobilized for war (the militia swelled to over 100 million and possibly many more). During the 1950s, however, Defense Minister Peng Dehuai had dismissed militia building as militarily useless, a waste of resources, and a potential source of disorder.[183] During the Cultural Revolution, the urban militia (particularly in Shanghai and Nanjing) became embroiled in political factional struggles when the radical Gang of Four attempted to build it up in an effort to have an armed counterweight to military forces controlled by their conservative opponents.[184] After the Cultural Revolution, Chairman Mao's death, and the arrest of the Gang, the militia was deemphasized, disarmed, and demobilized to a considerable

181. Li, ed., *Junshi Zuzhi Tizhi Bianzhi Juan*, p. 591.
182. See Edward McCord, *The Power of the Gun: The Emergence of Modern Chinese Warlordism* (Berkeley and Los Angeles: University of California Press, 1993); Edward McCord, "Local Militia and State Power in Nationalist China," *Modern China* 25, no. 2 (April 1999): 115–41.
183. This pithy description of Peng's position is taken from Jencks, *From Muskets to Missiles*, p. 169.
184. See Thomas C. Roberts, *The Chinese Militia and the Doctrine of People's War* (Washington, D.C.: National Defense University Press, 1983), pp. 51–75.

extent. In 1982, the CMC directed that the size of the national militia should be reduced by 60 percent to total only 10.7 percent of the national population.[185] If this percentage still is in effect, however, the size of China's militia today would be on the order of approximately 140 million!

Prior to the 1990s, the militia was under the dual command of the GSD Mobilization Department (Dongyuan Bu) and the People's Armed Forces Departments (discussed above), which had lines of command leading up to the Central Military Commission—although, for all ostensible purposes, the militia at the county level and below were mainly under the command of the local party committee secretary and the PAFC commander (who was the military subdistrict PLA commander). After the issuance of the Regulations on Militia Work by the State Council and CMC in 1990, the command and control of the militia came under the People's Armed Forces Committees (Renmin wuzhuang weiyuanhui),[186] but by the late 1990s, command and control of the militia was moved more firmly under military control. As codified in the 1997 National Defense Law, the militia is a constituent component of the active armed forces of China (together with the PLA, PAP, People's Armed Forces Committees, and reserves). As such, the militia is operationally controlled by the General Staff Department at the military region level, although ultimate authority resides with the Central Military Commission.[187]

Chinese sources also distinguish between the core *(jigan)* and common *(putong)* and the male and female militia.[188] According to the Military Service Law of the PRC, members of the militia must be between eighteen and thirty-five years of age, shall be physically fit, and "shall undergo military training and be prepared to join the armed forces, fight in wars, and defend the motherland at any time."[189] Training of the core militia is supposed to take place biweekly (although this is unlikely), to be conducted by the PAC at the county level and below, and to include training in formation drill, grenade throwing, shooting, demolition, martial arts, and combat fighting.[190] In addition, core militia units train members to be specialists in ground artillery, anti-aircraft guns, communications, engineering, chemical defense,

185. Li, *Junshi Zuzhi Tizhi Bianzhi Juan,* p. 597.
186. Ibid., pp. 593–94.
187. Zhang, ed., *Dangdai Shijie Junshi yu Zhongguo Guofang,* pp. 226–27.
188. Ibid., p. 228.
189. Nanjing Ground Force Command Academy, "Members of the Militia Must Undergo Training in Accordance with the Law," *Zhongguo Minbing,* no. 2 (February 1998), in FBIS–CHI, April 29, 1998.
190. Ibid.

and reconnaissance.[191] In addition to preparing for combat situations, the militia's main purpose is to mobilize for, and participate in, disaster relief operations. They have been so mobilized several times in recent years as China has fought floods. Other official sources specify further responsibilities of the militia: to assist in economic construction and public works projects; to protect strategic logistics depots, important local buildings, and transport hubs; and to assist in the maintenance of public order.[192]

Reserves

The PLA has been building up its reserve system since 1982, when the CMC issued Order No. 15 instructing lower-level units to organize reserve corps.[193] The reserves generally comprise demobilized servicemen, particularly infantrymen, and members of the militia who have received regular military training. Each service maintains its own reserve system, although at the local level, they are to be commanded by military district commanders. In 1998, the CMC stipulated that each province must have at least one division-size fully ready reserve unit,[194] and today total PLA reserves are estimated to number 500–600,000.[195] Effective January 1, 1997, reserve officers are required to wear uniforms, epaulets, and insignia.

Military Education

Like the militaries of most large nations, the PLA maintains an extensive system of professional military education (PME). China's current military education system dates from the Huangpo Military Academy of the 1920s. Germany, the Soviet Union, and the United States all contributed to developing the system before 1949, but the PLA has dramatically expanded the system since coming to power. Reforming the PME system has been a high priority of the PLA since 1998–99,[196] and a ten-year program to reform the

191. Ibid.

192. Zhang, ed., *Dangdai Shijie Junshi yu Zhongguo Guofang*, p. 227.

193. Liu Xiaohua, "Jiang Zemin Convenes Enlarged Meeting of Central Military Commission—Policy of Fewer, but Better, Troops Aims at Strengthening Reserve Service Units," *Guang Jiao Jing* (Hong Kong), May 16, 1998, in FBIS–CHI, June 10, 1998.

194. Ibid. For an approximate listing of these, see Mel Gurtov and Byong-Moo Hwang, *China's Security: The New Roles of the Military* (Boulder, Colo.: Lynne Reinner, 1998), p. 103.

195. International Institute of Strategic Studies, *Military Balance 2001/2002*, p. 188.

196. See, e.g., the symposium of articles in *Guofang Daxue Xuebao*, no. 1 (1999). Also see "Put Military Academy Education in a Strategic Position of Priority Development," *Jiefangjun Bao*, June 23, 1999, in FBIS–CHI, June 23, 1999.

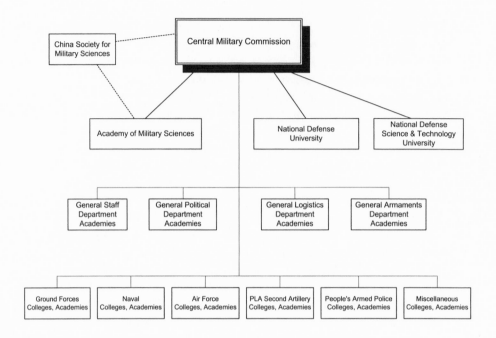

Figure 14. PLA professional military education structure. See figure 17 for subordinate bodies.

system began in 2000.[197] After 1983, it was stipulated that all officers at the platoon level and above should undergo some form of PME. As a result, PME has become a principal criterion for promotion in the PLA officer corps. Pre-military education has also become increasingly important, because all recruits must now possess a senior middle school education, and NCOs and officers should preferably have college degrees (although in practice, this standard has been hard to meet).

Some military educational and research institutions are centrally administered by the CMC—the National Defense University, National Defense Science and Technology University, and Academy of Military Sciences—while all four general headquarters departments and each service arm maintains its own network of academies, staff colleges, and training schools. Key academies and military training colleges are identified in figure 14.

197. For a recent assessment of PME in the PLA, see Thomas Bickford, "Professional Military Education in the Chinese People's Liberation Army: A Preliminary

This military educational system has evolved considerably over time.[198] PLA educational institutions grew substantially after the Korean War (to 232 by 1956), contracted greatly during the Cultural Revolution decade (from approximately 137 to 43), began to be rebuilt in the 1980s (to 103 by 1986), and were consolidated during the 1990s (to approximately 75 by 2000).[199] In 1999, after the 14th All-PLA Military Academies Conference,[200] PME underwent one of its most sweeping transformations, with the creation of some new institutions, the merging of several academies, and elimination of many others.[201] Most notably, a new National Defense Science and Technology University was established in Changsha. The goal was to reduce the overall number of PLA educational institutions by one-third by 2010.[202]

The PME curriculum has also undergone significant revision, in an effort to train a more professional officer corps skilled in modern warfare doctrine, strategy, and tactics.[203] By 1994, 378 separate fields of study were taught in PLA colleges.[204]

The National Defense University

The NDU was established in December 1985 by order of the State Council and CMC as the PLA's highest-level training institution. It is located at Hongshankou in northwest Beijing. The new NDU absorbed the PLA's former Military Affairs Academy, Political Academy, and Logistics Academy—drawing on the main academies of the three general headquarters (although the new institution was organized differently). The NDU is intended to be

---

Assessment of Problems and Prospects" (paper presented at the 2001 CAPS/RAND Conference, Washington, D.C., July 2001).

198. For an earlier assessment, see Lonnie D. Henley, "Officer Education in the Chinese PLA," *Problems of Communism*, May–June 1987, pp. 55–71.

199. Li Cheng et al., *Jianguo Yilai Junshi Baizhuan Dashi* (Beijing: Zhishi Chubanshe, 1992), p. 54; and *Directory of PRC Military Personalities*, 2000. The volume on the Cultural Revolution and the PLA cited earlier lists a total of 126 military academies and colleges in 1966 but only 84 in 1975. See Li and Hao, *"Wenhua Da Geming" zhong de Renmin Jiefangjun*, p. 373.

200. Luo Yuwen, "Military Academies Undergo Reform," Xinhua, June 22, 1999, in FBIS–CHI, June 25, 1999.

201. Xinhua, "Adjust the Structure of Military Academies," June 21, 1999, in FBIS–CHI, June 22, 1999

202. Academy of Military Sciences Strategy Department, ed., *2000–2001 Nian Zhanlüe Pinggu* (Beijing: Junshi Kexue Chubanshe, 2000), p. 148.

203. See James Mulvenon, *Professionalization of the Senior Chinese Officer Corps* (Santa Monica, Calif.: RAND Corporation, 1997).

204. Qian Taiqing, ed., *Zhongguo Junshi Zhidu Shi: Junshi Jiaoyu Xunlian Bianzhi Juan* (Zhengzhou: Dajia Chubanshe, 1997), p. 448.

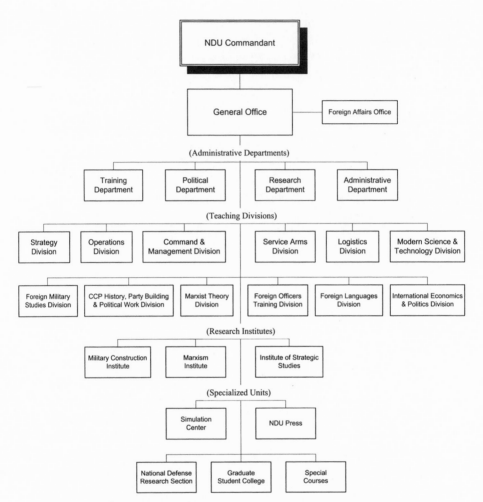

Figure 15. The PLA National Defense University. *Sources:* Yao Yanjin et al., eds., *Junshi Zuzhi Tizhi Yanjiu* (Beijing: Guofang Daxue Chubanshe, 1997); NDU brochures; interviews.

a joint service institution, where senior officers are trained. All division commanders and "leading cadres" of general headquarters departments and military region commands and above are required to take courses at the NDU, either intensive short courses *(jinxiuban)* or year-long classes. From 1986 to 1994, the NDU graduated 4,000 students,[205] and by 1998, it totaled more

205. Ibid., p. 20.

than 5,000 (including 400 Ph.D.s).[206] By 1998, more than 90 percent of "senior commanders" in the PLA had graduated from the NDU.[207]

The NDU is administratively directly under the control of the CMC and has a large number of departments. As figure 15 illustrates, the NDU is organized into:

- Four principal first-level administrative departments *(da bu):* Training, Political, Research, and Administration; twelve second-level teaching divisions *(jiaoyanshi):* Strategy, Operations, Command and Management, Service Arms, Logistics, Modern Science and Technology, Foreign Military Studies, Chinese Communist Party History/ Party Building/Political Work, Marxist Theory, Training of Foreign Officers, Foreign Languages, and International Economics and Politics

- Three research institutes: the Military Construction Institute, Marxism Institute, and Institute of Strategic Studies

- Several specialized units: the Simulation Center, Graduate Student College, NDU Press, and a variety of specialized courses for PLA and foreign officers[208]

The NDU Press publishes a large number of books and the monthly journal *Guofang Daxue Xuebao* (National Defense University Journal). Foreign interaction with the NDU is largely limited to the Institute of Strategic Studies, Foreign Military Studies Department, and CCP History Department. Visiting military dignitaries meet with the NDU commandant and his staff and are frequently given the opportunity to address staff and students, but direct interaction with most of the departments in the NDU is virtually impossible for foreigners.

The Academy of Military Sciences

The PLA Academy of Military Sciences was established in March 1958 on the order of Chairman Mao and the CMC, and was modeled on the Soviet General Staff Academy. It has always been under the direct leadership *(zhihui lingdao xia)* of the CMC, and was established to become the PLA's

206. Wang Yifei, "China's National Defense University: Cradle of Generals," *Guang Jiao Jing* (Hong Kong), December 16, 1998, in FBIS–CHI, January 7, 1999.
207. Ibid.
208. Yao et al., eds., *Junshi Zuzhi Tizhi Yanjiu,* p. 375; NDU Press, *The Chinese National Defense University* (Beijing: Guofang Daxue Chubanshe, 1995); "National Defense University PLA China—Introduction" (English, Russian, and Chinese pamphlet, no date); interviews with NDU personnel, 2001.

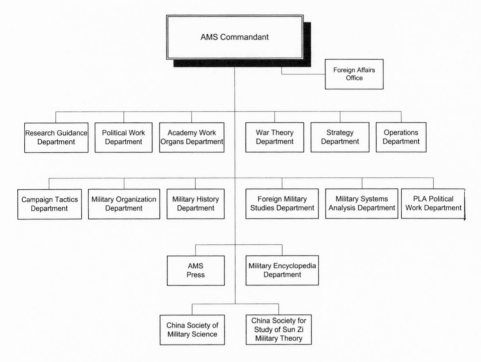

Figure 16. The PLA Academy of Military Sciences. *Sources:* Yao Yanjin et al., eds., *Junshi Zuzhi Tizhi Yanjiu* (Beijing: Guofang Daxue Chubanshe, 1997); Jiang Jianhua et al., eds., *Zhonghua Renmin Gongheguo Ziliao Shouce* (Beijing: Shehui Kexue Wenzhai Chubanshe, 1999).

"highest organ of research on military theory."[209] The research purview of the AMS covers the spectrum of military affairs, including considerable attention to the "revolution in military affairs" (RMA).[210] The AMS has always principally been a research institution, devoted primarily to studying doctrine (see chapter 3), although it created a doctoral program in 1988 (the first graduates matriculated in 1997). It is also located in northwest Beijing near the Central Party School and National Defense University. The AMS's full-time professional staff may number more than 500 officers, with roughly

209. Yao, *Junshi Zuzhi Tizhi Yanjiu.*
210. See many of the AMS authors/sources cited in chapter 3; and Michael Pillsbury, *China Debates the Future Security Environment* (Washington, D.C.: National Defense University Press, 2000), pp. 370–72.

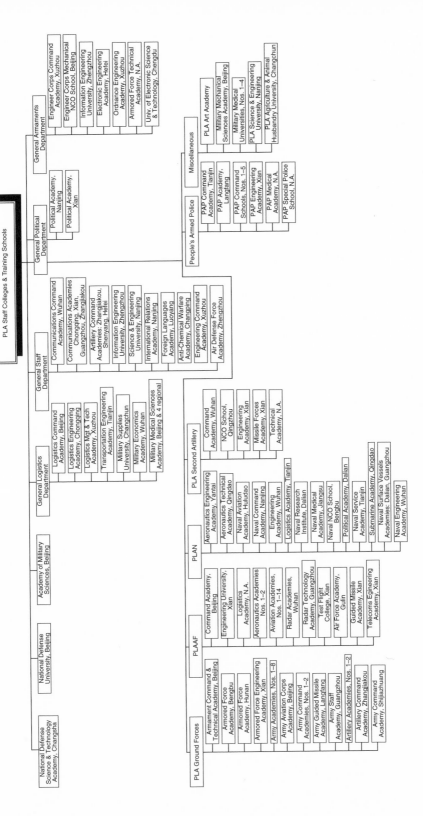

Figure 17. PLA staff colleges and training schools. *Source: Directory of PRC Military Personalities, 2000* (Honolulu: Serold Hawaii Inc., 2001).

50 to 60 officers per department.[211] The internal organization of the AMS, shown in figure 16, consists of twelve research departments: Research Guidance, Political Work, Academy Work Organs, War Theory, Strategy, Operations, Campaign Tactics, Military Organization, Military History, Foreign Military Studies, Military Systems Analysis, and PLA Political Work.[212]

With the distinct exceptions of the Foreign Military Studies Department and the Second Office of the Strategy Department, which carry out research on foreign militaries and international security, most of the research conducted at the AMS concerns issues internal to the PLA.[213] The AMS is also the principal PLA organization overseeing the work of two PLA-wide research associations: the China Society of Military Sciences (established in 1991) and the China Society for the Study of Sun Zi Military Theory (established in 1994).[214] As would be expected, the AMS Press is a major publisher of books on the PLA and military affairs, as well as a number of journals and the annual encyclopedia *World Military Affairs.* Limited interaction with, and visits to, the AMS by foreigners are possible, and in recent years AMS staff have increasingly traveled abroad as visiting scholars.[215]

ORGANIZATIONAL CHANGE IN THE PLA: IS IT ENOUGH?

This chapter has elucidated the considerable restructuring, streamlining, and change in the PLA in recent years. This process has not been easy, as it has resulted in the forced retirement of large numbers of officers and the demobilization of approximately one-third of the PLA rank and file. Significant organizational and financial interests have also been infringed upon, as the general headquarters have been revamped and the PLA has been forced to divest itself of its commercial interests. Meanwhile, the geographic purview of military regions has been expanded, while the structure of the ground

211. Ibid., pp. 368–69.

212. Yao, *Junshi Zuzhi Tizhi Yanjiu*, p. 375; Jiang Jianhua et al., eds., *Zhonghua Renmin Gongheguo Ziliao Shouce, 1949–1999* (Beijing: Shehui Kexue Wenzhai Chubanshe, 1999), p. 308; interviews with AMS personnel.

213. The Foreign Military Studies Department is subdivided into three regional research offices (the Americas; Europe, Russia/Ukraine, Central Asian republics; the Asia/Pacific region) and one comprehensive *(zonghe)* office that follows functional issues (including arms control). Interview with AMS staff member, October 2000.

214. Li Jijun, "Work Report of First Executive Council of China Society of Military Sciences," *Zhongguo Junshi Kexue* (June 2000), pp. 12–16, in FBIS–CHI, July 27, 2000.

215. For example, an AMS delegation toured the United States in August 2000.

forces is shrinking from divisions to brigades. Professional military education has been enhanced, and the reserves, militia, and paramilitary People's Armed Police have been expanded. Many other organizational reforms have been detailed above.

The organizational reform of the PLA is a work in progress. To be sure, it has had its jarring effects—for the reasons listed above, but also because so many reforms are being implemented simultaneously. It is true that the PLA has needed a wholesale makeover, but the sheer process of absorbing so many far-reaching changes at one time has itself been destabilizing. Nonetheless, they are all essential if the PLA is to transform itself into a force structure capable of fighting "limited wars under high-technology conditions." There will certainly be more changes to come, and it will be interesting to see if fundamental changes are made to the force structure, geographic configuration, or upper-level command and control. To date, the reforms outlined in this chapter have been incremental reforms to the existing system—akin to trimming the branches without replanting the tree.

As noted at the outset of the chapter, the PLA remains in essence a military heavily influenced by the organizational model adapted from the Soviet Union in the 1950s. Although there has been serious consideration given to adopting various American-style organizational reforms—such as a joint staff or theater war system—so far these have been deferred. If the PLA truly wants to overcome its rigidities and excessive compartmentalization, to become a more flexible and agile military, it must make basic changes to the existing organizational system.

5 Budget and Finance

Few areas of Chinese military affairs are more opaque and difficult to research than the revenue/expenditure and budget/finance domains—but perhaps none is more important to understand. PLA doctrine, force structure, threat perception, and organization are all more transparent and researchable than PLA economic affairs. Yet knowledge of the PLA's fiscal base is crucial to understanding these other areas. The allocation of financial resources is indicative of strategic priorities and calculations. In the case of the PLA, it is important not only to know where the money is going, but also where it comes from—as the military has always had extrabudgetary sources of revenue *(yusuanwai)* and significant hidden categories of expenditure in other ministerial budgets or secret accounts.

The official defense budget is only about half of the total revenue accruing to, and expended by, the PLA. It is therefore vital for analysts to think in terms of the total *revenue base* rather than simply of allocated *budget* when assessing the PLA's finances.

Like other facets of the PLA, the financial arena is undergoing comprehensive reform. There have been four principal areas of military fiscal reform in recent years.

The first concerns the commercialization and subsequent divestiture of commercial assets by the PLA. In the mid 1980s, the military was authorized to go into business *(bing shang)* to offset and compensate for low levels of state allocations to the PLA. Commercialization worked as intended—in fact, much better than intended. PLA units set up a plethora of enterprises and commercial activities. This helped refill depleted army coffers, but it also had the very deleterious effect of soldiers spending time in unprofessional business activity (much of it illegal) instead of training, diverting military resources for commercial purposes, and creating a significant "second economy" in China. After the negative effects of military commercialization became apparent in the late 1990s, the government and CMC issued several orders banning PLA business activities. They had little effect; indeed, the problem worsened. Only after the joint State Council, CCP, and CMC order of July 1998 did the PLA's commercial involvement truly begin to diminish.[1] Following the 1998 order, the commercial divestiture process passed through several phases, which are detailed later in this chapter.

The second reform was a regularization *(zhengguihua)* of accounting and auditing procedures in the PLA, beginning in the early 1990s. This move also met with resistance, particularly because military units sought to hide their assets and profits derived from their commercial activities. But gradually a regular auditing system was introduced from top to bottom.

The third principal reform has been the marketization and rationalization of the defense industrial procurement system. As discussed in chapter 6, a major institutional reform was inaugurated in 1998 with the creation of the General Armaments Department (Zong Zhuangbei Bu) and reorganization of the Commission on Science, Technology, and Industry for National Defense (COSTIND). The goal of this reform was to make the industrial and scientific/technological sectors of the armed forces more efficient and cost-effective. The introduction of a more market-based procurement bidding system had implications for the military budget. Also, following the 1999 Yugoslav War, the military was given a substantial boost in its allocations for weapons and other equipment—coming on top of double-digit real postinflation increases that the PLA had enjoyed since 1997.

The fourth area of reform was introduced in 2001 and concerned PLA budgeting. In a radical initiative, after 1997–98, zero-based budgeting (ZBB) was introduced to many ministries and entities under the State Council, on the order of Premier Zhu Rongji. This initiative was part of a package of phased fiscal and accounting reforms intended to make the government's entire fiscal system more efficient and accountable.[2] China's socialist economy was filled with accounting and budgeting irregularities that allowed for double counting, hidden assets, and a variety of off-budget revenues and expenditures. The PLA's fiscal management was no different, and probably worse. Under ZBB, all units were required to draw up their anticipated expenditure for the next fiscal year from zero, rather than from the previous system of taking the previous year's expenditure and adding a certain per-

---

1. The order was titled "Removal of the Military, People's Armed Police, and Political-Legal Units from Commercial Activities."
2. I am grateful to Christine Wong on this point.

centage. With this reform, "Units no longer are supposed to arrange their budgets on the basis of their base figures of the previous year. . . . They begin to calculate and examine their annual budgets and itemized budgets from 'zero,' with the arrangement of their budget [requests] in order of priority."[3] One important item apparently left out of ZBB initiative was personnel costs.[4]

This chapter explores the intricacies of these reforms, and PLA revenue flows and estimated expenditures. It also seeks to examine the primary data to better illuminate a very opaque subject. There exists a surprisingly large literature on Chinese defense economics *(guofang jingji)*, military finance *(jundui caiwu)*, military expenditure *(jundui feiyong* or *junfei)*, defense expenditure *(guofang feiyong* or *junfei)*, and logistics work *(houqin gongzuo)* on which to base research, although much of it is published and available only in China. The field of defense economics has, in fact, emerged as a bona fide field of teaching, research, and study in China.[5] These sources contain abundant information and a surprisingly systematic picture of the defense budgeting process and sources of revenue (although it is notably weak on precise figures). No doubt the PLA itself does not know the full extent of its earnings and expenditures. However, the "black box" of the budget process, the revenue base, and expenditure parameters can all be illuminated by a careful reading of these sources.[6] In addition, interviews with active

3. For an explanation of this system in the PLA, see Xiong Tingbin and Zhang Dongbo, "Central Military Commission Relays Plan for Reforming Compilation of Budgets for Armed Forces," Xinhua Domestic Service, March 22, 2001, in FBIS–CHI, March 22, 2001.

4. Thanks to Christine Wong for making this point.

5. The PLA runs a Military Economics Research Center in Wuhan (Junshi Jingji Yanjiuyuan), there is a national Chinese Society for Defense Economics (with branches in various cities), and a number of periodicals are devoted to the subject, e.g., *Jundui Caiwu* (Military Finance); *Junshi Jingji Yanjiu* (Defense Economics Research); and sometimes *Zhongguo Jungong Bao* (China Defense Industry News).

6. See, e.g., People's University Reprint Series, *Junshi* (Military Affairs); Lin Yichang and Wu Xizhi, *Guofang Jingjixue Jichu* (Basic Defense Economics) (Beijing: Academy of Military Sciences Press, 1991); PLA Logistics College Technology Research Section, ed., *Junshi Houqin Cidian* (Dictionary on Military Logistics) (Beijing: PLA Press, 1991); Chinese Military Encyclopedia Editing Group, ed., *Jundui Houqin Fence* (Section on Military Logistics) (Beijing: Academy of Military Sciences Press, 1985); Zhang Zhenlong, ed., *Junshi Jingjixue* (Military Economics) (Shenyang: Liaoning People's Press, 1988); Jin Songde et al., *Guofang Jingji Lun* (National Defense Economic Theory) (Beijing: PLA Press, 1987); Jiang Baoqi, ed., *Zhongguo Guofang Jingji Fazhan Zhanlue Yanjiu* (Research on the Strategy of China's Military Industrial Development) (Beijing: National Defense University Press, 1990); Gao Dianzhi, *Zhongguo Guofang Jingji Guanli Yanjiu* (Research on the Management of China's National Defense Economy) (Beijing: Academy of Military Sciences Press,

and retired PLA personnel in China and abroad can supplement the documentary data. Two native-speaking scholars have begun to mine these sources and have done much to illuminate the spending categories and budget process in the Chinese military.[7]

This chapter is divided into four sections. The first offers an overview of the official defense budget since 1949, with an emphasis on the evolution of the budget system. The second looks at the defense budget process and system in recent years. The third section attempts to account for areas of expenditure under the official defense budget and the PLA's off-budget revenue and expenditure. It attempts to estimate total PLA revenue and expenditure. The final section examines aggregate trends.

HISTORICAL PATTERNS OF CHINESE DEFENSE SPENDING AND FINANCIAL MANAGEMENT

Table 4 depicts the official Chinese defense budget from 1950–2001 in absolute terms, in terms of relative annual increases and decreases, and as a percentage of the annual central government expenditure (CGE) over time.[8] Figure 18 depicts the annual rate of growth, with both nominal and real change, in the defense budget after inflation for 1990–2001. The amount of expenditure converted into U.S. dollars varies, of course, depending on

---

1991); Sun Zhenyuan, *Zhongguo Guofang Jingji Jianshi* (The Construction of China's National Defense Economy) (Beijing: Academy of Military Sciences Press, 1991); Qiao Guanglie, ed., *Zhongguo Renmin Jiefangjun Houqin Jianshi* (History of PLA Logistics Building) (Beijing: National Defense University Press, 1989); Wang Dangying et al., *Guofang Fazhan Zhanlüe Yanjiu* (Research on National Defense Strategy) (Beijing: National Defense University Press, 1988).

7. See Arthur S. Ding, "China's Defense Finance: Content, Process, and Administration," in David Shambaugh and Richard H. Yang, eds., *China's Military in Transition* (Oxford: Clarendon Press, 1997); Wang Shaoguang, "Estimating China's Defense Expenditure: Some Evidence from Chinese Sources," *China Quarterly*, no. 147 (September 1996): 889–911; and Wang Shaoguang, "The Military Expenditure of China," in *SIPRI Yearbook, 1999* (Oxford: Oxford University Press, 1999). This chapter draws on several of the same sources as Ding and Wang, as well as their findings, so data drawing on the same source, or areas of agreement, will therefore not be footnoted.

8. Much of this section is based on Contemporary China Series Editing Group, ed., *Dangdai Zhongguo Jundui de Houqin Gongzuo* (Military Logistical Work in Contemporary China) (Beijing: Zhongguo Shehui Kexue Chubanshe, 1990), chs. 14–15; and *Dangdai Zhongguo Caizheng, Xia* (Finance in Contemporary China, Vol. 2) (Beijing: Zhongguo Shehui Kexue Chubanshe, 1988), pp. 257–63. However, in places, it also draws upon sources cited in footnote 6.

TABLE 4 Official Chinese Defense Expenditure

Year	Official Defense Expenditure (billion RMB)	As % of Total Central Government Expenditure (CGE)	% Increase/ Decrease[a]
1950	2.8	41.1	—
1951	5.2	43.0	89.0
1952	5.7	32.9	9.0
1953	7.5	34.2	29.0
1954	5.8	24.6	−29.0
1955	6.5	24.1	12.0
1956	6.1	20.0	−7.0
1957	5.5	18.1	−11.0
1958	5.0	12.2	−10.0
1959	5.8	10.5	16.0
1960	5.8	8.9	0
1961	5.7	13.6	−16.0
1962	5.7	18.7	14.0
1963	6.6	19.6	16.0
1964	7.3	18.3	11.0
1965	8.7	18.6	19.0
1966	10.1	18.7	16.0
1967	8.3	18.8	−22.0
1968	9.4	26.1	13.0
1969	12.6	24.0	34.0
1970	14.5	22.4	15.0
1971	16.9	23.2	17.0
1972	15.9	20.8	−6.0
1973	14.5	18.0	−10.0
1974	13.3	16.9	−9.0
1975	14.2	17.4	7.0
1976	13.4	16.7	−6.0
1977	14.9	17.7	11.0
1978	16.8	15.1	13.0
1979	22.3	17.5	33.0
1980	19.3	16.0	−15.0
1981	16.8	14.7	−15.0
1982	17.6	15.3	5.0

TABLE 4 *(continued)*

Year	Official Defense Expenditure (billion RMB)	As % of Total Central Government Expenditure (CGE)	% Increase/ Decrease[a]
1983	17.7	13.7	1.0
1984	18.1	11.7	2.0
1985	19.1	10.4	6.0
1986	20.1	8.6	5.0
1987	21.0	8.6	4.0
1988	21.8	8.1	4.0
1989	25.2	8.4	15.0
1990	29.0	8.7	16.0
1991	32.5	9.0	14.0
1992	37.0	9.1	15.0
1993	43.2	9.2	13.0
1994	52.0	10.0	29.0
1995	63.7	9.3	16.0
1996	72.0	9.1	15.0
1997	81.3	8.8	12.0
1998	93.5	8.7	12.0
1999	107.7	8.2	12.6
2000	121.3	8.3	14.6
2001	141.0	8.4	17.7

[a]Not adjusted for inflation; figures rounded.

SOURCES: Dangdai Zhongguo Congshu Bianjizu, eds., *Dangdai Houqin Gongzuo* (Beijing: Zhongguo Shehui Kexue Chubanshe, 1989), pp. 304–5; State Statistical Bureau, *Zhongguo Tongji Nianjian* (China Statistical Yearbook) (Beijing: Zhongguo Tongji Chubanshe, various years); *Beijing Review* (various years); *China's National Defense* (Beijing: Information Office of the State Council, 1998); SIPRI [Stockholm International Peace Research Institute] *Yearbook, 1992* (Oxford: Oxford University Press, 1992), p. 157; "China's Military Expenditure," in International Institute of Strategic Studies, *The Military Balance 1995/96* (Oxford: Oxford University Press, 1995); *SIPRI Yearbook, 1999* (Oxford: Oxford University Press, 1999), app. 7D, "The Military Expenditure of China"; Information Office of the State Council, *China's National Defense in 2000* (Xinhua, October 16, 2000); "Finance Minister Announces Government Budget," *China Daily*, March 11, 2001, Internet edition.

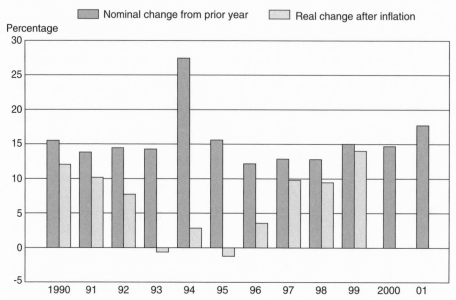

Figure 18.   Annual rate of growth in announced defense budget, 1990–2001.
Source: Central Intelligence Agency, from official Chinese statistics, 2001.

fluctuating exchange rates, and therefore has not been attempted. Broadly speaking, however, dollar conversion is not a particularly useful measure, because it does not represent the actual costs of goods and services in the Chinese economy, many of which are heavily subsidized by the government. The purchasing power parity (PPP) method favored by the International Monetary Fund (IMF) is therefore a more reasonable method of calculation, as in reality it is what the renminbi can purchase in the Chinese economy that matters (a relative measure illustrated by the *Economist* magazine's "Big Mac Index")—although this chapter does not attempt PPP estimates. The figures given below, though, are actual RMB amounts.

Measured as a percentage of central government expenditure, China's "defense budget burden" has been significant. Of course, in absolute terms, China's defense spending has been equivalent to only a small fraction of the defense spending of the United States, some other developed countries, or the former Soviet Union. Nonetheless, from 1950 to 2001, China spent an average of 16.7 percent of its national government expenditure on defense.[9] This figure must be considered even greater when extrabudgetary alloca-

9. Author's calculation.

TABLE 5 Allocation of Military Expenditure, 1998–2000
(in billions of RMB)

Category	1998	1999	2000
Personnel	32.3 (35%)	34.9 (32%)	40.6 (33%)
Operations and Maintenance (O&M)	29.8 (31%)	38.0 (35%)	41.8 (35%)
Equipment	31.4 (34%)	34.8 (33%)	38.9 (32%)

tions are taken into account. As a percentage of GNP, however, China's defense burden has been more modest. From 1950 to 1980, China's official national defense expenditure constituted approximately 6.35 percent of national income on average, but it dropped dramatically to approximately 2.3 percent for the 1980s and fell even further, to an average of 1.4 percent, during the 1990s.[10]

The important questions of what the money is being spent on and what the relative allocations indicate about intentions are discussed at greater length below. Suffice it to note here that personnel costs have always absorbed a disproportionately large percentage of Chinese defense expenditure. From 1950 to 1970, personnel expenditures (salaries, housing, medical care, support of dependents, etc.) accounted for 40 percent of official defense expenditure, dropping to 30 percent during the 1970s and rising again to approximately 40 percent during the 1980s.[11] During the 1990s, approximately 35 percent of the defense budget was devoted to personnel costs. China's 1998 Defense White Paper claimed that, in 1997, 36 percent of official military expenditure was spent on personnel-related costs, while 33 percent was spent on operations and maintenance (O & M), and an additional 31 percent on equipment.[12] The 2000 Defense White Paper revealed important adjustments in these relative allocations, as depicted in table 5.[13]

10. Contemporary China Series Editing Group, ed., *Dangdai Zhongguo Jundui de Houqin Gongzuo,* pp. 306–7, and author's calculations.

11. National Defense University Development Institute, ed., *Zhongguo Guofang Jingji Fazhan Zhanlue Yanjiu* (Research on China's National Defense Economy Development Strategy) (Beijing: National Defense University Press, 1990), p. 243.

12. Information Office of the State Council, *China's National Defense* (Beijing: State Council, 1998), pp. 84–85.

13. Information Office of the State Council, *China's National Defense in 2000,* Xinhua, October 16, 2000.

PLA sources also indicate that the official defense budget boosts of 1999–2000 (averaging 13.6 percent) have also primarily gone to increasing salaries in the wake of the 1998 commercial divestiture order; some interview sources indicate that, as of the 2000 budget, as much as 50 percent of the official military budget now pays for salaries.[14]

From these aggregate figures, it is, of course, difficult to ascertain the percentage of expenditure on different branches and services of the PLA, but one authoritative source revealed that for the period 1950–80, the PLA Air Force garnered an average of 31.37 percent of the defense budget and the Navy got a meager 18.4 percent, allowing the ground forces to absorb just over 50 percent of the budget.[15] Of the spending on equipment for the ground forces, this source revealed the following breakdown: 17.22 percent for vehicles; 7.4 percent for tanks; 9 percent for communications equipment; 8.88 percent for ordnance and munitions; 7.5 percent for "other equipment"; 30 percent on personnel; and 20 percent on operations and maintenance.[16] Funds allocated for weapons development are buried in other budgets, but nonetheless these figures are illustrative of how the PLA spends its money: it spends much more on people than on arms.

It is also interesting to note the fluctuations in annual defense expenditure. In most cases, China's defense budget reflected external tensions, but in others it reflected domestic considerations. As would be expected, a very high percentage of the national budget went to the military during the Korean War. Defense spending peaked in 1951 and then declined in percentage terms during the two years' stalemate preceding the armistice. The end of the war and concomitant demobilization brought about a dramatic drop in 1954, but the 1954–55 Taiwan Strait crises resulted in a brief turnaround. The defense budget continued to drop until the 1958 Taiwan Strait crisis, when it rose briefly, and then dropped again during the "three bitter years" *(san ku nian)* of the Great Leap Forward (1959–61). With the outbreak of Sino-Indian border hostilities, defense expenditure rose again—despite the fact that 1962 saw the nadir of the Great Leap catastrophe and a marked decline in overall national budgetary expenditure. Chinese defense expenditure continued to climb during the U.S. buildup in Vietnam, reaching a high in 1966. It is not quite clear why expenditure dipped in 1967–68, but the

14. Interviews with PLA officers, February 28 and May 16, 2000, Washington, D.C., and Beijing.

15. Contemporary China Series Editing Group, ed., *Dangdai Zhongguo Jundui de Houqin Gongzuo,* p. 307.

16. Ibid.

decline was in proportion to the overall drop in national income and expenditure. It no doubt had to do with the deleterious impact that the Cultural Revolution had on the industrial sector and transport system. Nonetheless, as a percentage of the state budget, defense held steady at around 18.7 percent during these years (1966–76).

Although Lin Biao is often perceived as a defense minister more interested in politics than professionalism, defense spending figures during the 1960s offer emphatic counterevidence. Also, to anyone who doubts the depth of the Chinese fear of Soviet attack during the tense period of 1968–71, defense expenditure offers proof positive. Defense spending nearly doubled in absolute terms during these three years. However, the rapid growth commenced prior to the Soviet invasion of Czechoslovakia and accelerated markedly following Lin Biao's famous Order Number 1 in October 1969, which called for national war mobilization. China was on a war footing during these years. The death of Lin Biao in 1971 and Sino-American rapprochement triggered a steady decline in military spending through the remainder of the decade, until the Sino-Vietnamese border war in 1979. This resulted in a brief two-year increase. By 1981, with Deng Xiaoping in charge of the Central Military Commission, the PLA was subjected to a decade-long erosion in its funding. The brief exception to this trend came in 1982, the year that China proclaimed its "independent foreign policy" and began to distance itself from the United States.[17]

Thus over the first forty years of the People's Republic, we see a close correlation between China's external threat environment and defense spending. In a couple of cases (the Great Leap and Cultural Revolution), austere domestic conditions produced a shift in defense expenditure, but, on the whole, defense expenditure paralleled China's security environment and posture.

The period since 1988, when the military budget began to increase appreciably, has demonstrated a deviation from the previous pattern. Although China's national security environment has never been better and there is no pressing external threat (see chapter 7), its defense spending is rising sharply. China's official military spending rose from 21.8 billion RMB in 1988 to 141 billion in 2001. While China suffered inflation from 1988 to 1997, most of the increases in official defense expenditure in recent years have come in real terms after inflation and in terms of a percentage of national expenditure.

17. See Carol Lee Hamrin, "China Reassesses the Superpowers," *Pacific Affairs*, Summer 1983, pp. 209–31.

THE DEFENSE BUDGET SYSTEM AND PROCESS

As would be expected, the Chinese defense budget process has evolved over time. Perhaps it is more appropriate to say that it has *devolved*. As in much of the rest of the Chinese economy, central management and planning have been reduced since the 1980s, with responsibility for revenue generation falling increasingly on individual units at all tiers of the system. Like the civilian sector of the Chinese economy, the defense finance *(guofang caiwu)* system is in a halfway house between the plan and the free market. To understand how it got to this point, it is useful to briefly review the history of the defense budget process in the PRC.[18]

The Evolution of the Defense Finance System

On March 24, 1950, the State Council adopted the "Decision on Unified Management of Revenue and Expenses," which stipulated that: "Military expenditure is to be allocated to the armed forces according to monthly and quarterly budgets worked out by it [the PLA] and approved by the Ministry of Finance."[19] As a result of this decision, the Finance Bureau of the General Logistics Department (Houqin Bu Caiwu Chu) was created and placed in charge of a system of "unified control." This system, mirrored by the state planning and revenue system for civilian state industry, was adapted from the Soviet model. Under the system of "unified control," General Logistics Department (GLD) finance bureaus were created down to the military district level and were put in charge of dispersal and collection of funds. The finance bureaus dealt with one another in a vertical fashion up to the parent bureau inside the GLD in Beijing, which in turn dealt directly with the Central Military Commission and the Ministry of Finance. This system remains essentially intact today, although the bureaus now reach down to the regiment level and their power has been diluted by unit-generated revenue. Under the old system, 100 percent of PLA funds were allocated from the center, and units were reimbursed at year's end for any shortfalls. Conversely, any surpluses had to be returned. During the period of PLA involvement in business (roughly 1985–99), these principles were reversed, and units retained most, if not all, of the revenue they generated.

The system changed somewhat in 1956 following Mao's speech on the "Ten Great Relationships." Mao's call for a shifting of planning priorities

---

18. The following also draws on Contemporary China Series Editing Group, ed., *Dangdai Zhongguo Jundui de Houqin Gongzuo.*
19. Ibid., p. 261.

had an impact on military expenditure. Mao pointed out in the speech that military spending during the First Five-Year Plan (1952–57) had averaged 30 percent of central government expenditure (CGE), and he opined that this was too high. He mandated that, in the Second Five-Year Plan (1958–63), military expenditure should be reduced to 20 percent. Following Mao's order, an enlarged meeting of the Central Military Commission approved a proposal put forward by Yu Qiuli, then vice director of the GLD, known as the "Ten Improvements" and "Four Management Methods." These were adopted by the CMC as the "Second Military Financial Laws and Regulations." Yu Qiuli had argued that the "unified system" had resulted in considerable waste, with budgets being padded without need and appropriations being made without checking. This had resulted in a situation of "documents going up and down without supervision."[20]

The new defense budgeting system and regulations resulted in a devolution of discretionary spending power. Unit commanders down to the regiment level were given leeway to spend funds that were not earmarked for specific purposes. This reform resulted in the first signs of a budget bidding process within the PLA. Commanders down to the regiment level would, in coordination with the GLD Finance Bureaus, work out estimated expenditures under various headings for the coming fiscal year, which would be put forward and authorized. The categories for allocations operated under a quota system *(zhibiao kongzhi)*,[21] under which commanders were given certain discretionary power within general guidelines promulgated by the GLD. The auditing system was tightened up, and receipts had to be kept for all expenditure.

This system was reaffirmed by the CMC in 1959 in the form of the "Decision on Improving the Management of Military Finance," in line with the general economic devolution ethic of the Great Leap. The system remained in effect until the eve of the Cultural Revolution, when the GLD's chief, Qiu Huizuo, labeled the "Four Methods" and "Ten Improvements" as "dictatorship in every field." In February 1965, Qiu Huizuo (who was a close accomplice of Lin Biao) issued a new directive on behalf of the GLD that authorized "Party committee *[dangwei]* management of finance in a unified way" and a "Plan for Reforming Military Financial Management." Neither document was approved by the GLD or CMC, but they nonetheless took effect. This initiative paralleled a similar shift in the civilian sector at the time. As a result, financial decision making in the armed forces was taken

20. Ibid., p. 312.
21. Ibid.

out of the hands of the GLD financial bureaus and local commanders, and was shifted to PLA Party secretaries *(dangwei shuji)* under the general control of the General Political Department. Consequently, funds were apparently diverted and mismanaged, causing "great difficulties."[22] In September 1969, at the height of the Cultural Revolution, the financial system under the GLD was closed altogether. Personnel were merged into other agencies, notably the Logistics Supply Bureau.

It was not until December 1977, with the CMC's "Decision on Rectifying and Strengthening the Financial Work of the Armed Forces," that moves were made to reorganize the PLA's budgetary system. By this time, Deng Xiaoping had been restored to the position of PLA chief of staff, and one of his first moves was to reform the military financial system. By early 1981, a series of "test point" *(shi dian)* experiments for devolved financial management in the armed forces commenced, and new military financial regulations were enacted by the GLD (its own financial system having been restored). These experiments and new regulations allowed a unit direct and complete management of its financial resources. Each test unit would continue to bid for funds based on estimates for the forthcoming year, but they would be allocated to each level with considerable discretion for their ultimate disbursement. This meant, for example, that funds allocated to areas *other* than salaries, training, and weapons maintenance could be moved from one heading to another or invested. Of equal importance, test units were given the go-ahead to considerably broaden their sideline commercial activities and generate their own revenue. By 1983, the new system was extended to some military districts and the air force.

Commercial Revenue: The PLA in Business

Since its inception, the PLA has grown much of its own food, raised its own animals, and engaged in local construction activities and sideline businesses. It has also manufactured a variety of the items it commonly uses, such as uniforms, boots, helmets, insignia, and so on. By 1987, PLA units had a total of 4 million *mu* of land under cultivation (a *mu* is equivalent to 0.164 acres) and raised 104 million kilos of meat, 650 million kilos of vegetables, and 500 million kilos of grain.[23] But in the mid 1980s, the PLA's involvement in commercial activity took an entirely new turn.

In January 1985, the Central Military Commission promulgated the "Decision on Strengthening Financial Work in the Armed Forces," which

22. Ibid., p. 315.
23. Ibid., pp. 553–54, 558–61, 569–73.

extended the new responsibility system throughout the military, and the General Logistics Department subsequently issued an important series of documents known as the "Eight Financial Rules and Regulations." These are: "Regulations on Financial Work"; "Budget and Final Accounting System"; "Accounting System"; "Management System of Extra-Budgetary Funds"; "Management System for Operating Expenses"; "The Valuation and Accounting System for Materials"; "The Financial Management System for Basic Construction"; and "Trial Loan Methods for the Basic Construction of the Armed Forces." These reforms strengthened certain financial powers of the GLD, but discretionary power was simultaneously devolved to units. The GLD continued to control allocations to certain core elements of the PLA, while individual units were cut loose to generate their own funds.

There are several aspects of the "responsibility system" in the PLA worth noting. The first concerns loans granted by the GLD to units seeking to start commercial activities, for which a fixed ratio of interest was paid if a profit was made.[24] The second feature concerns taxes paid by the armed forces to the state for earnings from commercial ventures. Prior to 1988, a 55 percent flat tax was levied on all military enterprises and units, but in that year a policy of tax holidays and preferential tax treatment was enacted by the State Council for the armed forces, decreasing the tax base rate to 10 percent.[25] This meant, in practice, that PLA enterprises could keep virtually all of their earnings. Third, in order to "enliven the military commercial environment," PLA units were authorized in 1988 to invest laterally in each other's ventures and to form joint ventures with other military or civilian concerns. Such "lateral capital flow" was not only permitted but actively facilitated by the setting up of "dedicated [investment] agencies" under the GLD finance bureaus. Such agencies were set up in Shanghai, Beijing, Guangzhou, Shenyang, Wuhan, Chengdu, Nanjing, and Xian to "adjust capital flow" and stimulate investment.

In the 1990s, the People's Liberation Army, Inc., as it became known abroad, cashed in on its comparative commercial advantages.[26] These came,

24. Ibid., p. 318. An elaborate progressive scale of remuneration is described for increasing levels of military enterprise output and earnings.

25. Ibid., p. 319.

26. The best studies of the PLA in business are James Mulvenon, *Soldiers of Fortune: The Rise and Fall of the Chinese Military-Business Complex, 1978–1998* (Armonk, N.Y.: M. E. Sharpe, 2001); Solomon Karmel, *China and the People's Liberation Army* (New York: St. Martin's Press, 2000); and Tai Ming Cheung, *China's Entrepreneurial Army* (Oxford: Clarendon Press, 2001). Also see Tai Ming Cheung, "China's

not only from converted defense industries, but also from a wide range of investment and production schemes. The PLA owned some of China's prime real estate and leased it out at high rents. Many local airlines were owned and managed by PLA front companies. Numerous hotels and guest houses were opened. The PLA Construction Corps charged localities hefty fees for heavy construction work that was previously undertaken without charge as a symbol of the Army's selfless devotion to the people. The military capitalized on mines under its control by selling metals and minerals at market and above-market prices. The PLA's formerly elite hospitals began to admit paying civilians.[27] Virtually every military unit set up some form of cottage industry, and many were involved in joint ventures with foreign entities. PLA ships, planes, and other modes of transport were put to commercial (and sometimes illicit) use. The General Staff Department invested in several five-star hotels in China, including Beijing's luxurious Palace Hotel and Guangzhou's Garden Hotel. Many PLA commercial ventures were less than respectable; the military became deeply involved not only in running brothels, karaoke bars, and prostitution rings, but also in smuggling. This illicit activity had much to do with the party's decision in 1999 to ban the army's involvement in business. Not all PLA companies were such headline-grabbing conglomerates. Most were small-scale tertiary, agricultural, or sideline enterprises. Many army units in the interior of the country also ran mines.[28]

The most famous and most profitable of the military-run enterprises were the giant conglomerates *(jituan)* run by the general departments under the CMC (see figure 19). The GSD established the Poly Group and China Huitong Corporation, the GPD ran Kaili Corporation and China Tiancheng Corporation, and the GLD ran Sanjiu (999) Enterprises and Xinxing Corporation. The three armed services all ran their own corporations as well. Each of these pyramid-style conglomerates employed 150,000 to 250,000 employees and contained 100 to 150 large and medium-sized enterprises and subsidiaries. Each conglomerate had a diversified portfolio. Poly Technologies

Entrepreneurial Army: The Structure, Activities and Economic Returns of the Military Business Complex," in C. Dennison Lane et al., eds., *Chinese Military Modernization* (London: Kegan Paul International; Washington, D.C.: AEI Press, 1996), pp. 168–97.

27. Interview with military doctor in the PLA's famous 301 Hospital, April 1994.

28. By 1987, there were more than 3,700 PLA-run mines, with more than 170,000 employees, 2 billion RMB in fixed assets, and annual output of 4.5 billion RMB. "Jundui Gongye he Di San Chanye," in Contemporary China Series Editing Group, ed., *Dangdai Zhongguo Jundui de Houqin Gongzuo,* p. 596.

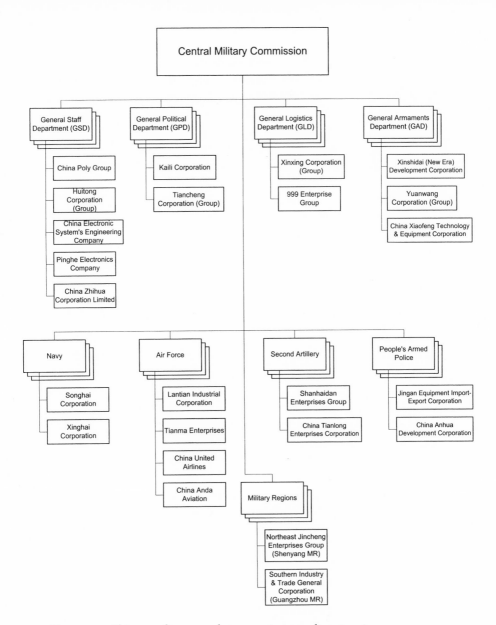

Figure 19. Chinese military conglomerates (prior to divestiture).

was involved in arms trading, satellite launching, infrastructure development, commercial real estate development, electronics, shipping, and foreign investment. Xinxing capitalized on its Logistics Department connections to produce vehicles, food, clothing, construction materials, fuel and petroleum products, and mining products. Kaili Corporation became deeply involved in the telecommunications business, striking up lucrative joint ventures with Motorola, AT&T, and Unisys in the mobile phone and paging business.

In addition to these large enterprises run by the PLA general departments, numerous others existed at regional levels. In his definitive study, Tai Ming Cheung counted more than thirty conglomerates at the central and regional levels.[29] "PLA Inc." reached its prime in the mid 1990s, when somewhere between 15,000 and 20,000 PLA companies were known to exist. Their assets and their profits ballooned. One Chinese source claims that total PLA assets totaled 180 billion RMB ($20.2 billion).[30] Foreign estimates of annual profit range from $1 to 3 billion, although the General Logistics Department claimed in 1998 that the figure was on the order of $600 to 700 million per annum.[31] Poly Technologies did particularly well (its name, *baoli*, literally means to "keep the profits"). By 1998, Poly's entrepreneurial empire had total assets of over $1 billion—including a $700 million real estate portfolio, a dozen Hong Kong–based container freighters with a 400,000-ton capacity, steel mills, and power plants, and a large portion of China's arms sales trade.[32] Its commercial tentacles spread into Hong Kong, Southeast Asia, America, Russia, and Europe, and many of its subsidiary companies stashed their earnings in offshore bank accounts in the Grand Cayman Islands, Channel Islands, and Switzerland. Many PLA conglomerates were controlled by PLA "princelings"—children of high officials. Poly Technologies involved the daughter of Deng Xiaoping, the son of Marshal He Long, the son of General Wang Zhen, and the daughter of Admiral Liu Huaqing. Poly gained particular notoriety when Wang Zhen's son Wang Jun attended a coffee klatsch with President Clinton in the White House in 1996. Thereafter, U.S. federal investigators found extensive links between PLA Inc., Chinese military intelligence, and attempts to buy influence in the Demo-

29. Tai Ming Cheung, *China's Entrepreneurial Army*.

30. Lu Zhuhao, ed., *Zhongguo Junshi Jingfei Guanli* (China's Military Budget Management) (Beijing: Jiefangjun Chubanshe, 1995), p. 155.

31. Interview, GLD, December 8, 1998.

32. David Jackson, "Poly Technologies: Buying Assets and Peddling Influence," *Chicago Tribune*, February 14, 1997; Simon Holberton and Tony Walker, "The Generals' Big Business Offensive," *Financial Times*, November 28, 1994.

cratic Party during the 1996 election. In July 2000, the most senior PLA officer closely associated with the scandal, Major General Ji Shengde, was convicted by Chinese prosecutors in connection with a massive embezzlement and smuggling case. General Ji, the former director of PLA intelligence and the individual accused by the Democratic Party fund-raiser Johnny Chung of having given him $300,000 in cash for President Clinton's re-election, was accused of corruption totaling $12.5 million in connection with the largest official corruption and smuggling case reported in China since 1949.[33] No doubt, some of General Ji's culpability had to do with his role in siphoning funds to buy influence in the United States.

The vast majority of the earnings of PLA enterprises remained with the unit that generated them and did not make their way into the General Logistics Department's budget stream. They helped to defray local operating costs and compensate for the inadequate allocations from the center. The commercialization of the PLA saved many military units from destitution at the very time that their central allocations were being drastically cut back, but the PLA's rapidly growing involvement in the market economy was having a deleterious effect on military professionalism.[34] Morale was low and recruitment difficult, because soldiers earned considerably less than merchants or peasants.[35] Concomitantly, the ranks were filled with soldiers anxious for demobilization in order to take advantage of business opportunities. Commercial priorities ran at cross-purposes with the corporate ethos that the PLA High Command was trying to instill. Incidents of corruption, speculation, profiteering, smuggling, illicit sales and purchases, and other "unhealthy tendencies" became widespread. The official *Jiefangjun Bao* (Liberation Army Daily) reported in 1990 that soldiers were often absent from duty, and even hired substitutes to cover their jobs, while they moonlighted in the free market.[36] A Shenyang Military Region inspection team discovered that many units were falsifying training reports while instead engaging in sideline production and commercial activities.[37] The diversion of military resources for commercial purposes is equally serious. For example,

33. John Pomfret, "Beijing to Indict Ex-Army Spy Chief," *Washington Post*, July 18, 2000.

34. For an interesting exposition of the financial problems that arose, and how the General Logistics Department attempted to cope, see the symposium on military logistical work in *Guofang Daxue Xuebao*, February 1993, pp. 64–71.

35. See Ellis Joffe, "The PLA and the Chinese Economy: The Effect of Involvement," *Survival* 37, no. 2 (Summer 1993): 24–43.

36. *Jiefangjun Bao*, August 31, 1990.

37. Ibid., September 3 and November 28, 1989.

a Jinan Military Region investigation discovered that a tank regiment had diverted 53 percent of its training fuel, and an artillery regiment 70 percent of its allocated fuel, to commercial endeavors.[38]

Thus the long-standing tension between politicization and professionalism in the PLA was supplemented during the 1990s with a new tension between commercialization and professionalism. The PLA's involvement in the economy cut two ways. On the one hand, it gave the PLA a strong institutional stake in the party's economic reform program, insofar as it benefited from the marketization of the economy. On the other hand, because so many PLA-run factories and state farms benefited from protectionist subsidies, not all of the PLA benefited from the reform policies. Just as in other sectors of the economy, there were winners and losers.

Some of the commercial latitude granted to military units began to be restricted with the promulgation of a series of regulations in November–December 1993 that banned units below the group army level from engaging in commercial dealings. These strictures were only partially successful, and they were revised in 1995 to ban business activities beneath the military region level. This effort was generally not successful either. Finally, in July 1998, the Central Military Commission, State Council, and Chinese Communist Party jointly announced that *all* military units, People's Armed Police units, and public and state security organs would have to divest themselves completely of all equities and commercial earnings by December 15, 1998.[39]

The senior leadership seemed to be serious this time. Like all major policy initiatives, this one resulted from the formation of a coalition of interests and individuals at the highest level. The senior PLA leadership, notably Chief of General Staff Fu Quanyou, who was aware of their negative impact on training and readiness, had been arguing for some time that PLA business activities should be curtailed. The second element of the coalition, the senior party leadership, came on board in early 1998, by which time smuggling by PLA units in the south had become endemic and corruption was spreading from society and the party into the armed forces. The third element of the coalition was the new premier, Zhu Rongji, who argued that if China was to create a "level playing field" for domestic and foreign investors and meet the requirements for entering the World Trade Organization, the military must exit from business and divest itself of its financial assets. Zhu recognized the stranglehold that the military and other security organs had over important real estate, transport hubs (including airports,

38. Ibid., April 7, 1989.
39. See Mulvenon, *Soldiers of Fortune*, ch. 7.

harbors, roads, and railways), and various equities across China. Domestic and foreign investors were either forced into partnership with the PLA, making various side payments to participate in joint ventures with it, or restricted from operating altogether. Thus, in the first half of 1998, this powerful tripartite coalition was forged at the top of the Chinese political system, and the order to divest the PLA of all financial and equity assets was promulgated with a seriousness that had been absent in previous efforts.

Still, this order did not ensure complete compliance. Many PLA units hid assets and parked money and other financial instruments in offshore bank accounts. One report in *Shidai Chao*, a magazine published by the official *Renmin Ribao* (People's Daily), reported that an early 1999 audit had found that 10 percent of the businesses covered by the divestiture order had failed to comply. Still, the report noted, 2,937 businesses had been transferred to the state, and an additional 3,928 had been closed by the initial December 1998 deadline.[40] Given the partial compliance with the first order, a second deadline was set for August 1999—by which time an additional 3,530 military enterprises had been handed over, totaling 230,000 additional employees.[41]

There is no doubt that the divestiture caused a lot of grumbling and obfuscation in the armed forces.[42] The postdivestiture auditing of accounts identified numerous anomalies and cases of corruption.[43] At least two dozen PLA corporate executives holding the rank of major general or higher reportedly fled the country.[44] The major surprise produced by the audits was not the amount of total assets or profits made by the military, but the enormous level of debt it carried. Many of the medium- and small-sized companies were, in fact, operating at a loss—and, like many other state-owned enterprises (SOEs), were saddled with extensive "triangular debt" with local governments and banks. Apparently the special National Handover Work Office of

40. Cited from the journal *Shidai Chao*, in Susan V. Lawrence, "A Model People's Army," *Far Eastern Economic Review*, July 13, 2000.

41. Ibid.

42. See Susan Lawrence and Bruce Gilley, "Bitter Harvest: The Handover of the Military's Business Empire Has Stirred Up a Hornet's Nest," *Far Eastern Economic Review*, April 29, 1999, pp. 22–26; John Pomfret, "Chinese Army Out of Business?" *Washington Post*, January 23, 1998; Matt Forney, "Chinese Army's Exit from Business Leaves Partners Guessing Next Move," *Wall Street Journal*, May 21, 1999; James Kynge, "China's Army Slow to Let Its Businesses Go," *Financial Times*, December 16, 1998.

43. "Commercial Disengagement of Military Enterprises Beset with Chaotic Accounts," *Inside China Mainland*, July 1999, pp. 34–38; "PLA Business Activities Fraught with Abuses," *Inside China Mainland*, November 1998, pp. 26–30.

44. Lawrence and Gilley, "Bitter Harvest."

the State Economic and Trade Commission (SETC) reported that of the first 14,730 enterprises audited "bad or false accounts" totaled 315 billion RMB, while 3,720 enterprises had a combined debt of 47 billion RMB.[45]

James Mulvenon describes the several phases of the divestiture process in his landmark study.[46] First, following the July 1998 order, various units at the central and provincial levels reiterated the order and convened meetings to implement it. The second phase, which lasted until December 1998, involved the formal registration and valuation of assets, and the initial transfer of some large-scale entities. The third phase lasted until mid 1999 and involved intense bargaining over the terms and extent of divestiture, resulting in some exceptions. Within a year, however, the divestiture process resulted in approximately 90 percent of PLA enterprises (including *all* of the conglomerates) having their assets transferred to the holding entity known as the SETC Handover Office. These included the major PLA flagship conglomerates such as Poly Technologies, Xinxing, and Sanjiu. There were, of course, significant exceptions to the order. Following a reorganization and some divestiture, the Xinshidai (New Era) Enterprise Group was still reported to control twenty-six military enterprises in thirteen provinces, with total assets worth more than 6 billion RMB.[47] The PLA Air Force continues to operate China United Airlines, and the arms sales functions of Poly Technologies were transferred to the new General Armaments Department. The most glaring exemptions are PLA-affiliated corporations known to still have major financial interests in the lucrative telecommunications and wireless telephone industries (the PLA monopolizes the commercial CDMA frequencies).[48] PLA companies involved in aviation, agriculture, and some industries also seem to have been exempted from (or to have circumvented) the divestiture order. To compensate the PLA, there appears to have been a one-time payout in December 1998 that increased salaries by 25 percent, as well as an additional 3.2 billion RMB ($400 million) built into the defense budget base—but this amount still falls short of the estimated $1–3 billion net profit that these companies generated every year.[49]

45. *Dong Xiang* (Hong Kong), May 1999, quoted in "Commercial Disengagement of Military Enterprises," *Inside China Mainland*, July 1999.

46. Mulvenon, *Soldiers of Fortune.*

47. DSTI Monthly Report, December 1999, p. 14, based on report in *Wen Hui Bao* (Hong Kong), December 1, 1999.

48. See, e.g., Matt Forney, "China's Army Plays Wireless Mogul Role," *Wall Street Journal*, March 2, 2000; Matt Pottinger, "China's Military Building Mobile Phone Empire," *Reuters World Report*, February 15, 2000.

49. Interviews with PLA General Logistics Department, December 1998.

The Defense Budget Process

Chinese sources reveal three different processes for the assembling and promulgation of the defense budget: the centralized, decentralized, and combined systems *(tongguan, fenguan,* and *jiguan).*[50] It seems that during the 1990s, all three systems operated simultaneously. The centralized system predominated and was supplemented by the other two. Historically, the defense budgeting, allocation, and finance system has oscillated between a centralized Soviet-style distributive system and a more decentralized system. Key policies to decentralize funding sources and spending and auditing requirements came with the Great Leap Forward in 1958, the Cultural Revolution in 1966, and the Zhao Ziyang reforms in 1985, while efforts to centralize the system were made in 1952, 1954–55, 1965, 1978, and 1991.[51] The reforms of 2001 to institute zero-based budgeting were intended simultaneously to decentralize the system again so as to increase unit accountability, and to streamline the method of allocation, giving total discretion to higher-level authorities and preventing units from accruing off-budget sources of income. But the 2001 reforms do not change the structural aspects of the defense budget bidding process, as depicted in figure 20.

The centralized defense budget system is the one where central *allocations* are made to central, military region, and military district levels. The process adopts a "down-up-down" system *(zishang erxia)* whereby the central-level GLD first works in conjunction with the Central Military Commission and Ministry of Finance to establish total expenditure targets, and then initiates a bidding system from military region/district levels, after which final expenditure figures and the central defense budget are set. The centralized military budget system cycle apparently works on an April-to-April fiscal year and in an interactive vertical process between central, regional, and district levels. In March of every year, at the National People's Congress, the annual national and defense budgets are announced by the minister of finance. This figure (for defense) should be viewed as both the culmination and initiation of the centralized defense budget process. That is, the total figure announced is both the outcome of a year-long bidding and negotiating process and the catalyst for the next budget cycle. The aggregate figure

50. Wang Qincheng and Li Zuguo, eds., *Caiwu Daquan* (Urumqi: Xinjiang Renmin Chubanshe, 1993), pp. 501–6. The following description of the three budget systems is drawn primarily from this source.

51. See the discussion in Long Youcai and Wang Zong, eds., *Jundui Caiwu Jianshe* (Beijing: PLA Publishers, 1996), pp. 122–25.

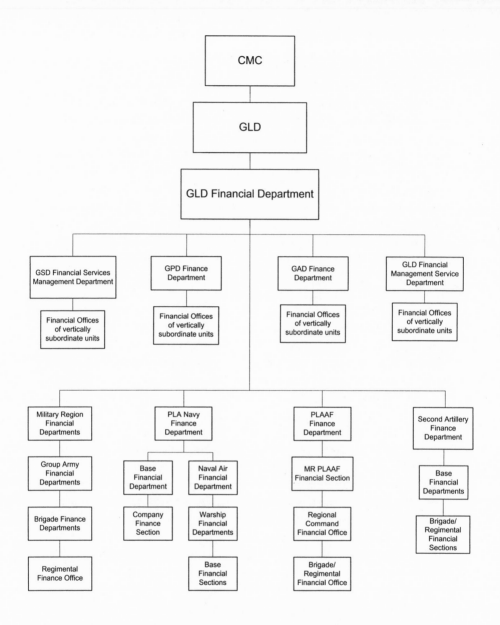

Figure 20. The military financial structure. *Sources*: Long Youcai and Wang Zong, eds., *Jundui Caiwu Jianshe* (Beijing: Jiefangjun Chubanshe, 1996), p. 145. Presumed GAD structure added.

announced is, in effect, the total allocated pool of funds released by the State Council that military units can bid for to receive central allocations.

After the NPC, between April and June of every year, the GLD financial bureaus (GLD/FB) down to the division (and now brigade) level assess their needs and put together budget submissions for the coming year. This pertains to all ground force, air force, and naval units, but *not* the four general departments (GAD, GSD, GLD, GPD), the Second Artillery, the Academy of Military Sciences, or the National Defense University—all of which are under direct control of the Central Military Commission. These estimates are passed up to military districts (still in the GLD/FB *xitong*) in July, where they are assembled and forwarded to the respective military regions in August or September. In the early autumn, the GLD/FB in Beijing begins the process of collating and assessing budget requests. When this process is completed, an annual "All Army Logistics Conference" is convened in Beijing, usually in November, but sometimes December. Following the conference, final accounts are prepared by the GLD/FB for the past year's expenditures as well as the coming year's bids. These are forwarded to the Central Military Commission for consideration at year's end. At this stage, seven central-level PLA institutions are required to submit their bids directly to the CMC (bypassing the GLD system): the General Staff Department; the General Political Department; the General Logistics Department itself; the General Armaments Department; the Ministry of Defense; the Second Artillery (missile forces); and military staff colleges directly under the control of the CMC (the AMS, NDU, and University of Defense Science and Technology). Prior to placing COSTIND solely under control of the State Council in 1998, it too entered the budget process at this stage.

Thus, there is really a two-tier budget system for forces in the field and this group of central departments. To be sure, not all of these late budget bids by key central departments are built into the annual announced official budget figure. For example, as is seen below, numerous research and development costs are buried in other state budgets or are borne by individual factories in the defense industrial system. The Central Military Commission also has a large discretionary fund set aside specifically for purchase of foreign weapons systems, while People's Armed Police, reserve, and militia costs are passed through other central and local budgets.

Usually after the annual November/December GLD conference, the Central Military Commission collates total budget bids and makes allocations. These recommendations are then forwarded to the Ministry of Finance (Caizheng Bu) under the State Council, no later than the Chinese New Year (typically late January). The Ministry of Finance—in consultation with state councilors, the Premier's Office, and certain leadership small groups under the Politburo—then prepares final accounts for the previous year and comes to a final determination for military expenditure in the coming year. These figures are subsequently announced by the minister of finance in his annual speech to the National People's Congress in March. These figures form the basis of the centralized system, which then begins all over again.

In contrast to the centralized management system, the decentralized system *(fengguan zhidu)* is one in which personnel and operating costs for military units are shared between the general department, military region, and district levels. This system is informally referred to as the "three-thirds" system *(san fenzhi san zhidu)*. In this system, military units at all three levels receive allocations outside the defense budget *(yusuanwai)* from provincial, municipal, county, and local governments. These contributions are themselves a kind of subsidy made by governments below the national level. For central units in Beijing and those at the military region level, provincial governments contribute funds, while the centrally administered municipalities of Shanghai, Tianjin, and Chongqing contribute to locally garrisoned forces. County, city, and township governments do the same at the military district and individual unit levels.

In reality, the "three-thirds" defense finance system (the combined centralized/decentralized one) has characterized the PLA budget process since the late 1980s. It is not yet clear, however, what the effect of the zero-based-budgeting system introduced in 2001 will be on the "three-thirds" system. Since the intention of the central government since the 1998 divestiture order has been to create a military budget system that relies solely on central government allocations, based on a rational budget submission process, it is quite likely that the contributions of noncentral governments to locally garrisoned PLA units will decline or cease.

In all three systems, the General Logistics Department has traditionally been the key player in the defense budget process, particularly the GLD's Finance Bureau (Houqinbu Caiwu Chu). While the GLD/FB plays a central role in the budget process, it is a coordinating role without any real decision-making power. It assembles the budget in consultation with the General Staff Department, service arms, and military regions, and forwards it to the CMC—which, in turn, negotiates the final annual budget package with the Ministry of Finance and State Council.[52] After the final budget is negoti-

---

52. This judgment is based on several published Chinese sources, interviews, as well as a CIA analysis—see James Harris et al., "Interpreting Trends in Chinese Defense Spending," in Joint Economic Committee of the Congress of the United States,

ated and set, the extensive nationwide GLD banking system (euphemistically known as the *houqin fuwu ju*, or "logistics service bureaus") allocates funds.

Needless to say, the entire process is fraught with intense lobbying. This usually takes place behind the scenes, but at the 1994 National People's Congress an unusual display of public lobbying took place. The PLA delegation introduced ten motions to the Congress aimed at increasing the defense budget. One of them proposed linking annual military outlays to growth in the economy and inflation by indexing. They argued for indexed increases of at least the inflation rate, and a year-on-year increase of 3.5 percent of gross national product (GNP).[53] The PLA deputies who signed the petition (104 out of 260), pointed out that Chinese defense spending was only 1.7 percent of GNP—well below the needs of the PLA.

The idea of fixing the rate of annual increase in the defense budget, or indexing it to GNP growth or inflation, began to surface in PLA circles in 1992 and continued throughout the decade. Frustrated that defense spending was barely holding even with inflation or was actually declining in nominal terms, senior generals sought some way to ensure adequate (i.e., indexed) annual increases. It seems that the idea of indexing arose out of frustration in the PLA High Command over a range of issues. Officers grumbled that their pay, insufficient to begin with, had not risen to keep pace with inflation. Because wages in the armed forces were so low, recruitment was becoming more difficult. Housing and other funds for troops were woefully inadequate. There were reports of inadequate fuel and spare parts for training exercises. And new weapons systems were underfunded. For example, when it became apparent in the spring of 1993 that the current defense budget was not adequate to pay for the high-priority fighter and submarine programs, the CMC, General Staff Department, and Ministry of Defense reportedly submitted a request for "Special Appropriations for the Production of Aircraft and Ships with Finalized Models" to the State Council and Central Committee.[54] The document outlined the equipment development plans of the air force and navy over the period 1993–96 and requested a special allocation of 31.5 billion RMB to meet es-

ed., *China's Economic Dilemmas in the 1990s* (Armonk, N.Y.: M. E. Sharpe, 1992), pp. 676–84.

53. *Jiefangjun Bao*, March 17, 1994.

54. This case was reported in Luo Bing and Li Ziqing, "Jiang Zemin Enhances Political Standing of the Generals, Now Numbering Ten," *Zhengming*, no. 191 (September 1, 1993), in FBIS–CHI, September 7, 1993.

sential development costs. The Central Committee and State Council, however, only agreed to a special appropriation of 8.5 billion RMB to pay for the J-10 and submarine programs. The money was reportedly transferred from the State Capital Construction budget, and the PLA was apparently given a "promissory note" that these special appropriations would be reviewed in 1994–95. Unsatisfied with this outcome and concerned with the longer-term implications, the CMC, GSD, and MND reportedly sent another document to the State Council and Central Committee. Known as "Reference No. 93003 of the Policy Research Office of the General Staff Headquarters of the Central Military Commission and the Strategic Research Office of the Ministry of National Defense," this document called for an annual minimum increase in the defense budget of 16 to 22 percent and an overall budget in the range of 95 to 115 billion RMB for 1994–95. The Hong Kong media reported similar requests throughout the remainder of the decade, but such indexing never took place.[55]

DECIPHERING CHINESE MILITARY EXPENDITURE

Accurately estimating PLA expenditures is a notoriously difficult and frustrating process because of the lack of transparency on China's part.[56] Although the PLA adamantly maintains that its officially announced defense budget constitutes its total military expenditure, most foreign analysts believe that the official defense budget figure constitutes only a fraction of the total revenue available to the People's Liberation Army. Western estimates range from two to twelve times the announced official budget. The operative questions are: what fraction of expenditures does the official budget represent, and how are other military expenses paid for? The data and analysis presented below suggest that official figures represent approximately one-half of total Chinese military expenditure. That is, I es-

---

55. See, e.g., Li Tzu-ching, "The Military Presses Jiang Zemin and Zhu Rongji to Increase Military Funding," *Zhengming*, April 1, 1999, in FBIS–CHI, April 1, 1999.

56. For an analysis of the problems associated with calculating Chinese defense expenditure, see "China's Defense Expenditure," in International Institute of Strategic Studies, *The Military Balance 1995/96* (London: IISS, 1995), pp. 270–75. Also see Bates Gill, "Chinese Defense Procurement Spending: Determining Intentions and Capabilities," in James Lilley and David Shambaugh, eds., *China's Military Faces the Future* (Armonk, N.Y.: M. E. Sharpe, 1999), pp. 195–227.

timate that total PLA expenditure is from two to two and a half times larger than the official budget. Because one year's surplus funds are often rolled over into the next fiscal year, funds for the PLA are buried in other budgets, and the military enjoys extrabudgetary commercial revenues, the total revenue available to the Chinese military is unknown, probably even to the PLA itself.

Categorizing Chinese Defense Expenditure

Any attempt to calculate Chinese military expenditure must begin with consideration of the *categories* of inclusion and exclusion in the Chinese defense budget. China does not apply the same categories that are standard in the international community—as used by NATO, the United Nations, the ASEAN Regional Forum, the World Bank, or leading international institutes such as the International Institute of Strategic Studies or Stockholm International Peace Research Institute (SIPRI). To be sure, these organizations are not themselves in complete agreement on appropriate categories, but their methodologies are all considerably more detailed than China's official budget breakdown.[57] Some organizations, such as the International Monetary Fund and the U.S. State Department's Arms Control and Disarmament Agency, employ a purchasing power parity (PPP) model, although their categorization is similar to the standard model employed by NATO's.

Officially, China's 1998 and 2000 Defense White Papers distinguish three broad categories of expenditure: personnel, maintenance, and equipment. This elementary breakdown was offered first in 1998, in response to considerable pressure from abroad for increased budget transparency; previously, only a single lump-sum figure was provided. The 1998 White Paper defined these three categories as follows:

· Personnel expenses, "mainly including pay, food and clothing of military and non-military personnel"

· Maintenance expenses, "mainly including military training, construction and maintenance of facilities and running expenses"

57. For an excellent summary of the similarities and differences used by these different organizations, see Somnath Sen, "Military Expenditure Data for Developing Countries: Methods and Measurement," in Geoffrey Lamb and Valeriana Kallab, eds., *Military Expenditure and Economic Development: A Symposium of Research Issues*, World Bank Discussion Papers, no. 185 (Washington, D.C.: World Bank, 1992), pp. 1–18.

· Equipment expenses, being "costs for equipment, including research and experimentation, procurement, maintenance, transportation, and storage"[58]

The 1998 White Paper goes on to say, "In terms of the scope of logistic support, these expenditures cover not only active service personnel, but also militia and reserve requirements. In addition a large amount of spending is used to fund activities associated with social welfare, mainly pensions for retired officers, schools and kindergartens for children of military personnel, training personnel competent for both military and civilian services, supporting national economic construction, and participating in emergency rescue and disaster relief efforts."[59]

Fortunately, other Chinese sources go much further in defining and delimiting expenditure on and by the PLA. One study of military economics divides military expenditure *(junfei)* into three broad categories and several subcomponents:

· Living expenses *(shenghuo fei):* (a) food, clothing, utilities, housing, travel; (b) cultural education, including military cultural studies, professional culture, and television studies

· Military education and research expenses *(junshi jiaoyu keyan fei):* (a) military academy education, including teaching, research, and wargaming and simulation; (b) military scientific research, including research and experimentation; (c) military training and simulation

· Equipment, installation, procurement and building, and maintenance: (a) the conduct of war, including tactics, command, logistics, and security; (b) maintenance labor, including individual unit and repairs in the field; (c) military architecture, including defense factories and reserve factories[60]

Other internal Chinese sources suggest even more detailed categories. The most detailed and definitive is the *Zhongguo Junshi Caiwu Shiyong Daquan* (Practical Encyclopedia of China's Military Finance),[61] which lists fifteen separate categories and extensive subsidiary descriptions (see table 6).

---

58. Information Office of the State Council, *China's National Defense* (1998).
59. Ibid., p. 82–83.
60. Zhang Xulong, ed., *Junshi Jingjixue* (Shenyang: Liaoning Renmin Chubanshe, 1988), p. 382.
61. China Academy of Military Sciences Editing Group, *Zhongguo Junshi Caiwu Shiyong Daquan* (Beijing: Jiefangjun Chubanshe, 1993), pt. 3 (pp. 221–403).

TABLE 6 Chinese Defense Budget Categories

Budget Category	Items Covered
1. Living Expenses *(shenghuo fei)*	Salaries for officers, civilian staff *(wenzhi ganbu)*, NCOs, soldiers, and trainees; subsidy for grain purchase; nurses' and teachers' subsidies; regional subsidies; professional subsidies; physical education allowances and bonuses for coaches and athletes; duty allowances for local officers and soldiers; salaries and living subsidy for retired cadres; housing subsidies; hygiene expenses for female soldiers; pension funds and demobilization stipends; welfare subsidies; storage, bedding, and uniform expenses.
2. Official Expenses *(gongwu fei)*	Official incidental expenses; special expenses; provision and equipment expenses; furlough expenses; business trip expenses; water, electricity, and heating expenses.
3. Operating Expenses *(shiye fei)*	Intelligence; technological detection; meteorology; cartography; confidential document management; electronic countermeasures; militia; political work; publishing; health and hygiene; military transportation; barracks management; management of matériel, bedding, uniforms, and militia equipment; defense factories management; administrative expenses.
4. Education and Training Expenses *(jiaoyu xunlian fei)*	Training equipment and installation expenses; military academies and schools management expenses.
5. Equipment Procurement Expenses *(zhuangbei gouzhi fei)*	Seventeen separate procurement categories: naval; air force; Second Artillery; armored units; engineering corps; communications corps; artillery corps; General Staff Second and Third Departments; antichemical corps; meteorological corps; survey, mapping, and cartography corps; confidential work; electronic countermeasure procurement; ground force's air defense; military ordnance; vehicle repair.
6. Logistics Procurement and Maintenance Expenses *(houqin zhuangbei gouzhi weixu fei)*	Procurement and maintenance of logistics equipment and spare parts; storage and related equipment for logistics support.
7. Weapons Maintenance Management Expenses *(zhuangbei weichi guanli fei)*	Repair and maintenance of weapons and equipment; spare parts, tools, and auxiliary materials.

TABLE 6 *(continued)*

Budget Category	Items Covered
8. Fuel Expenses *(youliao fei)*	Costs of procuring fuels domestically and abroad; refining; storage; transportation.
9. Basic Construction Expenses *(jiben jianshe fei)*	Military buildings, facilities, civil air defense, and other national defense works.
10. Scientific Research Expenses *(kexue yanjiu fei)*	Equipment and research materials for research in military sciences and military medicine (not weapons and technology); external coordination; professional work and achievement awards.
11. War Preparation and Combat Expenses *(zhanbei zuozhan fei)*	Strategic stockpile storage and "combat expenses."
12. Miscellaneous and Flexible Expenses *(qita he jidong jingfei)*	Foreign affairs; unexpected expenses; horse purchasing.
13. Central Military Commission Reserve Funds *(Jun Wei dingwu fei)*	Administrative expenses for running CMC and affiliated organs; special support for general departments; special funds for commissioned reports and investigations. No mention of funds for foreign weapons purchases, although likely.
14. Militia Expenses *(minbing fei)*	Militia training and operating costs; militia equipment purchase costs; militia management administration.
15. People's Air Defense Expenses *(renmin fangkong fei)*	Construction and maintenance of civil air defense network (centrally met costs).

SOURCE: *Zhongguo Junshi Caiwu Shiyong Daquan* (Practical Encyclopedia of China's Military Finance) (Beijing: Jiefangjun Chubanshe, 1993).

Given the internal PLA classification of this source and the length of the volume (over 800 pages), this breakout of the official defense budget should be considered quite definitive. It also roughly corresponds to another key source: the 700-page *Zhongguo Junshi Jingfei Guanli* (Management of China's Military Expenditure).[62] These definitive sources, intended for inter-

62. Lu Zhuhao, ed., *Zhongguo Junshi Jingfei Guanli* (Beijing: Jiefangjun Chubanshe, 1995), esp. pp. 351–550.

nal PLA use, indicate that the official PLA budget is quite comprehensive. However, two key facts need to be borne in mind when evaluating these data: first, this constitutes only the centrally apportioned percentage of defense expenditure, and, second, several categories of funding fall entirely outside this budget framework.

As noted above, the PLA has shared costs with subnational governments, and units throughout the armed forces generate their own revenue from a variety of extramilitary endeavors. It is unknown precisely what proportion of maintenance costs—particularly housing and food subsidies—or personnel overhead costs are met by noncentral allocations, as these are not generally reported in provincial statistical yearbooks.[63] Nor is it known how, prior to the 1998 divestiture, the commercial profits were distributed (estimates of these range from $600 million to $10 billion). The aforementioned categories cover only the central portion of military expenditures. However, they do illustrate the totality of expenditure categories covered by the official budget, thus revealing extrabudgetary categories and funds passed through other state budgets—and this is an important discovery.

Civil defense expenditure is normally excluded from internationally recognized categories of defense spending, as are military pensions to veterans or demobilized servicemen (these are considered transfer payments). Conversely, military aid, funds for paramilitary organizations, reserves and National Guard, *all* military-related research, development, testing, and evaluation (RDT&E) input costs, military space activities, and revenues from arms sales accruing to the military or its affiliated companies are all normally included. None of these are included in Chinese categories.[64] SIPRI specifically excludes some categories that have been regular components of the PRC military budget and PLA expenditure, such as veterans' benefits and demobilization costs, and funds for defense conversion and weapons destruction.

What Doesn't the Chinese Defense Budget Cover?

The official central budget, then, covers a fairly large range of defense expenditure costs. These allocations are supplemented by allocations and revenue streams from subcentral governments, industries, factories, and commercial

63. If taken literally, the "three-thirds" policy would suggest a tripling of the official central defense budget figure, but Chinese sources insist that this phrase indicates more a division of labor than division of actual running costs.

64. See "Sources and Methods for Calculating Military Expenditure," *SIPRI Yearbook, 1999*, p. 328.

endeavors. By the late 1990s, individual units were thought to generate approximately half (in some cases more) of daily operations and maintenance costs through their commercial activities. This notably included food production. The PLA also continues to manufacture a variety of the equipment it uses on a daily basis (in fact, a form of "in-kind" payment). Salaries and a variety of daily maintenance costs are also supplemented with proceeds from units' extracurricular activities. In addition, a variety of costs are paid for through other budgets or from off-budget revenue.

The official defense budget does not appear to include all funds for: (1) Chinese-made weapons and equipment production (as distinct from procurement); (2) some RDT&E costs; (3) the paramilitary People's Armed Police (Wu Jing) and reserves; (4) funds for special large weapons purchases from abroad; (5) funds directly allocated to military factories under the control of the GAD and funds for defense industry conversion; and (6) military aid. How are these six categories of costs paid for? First, the PLA does not buy everything that defense factories produce. Some of these factories now produce goods for civilian consumption. More to the point, however, is that production in many of these factories remains driven by socialist-style quotas or supply-side factors (e.g., maintenance of full employment) rather than by demand. For years, the PLA has complained that it does not want to buy much produced by its own defense industrial system (see chapter 6) but is forced to do so either for lack of alternative suppliers or because it is ordered to do so by the state. The defense industries share many of the burdens of other state-owned enterprises (SOEs).

When the ground, air, or naval forces seek to procure a given weapons system, these procurement (i.e., purchase) costs are apparently borne by the given service arm, as allocated through their annual appropriation as part of the defense budget. The revenue available for procurement, however, is fixed in the defense budget and calculated during the annual budget bidding process overseen jointly by the General Armaments Department and the Finance Bureau of the PLA General Logistics Department. When a service seeks to procure a given system, it contracts with the relevant ministry, which subcontracts to the factories concerned. Before the 1998 reorganization of the defense industries (when competitive bidding was introduced) and creation of the General Armaments Department, the price of the hardware was fixed by COSTIND at an arbitrarily low level. Once prices were set and contracts signed, payment was made, apparently for finished items upon delivery. Thus procurement prices did not meet production costs, which had to be borne by the defense industries concerned. Therefore, under the pre-1998 system, the defense industries were largely responsible for their production costs while sharing R&D costs with COSTIND; the deficit was compensated for or offset through direct subsidies to defense industries. It is too early to say how this has changed under the new system, which is still being worked out. While difficult to estimate, redundant and subsidized production in the defense industrial sector may easily amount to $1 billion annually.

The second area of defense expenditure not fully covered in the official budget is research and development (R&D). Estimating the channels and amounts of funding for this sector is a real conundrum. Funds appear to be derived from four sources—the General Armaments Department (GAD), COSTIND, the Ministry of State Science and Technology, and the defense industries themselves—although the division of labor and investment among them is unclear. Of the three, COSTIND has clearly been the principal source of R&D funds, although this is apparently changing with the creation of the GAD.[65] Following the 1998 reforms, COSTIND's budget now derives entirely from a specific line-item allocation from the State Council. Another source of R&D funds is the Ministry of State Science and Technology (MOST) budget, although the amount is unclear. A certain amount is also paid through the separate line-item defense industry budgets (see below), although presumably this pertains to upgrading production technology (applied research) rather than basic research on systems design and performance. The latter is undertaken in a sprawling number of (numbered) military research institutes and factories. In some cases, these institutes are affiliated with the ministerial defense industries; in others, they are independent entities. It would not be surprising if these extra sources together added $1 billion to the military R&D expenditure every year.

The third area of defense expenditure not included in China's official military budget pertains to the paramilitary forces and reserves. It is surprising not to find a line item in the detailed categories above for reserve forces, now estimated at 500–600,000 and growing.[66] The costs of supporting these forces must be borne entirely by contributions of provincial and local governments. In this regard, it is odd to find costs for maintaining the militia included in the official budget (although, to be certain, a considerable portion of this expense is met locally). However, the omission of the 1.5 million-

65. See Harlan Jencks, "COSTIND Is Dead! Long Live COSTIND!" in James C. Mulvenon and Richard H. Yang, eds., *The People's Liberation Army in the Information Age* (Santa Monica, Calif.: RAND Corporation, 1999), pp. 59–75.

66. International Institute of Strategic Studies, *The Military Balance 2001/2002* (Oxford: Oxford University Press, 2001), p. 188.

strong People's Armed Police is striking.[67] The *Zhongguo Junshi Caiwu Shiyong Daquan* explicitly states that the PAP is primarily funded directly by the Ministry of Finance and also through the Ministry of Public Security budget, although some sources indicate that it is partially paid for out of Ministry of State Security funds.[68] Strengthening the PAP is a high priority for China's leaders, and funding has followed. Wang Shaoguang's research, based on the Ministry of Finance's *Public Finance Yearbook*, reveals an allocation of 12.8 billion RMB for 1998, with an additional contribution of 334 million RMB from local sources. This is scarcely credible, of course, because it would imply an average annual expenditure of roughly 1,100 RMB for every PAP soldier, to say nothing of operations, maintenance, and equipment costs. Annual expenditures for the PAP on the order of $2–3 billion would be a reasonable estimate.[69]

An important fourth category of spending outside the official defense budget is specially earmarked for foreign weapons purchases. During the 1990s, China bought an estimated $6.75 billion worth of weapons and equipment from Russia. Some of these early purchases, such as the first batch of Su-27 fighters, were paid for with one-third foreign exchange ($400 million) and two-thirds barter in consumer durables and agricultural goods. The cash portions of these purchases were paid for from a separate category of funds earmarked for foreign procurement by the Central Military Commission. After 1993–94, Moscow began to demand full payment in foreign currency. In recent years, the PLA has been spending approximately $750 million per annum on Russian weaponry. Sukhoi-27 fighters cost about $32 million each "off the shelf" (and approximately 50 percent more for the kit assembly of 200 at Shenyang); Su-30 fighters cost approximately $47 million each; Sovremenny-class destroyers cost approximately $1 billion each; Kilo-class submarines cost $350 million each; and S-300 surface-to-air missile systems cost $500 million in 1995.[70]

Central government allocations made directly to defense industries constitute a fifth category of extrabudgetary allocations that have benefited the PLA, although, strictly speaking, these factories and companies are not owned by it. These large subsidies are paid directly by the State Council to defense industries or those factories that produce partially for the military

67. Ibid., p. 191.
68. *Zhongguo Junshi Caiwu Shiyong Daquan*, p. 424.
69. Wang Shaoguang, "Military Expenditure of China." For further discussion of Special Forces, see chapter 4. These forces are not to be confused with the Special Police, which are SWAT teams subordinate to the Ministry of Public Security.
70. I am indebted to Ken Allen for this information.

(e.g., electronics), but are administratively under one of the ten State Council corporations (see chapter 6). Many weapons production costs are thus defrayed by the State Council through its subsidies to the relevant defense industry or corporation, rather than carried in the defense budget. These corporate (ministerial) budgets are not made public in the finance minister's annual budget speech, nor are they available in the *Tongji Nianjian* (Statistical Yearbook). These direct line-item allocations to the defense industries could easily amount to an average of $500 million per defense corporation, or $5 billion collectively for the ten major defense corporations that exist today—not to mention the extrabudgetary earnings by the corporations themselves.

Funds allocated for defense industry conversion and earnings by these industries are an important subset of this category of extrabudgetary subsidies.[71] Nearly 70 percent of the output value of military factories is now accounted for by production of civilian goods, and during the Seventh Five-Year Plan (1991–95), the State Council earmarked 6 billion RMB ($1.14 billion) for facilitating conversion. That amount declined during the latter half of the 1990s and probably only amounts to approximately $500 million in the Ninth Five-Year Plan (2000–2005). To be sure, most of China's estimated 50,000 defense industrial factories—which employ up to 2.5 million staff—have not converted successfully. Hence they require substantial state subsidies. One report has noted that 50 percent of defense industry production capacity remains idle, and describes such factories as "an unbearable burden on the national economy."[72] Wang Shaoguang estimates that these subsidies to loss-making military enterprises and for conversion amounted to four billion RMB in 1998.[73] Thus one can assume that conversion subsidies, while considerably down from the early 1990s, still amount to approximately $500 million per annum.

Finally, China still provides military aid to a handful of Asian and African states.[74] Much of this goes to Pakistan, Burma, and Bangladesh and comes

71. See Paul Humes Folta, *From Swords to Plowshares? Defense Industry Reform in the PRC* (Boulder, Colo.: Westview Press, 1992); Mel Gurtov, "Swords into Market Shares: China's Conversion of Military Industry to Civilian Production," *China Quarterly*, no. 134 (June 1993): 213–41; and Ding, "China's Defense Finance."

72. Jiang Baoji et al., "Lun Wo Guo Guofang Jingji Tizhi Mianlin de Wenti ji Gaige Shexiang" (A Discussion of Problems Facing Our Nation's National Defense Economic System and Considerations for Reform), *Junshi Jingji Yanjiu*, no. 12 (December 1990): 14.

73. Wang, "Military Expenditure of China, 1989–98."

74. According to SIPRI, military aid should be counted as an element of military expenditure. Since it is not formally listed as a component of the official defense

in the form of officer training at the PLA National Defense University and military academies ("tuition" is usually fully paid for by China), and technical assistance accompanying arms transfers (see below).

While these seem to be the principal areas of military-related expenditure outside the scope of official defense budget categories, cost sharing through other state budgets and local government allocations is also significant. The PLA still apparently adheres to the "three-thirds" policy whereby many personnel and maintenance costs are proportionately split among central, provincial, and local governments. Pensions and demobilization are a prime example. From 1987 to 1997, the PLA demobilized approximately 1.2 million troops;[75] in 2000, it demobilized an additional 500,000. It is estimated that approximately 10 percent of those demobilized were officers, high-ranking officers who demand large pensions and perquisites. They continue to receive their salaries, plus retirement bonuses and pension, housing, travel allowances, free health and hospital care, and often a car and driver. Lower-ranking officers and enlisted personnel receive a one-time demobilization payment. These costs are partly covered in the official defense budget, but are also paid for through the Ministry of Civil Affairs budget, which is responsible for civilian cadre retirements as well. County, municipal, and local governments also underwrite, directly and indirectly, a large portion of the associated costs. Jiang Zemin and senior military officials have frequently commented on the need to give "high priority" to these demobilizations. Wang Shaoguang estimates, based on a survey of public finance and provincial statistical yearbooks, that annual noncentral allocations to demobilized personnel amounted to 3.6 billion RMB in 1998,[76] but many of the subsidies are disguised. Since pensions and demobilization costs are not usually included as defense expenditures, I do not include these expenditures in the off-budget spending of the PLA.[77]

The "three-thirds" policy also applies to housing and related garrisoning costs, as well as local contributions to energy expenditure (fuel costs) for some units. If one accepts the 1998 Defense White Paper's claim that 38 percent of official military expenditure is for personnel costs, and that this amount constitutes the *central* government's allocation, under the "three-

budget, it is categorized here as extrabudgetary expenditure. See *SIPRI Yearbook, 1999*, p. 328.

75. See Yitzhak Shichor, "Demobilization: The Dialectics of PLA Troop Reduction," in Shambaugh and Yang, eds., *China's Military in Transition*, pp. 72–95.

76. Wang, "Military Expenditure of China, 1989–98."

77. See *SIPRI Yearbook, 1999*, p. 328.

thirds" policy, provincial and local governments would have spent $8.99 billion (at official exchange rates) in "matching funds" in the 2000 fiscal cycle. This amount should then be added as a category of extrabudgetary expenditure.

Two other sources of revenue deserve mention: proceeds from commercial activities and arms sales. While the PLA's divestiture of its commercial investments has proceeded remarkably well since the 1998 order, it has certainly not been complete. As noted above, it is estimated that as many as 20 percent of the units involved in extracurricular commerce have carried on their activities—which would yield approximately $2 billion per year in revenue. Proceeds from arms sales are not normally counted on international defense budget ledgers, because such funds normally accrue to private sector defense contractors; but in most countries defense industries are not government-controlled, whereas in China some of the principal arms export companies are attached to one or more general departments of the PLA (see figure 18), and others are State Council entities.[78] Normally, proceeds from arms sales are paid directly by the foreign purchaser to the Chinese export company concerned—once production, storage, and transport costs are recovered, the company is supposed to remit one-third of the profits to its parent general department and one-third to the CMC, keeping one-third for itself.[79] In practice, China's arms export companies tend to keep whatever profits they can and probably obfuscate account books to conceal money made.

Arms sales provided China's defense industries with significant extra revenue during the 1980s, but they declined precipitously during the 1990s. At their height during the Iran-Iraq War, when China was selling to both sides, its arms export companies earned an average of $1.5 billion per annum in gross proceeds.[80] They garnered a total of approximately $12 billion between 1985 and 1992.[81] According to Arms Control and Disarmament Agency figures, China's exports topped out at $3.75 billion in 1988 but dropped to $0.58 billion by 1996.[82] China officially admits to selling $2 billion worth of

78. Also see John W. Lewis et al., "Beijing's Defense Establishment: Solving the Arms Export Enigma," *International Security,* Spring 1991.

79. Interviews with Northern Industries Company and General Logistics Department personnel, November 1993.

80. Arms Control and Disarmament Agency, *World Military Expenditures and Arms Transfers, 1991–1992* (Washington, D.C.: ACDA, 1993), p. 100.

81. Richard Grimmett, *Conventional Arms Transfers to the Third World, 1985–1992* (Washington, D.C.: Congressional Research Service, 1993), p. 60.

82. Arms Control and Disarmament Agency, *World Military Expenditures and Arms Transfers, 1997* (Washington, D.C.: ACDA, 1998), p. 265.

weapons in 1987, acknowledges a drop to $900 million in 1991, and claims that the "volume of contracted business" did not exceed $1 billion in subsequent years through 1997.[83] Since 1998, revenue from arms sales has plummeted to approximately $600 million per year—with China's major customers being the destitute nations of Pakistan, Bangladesh, and Burma. While these levels are not high, certainly when compared to other major arms-exporting nations, they do represent an additional source of revenue flowing into the coffers of China's military-industrial complex. It is important to note that these earnings do not directly go to the PLA, although they benefit it indirectly. Another way of stating this is that this money benefits China's armed forces and defense establishment, although not the PLA directly.

If these estimates of extrabudgetary sources of revenue are added to the 2000 official defense budget of $14.5 billion, one arrives at a total military revenue base of approximately $31.6 billion (see table 7). This total would rank China third in the world in total military expenditure behind the United States and Russia, and just ahead of France, Japan, the United Kingdom, and Germany.[84]

Some will surely challenge these estimates as excessively high, while others will no doubt find them low. They are simply the most realistic—yet admittedly approximate—estimates I can offer based on knowledge of the extra categories of revenue available to the PLA and the likely amounts in each category. Some categories are fairly well-known and accurate (foreign arms purchases, arms sales, military aid), while others are far less precise (subsidies, research and development, cost-sharing, commercial revenue). But the bottom line is that the PLA's official budget presents only a part of the story.

Aggregate Trends

These estimates reveal revenue available to the PLA, and total military spending of, a little more than twice the official budget for the 2000 fiscal year. As noted above, this would place China third globally in aggregate defense spending, making its military expenditure very comparable to that of medium-sized powers such as France, Britain, Japan, and Germany. But while these other nations' military budgets have been declining in the post–Cold War period (the "peace dividend"), China's military spending has been steadily rising. While China's military expenditure was closely correlated

83. Information Office of the State Council, *China's National Defense, 2000*, p. 128.

84. International Institute of Strategic Studies, *The Military Balance 1999/2000* (Oxford: Oxford University Press, 1999), pp. 300–302.

TABLE 7 Estimated PLA/Military Establishment Revenue, 2000

Item	Revenue (U.S.$ billions, approximate)
Funds Going Directly to the PLA	
Official Defense Budget	14.5
Foreign Arms and Technology Purchases	1
Provincial/Local Cost-Sharing	5
TOTAL DIRECT ALLOCATIONS	20.5
Funds Indirectly Going to Armed Forces and Military-Industrial Establishment	
Redundant Production and Subsidized Cost Overruns	1
Extrabudgetary Defense R&D	1
People's Armed Police	3
Direct Subsidies to Defense Industries and Defense Conversion	5.5
Arms Sales Revenue	0.6
TOTAL INDIRECT ALLOCATIONS	11.1
TOTAL ESTIMATED REVENUE	31.6

to its external threat environment for the first forty years of the PRC, during the past ten years, when there has arguably been no pressing external threat, Beijing's military spending has doubled in real terms. The official budget has risen at double-digit rates since 1989—with an average annual increase of 15.5 percent. To be sure, during 1993–97, China suffered inflation at approximately the same level (thus nullifying the increases), but in 1989–92 and 1997–2000, China's economy suffered deflation, so for much of this period, the increases have been real and substantial.

While China continues to spend a high proportion of net government funds available in the annual budget (an average of 17 percent over the past fifty years and 8.6 percent from 1989–2000) relative to other countries, its "defense burden" nevertheless remains modest in terms of the percentage of GDP spent on defense (approximately 1.4 percent of the official budget). Even if this figure is tripled to allow for the extrabudgetary revenue available to the PLA, it puts China in the same league as the United States (in percentage terms) and far below the Cold War levels of the former Soviet Union (which spent nearly 20 percent of GDP on defense). Although Chinese military expenditures have increased at a substantial rate since 1989, it is inaccurate to speak of any kind of "crash" buildup to date. China is not spending excessive available funds on the military, nor is there any evidence of heavy investment into particular programs (except perhaps short-range ballistic missiles since 1996 and cruise missiles since 1998). Over time, however, double-digit annual increases combined with low or no inflation—if continued—will have a significant impact on the PLA's weaponry and capabilities.

The extra funds for the military are also going much further because of the significant reduction in personnel. This has permitted an increase in per capita personnel expenditure and improvements in salaries, housing, and troop maintenance—thus permitting the military to recruit and retain better-educated soldiers and officers. As noted in chapter 3, most of the personnel reductions have come out of the ground forces—thus permitting an increase in recruitment into the air force and navy. Mothballing of antiquated equipment in recent years (particularly aircraft and armored vehicles) has also saved considerable money, spare parts, and personnel. In other words, as the PLA has downsized, it has become more rationalized and cost-efficient. In addition to freeing up funds for personnel, it has also increased the money available for weapons procurement at home and abroad. Purchases of advanced equipment from Russia and Israel are indicative of this new liquidity, but it will become particularly apparent when new indigenous systems (fighters, surface combatants, and submarines) begin to come on stream around 2004–7.

But if the PLA still spends nearly 40–50 percent of its budget on personnel, this does not leave a great deal to invest in procurement and R&D. This is where extrabudgetary funding comes in. The plowing back into the defense industrial system of funds generated by units and firms has been noted above. These amounts have been reduced as the PLA has proceeded to largely divest itself of its commercial business empire.

Finally, the revenue from China's arms sales has plummeted over the past fifteen years. Simply put, Chinese weapons are a last resort for most developing nations, and Beijing's failure to compete at all in the international arms market is further testimony to the pathetic state of China defense industries (see chapter 6). China's military aid has also plummeted over the same period of time.

In sum, the PLA has more money available than ever before and is spending it in a much more rational manner, but there still is scant financial evidence of a significant military buildup.

Plate 1.   *Top:* Deng Xiaoping, former chairman of the Central Military Commission, viewing naval exercise, July 1979 (Xinhua News Agency).

Plate 2.   *Bottom:* Jiang Zemin, chairman of Central Military Commission, reviewing troops at the PRC's fiftieth anniversary parade, October 1, 1999 (Xinhua News Agency).

Plate 3.   Members of the Central Military Commission, September 22, 1999 (Xinhua News Agency). Left to right: General Xu Caihou, General Cao Gang-chuan, General Wang Ke, General Fu Quanyou, General Zhang Wannian (vice-chairman), President Jiang Zemin (chairman), Vice-President Hu Jintao (vice-chairman), General Chi Haotian (vice chairman), General Yu Yongbo, General Wang Ruilin, General Guo Buoxiong.

Plate 4.   Mountain warfare exercises by Nanjing Military Region armored units in simulation of Taiwan invasion, June 7, 1999 (Xinhua News Agency).

Plate 5. *Top:* Armored personnel carriers of the Zhuhai-Macao Military District, November 19, 1999 (Xinhua News Agency).

Plate 6. *Bottom:* Mi-17 troop transport helicopters in rapid reaction unit exercises, July 25, 1999 (Xinhua News Agency).

Plate 7.   PLA Air Force Su-27 unit based at Wuhu, Anhui Province, November 9, 1999 (Xinhua News Agency).

Plate 8.   *Top:* DF-15 (M-9) short-range ballistic missile on display at the PRC's fiftieth anniversary parade, October 1, 1999 (Xinhua News Agency).

Plate 9.   *Bottom:* HQ-2 surface-to-air guided missile being fired in Taiwan Strait exercise on March 30, 1996 (Xinhua News Agency).

Plate 10.   DF-15 (M-9) short-range ballistic missile being fired toward Taiwan, March 18, 1996 (Xinhua News Agency).

Plate 11.   *Top:* PLA Navy Luda-class destroyers, led by the *Zhuhai,* exercising in the Taiwan Strait, March 30, 1996 (Xinhua News Agency).

Plate 12.   *Bottom:* PLA Navy Luda III–class destroyers, led by the *Zunyi,* on patrol in the South China Sea, March 31, 2000 (Xinhua News Agency).

Plate 13.   *Top:* The PLA Navy's first Luhu-class guided missile destroyer, the *Harbin*, gets under way from port, March 4, 2000 (Xinhua News Agency).

Plate 14.   *Bottom:* The PLA Navy's new Song-class submarine on sea trials in Bohai Gulf, June 7, 1999 (Xinhua News Agency).

Plate 15.   *Top:* The PLA's new soldier, the information warrior, in training at military academy, June 30, 1999 (Xinhua News Agency).

Plate 16. *Bottom:* The author, U.S. Ambassador Chas W. Freeman Jr., Chief of General Staff General Fu Quanyou, and Deputy Chief of Staff General Xiong Guangkai, December 1998 (author's photo).

6 Defense Industries and Weapons Procurement

There is probably no area of China's national defense establishment more in need of modernization than its defense industries (military-industrial complex). During the half-century of the People's Republic and the entire period since China first embarked on a policy of "self-strengthening" *(zi qiang)* in the 1870s, centered on a policy of building "shipyards and arsenals,"[1] China's defense industries have proven woefully inadequate to the task of producing weaponry and defense technology of an international standard.

This long failure has not been for lack of effort. Generations of Chinese leaders and soldiers have placed emphasis on building up an indigenous defense industrial base. Over the fifty years of the PRC, the country's defense industries have undergone one organizational change after another. Yet these repeated reforms are tacit admission of failure. In their attempts, they have periodically sought to buy and borrow from abroad, while at the same time persistently seeking to make China's own defense industrial establishment "self-sufficient" *(zili gengsheng)*. The process of trying selectively to graft foreign technologies onto an indigenous Chinese base and achieve autonomy in production capacity has also generally caused more problems than it has solved. China's persistent search abroad for military technology and hardware has been born of necessity and is a clear indication of indigenous failure: China's own industries, scientists, and technicians have consistently failed to keep pace with either their nation's defensive needs or global standards. To be sure, China has never had ample access or funds to purchase foreign technologies and weapons unabated on the international market, but even when it has successfully acquired a given system, the Chinese mili-

---

1. See, e.g., Thomas L. Kennedy, *The Arms of Kiangnan: Modernization in the Chinese Ordnance Industry, 1860–1895* (Boulder, Colo.: Westview Press, 1978).

tary has over the past century faced substantial problems of assimilation and maintenance.

THE PRE-REFORM MILITARY-INDUSTRIAL COMPLEX

The base of China's defense industries was formed through the massive material and technical assistance provided by the Soviet Union in the 1950s.[2] China's military-industrial and manufacturing capacity, such as existed, was then concentrated in the war-damaged Manchurian region and in the coastal cities of Tianjin and Shanghai. By 1950, forty-five factories were producing ordnance again, employing 100,000 workers.[3] They largely manufactured light weapons, ammunition, and artillery. But under Soviet tutelage, facilities were built to produce aircraft, naval vessels, electronic equipment, land armaments, and a wide range of ordnance. In addition, the Soviet Union transferred the know-how for thermonuclear weapons, although Nikita Khrushchev reneged on a promise to provide a sample atomic bomb.[4] Structurally, the defense industries were vertically integrated in the Soviet organizational mode, whereby each plant was composed of as many components as the whole manufacturing process required. Following Mao's decision in 1956, announced in his "Ten Great Relationships" speech, to expand industrial development in the interior of the country, many defense plants were built in or near cities such as Taoyuan, Luoyang, Lanzhou, Chengdu, Chongqing,

2. The following discussion is drawn in part from my "China's Defense Industries: Indigenous and Foreign Procurement," in Paul H. B. Godwin, ed., *The Chinese Defense Establishment: Continuity and Change in the 1980s* (Boulder, Colo.: Westview Press, 1983), pp. 43–86. Other useful sources include James Blaker, "The Production of Conventional Weapons," in William H. Whitson, ed., *The Military and Political Power in China in the 1970s* (New York: Praeger, 1972), pp. 215–28; Harlan W. Jencks, *From Muskets to Missiles: Politics and Professionalism in the Chinese Army, 1945–1981* (Boulder, Colo.: Westview Press, 1982), pp. 189–222; and Ellis Joffe, *The Chinese Army after Mao* (Cambridge, Mass.: Harvard University Press, 1987), pp. 94–118. Two extremely useful Chinese studies on the development of PRC defense industries and military R&D are Deng Liqun, ed., *Dangdai Zhongguo de Guofang Keji Shiye* (Contemporary China's Defense Science and Technology Enterprises), vols. 1 and 2 (Beijing: Dangdai Zhongguo Chubanshe, 1992), and *Dangdai Zhongguo Bingqi Gongye* (Contemporary China's Weapons Industries) (Beijing: Dangdai Zhongguo Chubanshe, 1993).

3. *Dangdai Zhongguo Bingqi Gongye*, p. 25.

4. See Harold Ford, "Modern Weapons and the Sino-Soviet Estrangement," *China Quarterly*, no. 18 (June 1969): 160–73; and Odd Arne Westad, *Brothers in Arms: The Rise and Fall of the Sino-Soviet Alliance, 1945–1963* (Washington, D.C.: Woodrow Wilson Center Press; Stanford, Calif.: Stanford University Press, 1998).

Kunming, and Wuhan. This process was given further impetus in the mid to late 1960s by the Chairman's decision to create the "third line" *(san xiam)* or Third Front, whereby factories were built deep in the interior of Sichuan and Guangxi provinces in particular (so as to reduce their vulnerability to attack by the Soviet Union or United States).[5] The Third Front's guiding principle of "decentralization, closeness to mountains, and concealment" *(fensan, kaoshan, yinbi)* dictated that sprawling complexes be constructed in remote mountainous and forested areas, with newly laid rail lines connecting them to sources of raw materials and larger cities. The program continued until the late 1970s. Altogether, under the Third Front initiative, a total of 483 factories and 92 research academies and institutes were located in China's remote hinterland.[6] While it may have made sense from a national security perspective (and even that is debatable), the Third Front lacked any kind of economy of scale and resulted in the squandering of incalculable resources. China's defense industries have been paying the price of Mao's decision ever since. In fact, some of the most intractable and laggard enterprises of China's ossified state industrial system are Third Front factories.

Although the construction of a comprehensive defense industrial base proceeded fairly well with Soviet assistance following the Korean War—producing first generations of fighter aircraft and transports, tanks and armored personnel carriers, surface ships and submarines, and general ordnance—development was interrupted by the Great Leap Forward in 1958–60, which drained capital, equipment, and manpower for other industrial initiatives and mindless "backyard" steel production. Some of this steel was supplied to military factories, but its shoddy quality resulted in production of inadequate goods, from airframes to tanks. Productivity dropped off: the machine-building industry's growth rate slipped from first to third behind chemical fertilizer production and petroleum production.

The abrupt withdrawal of Soviet advisers and assistance in the summer of 1960 left a wide variety of industrial projects unfinished. CIA analysts estimated that 100 of the 166 key heavy industrial projects were in the machine-building industries, with the majority of these in the defense sector.[7] Other

5. See Barry Naughton, "The Third Front: Defense Industrialization in the Chinese Interior," *China Quarterly,* no. 115 (September 1988).

6. John Wilson Lewis and Xue Litai, *China's Strategic Seapower: The Politics of Force Modernization in the Nuclear Age* (Stanford, Calif.: Stanford University Press, 1994), p. 94.

7. J. Craig, J. Lewek, and G. Cole, "A Survey of China's Machine Building Industry," in U.S. Congress Joint Economic Committee, *The Chinese Economy Post-Mao,* vol. 1 (Washington, D.C.: Government Printing Office, 1978), p. 287.

estimates place the number of defense-related factories lower, at 41 of the 156.[8] The aeronautic and nuclear programs were especially hard hit. The defense industries retrenched with the rest of the economy from 1961 to 1963. The reorientation of economic priorities following the post–Great Leap depression, under Chen Yun and Deng Xiaoping's aegis, rejected the Soviet emphasis on heavy industry, especially to serve military needs (indeed, this had been one of Mao's own criticisms, dating back to 1956). The defense industrial sector thus atrophied. As the China military specialist Paul H. B. Godwin pithily put it, "In the years following the termination of Soviet assistance in 1959–60, China's defense industrial base and research and development infrastructure eroded into obsolescence."[9] The onset of the Cultural Revolution (1966–69) did not help matters, as production was disrupted, factories came to a standstill, soldiers became involved in clashes with Red Guards, and scientists and bureaucrats were purged. Overall production dropped sharply, although the curtailment of military production was estimated by the CIA not to have been as severe as during the Great Leap Forward.[10] Some defense industries, notably the nuclear and strategic submarine programs, were insulated from the chaos of the Cultural Revolution by executive order of Chairman Mao, Premier Zhou Enlai, and Minister of Defense Lin Biao. But the aircraft industry and conventional weapons production atrophied. By 1968, the defense industries began to be revived, as the tensions with the Soviet Union grew intense. Defense production rose rapidly, reaching an all-time peak in 1971—more than double the output of 1967!

This trend was not to last. In mid 1971, a major policy debate between civilian and military planners surfaced in the Chinese media. The controversy went by the rubric of the "electronics versus steel" debate. At issue was not civil versus military production (guns versus butter), but rather a more refined argument as to budgetary allocation within the defense industries. It appeared that the ground forces were arguing for more "steel," while the air and nuclear forces made the case for more investment in high technology (i.e., "electronics"). This disguised debate was the first indication of dissatisfaction in some sectors of the PLA with the "people's war" doctrine. The issue polarized national security planners at the elite level. As-

8. Lewis and Xue, *China's Strategic Seapower*, p. 76.
9. Paul H. B. Godwin, "China's Defense Modernization: Aspirations and Capabilities," *Washington Journal of Modern China* 6, no. 1 (Spring 2000): 15.
10. Sydney H. Jammes, "The Chinese Defense Burden, 1965–1974," in U.S. Congress Joint Economic Committee, *China: A Reassessment of the Economy* (Washington, D.C.: Government Printing Office, 1973), p. 463.

sessment of external threat was an integral part of the question. Defense Minister Lin Biao, Chief of Staff Huang Yongsheng, the Communist Party ideologue Chen Boda, and other "radicals" took the "electronics" side of the debate. They believed the United States was China's principal threat and hence that the PLA needed a stronger air force and nuclear deterrent. The "steel" faction consisted of a coalition of party officials, headed by Premier Zhou Enlai, and civilian economic planners. They identified the former Soviet Union as the main enemy, feared a land invasion from the north, and advocated strengthening tank divisions and the ground forces. Because this was more in line with Mao's own strategic assessment, "steel" was favored over "electronics."

This debate was a watershed for Lin Biao. Given what is now known about the sensitive signaling with the United States at the time, which brought about the Sino-American rapprochement, the defeat of the "electronics" faction was simultaneously a rejection of Lin's "dual adversary" policy.[11] Lin Biao's policy defeat was followed by his own demise on September 1971, when his aircraft crashed into the Mongolian desert.[12] The fact that many of his apparent co-conspirators were affiliated with the air force may help to explain the anti-American, pro-electronics faction's position.

Following Lin's death and the opening to the United States and the West, China's defense industrial modernization entered a new period. As in the civilian sector, foreign assistance became an integral part of Premier Zhou Enlai's plan for comprehensive modernization. The critical question for Chinese policymakers was whether to favor the defense industries in such purchases (as they had during the 1950s). Initial purchases indicated the adoption of a middle position. From the outset China made it clear that it was interested in minimizing dependency on foreign suppliers and, if possible, acquiring the means of production for a range of military equipment. In areas where needs were pressing, whole weapons systems would be sought. PLA delegations fanned out across western Europe and "window-shopped" for a wide range of components and systems. Aside from some anti-air and

11. See Thomas Gottlieb, *Chinese Foreign Policy Factionalism and the Origins of the Strategic Triangle* (Santa Monica, Calif.: RAND Corporation, 1977); and Central Intelligence Agency, *Policy Issues in the Purge of Lin Biao* (1972), declassified under the Freedom of Information Act in November 1978.

12. For two excellent recent studies of the Lin Biao affair, see Jin Qiu, *The Culture of Power: The Lin Biao Incident in the Cultural Revolution* (Stanford, Calif.: Stanford University Press, 1999); and Frederick C. Teiwes and Warren Sun, *The Tragedy of Lin Biao: Riding the Tiger during the Cultural Revolution, 1966–1971* (Honolulu: University of Hawaii Press, 1996).

anti-tank missiles, however, very little was in fact purchased. Limited foreign exchange proved to be a real constraint, but so too did China's penchant for "self-reliance" and desire to avoid dependency on foreign sources of supply. A better and cheaper strategy, Chinese planners reasoned, was to selectively purchase key systems and attempt to "reverse engineer" and duplicate them. This strategy proved an utter failure. Either European suppliers did not wish merely to sell one or two prototypes or, when the Chinese did get their hands on them, the technologies proved far too complex for copying. As a result, China's defense industries continued to languish.

This situation persisted throughout the 1980s. Although the United States and China did agree to cooperate on some joint projects to improve a few select PLA capabilities—such as the "Peace Pearl" project to upgrade the avionics in the F-8 II fighter and some large-caliber ammunition production projects—China's defense industries did not benefit from the opening to the West. What little progress was made in weapons production during the 1980s came as a result of extensive investment and concentration of resources, as in ballistic missiles. Apart from a few "islands of competence," China's military-industrial complex remained a sea of mediocrity, backwardness, and redundancy. The June 4, 1989, massacre in Beijing terminated these projects, as the United States and European Union (EU) suspended most technological assistance to the PLA. Although the EU delivered components that had been contracted prior to June 4 (delayed until 1992–93), the European nations individually maintain a voluntary embargo on all lethal weapons and a very strict review process for sale of defense technologies to China. For its part, Washington's sanctions are enshrined in law and executive order.

Severed from Western sources of supply, the military-industrial complex and PLA again languished until the mid 1990s, when Moscow and Beijing resurrected their defense industrial relationship after more than thirty years (discussed at greater length below). Israel also became a supplier of military equipment and technology during the 1990s.

ORGANIZATIONAL EVOLUTION AND STRUCTURAL REFORM OF THE MILITARY-INDUSTRIAL COMPLEX

On May 5, 1950, China's defense industries were overseen by the newly created Military Industries Office of the Ministry of Heavy Industry.[13] A

---

13. Deng, ed., *Dangdai Zhongguo Bingqi Gongye*, p. 25.

TABLE 8 China's Defense Industries in 1960

Ministry	Responsibility
First MMB	Civilian
Second MMB	Atomic energy and nuclear weapons
Third MMB	Aircraft and nonballistic missiles
Fourth MMB	Electronics and telecommunications
Fifth MMB	Conventional ordnance
Sixth MMB	Naval equipment and shipbuilding
Seventh MMB	Ballistic missiles

year later the CCP Central Committee established a Military Industry Bureau *(Zhongyang Binggong Zongju)* under the State Council to provide more centralized control.[14] Under Soviet advice, a reconfiguration of the entire industrial sector took place in 1952, and two ministries of machine building were created—the first oversaw civilian production and the second military production. This system essentially held until after the Sino-Soviet Split in 1960, when they were reconfigured into eight separate ministries of machine building (MMBs). These are shown in table 8.

An eighth MMB, charged with producing agricultural machinery, was created in the mid 1960s but merged with the first MMB in 1970.[15] In 1979, these functions reverted to the first MMB and an entirely new eighth MMB was inaugurated, this time charged with space programs (rockets and satellites) and production of tactical missiles. In 1981–82, a further reorganization was undertaken. The eighth MMB merged with the seventh MMB and all other MMBs were renamed, although their functions did not change. As a result, the organization of China's military-industrial complex was as shown in table 9.

In 1988, these ministries were reorganized and consolidated again, shrinking to four ministerial-level organs. In effect, the ministries of Aviation and Space Industries were combined, as were the ministries of Electronics, Ordnance, and Machine Building. The Ministry of Nuclear Energy was renamed and merged with the ministries of Coal and Electric Power into a new Ministry of Energy Resources. While perhaps meeting the government goal of reducing the overall number of ministerial-level organs, this

14. Ibid., p. 42.
15. Jencks, *From Muskets to Missiles,* p. 194.

TABLE 9 China's Defense Industries in 1982

Ministry	Production Line
Ministry of Machine Building	Civilian production
Ministry of Nuclear Energy	Atomic energy and nuclear weapons
Ministry of Aviation Industry	Aircraft
Ministry of Electronics Industry	Electronics systems
Ministry of Ordnance Industry	Munitions and conventional arms
China State Shipbuilding Corp.	Naval and merchant shipping
Ministry of Space Industry	Space systems and ballistic missiles

TABLE 10 China's Defense Industries in 1988

Ministry	Production Line
Ministry of Energy Resources	Nuclear, coal, and electric power
Ministry of Aerospace	All civil and military aviation, space and missiles (tactical and ballistic)
Ministry of Machine Building and Electronics Industry	All civilian and military machinery, electronics, and ordnance
China State Shipbuilding Corp.	All merchant and military shipbuilding

round of bureaucratic restructuring and consolidation actually significantly decreased efficiency and economies of scale. For the defense industries, it was a definite step backward. The 1988 reorganization left the structure shown in table 10.

In 1993, the military-industrial complex was reorganized yet again. This reorganization, like those in 1982 and 1988, was part of a larger reorganization of the State Council ministries and commissions, intended to reduce the overall number and redundancy of functions, as well as to "corporatize" some ministries so as to inject some market-driven elements into the procurement and production processes. Although the previous round of restructuring in 1988 had left the defense industries overly centralized and controlled, this round moved to decentralize and more fully marketize them (although, as noted in chapter 5, they continued to receive central govern-

TABLE 11 China's Defense Industries in 1993

Ministry	Production Line
China National Nuclear Corp. (CNNC)	Nuclear power and nuclear weapons
Aviation Industries of China (AVIC)	All civilian and military aircraft
China Aerospace Corp. (CASC)	Space launch vehicles, satellites, missiles, and related equipment
China North Industries Corp (NORINCO) and China Ordnance Industry Corporation (COIC)	Conventional weapons and ordnance
China State Shipbuilding Corp. (CSSC)	All commercial and naval shipping

ment subsidies directly from the State Council, outside the defense budget). This move was also commensurate with the defense conversion program then under way. The 1988 restructuring halved the number of defense ministries from eight to four; the 1993 initiative recreated six ministry-equivalent bodies, plus a new Ministry of Electronics Industry and Ministry of Machine Industry (both of which now ostensibly produced entirely for the civilian sector), shown in table 11.

The most recent, and perhaps most sweeping, reorganization of the defense industries took place in 1998. In addition to creating the General Armament Department (GAD), a new suprabody to oversee the entire military-industrial establishment (see below and chapter 4), and redesigning the Commission on Science, Technology, and Industry for National Defense (COSTIND), the five ministerial-level corporations above were expanded into ten new corporate bodies *(gongsi)* and enterprise conglomerates *(jituan)*, shown in table 12.

Each reorganization over the past twenty years has represented a search for greater rationality and efficiency, yet each one was a tacit admission of the failure of previous attempts, and none has yet proved sufficient to the task. Quality has remained poor, particularly in the aerospace and ordnance industries, and production of platforms and weapons systems still lags substantially behind world standards.

TABLE 12   China's Defense Industries in 2000

Corporation	Production Line
China First Aviation Corp.	Fighter aircraft, bombers, transports, advanced training jets, commercial airliners
China Second Aviation Corp.	Helicopters, light trainers, unmanned aerial vehicles (UAVs)
China Aerospace Science Technology Corp.	Space launch vehicles, satellites
China Aerospace Machinery Electronics Corp.	Missiles, electronics, other ballistics
China North Industries Group Corp.	Tanks, armored vehicles, artillery, ordnance
China South Industries Group Corp.	Miscellaneous ordnance, trucks, automobiles, motorcycles
China State Shipbuilding Corp. (Northern Shipyards in Dalian)	Destroyers, submarines, large container and commercial vessels
China State Shipbuilding Corp. (Southern Shipyards in Shanghai and Wuhan)	Frigates and smaller surface combatants, submarines, merchant ships
China National Nuclear Corp.	Nuclear fuel, energy, and weapons
China Nuclear Engineering and Construction Corp.	Nuclear power plants

OVERSIGHT AND COORDINATION

The history of the bureaucratic organs coordinating and controlling China's military-industrial and research and development sectors is convoluted and complex. It, too, is a history of one reorganization after another, with organs being established, consolidated, divided, abolished, and recreated time and again. The sheer number of reorganizations is itself an admission of both the priority placed on military modernization (particularly the atomic and missile programs), and of the general failure of China's defense industries to produce modern (or even semimodern) weapons to meet the needs of the armed forces. While one study of the PLA's Commission on Science and Technology for National Defense by Benjamin Ostrov paints a picture of the bureaucratic rise and decline of the commission,[16] recently published

16. Benjamin C. Ostrov, *Conquering Resources: The Growth and Decline of the PLA's Science and Technology Commission for National Defense* (Armonk, N.Y.: M. E. Sharpe, 1991).

Chinese organizational histories of the national defense science and technology and ordnance industry sectors tell a more complex historical and bureaucratic story.[17] The highlights of this institutional history, as described in new Chinese documents, are as follows:

October 19, 1949: Ministry of Heavy Industry established, with oversight responsibilities for military industries.

May 3, 1950: Ministry of Heavy Industry establishes Military Industries Office (Binggong Bangongshi).

January 4, 1951: Central Military Commission establishes Military Industry Commission (Zhongyang Junwei Binggong Weiyuanhui).

April 17, 1951: State Council and CMC establish Aviation Industry Management Commission (Hangkong Gongye Guanli Weiyuanhui).

April 19, 1951: Ministry of Heavy Industry Military Industries Office renamed General Department for Military Industries (Binggong Zongju).

April 29, 1951: State Council orders Ministry of Heavy Industry to establish Central Bureau for Military Industry (Binggong Zongju), under the "leadership" of the CMC Military Industry Commission.

August 7, 1952: Second Ministry of Machine Building (Er Jixie Gongye Bu) established with responsibility for production of military industrial products and weapons.

April 13, 1956: Ministry of Defense establishes Aviation Industry Commission (Hangkong Gongye Weiyuanhui).

May 26, 1956: CMC establishes Missile Management Bureau (Daodan Guanli Ju) under Aviation Industry Commission.

June 5, 1956: State Council approves PLA General Staff Department Equipment Planning Bureau (Zong Canmou Bu Zhungbei Jihua Ju) to set up Military Industries Products Finalization Commission (Jungong Chanpin Dingxing Weiyuanhui).

August 7, 1956: Ministry of Defense sets up Fifth Bureau (Wu Ju) for missile development.

September 5, 1956: General Staff Department establishes Missile Testing Range Building Commission (Bachang Dengjian Weiyuanhui).

---

17. Deng et al., eds., *Dangdai Zhongguo de Guofang Keji Shiye* and *Dangdai Zhongguo de Bingqi Gongye.*

October 16, 1958: CCP Central Committee orders Aviation Industries Commission converted into new Ministry of Defense National Defense Science and Technology Commission (Guofang Bu Guofang Kexue Jishu Weiyuanhui) (hereafter NDSTC).

April 22, 1959: MoD Fifth Bureau merged into NDSTC.

December 1, 1959: CMC establishes National Defense Industries Commission (Guofang Gongye Weiyuanhui).

October 8, 1961: On the order of the CCP Central Committee, the State Council establishes National Defense Industries Office (Guowuyuan Guofang Gongye Bangongshi).

September 4, 1963: CMC abolishes National Defense Industries Commission.

May 5, 1965: CMC orders all research on missiles, nuclear weapons, conventional weapons, and naval weapons put under "unified management" of NDSTC.

May 13, 1967: National Defense Industry Management Leading Small Group (Guofang Gongye Junguan Lingdao Xiaozu) established by the State Council and CMC.

February 8, 1968: MoD NDSTC converted to the PLA NDSTC (along with eighteen research institutes).

April 1969: Central Committee establishes Conventional Weapons Industry Leading Small Group (Changui Wuqi Gongye Lingdao Xiaozu) under direction of CMC.

August 21, 1969: CMC and State Council establish Leading Small Group for Aviation, Shipbuilding Conventional Weapons, and Electronics Industry (Hangkong, Zaochuan, Changgui Wuqi, Dianzi Gongye Lingdao Xiaozu).

October 30, 1969: CMC Nuclear Engineering Leading Small Group (Heyan Gongcheng Lingdao Xiaozu) established.

December 22, 1969: Central Committee approves establishment of National Defense Industries Leading Group (Guofang Gongye Lingdao Xiaozu) under CMC, and abolishes State Council National Defense Industries Office (Guowuyuan Guofang Gongye Bangongshi).

January 23, 1970: CMC orders Defense Industry Management Small Group (Guofang Gongye Junguan Xiaozu) disbanded.

January 29, 1970: State Council and CMC order all defense industrial and engineering colleges and institutes placed under management by the National Defense Science Commission (Guofang Ke Wei). Although other sources mention that the Commission for Science and Technology for National Defense (Guofang Ke Gong Wei) was established in October 1958, this is the first mention of this Commission in these sources.

February 4, 1970: Mention of a CMC Industries Office (Junwei Gong Ban). Mention also made, for first time, of a War Preparation Leading Small Group (Huizhan Lingdao Xiaozu).

April 12, 1970: Central Committee, State Council, and CMC all approve establishment of Specialized National Defense Industries Leading Small Group (Zhuan Guofang Gongye Lingdao Xiaozu), to coordinate decision making on "all administration, production and research."

July 1, 1970: Nuclear Leading Group (Hexin Xiaozu) established under Fifth Ministry of Machine Building.

April 22, 1971: CMC reestablishes National Defense Industries Leading Small Group (Guofang Gongye Lingdao Xiaozu).

April 24, 1972: PLA Ground Forces establish Military Products Finalization Commission (Lujun Jungong Dingxing Weiyuanhui).

September 10, 1973: New State Council NDIO (Guowuyuan Guofang Gongye Bangongshi) formed.

February 13, 1974: CMC establishes Military Industrial Products Finalization Work Leading Small Group (Zhongyang Junwei Jungong Chanpin Dingxing Gongzuo Lingdao Xiaozu).

May 1, 1974: CMC promulgates "Directive Concerning the Readjustment of the National Defense Industry Management System," which ordered all relevant units of the defense industrial system placed directly under the authority of the CMC NDIO.

February 29, 1975: CMC and State Council establish new National Defense Scientific Research and Industrial Leading Small Group (Guofang Keyan Gongye Lingdao Xiaozu).

June 18, 1975: State Council and CMC establish Conventional Equipment Development Leading Small Group (Changgui Zhuangbei Fazhan Lingdao Xiaozu).

October 1977: CMC creates National Defense Science and Technology Equipment Commission (Guofang Kexue Jishu Zhuangbei Weiyuanhui, hereafter known as the Guofang Kewei).

July 14, 1979: Strategic Weapons Finalization Commission (Zhanlüe Wuqi Dingxing Weiyuanhui) established under CMC and State Council.

February 25, 1980: CMC and State Council establish China North Industries Corporation (Zhongguo Beifang Gongye Gongsi), NORINCO, to "manage import and export military technology."

May 4, 1982: Ministry of Ordnance Industry (Wuqi Gongye Bu) established under State Council.

May 10, 1982: CMC and State Council approve merger of National Defense Science Commission (Guofang Ke Wei), National Defense Industries Office (Guofang Gong Ban), CMC Research and Equipment Office (Junwei Ke Zhuang Ban), into the Commission on Science, Technology, and Industry for National Defense of the People's Liberation Army and People's Republic of China (COSTIND).

June 25, 1988: State Council and CMC jointly establish Military Industry Products Finalization Commission (Jungong Chanpin Dingxing Weiyuanhui).

January 21, 1989: China Military Industry Association (Zhongguo Binggong Xuehui) established.

January 18, 1990: State Council approves establishment of China Weapons Industries General Corporation (Zhongguo Bingqi Gongye Zong Gongsi).

April 3, 1998: State Council and CMC create the General Armaments Department (Zong Zhuangbei Bu) and reorganizes COSTIND. The GAD was created by amalgamating the equipment departments of the General Staff Department and General Logistics Department, the Special Arms Department (Te Bing Bu) of the PLA Army (Lu Jun), and the purely military weapons and associated R&D departments of COSTIND. The reorganized COSTIND was separated from the PLA chain of command, bureaucratically subordinated to the State Council, and made responsible for the research and development, converted defense industries, with some oversight responsibilities for the ten newly created defense industrial enterprises.

As this list illustrates, the oversight of the defense industrial sector has undergone constant reorganization—paralleling the reorganizations of the research and production facilities themselves. Sometimes these reorganizations have reflected priority projects—such as the quests to develop atomic and hydrogen weapons, ballistic missiles, and the strategic subma- rine program—but more often they have reflected a combination of the socialist preoccupation with central planning combined with continual frus- tration with the quality of output of the defense industries.

These last two factors have led the Chinese government and military to the faulty conclusion that the best way to improve production is to increase central planning and oversight—whereas most modern weapons-producing nations operate either a wholly or a semiprivatized defense industrial sector where corporations compete for government and military contracts (Rus- sia, France, and Brazil are exceptions to this rule). The penchant to plan, reg- ulate, and produce within huge vertically integrated enterprises *(xitong)*, all within state-administered hierarchies, has greatly handicapped China's defense industries. On occasion, this system has afforded concentrated ef- fort and resources in support of high-priority goals, but more often than not it has resulted in redundancy and inefficiency. Even the much-heralded creation of the General Armament Department and reorganization of COSTIND in 1998 was, in essence, an attempt to concentrate and central- ize management and channel investment and production lines even further (albeit within an ostensibly clearer division of labor among producers). The Chinese creation of the GAD was apparently modeled on the French sys- tem,[18] but even in France, which has a highly subsidized and relatively cen- tralized military-industrial complex, there is much larger scope for compe- tition between the large corporate contractors. When the five large defense industrial enterprise groups in China divided into ten in 1998 (see above), no real element of competition was introduced, although this was the stated intent. The new division simply cemented into place the existing division of labor in research and production, rather than empowering market mech- anisms and a bidding-based competitive system.

Another problem with the configuration of this system is that the GAD, and COSTIND and its predecessors before it, does not interact adequately either with the services (the end-users and "consumers") or with those units of the General Staff Department and Academy of Military Sciences responsible for defining doctrine and translating it to concrete equipment needs in the field. Worse yet, the GAD stands bureaucratically between the producer and the consumer, as an unnecessary matchmaker, whereas the procuring service (air, ground, navy) should be able to have direct contact, from design to finalization stages, with the factories concerned. They

18. Interview, GAD, December 11, 1998.

should also be able to directly negotiate price, but here again the GAD serves as an impediment by setting artificially low prices and channeling subsidies to the producers to maintain these prices. Inevitably, the GAD, like COSTIND before it, also has financial and bureaucratic interests in favoring certain tried-and-true production facilities over potential new sources of supply. Nor are the GAD or COSTIND necessarily able to anticipate new technologies or hardware needs; therefore they do not invest in retooling production lines or new research. Finally, the GAD and COSTIND effectively serve as a "firewall" between the civilian and defense technological sectors—inhibiting the very fruitful "spin-on" and "spin-off" that benefit many economies and provide the military with critical technologies developed in the private sector.

There is at least some awareness of this impediment in the PLA,[19] but altering a system with such deeply entrenched bureaucratic and financial interests is next to impossible. Nonetheless, in areas such as computer technology, biotechnology, missile and satellite technology, and especially microelectronics and telecommunications equipment, China's civilian and military R&D establishments often complement one another and may experience increased spin-on and spin-off in the future.[20] China is already one of the world's leading producers and assemblers of personal computers, its microelectronics industry only lags the state of the art by six to eight years, and a variety of its telecommunications transmission systems are approaching international standards.[21]

Despite this potential and recent reforms, the procurement process abounds with tensions arising from the overcentralized nature of the system.[22] In the end, the most important reform that the Chinese government could make to increase the efficiency of its military production would be to abolish the GAD and COSTIND, move toward privatization of the defense enterprise groups, and institute genuinely competitive market mechanisms into the bidding and procurement processes. But such a radical move would break not only with socialist tradition, but also with a tradition stretching

19. See, e.g., Quan Linyuan, "Lun Xin Shiqi Guofang Keji Gongye Shiju de Zhanlüe Tiaozheng" (Strategic Readjustment of the Defense Industries in the New Period), *Guofang Daxue Xuebao,* August 1999, pp. 76–79.

20. For further on this argument, see Roger Cliff, *The Military Potential of China's Commercial Technology* (Santa Monica, Calif.: RAND Corporation, 2001).

21. Ibid., pp. 11–18.

22. Also see Wendy Frieman, "Arms Procurement in China: Poorly Understood Processes and Unclear Results," in Eric Arnett, ed., *Military Capacity and the Risk of War: China, India, Pakistan, and Iran* (Oxford: Oxford University Press, 1997), pp. 76–83.

back to the 1870s when the Self-Strengtheners of the Qing Dynasty first tried to direct and manage military modernization. Old habits die hard. Today, such a move would also have devastating implications for the millions employed in former Third Front and other obsolete state industrial enterprises—a risk the regime is not yet prepared to take. Rather than move away from the centralized research and procurement system in the direction of a decentralized market-driven system, the emphasis is being placed on streamlining and tightening up the existing system. This was made clear by the director of the General Armament Department, General Cao Gangchuan, at the first national meeting on China's defense industries, convened by the GAD in August 2000, and by CMC executive vice-chairmen General Zhang Wannian and General Chi Haotian, as well as GLD director General Wang Ke, at the January 2002 national meeting on the defense industrial purchasing system.[23]

RECENT DOMESTIC AND FOREIGN PROCUREMENT TRENDS

The Size and Scope of the Defense-Industrial Complex

As noted above, the organization of China's defense-industrial complex (CDIC) has changed over time. By 2000, it had been organized into the ten large new companies *(gongsi)* and enterprise groups *(shi da jituan)* depicted in table 12. Each is an empire unto its own. No accurate estimate of the total size (i.e., number of factories and enterprises, affiliated academies and research institutes, and personnel) of the CDIC can be made, particularly as it is in the midst of radical downsizing at present. In the mid-1990s, the *Zhongguo Jingji Baike Quanshu* (Encyclopedia of the Chinese Economy) listed the State Council–run defense sector as encompassing 1,000 enterprises within the five conglomerates that then existed (each consisting of multiple factories and affiliated schools, research centers, etc.), and more than two hundred major research institutes and engineering academies.[24]

---

23. Xi Qixin, "Cao Gangchuan Demands Speeding Up the Pace of Reforms in Building the Army's Weapons and Equipment," Xinhua Domestic Service, August 18, 2000, in FBIS–CHI, August 18, 2000; PRC Plans Reform of Army's Purchasing System," Xinhua, January 9, 2002, in FBIS–CHI, January 9, 2002.

24. *Zhongguo Jingji Baike Quanshu* (Beijing: Chinese Academy of Social Sciences Press, 1993), p. 1754, as cited in John Frankenstein, "China's Defense Industries: A New Course?" in Mulvenon and Yang, eds., *People's Liberation Army in the Information Age*, p. 192.

This source estimated the total number of factory workers involved in the early 1990s at 3,000,000, plus some 300,000 engineers and technicians. These numbers appeared reasonable at the time, although they may have shrunk by one-third by the end of the decade, following reforms and reductions. Before the 1998 reforms, NORINCO alone employed an estimated 800,000 people, China Nuclear Corporation employed 300,000, and AVIC personnel numbered approximately 1.3 million.[25] Of course, each enterprise group had to support three or four times as many dependents and retirees.

Beneath this top tier of the CDIC exists a sprawling network of subcontractors and support services. These are heavily concentrated in the state-owned factories in the northeast and southwest of the country, and most are redundant workers. Many of the Third Front's workers fall into this category. Downsizing of personnel has been difficult because of the lack of alternative employment and job retraining programs. Layoffs and forced "retirements" are certainly proceeding, particularly since 1998. Anecdotal evidence of massive unemployment is plentiful (particularly in Liaoning, Jilin, and Heilongjiang), but it is difficult to gain firm statistics on the numbers cast off into the Hobbesian world. In his work report to the 1998 annual conference of the China Ordnance Corporation (which was split off from NORINCO), Minister Zhang Junjiu claimed that 90,000 workers had been laid off in the previous year—and that 74,000 of them had found other employment. As a result, annual losses had been reduced by 14 percent over the previous year.[26] AVIC claimed in 1999 that it had shed 34,000 workers over the previous year.[27]

It is clear that the CDIC is bloated and needs radical downsizing and restructuring. It is also clear that such reductions will reduce overheads and may improve economies of scale, but less certain that they will improve the quality of production, which will require increased automation of production and hiring of much better educated and trained personnel. But downsizing is the first step. While China's civilian, military, and local authorities have all exhibited reluctance to take this step, it seems clear that the 1998 reforms have indeed catalyzed the painful process.

25. Tai Ming Cheung, *China's Entrepreneurial Army* (Oxford: Clarendon Press, 2001), pp. 318–19.

26. Bie Yixun and Xu Dianlun, "Vice Premier Wu Bangguo Greets Opening of Ordnance Industry Meeting," *Jiefangjun Bao,* January 7, 1998, in FBIS–CHI, January 8, 1998.

27. As cited in Tai Ming Cheung, *China's Entrepreneurial Army,* p. 319.

Accomplishments and Impediments

It is not easy to identify concrete accomplishments of the CDIC, such as weapons produced or technologies mastered, because—when measured by the state of the art of military technology and hardware today—China has produced little of significance. Its history is one of repeatedly delayed and aborted projects. China does not perform well when measured against other major military producers in the world—the United States, Britain, France, Russia, Germany, and Japan. Even Sweden, Italy, Israel, and Brazil are able to turn out higher-end weapons, electronics, and associated technologies. In some areas, the defense industries of South Korea, Singapore, and India are more advanced than China's. The most important exception to this generalization lies in ballistic missiles: China's latest rockets, guidance systems, and warheads only lag about 10 to 15 years behind those of the other nuclear powers. In some conventional weapons categories, the CDIC also appears to be making improvements, but many of these—particularly in submarines, guided missile destroyers, and fourth-generation fighter jets—have yet to enter serial production and deployment.

It is thus premature to assert that China will close the gap with modern producers. Most Western analysts place the PLA's conventional capabilities at least twenty years behind the state of the art, with the gap widening. Today, China's best indigenous conventional military capabilities resemble European equipment of the early 1980s, and these constitute only a very small proportion of total equipment. Many technologies and hardware are of 1960s or 1970s vintage. Some even date back to the Korean War and the 1950s. The PLA is attempting to plug some of its most glaring gaps through purchases of equipment from Russia and Israel, but the PLA's overall order of battle (OB) remains extremely antiquated.

In the area of ballistic missiles, however, China's capabilities are considerably better—and improving. Chinese scientists have mastered the significant complexities of fission and fusion; atomic, hydrogen, and other radiation devices; inertial guidance; solid fuel propulsion; advanced warhead design (particularly miniaturization and MIRVing); submarine-launching and various land-based modes; and so on. Ballistic and cruise missiles are certainly a critical advantage in contemporary warfare, as they provide long-range strike capability with minimal exposure of forces. This capacity is the singular comparative advantage of China's military today. But the success of the nuclear weapons and ballistic and cruise missile programs has required dedicating extraordinary financial and political resources over a very long period to specific goals, sequestering the scientists and related design personnel, and building on inherent comparative advantages. Most nations do not have the resources necessary to make such a concentrated investment.

When one compares this advantage and China's military production capabilities with those of other developing countries, China's capacities are impressive. Certainly, no country in Africa, the Middle East (except Israel), or South or Southeast Asia (except India and Singapore in some areas) has anywhere near the comprehensive production base or technical and engineering capabilities that China possesses. But military production capability is not generally measured on a relative basis. While it is the case that weapons employed in war are context-specific and order of battle is measured relatively, defense production capacity is usually measured against the state of the art.

The U.S. Department of Defense's *Militarily Critical Technologies List, Part 1: Weapon Systems Technologies* is the principal means by which the U.S. Defense Department evaluates the military production capacity of other nations.[28] It assesses capability in 6,000 technologies, of which 2,060 are deemed "militarily significant" and 84 others are identified as "militarily critical." Nations are ranked on a five-point scale on these technologies:

0 indicates that a country has *no capability;*

1 indicates a capability in only a *limited set* of the critical elements of a technology;

2 indicates a capability in *some* critical elements;

3 indicates a capability in a *majority* of the technology area's critical elements;

4 indicates that a country is believed to have the production capability in *all elements* of a technology area.

Paul H. B. Godwin and Bernard Cole have undertaken very useful and pathbreaking research on China's production and development capabilities according to the MCTL-WST list.[29] They found that in most of the 84 technology areas critical to the development and production of advanced military

28. Department of Defense, Office of the Under Secretary of Defense for Acquisition and Technology, approved for public release June 1996.

29. Bernard Cole and Paul H. B. Godwin, "Advanced Military Technology and the PLA: Priorities and Capabilities for the 21st Century," in Larry M. Wortzel, ed., *The Chinese Armed Forces in the 21st Century* (Carlisle Barracks, Pa.: U.S. Army War College Strategic Studies Institute, 1999), pp. 159–216.

weapons, China has little or no capacity in all but two categories: nuclear weapons and nuclear materials processing. Even in the area of propulsion, inertial navigation and guidance systems, and vehicle control technology, where one would imagine China would score well given its ballistic missile and rocket science strengths, the PRC only scores a 2—ranking below the United States, Russia, Japan, Germany, Britain, and France. On the other hand, Godwin and Cole found the MCTL-WST list of China's weaknesses to be lengthy and qualitatively significant (see table 13).

To be sure, China is not the only nation with weaknesses—only the United States rated a 4 on all but two of the 84 militarily critical technology categories. Russia also has significant shortcomings in information systems technologies and command and control technologies, Japan in information warfare technologies, Germany and Japan in directed energy systems technologies, and Japan in some areas of sensors and laser technologies. But no nation among the major powers ranks nearly as low across the board as China.

There are many reasons for the weaknesses in China's military technologies and impediments to future development.[30] Clearly, lack of access to the international (i.e., Western) community of defense contractors and producers is a principal problem. Advancing science and technology requires close and regular interaction among professionals—at conferences, electronically or verbally, and through key publications. This applies to the military and defense realm as much as it does to civilian science. Since the founding of the People's Republic of China, defense scientists and technicians have had only partial and sporadic access to these Western sources of information, and some of that, allegedly, only through espionage.[31] Certainly, since the 1989 Tiananmen events and the resulting sanctions against China, particularly in the wake of the 1999 Cox Committee report, China's access to the American and European defense science and technological establishment has been next to nonexistent. The CDIC has had increased interaction with Russian scientists and technicians in recent years, although the extent is uncertain.

To some extent, China's cutoff from foreign military technology has also

---

30. For one of the more thoughtful discussions of these impediments, see Bates Gill, *China and the Revolution in Military Affairs: Assessing Economic and Socio-Cultural Factors* (Carlisle Barracks, Pa.: U.S. Army War College Strategic Studies Institute, 1996).

31. See *Report of the Select Committee on U.S. National Security and Military/Commercial Concerns with the People's Republic of China* (Washington, D.C.: Government Printing Office, 1999).

TABLE 13 China's Military Production Weaknesses

Category	Ranking
Aeronautic Systems Technology	
Fixed-Wing Aircraft	2
Gas Turbine Engines	2
Human Systems (Crew)	1
Marine Systems Technology	
Propulsors and Propulsion System	0
Signature Control and Survivability	1
Subsurface and Deep Subsurface Vehicles	1
Guidance, Navigation, Vehicle Control	
Aircraft and Vehicle Control Systems	2
Inertial Navigation Systems	2
Radio and Data-Based Navigation Systems	2
Directed and Kinetic Energy Systems Technology	
Lasers, High-Energy Chemical	2
Supporting Technologies	1
Weapons Effects and Countermeasures Technology	
Induced Shockwave from Penetrating Weapons	1
Sensors and Laser Technology	
Acoustic Sensors	0
Marine Active Sonar	2
Marine Passive Sonar	2
Marine Platform Acoustic Sensors	2
Electro-Optical Sensors	2
Gravity Meters	1
Lasers	2
Magnetometers	2
Radar	1
Signature-Control Technology	
Materials	2
Design Concepts	2
Application to Integrated Systems	1
Manufacturing	1
Logistics	1
Testing	2
Computer Codes	1
Space Systems Technology	
Computers and Electronics	1
Optronics	2
Power and Thermal Management	1

TABLE 13 *(continued)*

Category	Ranking
Space Systems Propulsion	2
Space Systems Sensors	2
Information Systems Technology	
C^{4}I Systems	1
High-Performance Computing	1
Human Systems Interface	1
Information Security	2
Intelligence Systems	1
Modeling and Simulation	0
Networks and Switching	2
Signal Processing	2
Software	1
Transmission Systems	1
Information Warfare Technology	
Electronic Attack	1
Electronic Protection	0
Optical Countermeasures	0
Optical Counter-countermeasures	0
Electronics Technology	
Electronic Components	1
Electronic Materials	2
Fabrication Equipment	2
General Purpose Equipment	2
Micro-Electronics	2
Opto-Electronics	1
Manufacturing and Fabrication Technology	
Advanced Fabrication and Processing	2
Bearings	2
Metrology	1
Nondestructive Inspection and Evaluation	1
Production Equipment	2
Robotics	1
Materials Technology	
Magnetic Materials	2
Optical Materials	2
Electric Power Systems	
Pulse and High-Power Systems	1

SOURCE: U.S. Department of Defense, Office of the Undersecretary of Defense for Acquisition and Technology, *The Militarily Critical Technologies List, Part 1: Weapons Systems Technologies,* June 1996.

been of its own doing, because the PRC has operated under a self-imposed "self-reliance" policy—which Evan Feigenbaum describes as "technological nationalism."[32] With an adamant preference for developing indigenous capacities or seeking to import the means of production instead of establishing a dependent relationship with a supplier, China has pursued a self-imposed path of autarkic development.

Another, related impediment has been China's poor record of technology assimilation and reverse engineering when it has been successful in acquiring foreign technologies or whole weapons platforms. China's failings in this area are legion, despite some successes with multiple rocket launchers and ship-to-ship cruise missiles.

Another set of impeding factors is organizational and administrative. Size is one dimension, while management is another. As noted above, the CDIC suffers from extreme overemployment and overcapacity. The CDIC has three times as many employees as are needed. Sweden's Saab aviation unit, with only 4,000 workers, has typically produced more aircraft per year than China's Shenyang Aircraft Corporation produces in a decade with 30,000 workers.[33] Also, as noted in the previous section, the sheer desire to centralize and control defense research and production instead of decentralizing and decontrolling it has proven a tremendous impediment to competition and innovation. This hierarchical "stovepiping" of administration has ironically also contributed to redundant production and overcapacity, although these problems also stem from the socialist planned economy. The defense production process itself is vertically integrated, rather than horizontally diffused. Rigid compartmentalization and obsessive secrecy have reinforced these organizational drawbacks. Of course, all of these organization impediments are by-products of the Soviet defense industrial system, which China copied in toto in the 1950s.

Traditionally, the CDIC has been a completely separate sphere of research and production from the civilian sector. As a result, there has been no "spin-on" to defense from inventions in the civilian sector and relatively few successful (i.e., marketable) "spin-offs" from the military to civilian sectors (see the section on defense conversion below). This traditional separation and lack of institutionalized horizontal information-sharing becomes especially problematic in the information age.

There has also long been a disconnect in Chinese science and laboratory

32. See Evan Feigenbaum, "Who's Behind China's High-Technology Revolution?" *International Security* 24, no. 1 (Summer 1999): 95–126.
33. I am indebted to John Frankenstein and Richard Bitzinger for this comparison.

research between applied and basic research, partly owing to the fact that the market does not play a role in driving research—instead, a researcher's agenda is dictated by quotas and research goals from above. The nation's many scientists and engineers have little, if any, experience in production, and those working in the production sphere have little experience in research—and there are few mechanisms for communication between them. *China Daily* reported in 1995 that China's enormous science and technology research establishment (which it put at 2.4 million researchers at 5,860 research institutes, 3,000 university research centers, and some 30,000 business-affiliated research units) produced some 30,000 patents the previous year, of which only about 5 percent wound up in production.[34] Seen from another perspective, however, this is in fact a positive trend, showing that innovative breakthroughs derive from basic research. Chinese science has long emphasized applied science to meet specific production goals—which stymied new innovations—which still seems to be the predominant case in the CDIC.

There are also long-standing, deeply rooted impediments and disincentives to innovation in the Chinese system, both military and civilian. Centuries of emphasis on cultural and social conformity and political emphasis on ideological conformity, both of which have reached new heights (or depths) during Communist Party rule in the People's Republic, have dulled the creativity of Chinese intellectuals and created a risk-averse research community. For these reasons, it is no wonder that mainland Chinese scientists have never won a Nobel Prize. In such a system it does not pay to take the initiative or be innovative—quite the contrary, there are strong disincentives to risk-taking. This normative imperative is reinforced by the Chinese educational system, where conformity to predetermined "correct" answers is rewarded, and deviation from the prescribed answer is penalized. Indeed, in China, both examination questions and answers are distributed beforehand in study booklets. The closer students come to giving the "correct" answer verbatim, the higher the grade. The whole system—cultural, social, political, economic, and educational—stresses and rewards conformity. This is not a recipe for innovation, invention, and advancement.

A related problem is the training of Chinese engineers and advanced scientific personnel in the defense sector. China's domestic institutions of higher education and vocational training—particularly the thirty-odd academies administered by the CDIC, which produce 90 percent of the techni-

---

34. *China Daily,* December 23, 1995, cited in Gill, *China and the Revolution in Military Affairs,* p. 11.

cians in the military research establishment—lag far behind world standards. China graduates no more than 110,000 engineers a year, and fewer than 10,000 mathematics and computer science majors.[35] Graduates with advanced degrees are far fewer. The best and brightest in Chinese science and engineering go to the West for their education—and the few that return do not go into the defense sector, where working conditions are poor and salaries are paltry.

A final impediment is financial. Despite high-profile initiatives like the "863 Program" (so named because it was initiated in March 1986),[36] the Chinese Government and PLA have not made much investment in science and technology R&D. The government spent only 0.7 percent of GDP on research in 1994.[37] In one study, the Stockholm International Peace Research Institute estimated expenditure of U.S.$1 billion on military R&D in 1994.[38] I estimate that the PLA and its affiliated enterprises spend an additional $1 billion on military R&D per year (see chapter 5). Taken together, these official and off-budget expenditures still fall in the $4–5 billion range for total spending on civilian *and* military research.

These facts go some way toward explaining the myriad problems that the Chinese defense industrial and scientific-technological establishments have suffered and why they have largely failed to produce better and more modern equipment. There are no quick fixes to military modernization or building a state-of-the-art defense industrial establishment. It takes time, money, personnel, and innovation. Until these impediments are rectified in China—which may require nothing short of a major transformation of the political system—China's defense industries can be expected to lag behind.

Defense Conversion

Although not directly relevant to assessing China's military *capabilities*, the issue of defense conversion *(jun zhuan min)* is pertinent here. Quite a lot has been written about China's defense production conversion program

35. Wendy Frieman, "The Understated Revolution in Chinese Science and Technology: Implications for the PLA in the Twenty-First Century," in James Lilley and David Shambaugh, eds., *China's Military Faces the Future* (Armonk, N.Y.: M. E. Sharpe; Washington, D.C.: AEI Press, 1999), p. 257.

36. See Feigenbaum, "Who's Behind China's High Technology 'Revolution'?"

37. *Zhongguo Kexue Jishu Zhibiao* (Chinese Science and Technology Indicators) (Beijing: Renshi Chubanshe, 1994) as cited in Frieman, "Understated Revolution in Chinese Science and Technology," p. 249.

38. See Eric Arnett, "Military Technology: The Case of China," in *SIPRI Yearbook 1995* (Oxford: Oxford University Press, 1995), p. 376.

since it was launched in 1982.[39] Suffice it to summarize some of this research briefly.

Deng Xiaoping's decision in 1982 to *jun-min jiehe, ping-zhan jiehe, jun-pin jiehe, yi-min yang jun* (combine the military and civilian, combine peace and war, give priority to military products, and let the civil support the military) was a tacit admission of the CDIC's overcapacity and redundancy, as well as a strategic economic decision to stimulate production of transportation and consumer durable goods such as motorcycles, minivans, trucks, cameras, consumer electronics, refrigerators, and optical instruments. Deng's decision was also premised on the desire to make the Third Front industries, in particular, more efficient and useful. Thereafter, the various components of the machine building industries began to retool for civilian production where possible. By 1994, the Communist Party's official *People's Daily* proudly proclaimed that fully 77.4 percent of the gross value of industrial output (GVIO) of the CDIC was in civilian products, up from 8.1 percent in 1978.[40] Some sectors had almost wholly converted—such as the electronics sector, which boasted in 1992 that 97 percent of its production was in civilian products.[41]

Despite official claims, the defense conversion effort has been mixed. On the one hand, it has certainly succeeded in producing vast quantities of consumer goods and modest means of transportation. It has even made a few factories profitable. It has resulted in retooling of production lines and retraining of workers. Indeed, it has provided gainful employment to thousands of idle staff (particularly in the rust belt northeast and the Third Front areas of the southwest). Some higher-end enterprises, particularly in electronics, have found markets overseas and have gone into partnership with foreign firms (indeed, the order to convert was the catalyst for the PLA to go into business more broadly).

However, many other factories and enterprises (approximately 65 percent) have not converted successfully and continue to bleed money, wallow

39. See, in particular, Paul Humes Folta, *From Swords to Plowshares: Defense Industry Reform in the PRC* (Boulder, Colo.: Westview Press, 1992); Jorn Brommelhorster and John Frankenstein, eds., *Mixed Motives, Uncertain Outcomes: Defense Conversion in China* (Boulder, Colo.: Lynne Reinner, 1997); Mel Gurtov, "Swords into Market Shares: China's Conversion of Military Industry to Civilian Production," *China Quarterly*, no. 134 (June 1993): 213–41.

40. As cited in Brommelhorster and Frankenstein, eds., *Mixed Motives, Uncertain Outcomes*, p. 3.

41. Ibid.

in debt, and require large subsidies to stay afloat. Indeed, these factories are at the soul of the stubborn state-owned enterprise problem. Some factories have not converted at all. Others have converted to produce civilian goods, but their quality is shoddy and, in an increasingly market-driven economy, no one wants to purchase their products. As a result, inventories accumulate and literally decay.

THE PLA'S WEAPONS INVENTORY

Over time, China's defense industries have developed a full panoply of ground, air, naval, and nuclear weapons. Although it still lags at least two generations behind the state of the art in most systems, China's military-industrial complex has produced hardware in large quantities in virtually every main category of equipment, as described below.[42]

Ground Forces

The PLA has always concentrated its manpower and expenditure in its ground forces, as warranted by its continental orientation and traditional fear of land invasion. Accordingly, the defense industries have been called upon to manufacture a range of tanks and anti-tank weapons; artillery, howitzers, multiple rocket launchers and mortars; armored personnel carriers and infantry fighting vehicles; trucks, half-tracks, jeeps, and light vehicles; radar and electronic warfare vehicles; surface-to-air and ground-to-ground missiles; and a full range of light infantry weapons.

Tanks and APCs

The International Institute of Strategic Studies estimates that the PLA at present has some 8,300 main battle tanks in its inventory, including 6,000 T-59s, 800 T-69s and modified T-79s, 500 T-80s, and 800 T-85s.[43] It is common nomenclature that the number designator reflects the year (1959, etc.) in which the unit first entered serial production, although, as is seen below, the actual production and integration of Chinese tanks into the force structure has usually taken place ten or more years later. Further sources reveal other model variants, including the newest T-90 and T-90-II tanks.

Numerically, the T-59 and its variants still dominate the force, and the PLA

42. I am particularly indebted to Thomas Sisk for his research assistance on this section.

43. International Institute of Strategic Studies, *The Military Balance 1999/2000* (Oxford: Oxford University Press, 1999), p. 186.

seems content to continually upgrade rather than to retire them. The original T-59 is really the T-54, which China acquired, renamed, and began to produce in large numbers at the Baotou tank factory in 1957. Throughout the 1970s, the factory turned out 500 to 700 T-59s a year, but it was producing 1,700 by 1983.[44] In 1986, when NORINCO began to receive inquiries and orders for export of the T-59 from Iran, Iraq, Bangladesh, Pakistan (where a coproduction plant was built), and other developing nations, the T-59 underwent a thorough retrofit (with Israeli assistance), which included fitting it with infrared night vision and a laser rangefinder, a stronger diesel engine (600 hp), a main gun turret stabilizer, a thermal fire-control system, an anti-biological and chemical system, Marconi radar systems, and a 105-millimeter main gun. While these upgrades made the T-59 more saleable for export in the low-end international tank market, it is nevertheless a relic on the modern battlefield.

Two smaller versions of the T-59 were spun off, the T-62 light tank and the T-63 amphibious model. Today, the PLA still fields 1,200 and 800 of these respectively. Both have been upgraded with more powerful engines. The T-63, for example, can reach a maximum speed of 64 km/h.

The withdrawal of Soviet advisers and termination of coproduction at Baotou in 1960 forced China's designers back to the drawing board. A decade later, China began to build prototypes of its first indigenously designed main battle tank (MBT), designated the T-69. However it took another ten years for the new tank to enter serial production, and it was not really fielded in the mobile units of north China until the early to mid 1980s (its first public appearance was on parade at Zhangjiakou in 1982). Thus, for nearly thirty years, from the mid 1950s through the mid 1980s, PLA ground forces were forced to rely on the T-59. Such was the impact of the Soviet withdrawal. In the early 1980s, a modified export version, designated the T-79, appeared. The T-69 and T-79 were very similar in weight, speed, powerplant, armament, and other features to the retrofitted T-59. A subsequent version (T-69 II) was additionally fitted with a computerized target acquisition system, laser rangefinder, and 12.7-millimeter anti-aircraft guns.[45] China began to export large numbers of the T-69/79 in the mid 1980s to Iran and Iraq—between 1,800 and 2,500 from 1984 to 1987.[46] Many were destroyed during the Iran-Iraq War, and those that remained in Iraq became easy fodder for the allied forces during the 1991 Gulf War.

44. *Jane's Armor and Artillery, 1992–1993* (London: Jane's Information Group, 1993), p. 12.

45. Ibid., pp. 9–10.

46. Ibid., p. 9.

The next generation of MBT, the T-80, appeared in several versions. The initial version, of which approximately 500 were produced, appeared in 1988 but it was quickly succeeded by the T-85 IIM—which appeared in 1989 and has become the principal MBT in the PLA inventory. It is roughly equivalent to the Soviet T-72 in its design and performance. The T-85 IIM possesses a number of improvements over previous generations: heavier armor (39 tons), a stronger engine (1,000 hp) improved power-to-weight ratio (23.98 hp/ton), and hence greater speed (65 km/h), and firepower. It has an advanced fire-control stabilization system that provides a much better "kill" capability than its predecessors. For the first time in a Chinese tank, a gunner can engage a moving target while the tank is on the move. Although the T-85 IIM is built with composite armor for the first time, it is not uniform and hence is vulnerable to heat-seeking projectiles. After a seven-year delay in prototype testing, the follow-on T-85 III reportedly entered production in 1995—but none have yet appeared in the force.

The newest MBT under development is designated the T-90 and T-90 II (the latter is also sometimes designated the T-98). The development of the T-90 was first revealed in late 1991, when the first prototype appeared.[47] Both versions possess significant improvements in design, armor, and firepower. It is equipped with a 125-mm main gun that can fire a variety of advanced projectiles, including HEAT (high explosive antitank), HE-FRAG (high explosive fragmentation) and APSDS-T (armor-piercing stabilized discarding sabot tank). The Type-90 has impressive mobility and power-to-weight ratio, despite a weight of 48 tons. The turret and hull are made of all-welded steel armor construction with an additional layer of well-distributed composite armor.[48] The composite armor is thought sufficient to deflect kinetic projectiles such as APSDS-T. NORINCO is also known to be developing a series of reactive armor plates that will be effective against a range of advanced projectiles (and which can be retrofitted on older tanks as well).[49] Finally, the combat suite of the T-90 and T-90 II has an integrated fire-control system that incorporates a laser range-finding system coupled with a gunner's all-weather sight and computerized control panel. While an impressive advance for China's MBTs and the first to incorporate laser targeting

47. Ling Xiang, ed., *Zhongguo Lujun* (Guangzhou: Chen Guang Chubanshe, 2000), p. 60.

48. *Jane's Arms and Armor, 1999–2000* (London: Jane's Information Group, 1999).

49. Christopher Foss, "China Develops Its Own Reactive Armor Family," *Jane's Defense Weekly*, May 7, 1997, p. 15.

and optics,[50] it is still no match for advanced Western tanks. Moreover, it still has not entered serial production, and there is no indication that either of China's two main tank factories are building it. When and if they do, it is at least as likely that it will be manufactured for export as built for, and delivered to, the PLA.

China has recently produced a newly designed light amphibious tank, designated the T-99. It carries a four-man crew and a 105-mm gun with a computerized fire-control system.[51] The T-99 was presumably designed with Taiwan in mind.

China also produces a range of armored personnel carriers (APC) and infantry fighting vehicles (IFV), and currently deploys about 5,500 (the People's Armed Police may also possess as many as 1,000). As with tanks, the majority deployed are old (2,000 T-63s), although during the 1990s China's defense industries began producing a series of T-85 and T-86 IFVs (many of which have been exported). Almost all can cruise at 65 km/h and carry 12.7- and 25-mm cannon. In recent years, variants of the T-90 IFV/APC series have begun to join the PLA infantry. The most modern of these is known as the WZ 523, which is wheeled rather than tracked, weighs 15 tons, carries a crew of twelve, can cruise at a rapid 80 km/h on land and 7 km/h in water, and has 600 rounds of ammunition for its 12.7-mm machine gun. Chinese sources reveal a similar model, designated the WZ 501, which carries anti-armor missiles mounted on the turret.[52] This source also shows an APC specially made for the People's Armed Police and crowd control (WJ 94).[53]

Taken together, the PLA ground forces field large numbers of tanks and APCs, but unless and until the T-90 series is produced and integrated into the force structure in the hundreds, the existing hardware will remain more than twenty years out of date. However, the PLA's focus on procuring air and naval systems to fight peripheral conflicts makes effective deployment of the T-90 doubtful, even in the event of a conflict with Taiwan. Taiwan's terrain is not conducive to tanks and IFVs and, in any event, the PLA lacks the sea and airlift capacity to transport much of this heavy equipment across the Taiwan Strait. With artillery (discussed below), the PLA fields a strong deterrent ground force against any potential aggressor—but it is doubt-

---

50. James Warford, "The Chinese Type 98 Main Battle Tank: A New Beast from the East," *Armor* (May–June 2000), pp. 12–14.

51. See "New Chinese Tank," *Jane's Defense Weekly*, November 22, 2000.

52. Ling Xiang, ed., *Zhongguo Lujun*, p. 71.

53. Ibid., p. 70.

ful whether any nation would be interested in invading China today or in the future. If China did encounter a more sophisticated adversary like the United States, its thousands of tanks and IFVs would be of little use, because such an adversary would likely prosecute a war with air bombardment and precision-guided munitions from a considerable distance. Thus, China's ground forces remain a testimony to times past, rather than to its likely future adversaries.

Artillery

Artillery has long been the mainstay of the PLA. Instead of being towed, today the PLA's artillery is increasingly mounted on tracked self-propelled vehicles—a hybrid of a tank and an IFV. The two most modern of these are the 155-mm and 203-mm self-propelled howitzers (SPH). The former was unveiled in 1988, although it has still not entered full serial production.[54] It weighs 32 tons, carries a crew of five, attains a maximum speed of 55 km/h, and has good firing accuracy of 4–5 rounds per minute at a maximum distance of approximately 39 kilometers. It is thought to be comparable to the U.S. M109 or British AS90. There is also a towed version of the 155-mm howitzer.

The 203-mm SPH is the latest and largest caliber Chinese howitzer. It also comes in mobile and towed versions. Its eight-inch (203-mm) gun fires standard size NATO ammunition, as well as a newly developed combustible shell with a maximum range of 50 kilometers. This makes it the longest-range artillery weapon in the world.[55] Since it has yet to be built in any numbers, it is not clear how the PLA will deploy the weapon. It could be used for ground bombardment, coastal defense, or even at sea. If mounted on board ship, it could be used to strike Taiwan from twenty to thirty miles offshore.

Air Defense Weapons

The PLA fields a number of surface-to-air missile (SAM) systems, ranging from shoulder-fired to fixed and mobile ground-launched to radio and radar homing missiles.[56] The most advanced is the SA-10 (S-300) purchased

54. Christopher Foss, "Chinese Self-Propelled and Towed Artillery Systems," *Jane's Intelligence Review*, June 1992, p. 273. Also see Ling Xiang, ed., *Zhongguo Lujun*, pp. 42–43.

55. Foss, p. 273.

56. For a full description of Chinese SAMs, see Wang Tianxi and Ma Hong, eds., *Zhong-Mei-E Xinxing Jianduan Wuqi: Zhongguo* (Chinese, American, and Russian New Types of Sophisticated Weapons: China) (Beijing: Guangming Ribao Chubanshe, 1997), pp. 68–101.

from Russia in 1995, three batteries of which are deployed around Beijing in conjunction with a phased-array radar capability. Sometimes compared to a Patriot PAC-2, the SA-10 is a very advanced SAM with solid-propellant propulsion. It carries a 130-kilogram warhead at Mach 6 speed up to a ceiling of 30,000 meters and at an operating range of 75,000 meters. The Chinese have developed a cloned version of the SA-10, which was first deployed during the 1996 Taiwan missile "crisis"[57] and has more recently been deployed along the Zhejiang coastline south of Shanghai in case Taiwan fires its own crude missiles (see chapter 7) at China. The most deployed indigenously produced SAM is the HQ-61A, which has radar guidance, carries a 42-kilogram warhead, flies at Mach 3, has an operating range of 2,500 to 12,000 meters, and can acquire targets up to a ceiling of 10,000 meters.

Another advanced SAM, designated the FT-2000, is also under development and is thought to include technology from the SA-10 and yet-to-be deployed HQ-9.[58] An anti-radiation SAM, the FT-2000 reportedly has a maximum range of about 100 kilometers with a maximum altitude of approximately 20,000 meters, carries a 60-kilogram fragmentation warhead, and is advertised as an "AWACs killer."[59]

PLA Air Defense also deploys unknown numbers of the KS-1 SAM, which can fire up to a ceiling of 25,000 meters at a range of 42,000 meters, and the HQ-2Y SAM, which can fire up to a ceiling of 27,000 meters over an operating range of 35,000 meters. The PLA also operates a variety of less sophisticated AAA from the 25- to 100-mm caliber family.

Taken together, Chinese air defense is formidable and getting better. Although stealth aircraft could probably penetrate Chinese air defenses, the PLA fields SAM defenses at least as capable as Iraq did in the Gulf War or Serbia during the Kosovo conflict.

In addition to developing a complete range of self-propelled and towed artillery systems, China has developed the largest family of multiple rocket launchers in the world. Some have been purchased from Israel and Brazil and cloned, but NORINCO also produces launchers capable of firing 4, 8, 10, 12, 19, 24, 30, and 40 rounds per minute and covering ranges from 10 to 80 kilometers. In addition, the Chinese have developed increasingly so-

57. *Asian Defense Yearbook, 1999–2000* (Kuala Lumpur: Syed Hussain Publications, 2000), p. 134.

58. U.S. Secretary of Defense, *Annual Report on the Military Power of the People's Republic of China*, Report to Congress Pursuant to FY2000 National Defense Authorization Act, June 2000, pp. 14–15.

59. Ibid.

phisticated fire-control systems and submunition warheads, which enable maximum ranges to be utilized.[60]

The PLA Air Force: Fighters and Bombers

When the Chinese Communists took power in 1949, they inherited no aviation industry. It was only after encountering superior American air power in the early stages of the Korean War, which was pummeling Chinese forces, that Mao and the Chinese leadership saw the importance of military aviation. Of course, they turned to the Soviet Union for assistance, which was forthcoming in 1951. Thereafter, as documented in two careful studies,[61] China has tried—and failed—to build modern fighter aircraft, bombers, airborne command and early warning aircraft, and in-flight refueling tankers. This systematic failure is due in part to the larger failings of the defense industries, as discussed above, and in part to the complexities of materials, fabrication, design, and engineering specific to modern aircraft production. It is one thing to build a tank, but quite another to build a high-performance interceptor. The failings of China's military aircraft industry became glaring in the 1990s, when the value of air power was put on display over Iraq and Serbia. At that time the PLA itself was reorienting its doctrine to prepare to fight limited wars along its periphery and to safeguard its far-flung maritime territorial claims—both of which required a fleet of fighters, refueling tankers, and airborne command and control.

Today, the PLA Air Force deploys some 3,000 fighters, 2,200 of them antiquated J-6s and J-7s (various models)—which were built in the 1960s.[62] The J-6 is a clone of the Soviet MiG-19, and the J-7 is a replica of the MiG-21. Both aircraft can operate up to a ceiling of about 18,000 meters at about Mach 1.5. The J-7 in particular has been through numerous upgrades over the years. The most recent, in the mid 1980s, produced the J-7 III, which is roughly equivalent to the MiG-21 MF, which entered the Soviet Air Force in 1972, or the American F-4C, which was the primary interceptor for the U.S. Navy and Marine Corps during the Vietnam War. The J-7 III is also roughly equivalent to the F5-E Tiger II operated by the Taiwan air force (al-

60. See Christopher Foss, "Chinese Multiple Rocket Systems," *Jane's Intelligence Review*, September 1992, pp. 418–22.

61. Kenneth W. Allen, Glenn Krumel, and Jonathan D. Pollack, *China's Air Force Enters the 21st Century* (Santa Monica, Calif.: RAND Corporation, 1995); and John Wilson Lewis and Xue Litai, "China's Search for a Modern Air Force," *International Security* 24, no. 1 (Summer 1999): 64–94.

62. International Institute of Strategic Studies, *Military Balance 1999/2000*, p. 188.

though with recently completed upgrade program, the F-5Es have a clear edge in radar and electronic warfare capabilities).[63] This aircraft represented a significant leap forward in electronics and avionics, providing the first all-weather radar in any Chinese fighter (although the rest of the avionics were not up to the same capability). The Chengdu Aircraft Corporation, where the J-7 is manufactured, has more recently produced prototypes of two other upgraded versions, designated the J-7E and J-7 MG, but it is not known what the differences with the J-7 III are or how many have been produced.[64]

In 1980, the Q-5 "Fantan" became the first completely domestically designed aircraft in the PLAAF's inventory. Designed in 1958, the first prototype flew in 1965—although various problems with hydraulics, brakes, and weapons systems delayed the testing phase, and the plane did not go into production until 1970. Like the J-6, the Q-5 is loosely modeled on the MiG-19. It too has undergone numerous upgrades over the years,[65] the most recent of which produced the Q-5C at the Nanchang factory in the mid 1980s. Despite the upgrades, the Q-5 is not a particularly nimble strike aircraft, and its limited electronics suite makes it capable of only daylight visual attack missions. It would be easy prey for any modern fighter—even the Taiwanese F-5E has precision strike and all-weather capabilities that the Q-5 could not match. It has a combat radius of about 600 kilometers, can carry 1,000 kilos of ordnance, and can reportedly fly at Mach 1.12.[66] The PLAAF currently deploys about 400 Q-5s.[67]

The next most advanced planes in the PLAAF inventory are the J-8 and J-8 II. Development of the J-8 began in 1960 after the Soviet advisers' pullout. It took nine years to develop a prototype suitable for flight-testing and another eleven years before it went into limited serial production (1980). At this point, the designers (not to mention the air force) were so frustrated that they essentially started afresh—and developed the J-8 II and "M" version for export. This plane only took four years to flight-test, and a mere twelve years before it went into production in larger numbers in 1992. Thus, the problems associated with developing the two J-8 models spanned thirty-

63. *Jane's All the World's Aircraft* (London: Jane's Information Group, 1999), p. 60.

64. See Ling Xiang, ed., *Zhongguo Kongjun* (Guangzhou: Chen Guang Chubanshe, 2000), p. 51.

65. Ibid., pp. 28–37.

66. Federation of American Scientists web page: www.fas.org/nuke/guide/china/aircraft (August 17, 2001).

67. International Institute of Strategic Studies, *Military Balance 1999/2000*, p. 188.

two years altogether! Still, according to IISS, the PLAAF only deploys 250 J-8 IIs today. This single-seated fighter is powered by two Liyang after-burning turbojet engines, weighs about 17.8 tons when fully loaded with fuel, and is large for a high-altitude interceptor (nearly 71 feet long with a 31-foot wingspan). According to the COSTIND Center for Defense Science and Technology Information Center, the J-8 II can climb at Mach 2 to a maximum altitude of 20,000 meters, and has a maximum combat radius of 2,200 kilometers.[68] It is outfitted with air-to-air missiles (PL-7s) as well as unguided free-fall rockets and free-fall bombs. There have been some speculative reports of the J-8 II being fitted with advanced Russian air-to-air missiles, but no evidence has materialized. The avionics of the "M" export version, which appeared in 1998, are fairly advanced; they include a Phazotron radar system capable of tracking ten airborne targets while targeting two simultaneously. Prior to 1989, the U.S.-sponsored "Peace Pearl" project was designated to upgrade the avionics suite of the J-8 II, but it was aborted as a result of the post-Tiananmen sanctions.

The newest domestically produced fighter to enter service is the JH-7 "Flying Leopard" (the FBC-1 is the export version). Produced by the Xian aircraft facility, this twin-engined, two-pilot fighter-bomber is another in a long line of frustrating stories of stymied aircraft production. First designed in the 1970s and planned around the acquisition of the British Rolls-Royce Spey MK 202 engine (China bought 50 Speys in 1977), the plane was not flight-tested until late 1988 and did not enter service with naval aviation (PLANAF) until 1995. The Xian engineers experienced protracted problems with thrust ratio between the engine and the airframe.[69] The JH-7 was supposed to fill the vacancy of a long-range strike aircraft for both the air force and navy, but it was rejected by the air force in favor of the Su-27. Thereafter, the navy adopted it as its main strike aircraft—although it is still not being produced in any significant numbers. It has a range of 1,600 kilometers, based on a fuel-tank capacity of 10 tons, and can fly at Mach 1.7.[70] Although the JH-7 has not entered production in any significant numbers and

68. China Defense Science and Technology Information Center, ed., *China Defense: Research and Development* (Beijing: CDSTIC, 1988), p. 166.
69. One Rolls-Royce engineer I met in Xian in 1988 complained bitterly that he had made nearly fifty visits over the previous decade and moaned, "They still can't get the damn thing off the ground!"
70. *DSTI Monthly Report,* October 1999, p. 9, citing *Wen Hui Bao* (Hong Kong), October 6, 1999. The plane flew in the October 1, 1999, parade commemorating the 50th anniversary of the PRC.

export orders for the FBC-1 version have been soft,[71] the Xian Aircraft Design and Research Institute has already embarked on a significant upgrade program that would be embodied in the JH-7A/FBC-2.[72] The new version would increase thrust of the aircraft's powerplant, possibly switching to the French Snecma M53-P3 turbofan engine (which powers the Mirage 2000, manufactured by Dassault), and make it stealthy with special paints on its fuselage.[73]

The final indigenously produced fighter is the long-awaited J-10 (a.k.a. F-10). This aircraft actually began as the J-9 in the late 1960s, but was subsequently designated the J-10 in the mid 1980s. It too has experienced chronic problems over time—ranging from the engine to airframe to avionics and weaponry. After numerous problems, Israel was invited to assist on a new design in the early 1980s, and full-scale cooperation commenced in 1984. Most of Israel's assistance went into the avionics and armaments of the plane. After three years, a design was unveiled, but it took until March 24, 1998, before the first prototype was flight-tested.[74] Prototype testing continues, and series production has still not commenced. Major problems apparently remain, with the engines generating too much thrust for the airframes to handle. As a result, China has apparently given up on its own engines for the J-10 and has turned to Russia for assistance. In July 2001, Russia agreed to sell 300 modified AL-31FN jet engines to the Chengdu Aircraft Industrial Group, which is responsible for the J-10.[75] This engine can produce maximum thrust of 27,560 pounds.

The J-10 is thus another story of failure. After taking more than three decades to literally get off the ground, the plane has still not been put into production. If and when it is, the J-10 will include Russian engines and radars and Israeli avionics (from the aborted Lavi program), but its onboard armament is not known. Some reports claim that the latest incarnation of the J-10 is a clone of the American F-16 A/B, of which China reportedly got one copy from Egypt, but one photograph of the J-10 published in a

71. Bruce Dorminey, "China Displays New (Old?) Attack Fighter," *Aviation Week and Space Technology*, November 23, 1998, pp. 22–23.

72. "China Considers Plans to Extend Fighter-Bomber's Capabilities," *International Defense Review*, January 1, 1999, pp. 63–64.

73. Ibid.

74. "First Flight for F-10 Paves Way for Production," *Jane's Defense Weekly*, May 27, 1998, p. 17.

75. Yihong Chang, "Beijing Engine Deal with Russia Heralds Up to 300 F-10s," *Jane's Defense Weekly*, July 4, 2001.

Chinese military magazine shows an aircraft with a delta wing canard configuration.[76]

With the abysmal failure of China's indigenous aircraft industry to produce modern fighter-interceptors, the PLAAF had no choice but to look abroad for a top-of-the line plane to meet its immediate needs. In 1990, China signed a contract with Russia for 72 Sukhoi-27 "Flanker" aircraft. The first twenty-six planes were delivered in 1992 and are at Wuhu air base in Anhui province central China. China reportedly paid the equivalent of U.S. $1 billion for the entire package (approximately $38 million per plane), but only 35 percent of this payment was in hard currency; the remainder was in bartered consumer and agricultural goods. As Russia expected a larger portion of the payment in hard currency, the delivery schedule stalled. Negotiations for the second batch of Su-27s reopened in 1994 and concluded two years later. This agreement resulted in the delivery of the final forty-eight aircraft (including two trainers), all of which were apparently sent to Suixi air base in Guangdong province in southern China.[77] The renegotiated contract was for $2 billion and included an agreement for the coproduction of two hundred Su-27s at Shenyang over a ten-to-fifteen-year period. The contract specifies that the first fifty aircraft will be assembled from kits before the transfer of production technology begins. Even by the end of the production period, the Shenyang Aircraft Corporation will build only 70 percent of the plane, the remainder coming from the Sukhoi factory at Komsomolsk.[78] The first two coproduced Su-27s were assembled at Shenyang with the assistance of over a hundred Russian engineers and were flight-tested in December 1998 (designated the J-11 by the Chinese).[79] The same report notes that the Shenyang factory plans to assemble fifteen more before 2002, after which time serial production will begin. Given that only six were produced between 1998 and 2000, it is doubtful whether such a production schedule can be met.

The Su-27 "Flanker" B version sold to China is a high-performance fighter primarily useful for high-altitude interception.[80] It was introduced in the Soviet Air Force in the mid 1980s and is often compared favorably with the American F-15C. Its capabilities are impressive in a number of re-

76. *Zhongguo Renmin Jiefangjun de Jing yu Fang,* no. 87 (2000): 41.
77. See Patrick Tyler, "China to Buy 72 Advanced Fighter Planes From Russia," *New York Times,* February 7, 1996.
78. *Jane's Defense Weekly,* June 10, 1998.
79. *DSTI Monthly Report,* May 1999, p. 9, citing *Liaoning Ribao,* January 1, 1999.
80. For detailed descriptions of different Su-27s, see Jon Lake, *Sukhoi-27 "Flanker"* (London: Aerospace Publishing, 1994).

spects. It has a remarkable range (930 miles) on internal fuel and can be re-fueled in the air if necessary. It flies at Mach 2.35, can climb to nearly 60,000 feet and is very maneuverable in high-altitude dogfights. Its avionics are sophisticated, with Doppler look-down/shoot-down radar, integrated fire-control, infrared search and tracking, and a laser rangefinder mounted on the pilot's helmet. The Su-27 can carry 6,000 kilograms of ordnance, as well as six radar-homing Alamo medium-range air-to-air missiles (AAM) and Archer infrared-guided AAMs. It is also outfitted with a 30-mm cannon. While far more advanced than any other fighter in the PLAAF's inventory, its air-to-air missiles and fire-control system are not as good as those of either the F-15C, F-16, or Mirage 2000.

While the Su-27 gives the PLAAF an impressive new capability, there have been real problems in assimilating the aircraft into the air force. Training time, approximately twenty hours a year, is much less than on China's other fighters, almost always in daylight hours and during good weather. While Su-27s have been used in some offshore exercises, this application has been minimal. They are never used in high-altitude simulated dogfights, and at least three planes have reportedly crashed during training exercises. Officials from Russia's Aeronautical Equipment Corporation, which has been involved in the manufacturing of the planes, claim that by late 2000, as many as half of the Su-27s were grounded.[81] Pilots are also said not to be given full tanks of fuel for fear that they might defect.

In December 1999, China also signed a contract for 40 Su-30 MKK fighters from Russia.[82] The deal was worth an estimated U.S.$1.8 billion. The first twenty of these fourth-generation "plus" fighters were delivered in 2000, and there is a distinct possibility that some will be phased into the Su-27 coproduction in Shenyang. The Su-30 MKK has all the air-combat capability of the Su-27 but also has a secondary all-weather ground attack capability. It is a twin-seat multipurpose fighter, optimal for long-range air combat roles, that was originally designed to challenge the U.S. F-15. It has a range of 3,000 kilometers without refueling, although it can be refueled

81. Lin Wei-chu, "Half of Mainland Principal Fighter Planes, Su-27s, Unable to Fly Due to Damaged Electronic Equipment Onboard, Says Russian Expert at Zhuhai Air Show," *Ming Bao* (Hong Kong), November 7, 2000, in FBIS–CHI, November 8, 2001.

82. See, e.g., Robert Sae-Liu, "Su-30 MK Purchase on Chinese Agenda," *Jane's Defense Weekly,* August 11, 1999, p. 6; Moscow Interfax, "Russia to Supply 20 Su-30 MKK Fighter Planes to China," December 18, 2000, in FBIS–Russia, November 18, 2000; Sergey Sokut, "Historic Flight: Russian Federation Supplies PRC with First Ten Su-30 MKK Fighters," *Nezavisimaya Gazeta* (Moscow), December 21, 2000, in FBIS–Russia, December 21, 2000.

TABLE 14 PLAAF Fighters

Fighter	Entered Production	Number in Force in 2000	Number in Force Projected for 2005
J-6	1963	1,800	500
J-7	1967	500	300
J-8II	1970	150	100
J-10	2005 (?)	0	100
JH-7	1995	20	100
Su-27	1999	72	150
Su-30	2001 (?)	0	100 (?)

in flight (China has developed in-flight refueling capability but rarely uses it). The Su-30 also has more advanced digital avionics and radar than the Su-27 and can be modified into a naval version for use on aircraft carriers if necessary. The Su-30's ordnance is also superior; it carries a dozen air-to-air and air-to-ground missiles, as well as 6,000 kilos of precision-guided "smart" bombs. All in all, the Su-30s add a distinct new capability for the PLAAF—for the first time giving it the capability to fly missions far from its coastline and patrol over the South China Sea.

Once all of these aircraft come on stream, and phased retirements of antiquated aircraft are completed, China will possess a diversified air force of several hundred third- and fourth-generation fighters—but this will not be until 2010–15 *if* all goes well in production and testing. One cannot be too optimistic on this score, given the chronic problems that have plagued the civilian and military aircraft industry in China. But, as table 14 indicates, these additions to the force structure will provide a more diversified fighter complement, and will give the PLA Air Force (PLAAF) a mixture of approximately 1,350 second-, third-, and fourth-generation fighter/interceptors. The U.S. Department of Defense estimates that the PLAAF will maintain "slightly more than 2200 [fighter] aircraft by 2020" and that approximately 4 percent of this force (150 fighters) will be fourth-generation.[83] This would be a substantial air force by regional standards.

To take advantage of these improvements, pilot training for combat situa-

83. U.S. Secretary of Defense, *Annual Report on the Military Power of the People's Republic of China*, p. 19.

tions in all-weather conditions, and regular maintenance, will be necessary— and again, the PLAAF's record on both scores has not been commendable to date. Chinese pilots, including those flying the Su-27, receive less than 100 hours of air time per year, rarely practice with live ammunition or in close combat, and almost never fly in bad weather conditions. Several Su-27s are known to have crashed in training in the past few years. Maintenance standards are questionable, and in any event, the Su-27 engines have to be returned to the Sukhoi factory in Komsomolsk for refitting after every 1,000 hours of flight time.

As China's fleet of fighters grows, it will also need airborne warning and control (AWAC). China had signed a contract with Israel for U.S.$250 million for the purchase of four Phalcon AWAC aircraft, but Israel reneged on the deal in 2000 under heavy political pressure from the United States. The planes had been built and were ready for delivery. As a result, Beijing turned to Moscow to meet this need. Russia agreed to sell up to four A-50E.[84]

Finally, the PLAAF has two principal bombers in its inventory, the H-5 and H-6. The former, of which there are more than 200 on duty, is modeled on the Soviet Il-28 "Beagle" and has a range of 1,850 kilometers. The latter, of which there are approximately 120 deployed, is modeled on the Soviet Tu-16 "Badger" bomber and is capable of carrying nuclear weapons. It has a range of 5,900 kilometers.[85] In recent years, there have been numerous reports of Chinese interest in acquiring the Soviet TU-22M "Backfire" bomber, but, as with much of China's weapons window-shopping, no sales or transfers have materialized.

The PLA Naval Forces

The PLA's new doctrine of peripheral defense has, of course, also included increased attention to developing a blue-water naval capability—although this ambition has been severely hampered by lack of funds, an indigenous production base that is inadequate (to produce, for example, heavy cruisers, aircraft carriers, and nuclear submarines), and lack of access to Western sources of supply for key technologies and armaments. Since 1989, as noted,

84. See John Pomfret, "Russia Moves in on Israel's Lost Jet Deal with China," *Washington Post*, December 8, 2000; David A. Fulghum, "China Slips Past U.S. AWACs Ban," *Aviation Week and Space Technology*, December 4, 2000; "China to Get Russian Air Patrol and Homing Radar Complexes in 2001," ITAR-TASS (Moscow), December 13, 2000.

85. Deployment estimates are from International Institute of Strategic Studies, *Military Balance 1999/2000*, p. 188.

China has been prohibited from purchasing Western military equipment, and there is little sign of a relaxation on this ban anytime soon, despite some loosening in European Union restrictions on some electronics.

Despite restricted access to Western naval technologies and platforms, the PLAN made significant progress during the 1990s.[86] It upgraded electronic countermeasures, radar and sonar, fire-control systems, and onboard armament on a few refitted Luda-class destroyers and Jianghu-class frigates. These are being supplemented by new generation Luhai-class and Luhu-class destroyers, and Jiangwei-class frigates. In all, the PLAN has added nearly twenty surface combatants to its fleet over the past decade. The most important addition are two Sovremenny-class destroyers built and sold to China by Russia, which has also supplied four Kilo-class diesel electric submarines in recent years, although the PLAN has experienced maintenance and operating difficulties with them. Also under construction in the Huludao shipyard are Chinese-built Song-class submarines;[87] three of these conventionally powered submarines have been launched. A new nuclear-powered ballistic missile submarine, the Type 094, is also planned. Another new nuclear-powered attack submarine (Type 093), which will not be armed with intercontinental ballistic missiles, is also under construction and may join the fleet around 2005, if all goes well. Submarine construction and operation is extremely complex, and the Chinese record in each has been very poor to date.[88]

Surface Combatants

The Chinese Navy currently deploys a total of 56 surface warships, including 21 destroyers and 35 frigates.[89] Like the Chinese Air Force, most of these are 20–30-year-old ships that have been retrofitted and upgraded over time, and their overall capabilities remain modest. Only a handful of these vessels can truly be considered blue-water capable; the vast majority constitute a coastal force that operates in brown and green water. In addition to these destroyers and frigates, the PLAN maintains approximately 676 coastal pa-

---

86. The best and most current assessment of the PLAN is Bernard D. Cole, *The Great Wall at Sea: China's Navy Enters the Twenty-First Century* (Annapolis, Md.: Naval Institute Press, 2001).

87. *DSTI Monthly Report,* October 1999, p. 10, citing *Naval and Merchant Ships* (in Chinese), October 4, 1999. Huludao is an island in the Bohai Gulf off Liaoning Province.

88. See Lewis and Xue, *China's Strategic Seapower.*

89. International Institute of Strategic Studies, *Military Balance 1999/2000,* p. 187. This total includes the one new Luhai-class and two new Sovremenny-class destroyers.

trol craft, 119 mine warfare vessels, 70 amphibious craft, and 160 support ships.[90]

The most advanced destroyer is clearly the Russian Sovremenny-class guided missile destroyer (DDG), built partially to Chinese specifications in the Severnaya Verf shipyards in St. Petersburg. The first Sovremenny sale was sealed in 1996 for a reported price of U.S.$840 million, and the second deal, reportedly worth $1 billion, was concluded in November 1997.[91] The PLAN has taken delivery of two of these destroyers, and it placed an order for two more in January 2002, worth $1.4 billion.[92] The first, named the *Hangzhou*, was delivered in February 2000, and the second in November 2000.

The Sovremenny class was designed in the 1970s and entered the Soviet fleet in 1980. It was designed both to escort aircraft carriers and to destroy them—particularly U.S. carriers and their Aegis escorts. The Sovremenny carries eight 3M-80E Zubr (SS-N-22) sea-skimming anti-ship missiles, dubbed "Sunburns," which are among the most advanced anti-ship missile deployed in the world today and against which there are limited counter-measures.[93] The Sunburn was specifically designed to penetrate the defenses of carrier battle groups (CVBGs). It can deliver a lethal blow with a 300-kilogram warhead over a range of 120 miles, at a velocity of Mach 2.5, and can avoid radar by flying 1.2 meters above water.[94] The *Hangzhou* carries eight Sunburns, 44 "Gadfly" short-range SAMs, and four torpedo tubes.[95] The ship displaces 7,940 tons fully loaded (6,600 tons standard) and can cruise up to 32 knots. It is an impressive destroyer and a significant improvement for the PLAN.

The decision to purchase the two Sovremennys must have been influenced by the 1996 Taiwan Strait "crisis," when the United States deployed two carrier battle groups east of the island. Since then, Chinese defense planners

90. Ibid.

91. Yelena Konnova, "Chinese Ceremonies—Russian Destroyer Joins Chinese Navy," *Kommersant* (Moscow), November 28, 2000, in FBIS–CHI, November 29, 2000.

92. "Russia: St. Petersburg Shipyard to Build Two Destroyers for China," *Agentstvo Voyennykh Novostey* (Moscow), January 3, 2002, in FBIS–Russia, January 3, 2002.

93. "People's Republic of China," in *Asian Defense Yearbook, 1999–2000*, p. 130.

94. He Chong, "China Purchase of Russian-Made Sovremenny-Class Destroyer Attracts Attention," *Zhongguo Tongxunshe*, Hong Kong, February 12, 2000.

95. Institute for Defense and Disarmament Studies, *Chinese Naval Forces, 2000* (Cambridge, Mass.: IDDS, 2000); *Jane's Fighting Ships, 1999/2000* (London: Jane's Information Group, 1999), p. 120.

have increasingly oriented their procurement and training around a series of Taiwan conflict scenarios with American intervention (see chapter 7).

In 1999, China also unveiled the first of its two new Luhai-class guided-missile destroyers, the 6,600-ton *Shenzhen*.[96] It was built in the Dalian Red Flag shipyards. A second, likely to be named the *Yantai*, is reportedly under construction and may join the fleet by 2003.[97] While built domestically, much of the equipment for the Luhai class is imported: two Ukrainian gas turbine engines, German electrical systems, French radars and Russian sonar, Russian helicopters, and Italian torpedoes. It also is equipped with sixteen C-802 ship-to-ship missiles, HQ-7 SAMs (cloned from the French Crotale), active and passive homing torpedoes, and 100-mm guns.[98] The new ships are reported to incorporate stealth-like features on the bridge (as on the French Lafayette-class frigates sold to Taiwan) that reduce the dangers of radar detection.[99] The Luhai class is an advance over the Luhu destroyers in many respects, but it still lacks effective air defense, ASW, electronic countermeasures, and over-the-horizon strike capability.

The PLAN also possesses two Type 052 Luhu-class guided missile destroyers. One, the *Harbin*, is depicted in plate 13. Built before the 1989 sanctions took effect, this class of destroyer is outfitted with a wide range of imported equipment. It is powered by two American gas turbine engines (General Electric LM 2500) and carries two French Dauphin-2 helicopters, 32 French Sea Crotale SAMs and cloned Exocet SSMs, German electronics, French radars, and Italian Whitehead torpedoes. This combination of systems, and the lack of spare parts and maintenance packages since 1989, has made operations and maintenance a logistical nightmare. The destroyer displaces 4,200 tons fully loaded, carries a crew of 280, and can cruise at up to 30 knots. Both Luhu-class destroyers are homeported in the North Sea Fleet.

The PLAN currently deploys sixteen Luda-class destroyers, which still remain the backbone of the surface fleet. The Luda is based on a 1950s-era Soviet Kotlin-class design, but a few have undergone upgrades over the years. Fifteen of them are the old Luda I (Type 051) DDGs. These ships displace 3,670 tons when fully loaded. The other one is a Luda II–class, which weigh slightly more (3,730 tons). The upgrades over the years have mainly

---

96. A photo of the Shenzhen (no. 167) is featured in Ling Xiang, ed., *Zhongguo Haijun* (Hong Kong: Chen Guang Chubanshe, 2000), p. 1.

97. The report on the *Yantai* is from *DSTI Monthly Report*, July 1999, p. 16, citing *Wen Hui Bao* (Hong Kong), July 11, 1999.

98. "China Launches a Powerful New Super Ship," *Jane's Defense Weekly*, February 3, 1999, p. 16; *Jane's Fighting Ships 1999/2000*, p. 122.

99. *DSTI Monthly Report*, July 1999.

been to outfit these ships, which previously only possessed deck-mounted guns, with ship-to-ship missiles, ASW torpedoes, and more modern electronics. The Luda I carries the C-801 SSM, and two of them are equipped with HQ-7 SAMs,[100] while the Luda II is outfitted with Italian Breda 70 caliber anti-aircraft mounts, cloned Exocet SSMs, and Whitehead torpedoes.[101] Yet these are far from state-of-the-art or reliable systems, and they lack over-the-horizon targeting. Nor are the fire-control systems trustworthy. These defects put the vessels at a serious disadvantage going up against even a mid-range modern navy. They cannot defend themselves against the modern strike capability carried by modern ships and aircraft. Even the seven World War II–vintage Gearing destroyers that constitute the dregs of the Taiwanese fleet have undergone sufficient modernization (including outfitting with Harpoon missiles) to outclass the Luda. The Luda II is slightly more sufficient, carrying the C-801 (the first generation of PLAN SSMs), but it would also be a sitting duck in any conflict with Taiwan, the United States, Japan, South Korea, or most Southeast Asian nations.

The PLAN's guided missile frigate (FFE) fleet has also been upgraded but still lacks modern mobility and firepower. The eight frigates of the Jiang-wei I and II classes built to date displace 2,250 tons fully loaded and cruise at a maximum of 25 knots. They carry six C-802 SSMs, which can deliver a 165-kilo warhead with active radar homing guidance at Mach 0.9 over a range of 120 kilometers.[102] They also carry the cloned Crotale (HQ-7) SAM, with an octuple launcher, and are outfitted with a combination of Western and Chinese electronics. Their anti-submarine warfare (ASW) capability is also considered weak, with minimum countermeasures and no torpedoes. Again, if these frigates went head-to-head with their counterparts in the Taiwanese navy (to say nothing of the U.S. Navy), they would not last long. Even more outmoded are the thirty-one variants of the Jianghu class FFGs (I, II, III, IV, and V). Everything about them is old, and they would have difficulty defending themselves against more capable foreign warships. They have limited ASW capability and must rely on gunnery for air defense.

The PLAN possesses about 100 fast-attack coastal combatants in the Huang, Houjian, and Houxian classes. While also essentially defenseless

100. *Jane's Fighting Ships, 1999/2000*, p. 122.

101. "New Ships for the PLAN," *Jane's Defense Weekly*, January 18, 1992, p. 88.

102. For description of this and other C-class (Yingji) SSMs, see Duncan Lennox, "China's New Supersonic Anti-Ship Missile," *Jane's Intelligence Review*, November 1992, pp. 512–13; Gordon Jacobs, "China's Naval Missiles," *Asian Defense Journal*, October 1990, pp. 65–74; "China's New Naval Missile," *International Defense Review*, July 1992, p. 636.

against air or subsurface attack, they are effective for patrolling China's long coastline. Most are now outfitted with C-801 SSMs. Five of the newest Houjian PPGs are now stationed in the Hong Kong Special Administrative Region. In addition, the PLAN has over 500 smaller patrol craft and about 120 mine warfare vessels, most of them in reserve.

The PLAN's amphibious capability is also relatively limited. It possesses eight Yukan-class and six Yuting-class landing ship tanks (LSTs), each of which can carry about 200 troops. The only difference between the two is that the latter is equipped with a helicopter flight deck for the Harbin Z-9A. The American counterpart to these ships is the Whidbey Island–class landing ship dock (LSD), which carries three times as many troops and four times more tanks/IFVs. The PLAN also has thirty-one older Yuliang-class (which can carry about 100 troops each), and twelve Yuhai-class ships (ferrying 250 troops). There are also four Qiongsha-class transport ships (with capacity of 400 troops and 350 tons of cargo).[103] Taken together, these vessels could ferry only approximately 12,000 troops across the Taiwan Strait (presuming they stayed afloat). No doubt, should China decide to undertake an amphibious landing on Taiwan (see chapter 7), many other civilian and naval ships would be commandeered for the purpose, but most experts calculate that the PLA would need enough troops to outnumber Taiwan's army by four or five times—that is, 1–1.25 million PLA soldiers. Other Western experts, though, calculate that any amphibious landing would be a "force insertion" operation putting an overwhelming number of troops into a concentrated area, opening up a beachhead or front, and then pushing inland. Certainly, however, the current PLA lift capacity is sufficient to seize one of the offshore islands.

Finally, mention must be made of the PLAN's plan for an aircraft carrier. There have been countless reports over the years of Chinese purchase or construction of a carrier, but none have materialized to date. Certainly, it is an important aspiration of the Chinese Navy, China's leaders, and the public—as much for status as for military reasons. Great powers have aircraft carriers and can project sea power, it is reasoned, and China looks with envy on the carriers of Thailand and India. The Chinese have, however, purchased several decommissioned carriers—the HMAS *Melbourne* from Australia, the *Varyag* from Ukraine, and the *Minsk* from Russia. The former was used for scrap (presumably after Chinese engineers scoured it for design information), the latter is now a floating casino in Macao, and the *Varyag*

103. International Institute of Strategic Studies, *Military Balance 1999/2000*, pp. 187–88.

is probably destined to become a floating theme park. Even reports that China had contracted with a Spanish shipyard to build a carrier have proven fallacious. Eventually, China will no doubt buy a carrier—as it certainly does not have the technological capacity to produce one—but this day likely remains some way off, as there are other, more pressing priorities on the surface fleet and submarine programs, for aircraft, and for nuclear weapons and missiles. Even if China did purchase a carrier, it would need a complement of destroyers, frigates, and submarines as escorts. Right now, forming just one carrier battle group (CVBG) would require using virtually every advanced vessel in the fleet. Nonetheless, there are reports that Chinese naval pilots are preparing for the day by practicing takeoffs and landings on a simulated 70-meter flight deck reportedly copied from the HMAS *Melbourne*.[104]

Submarines

The PLAN has only one strategic ballistic missile submarine (SSBN)—the Type 092 Xia-class—and sixty-nine tactical attack submarines, of which five, in the Han class (Type 091), are nuclear-powered. The remainder of its indigenous subs are old Romeo- and Ming-class vessels, although the fleet also includes four Russian diesel-powered Kilo-class submarines, and three new Song-class boats. As described below, a new generation of nuclear-powered attack submarines (SSN and SSBN) is currently planned or under construction. Numerically, this is clearly a formidable force, the largest in the Asia-Pacific region other than the American fleet, but like virtually every other aspect of the Chinese military, it is antiquated.

The single Xia joined the fleet in 1988 after sixteen years of development.[105] It conducted one successful live missile firing in that year, but is thought not to have left port since then, owing to problematic nuclear reactor and propulsion systems. The boat weighs 6,500 tons at diving depth (it can dive to a depth of 300 meters), is 120 meters long, carries a crew of 140, and can reach a top speed of 22 knots submerged. It carries twelve JL-1 inertial guidance ballistic missiles (SLBM), which have a range of 1,800 kilometers and carry 250-kiloton nuclear warheads. The Xia also carries eighteen YU-3 active/passive torpedoes. Compared to the ultraquiet Ohio-class SSBNs, the Xia is a relic—no match for Japanese SSNs or SSKs.

104. See Lin Mu, "The Aviation Dream of the Chinese People," *Shidian* (Beijing), July 8, 1994, in FBIS–CHI, August 24, 1994, pp. 35–38; and You Ji, "Chinese Military Modernization in the 1990s" (unpublished paper citing Chinese military sources).

105. *Jane's Fighting Ships*, 1999/2000, p. 116.

Although it may have been refitted in the late 1990s, the single Xia is due to be replaced by a new generation of nuclear-powered ballistic missile submarines (SSBN), the Type 094–class sub, which may carry sixteen JL-2 ballistic missiles with a range of 8,000 kilometers.[106] This second-generation SSBN is derived from the new land-based DF-31, and its missiles may be armed with up to six independently targeted warheads.[107] Development of this submarine began in the late 1980s, but it has reportedly encountered construction problems in a number of areas. Even if it is completed in the next decade, it will need to undergo extensive sea trials, missile testing, and crew training. Once operable, though, it will substantially augment China's sea-based nuclear deterrent.

The Type 093 is the new nuclear-powered attack submarine (SSN) under development. It may carry land-attack cruise and C-801 anti-ship missiles, as well as wake-homing torpedoes and mines.[108] The 093 is due for prototype testing sometime between 2005 and 2010.[109] Some analyses compare the 093 to the Soviet Victor III class, a late-1970s SSN. The 093 may displace 6,000 tons submerged, is powered by two nuclear reactors, and can attain a maximum submerged speed of 30 knots. Russian engineers are known to be assisting in the design and construction.

The Type 093 is really meant to replace the five Han-class SSNs in the fleet. The Han-class submarine was China's first attempt at an indigenously produced nuclear-powered submarine. Originally laid down in 1974, it encountered serious reactor and other problems and thus did not reach full operational status until the mid-1980s. All five Hans are based in the North Sea fleet and rarely go out on patrol (they are estimated to spend three-quarters of their time in port). It was a Han, however, that was tracked by ASW aircraft dispatched by the U.S. aircraft carrier *Kitty Hawk* in the Yellow Sea in October 1994, which prompted the PLA Air Force to scramble two J-7s to intercept the American aircraft. While not a serious incident between the two navies, it did stimulate the bilateral Military Maritime Accord in 1998 to avoid similar incidents at sea in the future. The Hans are noisy and are no match for U.S. Los Angeles–class or Japanese Harushio- and Oyashio-class submarines.

The first Song-class submarine was launched in May 1994 and commissioned in early 1996. The Song is much faster and quieter than its prede-

106. "JL" stands for *julang*, "big wave."
107. Institute for Defense and Disarmament Studies, *Chinese Naval Forces, 2000.*
108. "Asia-Pacific Submarine Survey," *Asian Defense Journal,* November 1999, p. 48.
109. Interview, Academy of Military Sciences, May 16, 2000.

cessor, the Ming-class diesel-electric-powered attack submarine (SS), and is apparently capable of launching YJ-8/CY-1 cruise missiles from its 533-millimeter torpedo tubes.[110] The PLAN has three in its fleet today. A Song cruising in the Bohai Gulf is shown in plate 14.

During the mid-1990s, the PLAN also procured four Kilo-class diesel-electric attack submarines from Russia, at a cost of around U.S.$1 billion. The Kilos represent an impressive leap forward for the PLA submarine forces, providing a more effective and quieter long-range attack submarine. The Kilo's hull is coated with anechoic tiles that reduce its susceptibility to sonar detection and diminish the noise from its diesel-electric engines.[111] The PLAN purchased two types of Kilos: the export version 877 EKM and the EKM 636 model used by the Russian Navy. They come with wake-homing and wire-guided torpedoes (something the PLAN has previously lacked), electro-optical and acoustic sensors, sonar-quieting countermeasures, and reinforced hull construction. In addition, the EKM 636 incorporates an advanced engine design that gives it longer endurance and greater submerged time without having to recharge its batteries. The Chinese seem to be having problems maintaining the Kilos, as two of the four have not been to sea for over a year and one had to be returned to Russia to have one of its electrical generators fixed. One of the Type 636s may also be disabled.[112] The Chinese seem to adopt the attitude of "if it isn't broken, don't fix it"—which, of course, is an approach not applicable to high-maintenance platforms. The Kilos have also required very different training regimens from what Chinese sailors are accustomed to, and hence the crews are not interchangeable with other submarines in the fleet. Nonetheless, the Kilo is a very capable submarine, as quiet as the Los Angeles–class submarines in the U.S. fleet but otherwise comparable to the soon-to-be-decommissioned Japanese Yushio submarines.

As noted, the remainder of the PLAN's submarines are of the older Ming and Romeo classes. The Romeo is an easy target. It first entered the Chinese fleet in 1969. In the mid-1980s, some were refitted to reduce the noise levels, but production ceased altogether in 1987. Since then twenty have been decommissioned, with the remaining twenty-six in various states of operational capability. The Ming class is a moderately upgraded version of the Romeo, but it too is obsolete. The only advantages of the Romeo and Ming

110. *Asian Defense Yearbook, 1999–2000*, p. 132.

111. Godwin and Cole, "Advanced Military Technology and the PLA," p. 188.

112. "Kilos No Longer in Operation," *Jane's Defense Weekly*, September 2, 1998, p. 17.

submarines is that they can operate in shallow waters off Taiwan and can be deployed in large numbers. Otherwise, they are fodder for more advanced attack submarines, as well as surface ships and ASW aircraft.

Ballistic Missiles

If the Chinese military has any truly modern capability, it lies in the realm of ballistic missiles. With an operational history of more than four decades, China's ballistic missile program has passed through several phases.[113] From 1965, when the first ballistic missile (DF-2A) was finally successfully flight-tested (following six years of failures), until 1981, the emphasis was on deploying first-generation intermediate-range missiles (IRBM) and one intercontinental-range missile (ICBM). These were all liquid-fueled, land-based, and equipped with heavy warheads. As their accuracy was poor, and China was trying to develop a minimum nuclear retaliatory capacity, these missiles were targeted on cities and other "soft" targets. Since 1982, the emphasis has been on developing the full triad of nuclear-capable delivery vehicles, which was achieved with the successful test of a submarine-launched ballistic missile (SLBM) in 1982. The second phase has also included the development of new generations of short, intermediate, and intercontinental missiles that are fueled with solid propellants, have longer range and better accuracy, and carry a variety of smaller and more powerful warheads. Developing and deploying MIRV missiles (multiple independently targeted reentry vehicles) is also a priority for the next few years, although the PLA's Second Artillery has possessed a rudimentary MIRV capability for nearly twenty years.

Today, as table 15 illustrates, the PLA has in service a full range of ballistic missile systems. The accelerated deployments of short-range ballistic missiles (SRBMs) opposite Taiwan, the successful test of the DF-31 (8,000-kilometer range) in August 1999, the development of a follow-on 12,000-kilometer range ICBM (sometimes dubbed the DF-41), the program to develop and deploy the JL-2 SLBM, and testing of land attack cruise missiles (LACMs), are all evidence of the central importance that China places on missiles as both offensive and defensive weapons.

As table 15 shows, the most credible Western sources are in general agreement about the variety, range, and payload of the missiles in China's arsenal but differ substantially on the number of missiles deployed, for three

113. Among the numerous sources detailing the history of China's missile and nuclear programs, see in particular John Wilson Lewis and Hua Di, "China's Ballistic Missile Programs," *International Security* 17, no. 2 (Fall 1992): 5–40.

principal reasons. First, China does not openly publish information about its missile and nuclear programs. Second, China is not involved in any strategic arms limitation negotiations with foreign powers, and hence does not need to reveal or limit its arsenal accordingly. And, third, the majority of China's land-based missiles are mobile and deployed in a variety of unconventional basing modes (including in caves, forests, and valleys). Although the principal missile brigades and test sites are publicly known abroad (see chapter 4), the actual numbers and physical deployment of China's ballistic missiles are far less certain. Without China being a party to international strategic arms control accords that include verification, there will always be a margin of error in the estimates of missiles and launchers deployed. If the Second Artillery really develops and deploys MIRV warheads, such estimates will become considerably more difficult.

The DF-3 (DF stands for Dong Feng, or "East Wind") is the oldest ballistic missile currently deployed (the DF-2 and 2A were all retired by the mid 1980s). It is a modified Chinese copy of the Soviet R-12 MRBM (designated the SS-4 by NATO), which entered the Chinese arsenal in 1971. The improved version, the DF-3A, entered service in the late 1980s. Because it is liquid-fueled (nonstorable alcohol and liquid oxygen), it requires approximately two hours to prepare for launch,[114] thus leaving it very vulnerable to a first strike. The DF-3A has better accuracy than the DF-3, with a circular error probability (CEP) of 1,000 meters (0.6 miles), and can deliver a 2,150 kilogram warhead (4,730 lbs.) about 2,800 kilometers (1,739 miles).[115] China sold thirty-six of these missiles (presumably with conventional explosive warheads) to Saudi Arabia in 1988.

The DF-4 was first tested in 1970 but thereafter underwent significant redesign before being deployed in 1980. The DF-4 was China's first limited-range ICBM, with a range of 4,750 kilometers, and was the first to be deployed in fixed underground silos (a version was also developed to be based in mountain caves and tunnels). This missile also requires significant fueling and preparation time, as it has to be brought to a surface launch position in its silo or rolled out onto a launch pad from its tunnel storage, erected on its launch stand, and fueled—a process requiring several hours.[116] Unlike the DF-3, the DF-4 and 4A are two-stage booster rockets. Similar to the

114. Robert S. Norris, Andrew S. Burrows, and Richard Fieldhouse, *British, French, and Chinese Nuclear Weapons* (Boulder, Colo.: Westview Press, 1994), p. 362.

115. Shirley Kan and Robert Shuey, *China: Ballistic and Cruise Missiles* (Washington, D.C.: Congressional Research Service, Library of Congress, 1998), p. 5.

116. Norris et al., *British, French, and Chinese Nuclear Weapons*, p. 363.

TABLE 15 China's Ballistic Missiles

System/Type	Status	Propellant	Estimated Range (km)	Warhead (kgs)	Estimated Number Deployed
DF-3/3A (MRBM)	deployed	liquid	2,800	2,150 1–3 megaton	50–120
DF-4 (ICBM)	deployed	liquid	4,750	2,200 1–3 megaton	20–30
DF-5/5A (ICBM)	deployed	liquid	12,000–15,000	3,200 3–5 megaton	7–20+
DF-11/M-11 (SRBM)	developed, under deployment	solid	185–300	500 350 kiloton	40+
DF-15/M-9 (SRBM)	deployed	solid	200–600	500–950 350 kiloton	100–200
DF-21/21A (MRBM)	deployed	solid	1,800	600 300 kiloton	20–40
DF-31 (ICBM)	tested	solid	8,000	700 300 kiloton	0

DF-41 (ICBM)	under development	solid	12,000	800 (MIRV?)	0
JL-1 (SLBM)	deployed	solid	1,700	600 300 kiloton	12–24
JL-2 (SLBM)	near testing	solid	8,000–10,000	700 (MIRV?)	0

SOURCES: Robert A. Manning, Ronald Montaperto, and Brad Roberts, *China, Nuclear Weapons, and Arms Control: A Preliminary Assessment* (New York: Council on Foreign Relations, 2000), table 3; Shirley Kan and Robert Shuey, *China: Ballistic and Cruise Missiles* (Washington, D.C.: Congressional Research Service, Library of Congress, 1998); Department of Defense, *The Security Situation in the Taiwan Strait* (Report to Congress Pursuant to the FY99 Appropriations Bill, February 1, 1999); International Institute of Strategic Studies, *The Military Balance 1999/2000* (Oxford: Oxford University Press, 2000); U.S. National Intelligence Council, *Foreign Missile Developments and the Ballistic Missile Threat to the United States Through 2015* (September 1999); Robert Norris, Andrew Burrows, and Richard Fieldhouse, *British, French, and Chinese Nuclear Weapons* (Boulder, Colo.: Westview Press, 1994); *Report of the Select Committee on U.S. National Security and Military/Commercial Concerns with the People's Republic of China* (Washington, D.C.: Government Printing Office, 1999); *Jane's Strategic Systems* (London: Jane's Information Group, 1998).

first-generation American Titan rockets, the DF-4 is also frequently used to launch Chinese and foreign satellites.

The DF-5, developed at the same time as the DF-4, is the backbone of China's land-based strategic force. With a range of 13,000 kilometers (8,073 miles), it remains the only Chinese missile capable of striking anywhere in the continental United States. Despite its range, the DF-5A is a "city buster" with a 4–5 megaton warhead and CEP of 500 meters (0.3 miles). Deployed principally in hardened silos near Luoyang in Henan Province since 1981, the DF-5 and 5A are also maintained unfueled and "unmated" (without their warheads fitted, in nuclear weapons parlance).[117] An estimated 17–20 DF-5s and 5As are known to be deployed, and are all presumably for use against the United States (although, technically, the 1998 bilateral nontargeting agreement forbids current targeting). One Chinese source contains a photograph of three DF-5 ICBMs deployed together in a single silo (separated by several feet of concrete)—a rather unusual, and vulnerable, basing mode.[118]

The DF-21 was first flight-tested in 1982 and began deployment in 1986. It can deliver a 600-kilogram (1,320 lb.) warhead up to 1,800 kilometers (1,118 miles). A modified version, the DF-21A, is thought to have a terminal guidance system and slightly better accuracy. Both versions were land-based spin-offs of the first generation SLBM, the Julang I. A road-mobile version, with transporter-erector-launcher (TEL), was successfully tested in 1985 and is also apparently in service. The DF-21 represented a significant step forward in Chinese IRBM capability, particularly because of its road mobility and partly because it was China's first solid-fueled ballistic missile. It also possesses an automatic command-control-firing system. Thus far, the Second Artillery has only deployed between 25 and 50 of this missile. The static numbers probably reflect the improved state of Sino-Russian relations in the 1990s, as the DF-21 series was initially developed during the height of Sino-Soviet tensions. If tensions with India or Japan magnify, we may see increased numbers built and deployed.

In terms of ground-based ICBM systems, China is known to be developing two new long-range missiles: the DF-31 and DF-41. Although still under development and not yet deployed, this new generation of missiles warrants brief mention.

The DF-31's rocket motor was successfully tested in 1995, and the

117. Briefing by Robert Walpole, U.S. National Intelligence Officer for Strategic and Nuclear Programs, at the Carnegie Endowment for International Peace, September 17, 1998.

118. China Defense Science and Technology Information Center, ed., *China Defense: Research and Development*, pp. 208–9.

mobile missile itself was successfully tested on August 2, 1999.[119] The new IRBM/ICBM is due to be phased into service by 2005. Originally designed as an IRBM with a range of 6,000 kilometers, the missile was redesigned to give it a more extended range of 8,000 kilometers—thus putting Alaska, Hawaii, and the northwestern continental United States within its range. Being road-mobile and solid-fueled, the DF-31 is really China's first true strategic nuclear deterrent. It has a faster launch time than earlier weapons and is difficult to target. Since it is a three-stage rocket, it will also be difficult for an anti-missile defense system to intercept. Furthermore, it is reported to have a sophisticated inertial guidance system that can be linked to GPS, and thus it may be feasible to alter the missile's trajectory in flight. It is on the DF-31 (along with the sea-launched JL-2 and presumably the land-based DF-41) that the Chinese version of the W-88 miniaturized warhead, which the Cox Commission alleges was stolen from the United States, will likely be mounted.[120]

The longer-range DF-31 (commonly referred to as the DF-41) represents the fourth phase in China's ICBM program. Ultimately, it will replace the DF-5 and 5A as the principal land-based ICBM. As it has not yet been flight-tested, not much is known about the new missile. But it is thought to have a range of 12,000 kilometers (7,452 miles), and will likely carry an 800-kilo (1,760 lb.) warhead with an explosive power of 250 kilotons.[121] Like the DF-31, it is a three-stage missile (although its third stage has much greater thrust),[122] uses solid fuel, has inertial guidance and GPS capability, and can be deployed in silos or in mobile-basing modes (road, rail, or river). If fitted with MIRV warheads, the DF-41 could be a formidable ICBM.

The PLA is also developing a second-generation submarine-launched ballistic missile, the JL-2, to equip the new Type 094 strategic submarine. Each submarine (the PLAN anticipates building five to seven) will carry sixteen JL-2s, which will—for the first time—provide the capacity for a sea-based strategic deterrent against the continental United States. If armed and miniaturized with the clone of the W-88 warhead used on U.S. Trident submarines, the JL-2 will significantly increase the quantity and quality of China strate-

119. "Dongfeng 31 Strategic Ballistic Missile Successfully Launched," *Wen Hui Bao* (Hong Kong), August 3, 1999.

120. See *Report of the Select Committee on U.S. National Security and Military/Commercial Concerns with the People's Republic of China* (Washington, D.C.: Government Printing Office, 2000), ch. 2.

121. Kan and Shuey, *China's Ballistic and Cruise Missiles*, p. 9; *Jane's Strategic Systems, 1998/99*.

122. *DSTI Monthly Report*, August 1999, p. 8.

gic nuclear deterrent. If successfully deployed, the JL-2 will certainly represent a marked improvement over the JL-1. The technical capabilities of the JL-2 are virtually the same as those of the DF-31 (see above).

While China has developed a full complement of ballistic missiles, possesses a triad of nuclear forces, and is accelerating its development of a new generation of missiles, it remains by far the most backward of the five nuclear powers and suffers from some severe weaknesses that would come into play in any potential conflict. Perhaps the greatest vulnerability of China's missile force is the lack strategic reconnaissance platforms—either space-based or a functioning over-the-horizon (OTH) radar network—to provide early warning. A second major impediment is that China's silo-based systems are not thought to be hardened to survive an initial strike. Even a powerful conventional warhead could easily disarm them. But perhaps the greatest vulnerability is that the missile force is a nonready force. The missiles are not fueled, and the warheads are not mated. Consequently, China's ground-based ICBMs have no ability to launch on warning (LOW).[123] They would be destroyed before they could ever be fueled and launched. The PLA is addressing all three of these vulnerabilities with new improvements in solid fueling and guidance systems, more diversified basing modes, and improved warhead design. If all goes well, within a decade or so, the vulnerabilities will disappear as the new generation of missiles comes on stream and the older ones are retired.

Finally, mention must be made of China's short-range ballistic missiles, which are of tremendous concern to the U.S. government because of their deployment opposite Taiwan and the possibility of exporting them to unstable nations. The two principal SRBMs in China's arsenal are the DF-15 (usually referred to as the M-9) and the DF-11 (a.k.a. the M-11). The Second Artillery also possesses a limited number of M-7 (the 8610 missile) SRBMs, which are two-stage missiles believed to have a range of 150 kilometers (93 miles) with a warhead of 190 kilos (418 lbs.). However, these missiles were developed exclusively for export, and a number have been sold to Iran.

The DF-15 entered service in 1995 and has become the mainstay of the PLA's SRBM inventory. In 2001, the U.S. Pacific Command estimated that China had approximately 300 ballistic missiles targeted at Taiwan, and this number may be increasing at the rate of 50 per year. This was the missile

123. Robert A. Manning, Ronald Montaperto, and Brad Roberts, *China, Nuclear Weapons, and Arms Control: A Preliminary Assessment* (New York: Council on Foreign Relations, 2000), p. 18.

that was "test" fired and impacted in close proximity to Taiwan in 1996. As a battlefield weapon, the DF-15 is quite capable. First, it is solid-fueled, which reduces preparation time for launch. Second, its variety of payloads can make it very flexible in combat situations. It can even be fitted with the enhanced radiation warhead (the neutron bomb), which China admitted to possessing (and the Cox Committee alleges was stolen) in 1999. Being a mobile missile, it is very hard to target (although the launch brigades are known). Third, because of the missile's strap-down inertial guidance and onboard digital computer, the missile's terminal velocity, reentry altitude, flight trajectory, and range can all be altered in flight, and it has relatively good accuracy of around 300-meters CEP (0.2 miles).[124] Also, the Second Artillery is attempting to make the DF-15 GPS-capable, and it may also become compatible with the Russian GLONAS (global positioning satellite) system.[125]

The DF-11/M-11 is similar to the DF-15 but has two stages and a shorter range of 300 kilometers (186 miles). It carries a 500-kilogram warhead—slightly heavier than the DF-15's, but less accurate. The DF-11 has many design similarities to the Soviet Scud-B, but is lighter and smaller. The DF-11 first flew in 1990 and apparently entered service sometime in 1992.[126]

Cruise Missiles

The PLA is also said to be hard at work on developing land-attack cruise missiles (LACMs). A variety of programs are under way—most trying to adapt the existing sea-launched C-801 and C-802 for air- and ground-launched systems. The reengineered C-801, which is cloned from the French Exocet and designated the YJ-8, could enter production as early as 2000. It has a 135-kilometer range, would incorporate GPS navigation and terrain contour mapping (TERCOM) guidance systems, and is likely to have an accuracy of within ten meters.[127] China may also turn to Russia to supply LACMs over the next few years.

Of course, the PLAN already possesses a number of sea-launched and subsurface-launched anti-ship cruise missiles (see above) including the HY-2/2A (a.k.a. the C-201 or "Silkworm"), the HY-3 (C-301), the HY-4 (C-201W), YJ-1, and the YJ-2 (C-802). The HY-3 was the PLAN's only su-

---

124. Kan and Shuey, *China: Ballistic and Cruise Missiles*, p. 7.
125. See John Pomfret, "Russians Help China to Modernize Its Arsenal: New Military Ties Raise U.S. Concerns," *Washington Post*, February 10, 2000, A17.
126. *Jane's Strategic Systems, 1998/99*.
127. Mark Stokes, *China's Strategic Modernization: Implications for the United States* (Carlisle Barracks, Pa.: U.S. Army War College Strategic Studies Institute, 1999), p. 86.

personic anti-ship cruise missile before the addition of the state-of-the-art SS-N-22 "Sunburn" anti-ship cruise missiles to the Sovremmeny destroyers.

The PLAN Air Force also possesses the C-601, an air-launched version of the C-201. This cruise missile, which can deliver a 513-kilogram warhead up to 68 miles, is deployed on the PLAAF's H-6D bombers in the naval air force. An improved version of this cruise missile, designated the C-611, is also known to be under development. It would have an increased range of 124 miles with improved propulsion, electronics, and terminal guidance, and it would use new high-energy fuel.[128]

OUTLOOK

While some progress has been made, and the Chinese military does field a large force and weaponry in most categories of conventional and strategic systems, the Chinese military-industrial complex remains constrained by a number of factors. Without access to equipment and technologies from the West, the PLA and China's military-industrial complex will never be able to close the weaponry and defense technology gap with Japan and the West. Transfers from Russia are meeting some of the PLA's needs, but they are far from sufficient to provide it with a power-projection capability.

Great emphasis is being placed on long-range precision strike capability and on mastering new information-warfare techniques associated with the revolution in military affairs (RMA).[129] China is actively studying these technologies (including laser-guided munitions, electronic countermeasures, computer viruses, anti-satellite weapons, high-powered microwave weapons, satellite photo reconnaissance, over-the-horizon sensors, phased-array radars, and high-speed telecommunications).[130]

One might infer from the desire to develop such technologies and weapons systems that China is preparing for asymmetrical military contingencies involving opponents possessing state-of-the-art militaries (e.g., Japan or the United States), particularly in a potential conflict over Taiwan. To a certain extent, this is true, but the PLA more likely has simply set its sights on becoming a modern military and is deploying its relative comparative advantages in an attempt to "leapfrog" several generations of its

128. Kan and Shuey and Kan, *China: Ballistic and Cruise Missiles,* p. 13.
129. Stokes, *China's Strategic Modernization;* and Michael Pillsbury, ed., *Chinese Views of Future Warfare* (Washington, D.C.: National Defense University Press, 1997).
130. Stokes, *China's Strategic Modernization.*

conventional backwardness and technological inferiority. Purchases of high-tech systems from Russia and Israel, however, prompt a different interpretation. China's acquisitions of aircraft, submarines, and destroyers from Russia all appear to be contingency-driven. They seem to indicate preparations to present a credible threat to Taiwan in the first decade of the twenty-first century (probably around 2007). Moreover, these purchases and the emphasis on improving ECM and IW capabilities further suggest a plan to engage and disrupt U.S. aircraft carrier battle groups in a Taiwan conflict. Persistent attempts to acquire in-flight refueling capability and the development of the F-10 and FBC-1 fighters perhaps indicate a desire to project air power into the South China Sea and beyond.

These factors aside, however, there is little evidence that PLA procurement patterns are driven by specific threat perceptions or contingency planning. China seems rather to be building on its strengths, consolidating "pockets of excellence," and seeking to close technology gaps in order to create a world-class military capability in the first quarter of the twenty-first century. In other words, PLA procurement seems driven by status factors more than specific contingency planning, except in the case of Taiwan. Either way, the PLA finds itself way behind on the R&D curve—and will be very hard pressed to catch up.

7 Threat Perceptions

> If Hegemonism dares to impose war on us, the Chinese
> people will be fully capable and confident of winning it.
>
> YAO YOUZHI AND ZHAO DEXI,
> "How Will China Handle War in the 21st Century?"

The threat perceptions of PLA and civilian Chinese leaders are fundamental to the posture of China's military and some of their priorities in the process of military modernization. To a large extent, the PLA's priorities and allocation of resources reflect the desire to develop a comprehensively modern military. Yet, certain exigencies intrude that force choices of allocation to meet more pressing threats and contingencies. This chapter taps into PLA writings and interviews with some of the PLA's leading strategic analysts to gauge the PLA's contemporary threat perceptions.

At the beginning of the twenty-first century, with the important exception of the volatile Taiwan situation, it would seem that China faces no tangible or immediate external military threat. Although the Asian financial crisis of the late 1990s pointed up distinct nonmilitary dangers to China's social stability and national security,[1] and further sensitized China's leaders to the volatile forces of interdependence and globalization and their relationship to China's security,[2] from an objective military standpoint China

---

Epigraph: Yao Youzhi and Zhao Dexi, "How Will China Handle War in the 21st Century?" *Liaowang,* January 10, 2000, in FBIS–CHI, February 14, 2000. Major General Yao Youzhi is director of the Strategy Department at the Academy of Military Sciences.

1. Some senior Chinese military intelligence officials also now speak of concerns over energy security, since China has become a net oil importer, and other nonconventional security threats, including terrorism, narcotics trafficking, and organized and transnational crime. Interview with GSD Second Department officers, December 6, 1998.

2. As China's Defense White Paper clearly states: "Economic security is becoming daily more important for state security. In international relations, geopolitical, military security and ideological factors still play a role that cannot be ignored, but the role of economic factors is becoming more outstanding, along with growing eco-

has never been more secure. Yet the assessment of China's security environment by the PLA's security analysts (depicted in this chapter) suggests that China lives in a dangerous neighborhood and that the PLA must be prepared for a range of potential threats, both external and internal.[3] Indeed, Chinese leaders and analysts have always viewed threats, security, and power in more comprehensive *(zonghe)* terms than many Westerners, who tend to adopt narrower external and militarily defined definitions.[4] In the more comprehensive context, domestic "stability" is always paramount (the Chinese term for security, *anquan*, means "complete stability"), and external threats are usually perceived in the context of aggravating domestic instability.[5]

CHINA'S NEW PEACE

At the outset of the twenty-first century, the PRC has been able to pacify its borders and build cooperative relationships with all nations on its periphery. This is no small diplomatic feat considering the numerous difficulties Beijing has had with its neighbors since the Chinese Communist Party came to power in 1949. China shares land borders with fourteen nations and maritime boundaries with seven. Territorial disputes have existed with Russia, the Central Asian republics, Japan, Pakistan, India, Nepal, Sikkim, Burma (Myanmar), Thailand, Vietnam, Malaysia, Indonesia, the Philippines,

---

nomic contacts among nations." Information Office of the State Council, *China's National Defense* (Beijing: State Council, 1998), p. 4.

3. One interesting exception is an article by General Xiong Guangkai, vice-chief of staff and CIISS president, "The International Strategic Situation and China's Security Environment," *International Strategic Studies,* January 2000, p. 3. Xiong states: "China enjoys a more favorable security environment than at any time since the founding of the PRC, despite the development of factors of instability in its surrounding areas."

4. See the discussion in Wang Jisi, "Comparing Chinese and American Perceptions of Security" (North Pacific Cooperative Security Dialogue [Toronto] Working Paper No. 17); and Wu Xinbo, "China: Security Practice of a Modernizing and Ascending Power," in Muthiah Alagappa, ed., *Asian Security Practices: Material and Ideational Influences* (Stanford, Calif.: Stanford University Press, 1998).

5. Some Chinese analysts, such as Colonel Peng Huaidong of the Academy of Military Sciences, even argue that Western societies glorify war and extol martial values, militarism, bravery, struggle, and violence, whereas Chinese society emphasizes morality, peace, stability, order, and intellectual rather than material strength. Peng Huaidong, "Lun Zong-Xi Zhanzheng Guanzhi Zhuyao Chabie" (A Discussion of the Major Differences in Chinese and Western Views of War), *Zhongguo Junshi Kexue,* no. 1 (1997): 127–31.

and Brunei. Border conflicts have erupted with the former Soviet Union, India, and Vietnam. For many years, China faced virtual military encirclement by antagonistic nations—including the United States and its Asian treaty partners, the Soviet Union, and India. At the height of tensions, the former Soviet Union alone maintained forty-four heavily armed mobile assault divisions on the Sino-Soviet frontier and threatened nuclear attacks against strategic targets in China's heartland. During the 1960s and 1970s, Beijing added to the tensions by actively supporting insurgency movements and the destabilization of governments in Southeast Asia, the Middle East, Africa, and Latin America.

The new peace is striking compared with China's insecurity in the past. A century ago, the moribund Middle Kingdom was experiencing colonial dismemberment and internal imperial decay, and had just been humiliated in the Sino-Japanese War of 1894–95. A half century ago, on the eve of the Chinese Communists' seizure of power, much of the country lay in ruins from three decades of internecine strife, civil war, and occupation by invading Japanese forces.[6] Although China was on the verge of territorial unification for the first time in more than a century, the soon-to-be-established People's Republic unknowingly stood on the precipice of bloody conflict in Korea and two decades of hot and cold war around its periphery.

Since the Cold War ended, these former threatening realities have been transformed. China has become more of a status quo power and has become much more deeply and constructively engaged in world affairs. China has joined a number of international governmental and nongovernmental organizations (IGOs and NGOs), including almost all key security regimes: the Comprehensive Test Ban Treaty; Nuclear Non-Proliferation Treaty; and Chemical Weapons Convention; the Bacteriological, Biological, and Toxin Weapons Convention; the Convention on Certain Conventional Weapons (and its various protocols for land mines, laser weapons, etc.); the Zangger Committee (for Nuclear Export Controls); and a series of Nuclear Free Zone treaties. While not yet a member of the Missile Technology Control Regime (MTCR), the PRC has abided by most of the regime's guidelines and parameters. China has also supported the early conclusion of the Convention on Banning the Production of Fissile Materials for Nuclear Weapons or Other Nuclear Explosive Devices (Fissile Material Cutoff); a Treaty for Non-First-Use of Nuclear Weapons; and a Treaty on the Ban of Weapons in Outer Space. Since 1990, China has also become more active in United Nations

6. See Edward L. Dreyer, *China at War, 1901–1949* (New York: Longman, 1995).

peacekeeping operations, although this involvement has been limited to dispatching observers rather than troops (the one exception being an engineering battalion sent to Cambodia). In 1997, China did agree to contribute "in due time" civilian policemen, more military observers, and engineering, medical, transportation, and logistics service teams to future UN peacekeeping operations. After the civil crisis in East Timor in 2000, China dispatched approximately 100 civilian policemen as part of the UN contingent.

The transformed nature of China's regional posture is perhaps nowhere more notable than in Sino-Russian relations, which have moved during the 1990s from the brink of nuclear war to a productive "strategic cooperative partnership."[7] This designation was first proposed by the Yeltsin government in April 1996, and has since become a blueprint for Beijing's relations with other major and medium-sized powers. Then, in July 2001, Moscow and Beijing concluded a twenty-year "Sino-Russian Treaty of Good Neighborly Friendship and Cooperation."[8] While not a security treaty and certainly falling short of the 1950 Sino-Soviet Alliance, Article 9 of the pact does call for mutual consultations in the event of threat:

> If one party to the treaty believes that there is a threat of aggression menacing peace, wrecking peace, and involving its security interests, and is aimed at one of the parties, the two parties will immediately make contact and hold consultations in order to eliminate the threat that has arisen.

The treaty of "friendship and cooperation" is also intended to show solidarity against a global order dominated by the United States and its European allies. The anti-American language of the treaty is scarcely veiled.

Despite an increased identity of views on security and international affairs, the Sino-Russian relationship remains lacking in other areas. Two-way trade between Russia and China remains relatively miniscule (U.S.$8 billion in 2000, representing only 2 percent of the PRC's total trade and less than 5 percent of Russia's) and is largely limited to compensation trade and

---

7. See Jennifer Anderson, *The Limits of Sino-Russian Strategic Partnership*, Adelphi Paper No. 315 (New York: Oxford University Press for the International Institute for Strategic Studies, 1997); Sherman W. Garnett, ed., *Limited Partnership: Russia-China Relations in a Changing Asia* (Washington, D.C.: Carnegie Endowment for International Peace, Russia and Eurasia Program, 1998); Sherman W. Garnett, ed., *Rapprochement or Rivalry? Russia-China Relations in a Changing Asia* (Washington, D.C.: Carnegie Endowment for International Peace, 2000).

8. Text is carried by Xinhua Domestic Service on July 16, 2001 and was translated in FBIS–CHI on the same day.

some exchange in the spheres of machine building, electronics, power generation, petrochemicals, aviation, space, and military technology and weapons. The two countries fell far short of their trade target of $20 billion by 2000, which was always unrealistic because the two actually have few economic complementarities. In an ironic historical reversal, Beijing even pledged a $5 billion concessionary loan to Moscow in 1998, in an effort to help its basket-case economy.

Cooperation in other areas is more impressive. Summits between the heads of state now take place annually. With the exception of two small sections, the two former enemies have now completely demarcated their long-disputed 4,340-mile border and have demilitarized the border region. Both sides have placed limits on ground forces, short-range attack aircraft, and anti-air defenses within 100 kilometers of the frontier. As part of two other landmark treaties—the Agreement on Confidence Building in the Military Field along the Border Areas and the Agreement on Mutual Reduction of Military Forces in the Border Areas—signed together with Russia, Tajikistan, Kazakhstan, and Kyrgyzstan in April 1996 and April 1997 respectively, China and the other signatories agreed to force reductions that will limit each to a maximum of 130,400 troops, 3,900 tanks, and 4,500 armored vehicles within this 100-kilometer zone. Other provisions of the agreements prohibit exercises exceeding 40,000 personnel; prior notification of exercises, and mandatory observers for any involving over 35,000 personnel; and a limit of one exercise each year of 25,000 personnel or above. China and Russia have also signed several other bilateral agreements to stabilize and enhance their mutual security—including a nuclear nontargeting agreement (1994) and an agreement to prevent accidental military incidents (1994).

In addition to the annual presidential summit meetings, ministerial-level officials regularly shuttle between the two nations. The two military establishments have forged particularly close relations—including the transfers of substantial numbers of Russian weapons and defense technologies (including training) to China. Since 1990, Russian arms exports to China have averaged $750 million per year, less than one-sixth of their total bilateral trade but 40 percent of Russia's total global arms exports and almost all of China's total foreign arms purchases. These transactions totaled $6.75 billion in sales between 1991 and 2000.

While it would be an exaggeration to claim that Russia has turned from China's adversary to its ally, and both countries profess that this is not their goal, the new "strategic cooperative partnership" has substantially enhanced their mutual and regional security. The two have also found common cause in opposing "hegemonism and power politics"—Beijing's code words for the United States.[9] In addition to the aforementioned "friendship and co-operation" pact, the two governments have increasingly begun to side together by voting against the United States and the United Kingdom in the UN Security Council and other forums. Thus far, Sino-Russian opposition to the United States and its allies has remained largely rhetorical, but it could become more tangible over time.

There is little doubt that Chinese leaders and strategists view the United States as the greatest threat to world peace, as well as to China's own national security and foreign policy goals. China's 1998 Defense White Paper is only thinly veiled on this point:

> Hegemonism and power politics remain the main source of threats to world peace and stability; the cold war mentality and its influence still have a certain currency, and the enlargement of military blocs and strengthening of military alliances have added factors of instability to international security. Some countries, by relying on their military advantages, pose military threats to other countries, even resorting to armed intervention.[10]

The 2000 Defense White Paper was similarly strident:

> In today's world, factors that may cause instability and uncertainty have markedly increased. The world is far from peaceful. . . . Hegemonism and power politics still exist and are developing further in the international political, economic, and security spheres. Certain big powers are pursuing "neo-interventionism," "neo-gunboat diplomacy," and "neo-economic colonialism," which are seriously damaging the sovereignty, independence, and developmental interests of many countries, and threatening world peace and security. . . . There are new negative developments in the security of the Asia-Pacific region. The United States is further strengthening its military presence and bilateral military alliances in the region, and is advocating the TMD [theater missile defense] system, and is planning to deploy it in East Asia.[11]

Similar assessments by PLA analysts of the Asian security situation express similar concern about the United States, Japan, and Taiwan.[12]

Despite this subjective pessimism, when viewed more objectively, China's

9. "China, Russia Presidents Sign Joint Statement on ABM Issue," Xinhua, July 18, 2000.

10. Information Office of the State Council, *China's National Defense*, p. 5.

11. Information Office of the State Council, *China's National Defense in 2000*.

12. See, e.g., the essays in Song Mingming, ed., *Ya-Tai Anquan Zhanlüe Lun* (Essays on Asia-Pacific Security Strategy) (Beijing: Academy of Military Sciences Press, 2000).

national security environment has never been better. In addition to repairing ties with Russia and establishing them with the newly independent Central Asian republics, during the 1990s China also mended fences with India and Vietnam.

While border disputes still exist with India, various confidence building and security measures have been put into place along the common borders and negotiations proceed to resolve more long-standing territorial disputes. The November 1996 Agreement on Confidence Building Measures in the Military Field along the Line of Actual Control in the China-India Border Areas was a very significant initiative to lower tensions and reduce the possibility of accidental conflict. Strengthened Sino-Indian ties were undermined by India's detonation of four nuclear devices in May 1998. Pakistan followed suit, and could not have done so without China's assistance to its nuclear development program over many years. Beijing was quick to join the international condemnation of India and subsequently worked to keep pressure on New Delhi to freeze its nuclear program and development of delivery systems. However, after a relatively brief hiatus, Beijing deemed its broader interests lay in stabilizing and strengthening bilateral ties with New Delhi, and since late 1999, they have improved. Nonetheless, as is discussed at greater length below, PLA national security analysts have long viewed India as a "regional hegemon." Many in India have long seen China as a threat to its security. In justifying its nuclear testing, the government in New Delhi cited the Chinese nuclear "threat," as well as a perceived containment policy by Beijing. As a result, Sino-Indian relations are filled with mutual suspicion, even if they have stabilized since the 1998 nuclear detonations.

Following the collapse of the Soviet Union and independence of Central Asian states, China moved quickly to establish diplomatic relations and has subsequently built strong ties with its new neighbors. Beijing was the driving force behind forming the "Shanghai Five" (China, Kyrgyzstan, Kazakhstan, Tajikistan, and Russia), a group that now includes Uzbekistan and is known as the Shanghai Cooperation Organization. The PRC has paid particular attention to Kazahkstan, with which it has signed several accords for joint energy exploitation. Central Asian oil reserves, estimated at about 200 billion barrels, have become strategically important to China, because the PRC became a net importer of crude oil in 1993 and relied on the Middle East for 53 percent of its total imports that year. One of Beijing's motivations for solidifying ties with the CIS states is its own fears of ethnic unrest among its Muslim and minority populations in Xinjiang province. Small arms and other support have flowed to insurgents in China's northwest from Iran, Afghanistan's Taliban, and sympathetic brethren in the CIS states. But Beijing and Moscow have managed to stem the tide through coordinated action with other Central Asia states. All in all, Beijing's diplomatic attention to Central Asia has paid off, and its long northwest frontier is now considerably more stable and secure.

During the 1990s, China also normalized diplomatic relations with the Republic of Korea, Mongolia, Singapore, and Indonesia—thus taking significant steps to stabilize its periphery and regional security. Despite ASEAN suspicions of China arising from contested claims to islands in the South China Sea, the China-Myanmar relationship, and China's military modernization program and long-range strategic objectives, Beijing has also been able to build amicable ties with Southeast Asian states. China-ASEAN trade reached U.S.\$26 billion in 2000 (quintuple that of 1990) despite the impact of the regional financial crisis. China's trade with South Korea has similarly mushroomed, rising from a negligible amount in 1990 to \$25.3 billion in 2000.

In foreign relations since the Cold War, China's relations with Japan and the United States have been the most difficult and strained. Sino-Japanese relations are imbued with much historical residue and complexity, and it is likely that they will continue to be characterized by a combination of friction and limited cooperation for some time to come.[13] The same can be said of U.S.-China relations (see below and chapter 8). However in neither case does China (yet) face an overt military adversary or a confrontational relationship.

China's improved regional relations are owed, in no small part, to Beijing's active diplomacy. Never before have China's leaders, Foreign Ministry officials, military brass, and other government representatives been as active in regional or international diplomacy.[14] As China has intensified its bilateral diplomacy, it has also more fully embraced multilateral organizations such as APEC and the ASEAN Regional Forum (I examine below how

13. See David Shambaugh, "Sino-American Strategic Relations: From Partners to Competitors," *Survival*, Spring 2000, pp. 97–115.

14. "In 1996 and 1997 alone, China sent more than 100 military delegations to most of its adjacent countries, and hosted over 130 military delegations from such countries" (Information Office of the State Council, *China's National Defense* [1998]). The now classic Western work on the subject of China's military diplomacy is Kenneth W. Allen and Eric A. McVadon, *China's Foreign Military Relations* (Washington, D.C.: Henry L. Stimson Center, 1999).

the PRC came full circle, in a relatively short period, from opposing to embracing multilateralism).

The "New Security Concept"

Parallel with this shift in its diplomacy, beginning in early 1997, Beijing also began to tout its "New Security Concept." First enunciated by Foreign Minister Qian Qichen and Minister of Defense Chi Haotian in 1997, the NSC melds several elements of Beijing's global strategic outlook. Some—like the Five Principles of Peaceful Coexistence and prediction of the emergence of a multipolar world—are long-standing trademarks of China's professed foreign policy goals. Other elements—such as the embrace of multilateral security mechanisms and "strategic partnerships" with other countries—are new since the Cold War. Some—such as strengthening trade and economic cooperation—are just self-interested and consistent with domestic reforms. The NSC should also be seen as a fuller enunciation of the "New International Political Order" floated by Qian Qichen in the early 1990s.

The NSC expresses China's alternative vision for regional and global international relations and security.[15] First, it clearly reveals China's dissatisfaction with the existing unipolar international system, dominated by American power. Second, it shows China's stated, normative aversion to settling disputes through coercion and the use of force.[16] Third, it illustrates Beijing's more proactive stance in world affairs and its aspirations to be treated as a global power. Fourth, it is obvious that the NSC was formulated in direct response to the expansion of NATO and efforts by the United States to strengthen its five bilateral security alliances in East Asia and nonallied security ties in East, South, and Central Asia. In this regard, the NSC is aimed substantially at China's neighbors. Chinese officials and analysts have been very concerned that the strengthening of U.S. alliances and defense relationships are implicitly or expressly aimed at China, particularly as regards Taiwan. The revised U.S.-Japan Defense Guidelines and possible deployment

15. I have benefited from discussions with David Finkelstein and Michael McDevitt on these points.

16. Word and deed must be distinguished here, as both the PRC and previous Chinese governments have demonstrated a high proclivity to escalate conflicts and settle disputes through force. Research by Alastair Iain Johnston is particularly germane in this regard. See his *Cultural Realism: Strategic Culture and Grand Strategy in Chinese History* (Princeton, N.J.: Princeton University Press, 1995), and "China's Militarized Interstate Dispute Behavior, 1949–1992: A First Cut at the Data," *China Quarterly*, no. 153 (March 1998): 1–30.

of TMD have been a particular source of concern, but the PRC has tended to view all of America's security relationships in the Asia-Pacific region through the prisms of "containment" and Taiwan.[17]

Despite its turgid and seemingly naive prose, the New Security Concept should not be dismissed as frivolous and irrelevant. It does represent, in its most systematic exposition, China's official prescriptive view of how international relations should be conducted and security maintained. The NSC is firmly rooted in modern Chinese history and Communist China's myths about fostering a world based on the Five Principles of Peaceful Coexistence: mutual respect for territorial integrity and sovereignty, mutual nonaggression, noninterference in each other's internal affairs, equality and mutual benefit, and peaceful coexistence. This schema is designed to shield Beijing from outside pressure over its "internal affairs," while, at the same time, articulating a genuine vision of international relations and security—a vision intentionally distinct from the American view that emphasizes alliances, deterrence, and military force.[18] As Defense Minister Chi Haotian claimed in a 1998 Singapore speech: "The Five Principles are the political basis and premise of global and regional security."[19]

Thus, in several ways, China has become more proactive in pushing its vision for international affairs and security. Beijing is also making an effort to incorporate elements of its NSC into the diplomatic documents signed with its new "strategic partnerships" with other nations and to criticize and undermine American global power.

Despite the strategic benefits that the end of the Cold War and China's diplomacy have produced, PLA planners still believe that they live in a dangerous neighborhood. Some other Asian militaries possess weapons and forces that are qualitatively superior, if quantitatively inferior. To be sure, American, Japanese, and Indian forces figure prominently in Chinese computer war-gaming and active contingency planning, and China also has territorial disputes with several Southeast Asian nations. Chinese military intervention on the Korean peninsula also cannot be ruled out. Finally, of course, the most likely use of Chinese force would be against Taiwan.

17. See Thomas Christensen, "China, the U.S.-Japan Alliance, and the Security Dilemma in East Asia," *International Security* 23, no. 4 (Spring 1999): 49–80.

18. See Luo Renshi, "The Struggle between Two Security Concepts," *International Strategic Studies*, April 2000, pp. 11–17.

19. Chi Haotian, "China's Defense Policy," speech delivered to the Institute of Defense and Strategic Studies, Singapore, November 27, 1998.

PERCEIVING CHINA'S POTENTIAL THREAT ENVIRONMENT

It is not easy to gain insights into PLA thinking about China's regional threat environment. Interviews with PLA officers are sometimes illuminating, and occasionally there is an insightful and informative article in *Jiefangjun Bao* (Liberation Army Daily), but the best sources are periodicals and books published by PLA think tanks. The PLA publishes nearly fifty journals, but they mainly concentrate on doctrinal and training issues.[20] The exceptions are those few that publish articles on regional and international security. One of the best is *Guoji Zhanlüe Yanjiu* (International Strategic Studies), published by the China Institute for International Strategic Studies (a research institute connected to the General Staff Department's Second Department); there is an English-language version of this journal. Another useful periodical, published since 1988, is the restricted-circulation *Guofang Daxue Xuebao: Zhanlüe Yanjiu* (National Defense University Journal: Strategic Research), edited by the Institute of Strategic Studies at the National Defense University (NDU). Other journals that publish about regional and global security include *Guofang* (National Defense) and *Junshi Kexue* (Military Science). In recent years, both the NDU and the Academy of Military Sciences (AMS), the PLA's two premier educational and research institutions, have also published annual assessments of international security. Other than these, one has to comb *Jiefangjun Bao* and military textbooks for indications of PLA analysis of regional and global security trends. What do these sources indicate about the PLA's threat perceptions?[21]

Comprehensive Security

PLA analysts like to offer broad overviews of regional and global security issues. But in contrast to their civilian counterparts, there tends to be a much greater range of views about the sources of strategic stability and instability. Also unlike civilians, military analysts tend to see greater sources of instability (perhaps it is the inherent nature of military analysis).

The director of the General Staff Department's First Bureau responsible for the "comprehensive international security situation," Senior Colonel Li

20. This figure comes from a survey by a researcher with access to the Academy of Military Sciences library.

21. Much of the following section draws upon my article "China's Military Views the World: Ambivalent Security," *International Security* 24, no. 3 (Winter 1999/ 2000): 52–79.

Qinggong, posits that U.S. "hegemonism and power politics" has become a major security problem in Asia and the world. Militarily, Li divides the world into a five-level military power hierarchy:

1. The United States and Russia (although he concedes that Russia is only a "second-rank military superpower")

2. The United Kingdom, France, China, and Germany

3. India, Israel, Iran, and Iraq

4. North Korea, South Korea, ASEAN, Brazil, Argentina

5. African and other Latin American countries[22]

In a later article, following the Kosovo conflict, Li identified a slightly different set of factors causing global instability:[23]

· American hegemony and the attempt to conquer the world by force

· Western "humanitarian intervention" and the "Clinton Doctrine"

· The increasing intensification of local ethnic conflicts, as in Chechnya, Eritrea, Indonesia, and Yugoslavia

· The decline of arms control efforts and the buildup of regional military forces

· The rise of ethnoreligious separatism and increase in terrorist acts

One of Li's senior Second Department colleagues adopts a less geographic approach, identifying a series of nonmilitary factors now important for Chinese security: the Asian financial crisis; environmental issues; transnational crime; terrorism; and drug trafficking. Allowing for these new considerations, this analyst also pointed to "problems of national division" *(guojia fenlei wenti)* and "disputes over territory and resources" *(lingtu yu ziran chongtu)* as potential factors that could lead China into military conflict.[24]

Another military commentator, an editor of the official *Jiefangjun Bao*, Colonel Zhang Yi, also sees an increase in the number of global hot spots,

---

22. Li Qinggong, "Wulun Leng Zhan Hou Shijie Junshi Geju de Bianhua" (An Examination of Changes in the Post–Cold War Global Military Structure), *Zhongguo Junshi Kexue*, no. 1 (1997): 112–19.

23. Li Qinggong, "A Review of and Prospects for the World Military Situation," *International Strategic Studies*, January 2000, pp. 29–33.

24. Interview, December 6, 1998.

but a concomitant decrease in their scope, duration, and intensity.[25] Interestingly, Zhang identified seven causes of such post–Cold War hot spots:

- American "power politics" and increased interventionism

- Power imbalance caused by the collapse of the bipolar system

- Contest and conflict between the (U.S.) global hegemon and "regional hegemons"

- A surge in nationalism, national separatism, "national extremism," and ethnic conflict

- An increase in religious movements and fundamentalism

- Struggle over territorial, sovereignty, and economic rights

- Internal factionalism and power struggles

Based on these factors, Zhang foresees a very turbulent world and prolonged strife.

Another Second Department intelligence analyst, Zhang Changtai, lists a somewhat different set of sources of international instability:[26]

- An increase in local wars between states

- Strengthening of military alliances by the United States

- Damage done to international arms control efforts by the South Asian nuclear tests

- Military interventionism by the United States

- Economic insecurity

- International terrorism

Luo Renshi of the China Institute of International Strategic Studies (CIISS) believes that a principal source of post–Cold War strategic instability lies in the revolution in military affairs *(xin junshi geming)*, which he believes has catalyzed a global "high-tech arms race."[27]

---

25. Zhang Yi, "Leng Zhan Hou Shijie Ri Dian yu Dangjin Guoji Zhanlüe Xingshi" (Post–Cold War Global Hotspots and the Contemporary International Strategic Situation), *Zhongguo Junshi Kexue*, no. 1 (1997): 103–11.

26. Zhang Changtai, "Several Factors Affecting Current International Security," *International Strategic Studies*, no. 4 (1998): 1–5.

27. Luo Renshi, "The Emerging High-Tech Arms Race and Its Impact on the International Strategic Situation and Arms Control," *International Strategic Studies*, no. 4 (1998): 6–11.

Thus there is no agreement among PLA analysts about the sources of potential instability when they survey the regional and international strategic landscape. Yet one commonality in such analyses is their view that the United States is a destabilizing force in international security affairs.

Worried about the Hegemon

By far the most discussed security problem for PLA analysts is the United States—both generally and in the particular contexts of Taiwan, Korea, and Japan. Numerous Chinese military analyses portray the United States since the Cold War as hegemonic, expansionist, and bent on global and regional domination. As retired General Chen Kaizeng, vice president of the CIISS and former PLA defense attaché to London and Washington, puts it: "The strength of the United States has intensified its lust for leading the world and its tendency of expansionism. . . . The attempt to maintain the hegemonist status and seek a monopolar world has constituted an important divergence between the United States and other powers."[28] Senior Colonel Li Qinggong (cited above) similarly states, "The biggest unstable factor of the global military situation at the turn of the century is that the U.S. has been trying to reign over the world and to seek hegemony by force."[29] One of Li's senior colleagues in PLA intelligence adds, "Just because America's hegemonic behavior is understandable from a historical perspective does not mean it is acceptable."[30] The director of the Strategy Department at the Academy of Military Sciences opined:

> Since the end of the Cold War the United States has been seeking to
> build a unipolar world exclusively dominated by itself. Relying on its
> strong military capabilities, commandeering the support of Western
> developed countries, and exploiting religious conflicts, ethnic contra-
> dictions, and territorial disputes around the world, it has willingly
> interfered in the internal affairs of other countries and intervened
> in regional conflicts, in an effort to expand its area of domination.[31]

Various means are identified as examples of the American quest for hegemony:[32]

28. Chen Kaizeng, "Prospects for the Relations among Great Powers in the New Century," *International Strategic Studies,* no. 2 (2000): 1.

29. Li, "Review of and Prospects for the World Military Situation," p. 29.

30. Interview, General Staff Department, May 4, 1998.

31. Yao and Zhao, "How Will China Handle War in the 21st Century?"

32. These views are expressed in a wide range of articles. See, e.g., Sa Benwang, "A Review of the U.S. Concept of 'Enlargement Strategy,'" *International Strategic*

- Domination of the international trading and financial systems
- An ideological crusade to "enlarge" democracies and subvert states that oppose U.S. hegemonism
- An interventionist emphasis on human rights
- Strengthening old and building new military alliances
- Reverting to military coercion in pursuit of political and economic goals
- Intervention in regional conflicts
- Manipulating arms control negotiations in order to "leverage" weaker states
- Manipulating and dominating regional multilateral security organizations

Most civilian and military analysts see the greatest check on the U.S. quest for hegemony *(baquanzhuyi)* as the rise of multipolarity *(duoyanghua)*. Most see the post–Cold War balance of power as being one of "one superpower, many strong powers" *(yi chao duo qiang)*, with the latter able to check the former.[33]

PLA analysts also pay particular attention to U.S. deployments overseas and development of new weapons and combat systems commensurate with the revolution in military affairs.[34] With regard to the former, some analysts argue that U.S. military forces are overextended and undersupported logistically and financially to achieve America's goals of achieving dominance in the Asia-Pacific, Middle East and Persian Gulf, Europe, and Latin American theaters simultaneously.[35] They do not believe that the United

Studies, no. 4 (1993); Zhang Linhong, "Focal Points of U.S. Global Strategy at the Turn of the Century," ibid., no. 2 (1997).

33. See the discussion in Pan Xiangting, ed., *Shijie Junshi Xingshi, 1997–98* (The World Military Situation) (Beijing: National Defense University Press, 1998), pp. 1–7.

34. See Wang Baocun, *Shijie Xin Junshi Geming* (The Global Revolution in Military Affairs) (Beijing: Jiefangjun Chubanshe, 2000), and the discussion of his work in chapter 3 above; and Lu Xinmei, "New Characteristics of the Plan for Arms Buildup of the New U.S. Administration," *International Strategic Studies,* no. 2 (1993): 18–21.

35. See, e.g., Fu Chengli, "The Post–Cold War Adjustment of U.S. Military Strategy," *International Strategic Studies,* no. 1 (1994): 27–33; Fu Chengli, "Xin Meiguo de Ya Tai Zhanlüe" (The New American Asia Strategy), *Guofang,* no. 5 (1996): 30–31.

States could wage and win two wars at the same time. Prior to the 1999 Kosovo crisis and NATO campaign against Serbia, they argued that U.S. forces will increasingly face small and limited conflicts (e.g., Bosnia, Haiti), to which the American military's overwhelming firepower and technological prowess are not well-suited. As is discussed in chapter 3, the PLA was generally heartened by Serbia's ability to withstand massive aerial bombardment. Other analysts, such as Academy of Military Sciences strategist General Wang Zhenxi, argue that the strengthening of U.S. alliances and non-alliance defense relationships are permitting greater flexibility in American strategic reach and have significantly extended U.S. "global dominance."[36]

PLA analysts are uniformly opposed to U.S. alliances, even if they moderated their tone after 1997. But some are more sanguine. One colonel affiliated with the GSD Second Department said, "In the long term, the U.S. presence in East Asia should decrease step by step; a rapid pullout would cause concerns. U.S. alliances [in the region] are not opposed to China ipso facto, but they should not be used to interfere in our internal affairs, i.e., Taiwan."[37]

Military analysts perceive U.S. policies toward China as part of an American quest for global domination. They are unequivocal about America's alleged desire to strategically and militarily contain the PRC. This is evidenced in numerous articles.[38] However, in 1996 and 1997, some authors interpreted the new Clinton administration policy of "engagement" as evidence of the futility and defeat of the previous policy of containment.[39] Nonetheless, many perceived "engagement" as merely a tactical adjustment, amounting to "soft containment."[40] In the words of one PLA analyst, "The United States will still try to exert maximum influence on China."[41] "The U.S. desire to

36. Wang Zhenxi and Zhang Qinglei, "Post–Cold War U.S. Alliance Strategy," *International Strategic Studies*, no. 3 (1998): 1–9.

37. Interview, May 4, 1998.

38. See, e.g., General Cai Zuming, "Meiguo Anquan Zhanlüe Sixiang Xin Fanxiang" (New Directions in American Security Strategic Thinking), *Guofang*, no. 1 (1994): 21–22; Huang Dong, "Dangqian Guoji Zhanlüe Xingshi De Tedian Ji Fazhan Qushi" (Special Characteristics and the Direction of Development in the Recent International Strategic Order), *Guofang*, no. 2 (1997): 10–11.

39. See, e.g., Colonel Guo Xinning, "Qianyi Kelindun Zhengfu de Ya-Tai Zhanlüe" (The Clinton Government's Asia-Pacific Strategy), *Guofang Daxue Xuebao* (March 1997); Xie Wenqing, "Adjustment and Trend of Development of U.S. Policy towards China," *International Strategic Studies*, no. 3 (1996): 14–20.

40. For further analysis, see David Shambaugh, "Containment or Engagement of China? Calculating Beijing's Responses," *International Security*, Fall 1996, pp. 180–209.

41. Guo, "Qianyi Kelindun Zhengfu de Ya-Tai Zhanlüe."

'shape' China, as is clear [in the Defense Department's 1998 *East Asia Strategy Review*]," said one PLA general, "is doomed to futility."[42] In addition to seeing a policy of strategic containment and political subversion, many argue publicly and privately that the United States seeks to permanently separate Taiwan from Chinese sovereignty.[43] Another PLA general stated bluntly: "The United States is opposed to China's reunification and seeks to keep separation permanent."[44]

Northeast Asia

PLA analysts express great suspicions about Japan. They see Japanese defense policy as shifting from being locally to regionally directed, and from passive to active defense.[45] Japan's new geographic strategic thrust is said to have shifted from the north (Russia and Korea) to the west (China) and south (ASEAN).[46] Some articles are very alarmist about Japan's military capabilities, including latent nuclear capabilities.[47] The redefined U.S.-Japan Mutual Security Treaty (1996) and revised Defense Guidelines (1997), and the 1995 National Defense Buildup Program are taken as key manifestations of Japan's new assertiveness and strategic ambitions.[48] Most PLA analysts view these initiatives as part and parcel of Japan's playing the junior partner in America's containment of China. "The common strategic goal of the U.S.-Japan relationship is to contain the 'China threat'—the newly strengthened alliance allows the United States to use Japan to restrain the growth of China," one National Defense University specialist says.[49] Another analysis cautioned, however, that while Japan did indeed have such ambitions to become a symmetrical (economic, political, military) great

42. Interview, December 8, 1998.

43. A good example is Xu Yimin and Xie Wenqing, "U.S. Hegemonism on the Question of Taiwan," *International Strategic Studies*, no. 3 (1995): 10–16.

44. Interview, December 8, 1998.

45. Liang Yang, "Riben Fangwei Zhengce Tiaozheng Jichi Dui Ya-Tai Anquan Xingshi de Yingxiang" (Adjustment of the Scope of Japan's Defense Policy and Its Influence on the Structure of Asian Security), *Guofang*, no. 9 (1996): 13–14.

46. Ibid.

47. Ji Yu, "Riben Junguozhuyi Miewang Furi" (Vigilance against the Revival of Japanese Militarism), *Guofang*, no. 9 (1996): 15–16.

48. Zhang Taishan, "New Developments in the U.S.-Japan Military Relationship," *International Strategic Studies*, no. 4 (1997): 28–33.

49. Jiang Lingfei, "Yingxiang Ya-Tai Anquan Xingshi de Sange Zhongda Wenti" (Three Big Factors Influencing the East Asian Security Situation), *Guofang Daxue Xuebao*, no. 3 (1997): 46.

power, a number of serious constraints (domestic and international) would limit its ability to realize its ambitions.[50] PLA analyses concentrate on changes in Japanese defense doctrine from "exclusive defense" of the home islands to enlarged "surrounding areas"; redeployment of forces from Hokkaido to western Japan (opposite China and Korea); streamlining of the Japanese Self-Defense Forces; procurement of new force-projection air and naval weapons platforms; and increasingly close integration with U.S. forces.[51] Japan's participation in the research and development aspects of the U.S. Theater Missile Defense program is particularly alarming to PLA strategists, and they are virulently outspoken in criticizing it.[52] Their objections seem to be less military in nature than disturbed by the strategic implications of U.S.-Japan cooperation in this area.

The anti-Japanese sentiment one encounters among the PLA at all levels is palpable. Distrust of Japan runs deep, transcends generations, and is virulent among the generation of PLA officers in their forties and fifties. Japan stimulates an emotional reaction not evident even in anti-American diatribes. In conversations with PLA personnel, Americans are regularly subjected to the view that the United States is naïve to consider Japan as an ally or partner, and they often counsel the United States to be wary of Japanese intentions and military ambitions.

If PLA analysts are worried about Japan, they seem strangely relaxed about Korea. In fact, they express a very different view of the security and humanitarian situation in North Korea than is found in Washington or Tokyo. Several military writings and interviews indicate a critical view of South Korea and the United States for exacerbating tensions and continuing the Cold War on the peninsula.[53] One PLA general attacked joint exercises and U.S. forces in Korea as "provocative" and called for the removal of U.S. forces from the peninsula.[54] Chinese officials and analysts, civilian and military alike, are strongly critical of what they describe as U.S. "pres-

---

50. Tang Yongsheng, "Riben Duiwai Zhanlüe de Tiaozheng Jichi Zhiji Yinsu" (Revisions to Japan's Foreign Strategy and Its Limiting Factors), *Guofang Daxue Xuebao*, no. 3 (1997): 44–49.

51. Zhang Taishan, "Japan's Military Strategy in the New Era," *International Strategic Studies*, no. 3 (1998): 17–20.

52. Numerous interviews, October and December 1998.

53. Pan Junfeng, "Zhanlüe Geju, Daguo Guanxi, Ya-Tai Huanjing" (Strategic Areas, Great Power Relations, and the Asia-Pacific Environment), *Guofang*, no. 1 (1997): 10–11.

54. Interview, December 6, 1998

sure tactics" against Pyongyang. "What is the purpose of U.S. pressure? To force North Korea into collapse or into changing and developing," asks one general.[55] "The tougher the U.S. response and pressure, the closer to the brink [North] Korean leaders will be willing to go," another general opined.[56] These PLA interlocutors argue that China does not wish to see weapons of mass destruction (WMD) on the Korean peninsula, and that the PRC seeks "stability" on the peninsula—but they downplay the humanitarian situation in the North. Chinese analysts often argue that "the North Koreans have a great capacity to endure hardship." Chinese analysts do not think that the country and the Kim regime are about to collapse. Some PLA analysts are even optimistic about North Korean behavior.[57] For China and the PLA, maintenance of North Korea as a viable state and security buffer is the highest priority. Beijing has been very supportive of the historic 1998 rapprochement between North and South Korean leaders and the gradual ensuing détente, and worked hard behind the scenes to facilitate it. During the course of the 1990s, China has also worked very hard to improve its ties with South Korea. Taken together, these two initiatives augur well for China's future security and stability on its northeastern frontier.

Uncertainty about the Neighbors to the North

Over the past decade, China's security calculations with Russia and the Central Asian republics to the north have fundamentally transformed. Moscow and Beijing have moved from the brink of nuclear war to a "strategic partnership."[58] Although Moscow and Beijing have a long history of distrust and hostilities, bilateral relations have not been better in four decades.[59] The 1999 Kosovo crisis and Yugoslav war helped to cement the newfound Sino-Russian strategic solidarity, but even before Kosovo, the two governments had increasingly begun to side together against the United States in the UN Security Council and other international forums. Since Kosovo, the anti-U.S. rhetoric has become more explicit and frequent—as was evident at the

55. Ibid.

56. Ibid.

57. Wang Dahui, "The Post–Cold War Situation on the Korean Peninsula," *International Strategic Studies*, no. 3 (1997): 31–36.

58. See Anderson, *Limits of Sino-Russian Strategic Partnership*, and Garnett, ed., *Limited Partnership*.

59. See, e.g., "China-Russia Relations at the Turn of the Century" (joint statement of Presidents Jiang Zemin and Boris Yeltsin, November 23, 1998), reprinted in *Beijing Review*, December 14–20, 1998.

August 1999 summit of Presidents Jiang Zemin and Boris Yeltsin and their counterparts from Kyrgyzstan, Kazakhstan, and Tajikistan.[60]

Improved Sino-Russian relations are not necessarily mirrored on the perceptual level. In contrast to civilian analysts, who portray Russia as a passive and weak power in decline and one that no longer threatens China, or a country with which China enjoys a solid "strategic partnership," some military analysts express reservations about Russia's long-term strategic ambitions and current defense policies. They argue that Russia seeks to rebuild and reassert itself as a great power,[61] and particularly to reassert itself across Eurasia and in East Asia.[62] In both cases, Russia is seen as trying to use collective security mechanisms as a wedge to reassert its strategic presence absent its former military presence in the region.[63] While PLA analysts recognize the problems affecting Russia's military forces,[64] not all assess the Russian military to be as atrophied as do civilian analysts. They point to an increased emphasis placed by the Russian armed forces on developing large-scale mobile assault forces while maintaining a robust nuclear deterrent.[65] This is a strategy of necessity, some National Defense University analysts believe, because the Russian Navy has collapsed.[66] Although some articles discuss the overall improved Sino-Russian relationship,[67] there was no commentary in these open-source journals on the extensive military-to-military relationship or on what Russia can do to assist PLA force modernization.[68]

Central Asia poses strategic challenges for China's security as well. On

---

60. See, e.g., "Anti-Western Edge to Russian-Chinese Summit," *Jamestown Foundation Monitor*, August 26, 1999, available at wwwjamestown.org/htrn/pub-monitor/htm.

61. Wang Rui and Zhang Wei, "A Preliminary Analysis of Russian Military Strategy," *International Strategic Studies*, no. 3 (1997): 42.

62. Xue Gang, "The Present Security Policy Framework of Russia," *International Strategic Studies*, no. 1 (1995): 22–27; Xue Gang and Xu Jun, "Russia's Asia-Pacific Strategy," *International Strategic Studies*, no. 4 (1995): 14–20.

63. Xue, "Present Security Policy Framework of Russia."

64. Xue Gang, "Retrospect and Prospect of Russia's Economic and Political Transformation," *International Strategic Studies*, no. 3 (1998): 13.

65. Wang and Zhang, "Preliminary Analysis of Russian Military Strategy."

66. Chen Youyi and Yu Gang, "Eluosi Zhanlüe Xingshi De Tedian ji Duiwai Zhengce Zouxiang" (Special Characteristics of Russian Strategy and Trends in Foreign Policy), *Guofang Daxue Xuebao*, no. 3 (1997): 42.

67. See, e.g., Xue Gang, "Sino-Russian Relations in the Post-Cold War International Structure," *International Strategic Studies*, no. 2 (1996): 12–16.

68. Pan Xiangting, ed., *Shijie Junshi Xingshi, 1997–1998* (The World Military Situation, 1997–1998) (Beijing: National Defense University Press, 1998), pp. 277–79, was one of the few surveys that even discussed military exchanges.

the one hand, China has taken advantage of the dissolution of the Soviet Union to build positive relations with the new Central Asian republics bilaterally and in the multilateral context of the Shanghai Cooperation Organization (SCO). Central Asian petroleum reserves are estimated at approximately 200 billion barrels, and this factor has become strategically important to China, given its increasing dependence on imported oil. Accordingly, the PRC has paid particular attention to Kazakhstan, with which it has signed several accords for joint energy exploration and transport to China.

Another principal motivation for Beijing to solidify ties with the Central Asian states is its own problem with ethnic unrest and separatist groups in Xinjiang province. Small arms and other support have flowed to insurgents in China's northwest from Iran, Afghanistan's former Taliban regime and al-Qaeda terrorists, and Chechnya.

This concern was a principal motivation for Beijing to quickly join the U.S.-led war on terrorism following September 11, 2001. Despite China's participation in the anti-terror coalition, however, many Chinese strategists— particularly in the PLA—are concerned about the implications for China's security of the U.S. military presence in Central Asia, Southwest Asia, and South Asia. Many PLA analysts perceive this presence as facilitating U.S. strategic encirclement of China (taken together with existing U.S. deployments in Northwest and Southeast Asia).[69]

ASEAN and Multilateral Regional Security

While China's relations with Southeast Asia are correct, there is a wariness in the region toward China and the PLA.[70] For their part, PLA analysts tend not to write about Southeast Asia and subregional security issues. Because China considers its maritime claim to the South China Sea to be a "domestic issue," a position similar to China's claim on Taiwan, *Jiefangjun Bao* and other PLA publications do not write about them. One senior PLA intelligence official defined the South China Sea issue as both a "sovereignty matter" *(zhuquan yinsu)* and a dispute over territory and resources *(lingtu yu ziran chongtu)*.[71]

69. Interviews with NDU and AMS analysts, March–April 2002, Washington, D.C.

70. See, e.g., Koong Pai-ching, *Southeast Asian Perceptions of China's Military Modernization*, Asia Paper No. 5 (Washington, D.C.: Sigur Center for Asian Studies, George Washington University, 1999); and Allen S. Whiting, "ASEAN Eyes China: The Security Dimension," *Asian Survey* 37, no. 4 (April 1997): 299–322.

71. Interview with General Staff Department Second Department official, Beijing, December 8, 1998.

PLA analysts are generally positive about the potential for regional co-operative security mechanisms, and for the same principal reason as civilian analysts: to constrain American hegemonic power and break through the perceived U.S.-Japan containment policy toward China.[72] Some analysts, notably Luo Renshi of the CIISS, tend to view the ARF and idea of cooperative security in their own right rather than as a means to counter the United States.[73] A former Chinese delegate to the Conference on Disarmament in Geneva, Luo is one of China's most knowledgeable experts on cooperative security institutions. His writings show an appreciation of the underlying norms of such regimes (including transparency), rather than viewing them as mere tactical instruments to pursue realpolitik. Some, such as Colonel Wu Baiyi of the Foundation of International Strategic Studies (FISS), are more explicit in promoting multilateral security and the New Security Concept as a means of countering U.S. hegemony and alliances.[74] Other CIISS analysts are more wedded to traditional geometric and balance-of-power approaches to Asian security, and pay little heed to multilateral institutional mechanisms,[75] while yet others see the ARF as simple evidence of the rising regional role of ASEAN as a "new power."[76]

Worries about South Asia

PLA analysts do not write a great deal about South Asia. Prior to 1998, they were even silent (unlike civilian analysts) about Indian "regional hegemony." But the nuclear tests of that year were a wake-up call to the military. "In-

72. Jiang Linfei, "Yingxiang Ya Tai Anquan Xingshi de Sange Zhong Da Wenti" (Three Major Issues Influencing the Asian Security Situation), *Guofang Daxue Xuebao*, no. 3 (1997): 13–17; and Wu Guifu, "The U.S. Asia-Pacific Strategy in Adjustment," *International Strategic Studies*, no. 3 (1992): 1–8.

73. See Luo Renshi, "Post–Cold War Strategic Trend in the Asia-Pacific Region," *International Strategic Studies*, no. 3 (1994): 5–13; "Progress and Further Efforts to be Made in Establishing Confidence Building," ibid., no. 2 (1995): 18–24; "New Progress and Trend in the Establishment of Confidence and Security Building Measures in the Asia-Pacific Region," ibid., no. 4 (1996): 6–12.

74. Wu Baiyi, "Dong Ya Guojia Anquan Zhengce de Tedian yu Yitong" (Similarities and Differences in East Asian Countries Security Policies) (unpublished paper May 1998).

75. See, e.g., Xu Yimin, "The Strategic Situation in East Asia and China's Place and Role," *International Strategic Studies*, no. 1 (1996): 16–24; Zhu Chun, "A Discussion about the Situation and Security Problems in the Asia-Pacific Region," ibid., no. 1 (1993): 18–22; Zhang Changtai, "Some Views on the Current Situation in the Asia-Pacific Region," ibid., no. 1 (1997): 27–32.

76. Senior Colonel Luo Yuan, "Dongmeng de Chuqi yu Ya-Tai Anquan Hezuo" (The Rise of ASEAN and Asian Security Cooperation), *Guofang*, no. 7 (1996): 23–24.

dia's Attempt to Seek Regional Hegemony Has Been Longstanding!" roared a headline in *Jiefangjun Bao* within days of the blasts.[77] Another *Jiefangjun Bao* article elaborated in unprecedented detail for readers on the composition and order of battle of Indian forces. (One wonders how Chinese readers felt when learning how much more advanced Indian forces are than the PLA in virtually all categories of conventional weapons.)[78] "Through fifty years of efforts, India now boasts a mighty army," the authors observed. To what end is the Indian buildup to be put? The *Jiefangjun Bao* article was clear: "The military strategic targets of India are to seek hegemony in South Asia, contain China, control the Indian Ocean, and strive to become a military power in the contemporary world. To attain these targets, since independence India has always pursued its military strategy of hegemonist characteristics." The authors continued to describe Indian policy of "occupying Chinese territory in the eastern sector of the border region" (saying nothing, of course, about the western sector, where Chinese forces occupy 14,500 square kilometers of Indian-claimed territory), targeting its missiles on southern and southwestern China, and "maintaining its military superiority in the Sino-Indian boundary region to consolidate its vested interests and effectively contain China." India, the authors concluded, "is waiting for the opportune moment for further expansion to continue to maintain its control over weak and small countries in South Asia, advance farther southward, and defend its hegemonist status in the region." Other PLA commentators alarmingly expressed fear of an accidental nuclear exchange between India and Pakistan, citing the situation on the subcontinent as "far more serious than the Cuban missile crisis of 1962."[79] By 2002, PLA commentators seemed slightly more sanguine about India's nuclear capability but still expressed concerns over India's regional ambitions and growing military capabilities.[80]

The PLA has seemingly found a new adversary in India. The only ques-

77. Liu Wenguo, "India's Attempt to Seek Hegemony Has Been Longstanding," *Jiefangjun Bao*, May 26, 1998, in FBIS–CHI, June 3, 1998.

78. Liu Yang and Guo Feng, "What Is the Intention of Wantonly Engaging in Military Ventures—India's Military Development Should Be Watched Out For," *Jiefangjun Bao*, May 19, 1998, in FBIS–CHI, May 21, 1998.

79. Yang Haisheng, "Harmful Effects of India's Nuclear Tests on the World Strategic Situation," *International Strategic Studies*, no. 4 (1998): 17.

80. Cao Yongsheng and Xu Yong, "India Seeks 21st Century Major Power Status," *Jiefangjun Bao*, February 11, 2002, in FBIS–CHI, February 11, 2002.

tion is how long it will be before Chinese analysts see the United States, Japan, Taiwan, and India as acting in cahoots.

THE SPECIAL CASE OF TAIWAN

> Taiwan independence means war and separation will lead to no peace. . . . the People's Liberation Army's millions of troops stand in combat readiness, are on high alert, and will never allow and sit idly by for any attempt to split China to succeed. . . . We will adopt all measures to firmly crush any attempts to divide China and will realize the complete reunification of the motherland.
>
> —*JIEFANGJUN BAO*, March 6, 2000

Clearly, Taiwan is at the top of the PLA's list of potential tensions and possible conflict. Given the primacy of Taiwan in PLA defense planning, it is surprising how little is written in available PLA publications about the military balance with Taiwan or scenarios for conflict. One exception can be found in the journal *Junshi Wenzhai* (Military Digest),[81] which carries a regular feature assessing Taiwan's military and defenses. These articles offer important insights into PLA planning and thinking about how to penetrate Taiwan's air and naval defenses. One special issue published in 1993 offered surprisingly detailed assessments of how to electronically "blind" Taiwan's intelligence, how to sink surface ships with submarines, how to neutralize Taiwan's superiority in fighters, how to invoke public panic with ballistic missile strikes, and so on.[82] Another issue published in 1997 discussed how to attack U.S. Navy aircraft carrier battle groups and how to "teach the United States a lesson,"[83] and a 1998 issue analyzes the new weapons sold to Taiwan by the United States.[84] The May 2000 issue carried an extensive assessment of Taiwan's defenses, with a particular focus on China's short-range ballistic missiles and Taiwan's potential ABM defenses.[85] Another journal, *Quanqiu Junshi Baodao* (World Military Report), carried a map in its March 2000 issue of all of Taiwan's military bases and conceivable strategic targets.[86] A recently published book, *Perspective on Taiwan's Military Situation*, written by anony-

81. Published by the Second Research Institute of China Aerospace and the Chinese Military Scientists Association.

82. *Junshi Wenzhai*, July 1993, pp. 3–45.

83. Ibid., October 1997.

84. Ibid., December 1998, pp. 10–12.

85. Ibid., May 2000, virtually the entire issue.

86. *Quanqiu Junshi Baodao*, March 2000, p. 13.

mous authors under an unknown editor, catalogues in some detail Taiwan's weapons and equipment, command and control, organization and deployments, services, military education, air defenses, electronic warfare capabilities, and other aspects—but this published volume is unique in China.[87] All of these sources are quite detailed and relatively straightforward in their descriptions of Taiwan's defense capabilities, but they tend to avoid discussion of the PLA's own offensive capabilities and how the two would fare in a conflict.

Chinese military officers are also usually reticent about discussing the military dimensions of the Taiwan situation with foreigners. At one 1998 conference with the PLA National Defense University on the regional military balance in the Asia-Pacific, in which I participated, the Chinese side politely listened to an American expert present a detailed assessment of the cross-strait balance. The American was then bluntly told by a PLA general that "since this was an internal affair, no further discussion was warranted." There have been a few exceptions to the general ban on discussing Taiwan military scenarios (as distinct from political scenarios). One was a paper presented by Academy of Military Sciences Strategy Department deputy director, Senior Colonel Luo Yuan, to a conference at the Center for Strategic and International Studies in Washington. In terms of "comparative military capacity" Luo observed that:

> In terms of hardware inventory, each side has its respective strengths and weaknesses—but the PLA's comprehensive capacity enjoys an edge over Taiwan. . . . There exist some serious deficiencies in the overall hardware system of Taiwan's armed forces. First, their weaponry does not form a unified and integrated system, which makes it difficult to really translate into effective fighting power. Modern wars are confrontations between systems, and a few pieces of advanced weapons alone cannot determine the final result of wars. Second, Taiwan's military industry can ill afford a long war of attrition. Third, the strategic territory of Taiwan is limited, which does not provide enough space for military maneuver. Fourth, its strategic targets are overconcentrated and are not effectively protected. These are Taiwan's inherent defects, for which remedies are not available. . . . Regarding software, the mainland has a decided advantage over Taiwan. . . . It can be said that the PLA has an upper hand in its psychological preparation and in its battlefield experience. Further, the initiative for taking military action will be in the hands of the PLA—when, where, and what action will be up to the PLA, and the armed forces of Taiwan can only wait to take a beating. Moreover, the mainland enjoys higher morale and stronger popular support than Taiwan.

87. Liu Shuixin, ed., *Taiwan Junqing Toushi* (Beijing: Jingji Guanli Chubanshe, 2000).

We are fully ready to fight a tough war. Although we prefer to fight a short war to force a quick end, we are also prepared to fight a protracted war. . . . We will not stop until we accomplish our goal. If the first attack is unsuccessful, we will undertake another one and another one until complete victory.[88]

Another interesting insight comes from Senior Colonel Wang Baoqing of the Academy of Military Sciences, who outlined three possible avenues of attack.[89] The first was an all-out attack on the island of Taiwan—"first using missiles to paralyze Taiwan's command system and important military targets in order to gain air superiority and command of the sea," to be followed by a joint army-navy-air operation that "would cross the Strait, land on Taiwan, and thoroughly annihilate Taiwan's troops." Wang's second scenario was a naval blockade "to cut Taiwan's economic exchange with other countries so that it will collapse without fighting a war." This would be done, according to Wang, with extensive mining of ports and navigational channels, backed up by submarines and surface combatants. Third, Wang posited the seizure of offshore islands before attacking Taiwan itself. While Wang did not reveal his preference, he did say that the PLA was prepared for U.S. intervention—but opined that the United States would not become directly involved in combat and would only supply military aid to Taiwan and apply sanctions to China. This "limited intervention," Wang reasoned, would be because a major war would "seriously impair U.S. economic interests."

Concerning American intervention in a Taiwan crisis, in one candid interview in May 2000, a senior colonel in the Institute of Strategic Studies of the National Defense University bluntly warned that:

If force is used to reunify [with Taiwan], we must be prepared for war with the United States. If the United States wants to intervene, you are welcome! In order to fight against the United States, the PLA must: (1) maintain a nuclear retaliatory capability; (2) be able to destroy nuclear aircraft carriers; and (3) try to deprive the United States [of the] right to use foreign bases—we shall tell Japan that if they allow the United States to use bases there [in the conflict], we shall have to strike them![90]

When questioned about the PLA's capability to seize the island with military force, he responded:

88. Luo Yuan, "The Military Factor in the Cross-Strait Situation" (paper presented at CSIS conference on "The Taiwan Issue in U.S.-China Relations," April 4, 2000).

89. "Military Expert Wang Baoqing Envisages War with Taiwan," *Zhongguo Xinwenshe* (Beijing), September 7, 1999, translated in FBIS–CHI, September 8, 1999.

90. Interview, Institute of Strategic Studies, National Defense University, Beijing, May 18, 2000.

We are accustomed to asymmetric war—we may not possess superiority in weapons over Taiwan, but our whole history of the PLA is to achieve victory over superior forces. The gap today is not nearly as great as in the Korean War. The PLA is not well prepared for war against Taiwan, but we have never been well prepared for past wars and have always met our objectives. Our capabilities in information warfare and electronic warfare are not that strong, but more likely are missile and air attacks and possibly blockades.[91]

A report from a Hong Kong newspaper cites a reported meeting of a "forum on war in the Taiwan Strait" convened by the General Staff Department in May 2000.[92] While reporting in the Hong Kong press of such alleged meetings must always be taken with a large grain of salt, the reported considerations were interesting. The five-day meeting allegedly considered a range of possible actions, of which a 36-hour lightning strike was the most likely. This, according to the report, would involve a first-wave missile attack on more than 200 targets, a second-wave aerial bombardment of these targets to ensure their destruction, followed by a third-wave large-scale invasion. As for American intervention, conferees concluded that a variety of cruise missiles could destroy carrier battle groups. Of course, if these arguments were really put forward at the PLA conference, they must all be judged fallacious, because none of these objectives could be achieved in reality.

Perhaps the most remarkable source discussing the possible use of force against Taiwan is an alleged General Office of the Central Military Commission document (No. 65 of 1999), promulgated by the General Political Department on August 1, 1999, which comes to the sobering conclusion that:

> Taking into account the possible intervention by the United States and based on the development strategy of our country, it is better to fight now than future—the earlier, the better. The reason being that, if worse comes to worst, we shall gain control of Taiwan before full deployment of U.S. troops. In this case, the only thing the United States can do is fight a war with the purpose of retaliation, which will be similar to the Gulf War against Iraq or the recent bombing of Yugoslavia.[93]

These sources offer rare glimpses into PLA thinking and planning for combat contingencies with Taiwan and the United States. To be sure, a con-

91. Ibid.

92. Wen Jen, "PLA Deliberates Military Tactics against Taiwan," *Taiyang Bao* (Internet version), Hong Kong, June 5, 2000, in FBIS–CHI, June 5, 2000.

93. Office of the Central Military Commission of the Communist Party of China, OCMC No. [10999] 65, Directive to All Military Regions and General Departments,

siderable amount of such thinking and planning goes on in PLA institutions. For example, my visit to the National Defense University in December 1998 revealed a course being taught to the current class of commanding officers on "Taiwan's Weaponry and Military." The Academy of Military Sciences also includes an intelligence research office specializing in the Taiwan military. Exercises, particularly in the Nanjing Military Region and by the South and East Sea Fleets of the PLAN, have increasingly focused on the Taiwan scenarios in recent years.

If Conflict Erupts

Setting aside these subjective judgments and propaganda statements by some in the PLA, how would a conflict over Taiwan likely play out, and what is the balance of forces that would come into play?

Most military experts do not consider the total balance of forces and order of battle between the PLA and Taiwan's armed forces to be a very useful measure, because it is highly doubtful whether the PRC could employ anywhere near all, or even a significant portion of, its military against Taiwan. The PRC need not do so. It can be reasonably argued that the PRC need only use minimal force, or even the threat of force, to bring considerable pressure to bear on the island and deter Taiwan's independence. If Beijing has another goal, such as the physical occupation of the island by invasion to force "reunification," that is another story, as the PLA currently lacks the conventional capabilities for a successful invasion.

Even if one compares the order of battle, quality of weaponry and manpower is far more important in combat than quantity. Ultimately, however, the employment of military forces is contingency-specific. Taiwan Air Force personnel calculated in 1995 that with the full deployment of 340 fighters coming on stream (150 F-16s, 60 Mirage 2000s, and 130 IDF fighters) by 2000–2001, its fighter force could last approximately one month given an estimated 15 percent loss rate per day.[94] These caveats are necessary when considering table 16.

Affiliated to the Central Military Commission, All Arms and Services, All Corps Headquarters, All Provincial Garrisons, and All Prefecture Garrisons, "Watching Closely for Changes in the Relationships with Taiwan and Enhancing the Awareness by Military Leadership of the Current Situation" (Confidential). This document, in translated form, circulated among nongovernmental specialists on the PLA in the United States.

94. Interview with Taiwan Air Force personnel and military specialists, Taipei, July 9–10, 1995.

TABLE 16 The Balance of Forces: China and Taiwan, 2002

	China	Taiwan
Total Armed Forces (active duty)	2,310,000	370,000
Total Reserves	500,000–600,000 1.5 million People's Armed Police	1,657,500
Defense Budget (U.S.$ billions)	14.5 (2000 official)	12.8 (2000 official)
Strategic Missile Force Personnel	110,000+	0
Ballistic Missiles	20+ ICBMs 130–150 IRBMs 12 SLBMs 335 SRBMs	0
Total Ground Forces	1,600,000	240,000
Main Battle Tanks	8,000 total, including: 5,500 T-59 150 T-69 500 T-79 900 T-88 10+ T-98 700 light and amphibious	1,644 total, including: 100 M-48 A5 450+ M-48H 189 M-60A3; 230 M-24; 675 M-41/T-64
Armored Personnel Carriers	5,000	950
Towed Artillery	13,000	650
Total Air Force Personnel	420,000	68,000
Bombers	150	0
Fighters	2,724 total, of which: 1,500 J-6 624 J-7 170 J-8 300 Q-5 90 Su-27 40 Su-30	444 total, of which: 90 F-5 146 F-16 A/B 58 Mirage 2000–5 128 Ching-kuo IDF 22 AT-3
Helicopters	170	18
Transports	513	34
Airborne Early Warning	None at present	4 E-2T

TABLE 16 *(continued)*

	China	Taiwan
Total Naval Personnel	250,000, including: 26,000 Naval Airforce; 10,000 marines	62,000, including: 1,700 Naval Airforce; 30,000 marines; plus 16,000 Coast Guard
Principal Surface Combatants	62, of which: 21 destroyers 41 frigates	32, of which: 11 destroyers 21 frigates
Submarines	69, of which: 1 SSBN 5 SSN 1 SSG 61 SS	4 SSK
Mine Warfare Ships	39	12
Coastal Patrol Craft	368	59
Amphibious Ships	56	18
Supply and Miscellaneous	163	20

SOURCE: All data derive from International Institute of Strategic Studies, *The Military Balance 2001/2002* (Oxford: Oxford University Press, 2001).

Table 16 indicates a substantial numerical advantage for PRC forces; but unless the PLA threw everything it had at the island at once, Taiwan's conventional defenses appear adequate to repel an invasion. The qualitative edge that Taiwan currently holds, particularly in air and naval platforms, accrue to its substantial advantage for the time being—but with the mainland's weapons systems coming on stream in the early twenty-first century, Taiwan's "window of superiority" will narrow. Continued and expanded provision of advanced U.S. weapons to Taiwan can serve to maintain its advantages, but not forever.

Maps 2–5 also reveal the PRC's numerical advantages in Taiwan-estimated deployments in military regions contiguous to the Taiwan Strait theater. As these maps indicate, the PLA has a sizable force within easy striking distance of Taiwan, although they would encounter great difficulty in moving even a small fraction of it across the Strait. In the Nanjing Military Region alone (directly opposite Taiwan), PLA ground forces total approximately

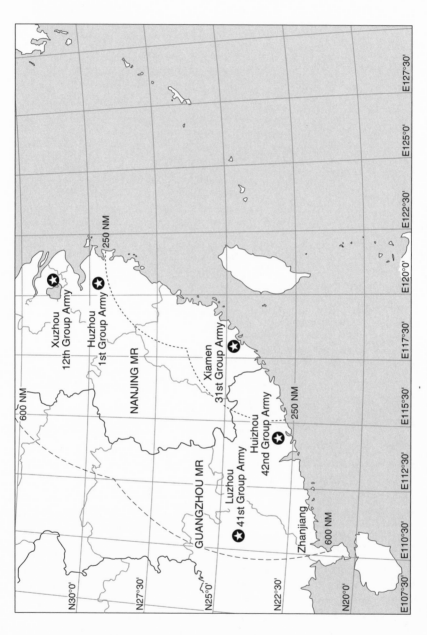

Map 2. PLA Ground Force deployments in the Taiwan theater. Adapted from Defense Mission of the Taipei Economic and Cultural Representative Office in the United States data.

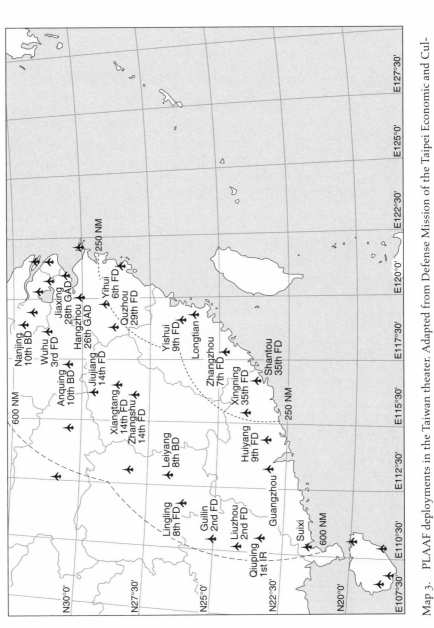

Map 3. PLAAF deployments in the Taiwan theater. Adapted from Defense Mission of the Taipei Economic and Cultural Representative Office in the United States data.

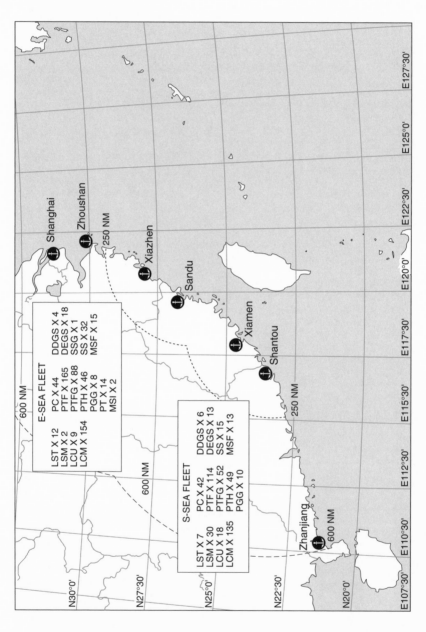

Map 4. PLAN deployments in the Taiwan theater. Adapted from Defense Mission of the Taipei Economic and Cultural Representative Office in the United States data.

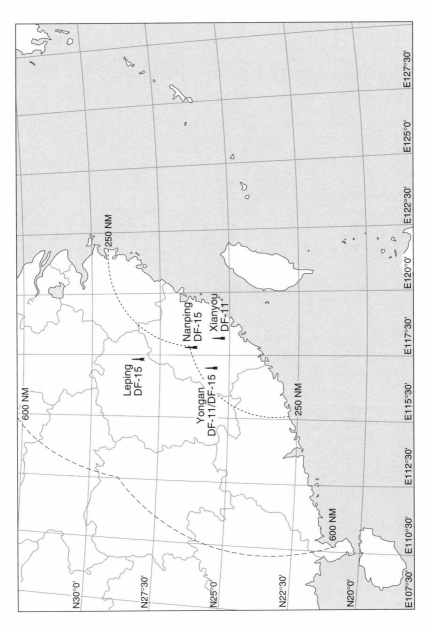

Map 5.   PLA Second Artillery SRBM deployments in the Taiwan theater. Adapted from Defense Mission of the Taipei Economic and Cultural Representative Office in the United States data.

250,000 troops, deployed in three group armies—with 70,000 deployed directly across the Strait in Fujian.[95] But the nearby Jinan and Guangzhou MRs could easily redeploy at least as many combat troops in a short period.[96] Although ground force deployments in the Nanjing MR have held steady for fifteen years (since the normalization of Sino-American relations), there are signs of moderate increases in troop strength since 1995. Approximately 1,000 planes of various types and an estimated 250 combat aircraft are deployed within 600 nautical miles of Taiwan.[97] An additional 1,500 fighters (including the Su-27s) are based within 500 nautical miles of the Taiwan Strait. The Su-27s based both at Wuhu in Anhui and at Suixi in Guangdong are well within range of Taiwan (810 nautical miles). Also, the North, East, and South China Sea fleets are all within easy range (although the PLAN's amphibious lift capability is extremely limited). Finally, the PLA can easily bring short-range ballistic missiles to bear on the Taiwan theater. Since 1998, the PLA's Second Artillery has been building up its deployment of M-9 and M-11 SRBMs opposite Taiwan. At the current pace of deployment of fifty per year, it is reasonable to estimate that there will be six hundred SRBMs deployed in bases in Jiangxi, Fujian, and Zhejiang by 2005.

These numerical advantages must not be ignored under conditions of total war, but this seems unrealistic for at least five reasons. First, the PRC would suffer inestimable political fallout and isolation in the world as a consequence of an all-out attack on Taiwan. Second, the PRC would likely incur substantial loss of life and physical destruction in Taiwan's retaliation. Third, the PRC could probably not succeed in a total attack on, and occupation of, the island unless the conflict was protracted *and* the United States and other nations stayed out of it (neither resupplying Taiwanese forces nor deploying their own). The Taiwan Strait and Taiwan itself present formidable geographic obstacles. Fourth, total annihilation is not a feature of either traditional or contemporary Chinese military doctrine, which emphasizes subduing and humiliating an enemy with minimal use of force. Fifth, and most important, Beijing's overwhelming objective is to deter Taiwanese independence and facilitate political reunification with the mainland. Full-scale conflict facilitates neither goal. Rather, the use of carefully applied limited

---

95. ROC Ministry of National Defense, *2000 National Defense Report,* Internet version, August 2000, p. 13.

96. During the severe flooding of 1998, 110,000 PLA troops were redeployed by rail and air. Interview, December 8, 1998.

97. ROC Ministry of Defense, *2000 National Defense Report,* p. 14.

force and coercive diplomacy is a far more efficacious strategy for the PRC to pursue.

Conversely, Taiwan's defense doctrine is aimed neither at retaking the mainland *(guangfu dalu)* by force nor annihilating PRC forces. Rather, it is oriented solely toward defending the main island, offshore islands, airspace, and surrounding seas. "We do not want war but are prepared to prevent an invasion," Commandant Xu Bosheng of Taiwan's Joint Forces War College says. "We are prepared for a wide spectrum of conflict—including high-, medium-, and low-intensity conflict. Our deterrent is based not only on fighting as best possible to protect the country, but also in making the PRC pay too high a price."[98]

For these reasons, it is more useful to consider a variety of conflict contingencies and to assess how Taiwan's military might cope with each.[99] Five scenarios are plausible: (1) provocative interdiction; (2) blockades; (3) air and sea battle; (4) strategic strikes; and (5) amphibious assault.

Provocative Interdiction

The first scenario envisions PRC fighter aircraft violating the "rules of operation" over the Taiwan Strait or elsewhere in Taiwan airspace, thus provoking the Taiwan Air Force to respond, and thereby providing the context or excuse for "a defensive counterattack" by PRC forces (as happened in the wars with Vietnam in 1979 and India in 1962). Violations of the naval rules of operation are equally possible. For many years the PLA Air Force and the Taiwan Air Force have observed the "Strait Central Line" *(haixia zhongxian)*, the unwritten rules being that PLAAF planes remain west of this line, while Taiwan aircraft have the right to resupply Jinmen and Matzu. The Central Line is sixty nautical miles from the west coast of Taiwan and just east of the offshore islands. It is thus not actually the midpoint in the Strait, but has served as the operative defense perimeter for Taiwan. Until recent years, when Taipei acquired E-2T airborne warning aircraft from the United States, this line represented the limit of Taiwan's radar capabilities, as well

98. Interview, Joint Forces War College, Taipei, July 10, 1995.
99. There is no shortage of analyses of potential conflict scenarios involving Taiwan, China, and the United States. See, in particular, Harlan Jencks, "Wild Speculations on the Military Balance in the Taiwan Strait," in James Lilley and Chuck Downs, eds., *Crisis in the Taiwan Strait* (Washington, D.C.: National Defense University Press and AEI Press, 1997), pp. 131–65; and Paul H. B. Godwin, "China's Defense Modernization: Aspirations and Capabilities," *Washington Journal of Modern China* 6, no. 1 (2001): 13–37.

as its anti-air and antiship missile range.[100] On the naval side, Taiwan maintains an exclusion zone of twelve nautical miles for PRC submarines or surface combatants.[101]

The first scenario thus envisions gross, repeated, and provocative PRC violations of these zones, which would precipitate an air and/or naval response from Taiwan forces, with unpredictable consequences. Over the years, the PLAAF has fairly strictly observed the Strait Central Line, but tensions rose in July and August 1999, following Lee Teng-hui's provocative proclamation of the "two states theory" *(liang guo lun),* and Chinese fighters were increasingly brazen in their violation of the Strait Central Line and Taiwan airspace. If a conflict erupted in this way, the Chinese aim would likely be to "punish" Taiwan rather than to trigger a wider conflict. That is, the campaign would likely be limited dogfights over the Strait, combined with some air and/or missile strikes.

Blockades

There are three principal types of blockade scenarios: low, medium, and high. In the first instance, the PRC would simply announce a blockade of Taiwan, the offshore islands, and possibly Taiping Island in the South China Sea (controlled by Taiwan). In this scenario, the PRC would board and turn back any ships seeking to breach the blockade zone. Certain categories of shipping might be exempted from the blockade (as was the case during the Cuban Missile Crisis quarantine). The second type would involve the same proclamation of an exclusion zone, possibly also with some exemptions, but with the additional deterrent that any ships seeking to break the blockade would be fired upon. A high-intensity blockade would involve a total quarantine with the threat to fire on and sink any transgressors. All three naval blockades could be coupled with limited to full air quarantine.

Any of these scenarios would wreak havoc on the Taiwan economy, given its dependence on shipping. It could throw the Taipei stock market and business confidence into free fall and raise insurance rates for freight to unacceptably high levels. During the 1996 crisis, the stock market plummeted 1,000 points (21 percent) and U.S.$15 billion in investment fled the island.[102] The effect on Taiwan's energy needs would be equally devastating, insofar as it is completely dependent on crude oil imports. Taiwan consumes 250,000

100. Interview with Taiwan military expert, Taipei, July 9, 1995.
101. Ibid.
102. John Pomfret, "Taiwan's War Readiness and Military in Doubt," *International Herald Tribune,* July 28, 1999.

barrels of crude every day, and a supertanker docks in Kaohsiung harbor every third day. Moreover, Taiwan is very short on oil: the 120-day strategic reserve built up after the 1995–96 crises had shrunk to a mere 18-day reserve by 1999.[103] The port of Kaohsiung, through which the majority of trade and energy imports pass, is extremely vulnerable. Blockading or mining the maritime approaches to the harbor could close down the port altogether (particularly if the PLA sank ships at the mouth of the harbor or hit the large oil storage tanks and refineries nearby). It was no accident that the missiles fired by the PLA in 1996 landed in the approaches to the harbors of Kaohsiung and Jeelung.

Submarines also present a real threat to Taiwan. Some experts argue that the Taiwan Strait is conducive to anti-submarine warfare, because it is relatively shallow and submarines cannot hide easily (American submarines scored several key victories against Japan in the Strait during World War II). But Taiwan's Navy has limited ASW capability and only two antiquated World War II–vintage (Guppy-class) and two Dutch-built Zvaardvis diesel submarines of its own. The offer by the Bush administration in 2001 to sell or manufacture eight diesel submarines has not come to fruition. Taiwan's airborne ASW capability is presently poor, but surface capabilities have improved with receipt of Perry-, Knox-, and Lafayette-class frigates (indeed, the Knox-class frigate is primarily an ASW vessel). More Hughes and Sikorsky ASW helicopters are also in the pipeline. It was the Hughes MD-500 that apparently successfully detected and tracked a PLAN submarine during the Hankuang No. 10 exercises near the Penghu Islands in May 1994.

Many experts (including some in the Taiwan military) believe that a blockade is the PRC's best and most likely option to exert military pressure on Taiwan. It is argued that the PRC could rather easily accomplish its political purposes without significant military engagement. However, the blockade scenarios presume the PLA Navy's capability to enforce one. At present, judging from the PLAN's inventory, a blockade of the entire island would be infeasible, but a naval blockade of Jeelung and Kaohsiung harbors is probably within its capacity. But a blockade would undoubtedly be resisted. Blockades can be alleviated by airlifts or broken by concerted naval effort. Despite the overall numerical advantages the PLAN enjoys in destroyers, guided missile frigates, and submarines, in qualitative terms, the surface combatants are still inferior to Taiwan's naval forces, and Taiwan has placed the highest priority on improving its ASW capability. Only the PLAN's two Luhai- and Luhu-class destroyers are a match for Taiwan's Knox- or

103. Ibid.

Gearing-class surface combatants, while at present the PLAN's only match for the stealthy Lafayette or new Perry frigates is the Sovremenny. The PLAN's refitted Luda-class destroyers or Jianghu and Jiangwei frigates are also inferior in speed and onboard armaments to Taiwan's fleet.

Any attempt by Taiwan to break a PLAN blockade by force would risk a rapid escalation in conflict that would no doubt quickly go beyond the naval theater. Taiwan's attempts to break blockades would undoubtedly require the mobilization of air assets, which could quickly escalate to a fuller conflict. Just as in the Cuban Missile Crisis, one never knows the outcome of naval blockades. They are considered an act of war under international law. They are *not* a low-level deterrent, and they can rapidly escalate into full-scale combat.

Air and Sea Battle

The third principal scenario envisions full-scale combat at sea and in the air in the Taiwan Strait theater, but not a land invasion of Taiwan. Such a scenario, which is quite straightforward, would involve a full range (but not full force) of the air and naval forces outlined in table 16. Taiwan's Air Force would likely fare well in aerial combat over the Strait, given its more modern fighters and better-trained pilots. In a protracted air war, however, attrition might become a problem. Taiwan's navy would presumably also cope well in sea battles not far from Taiwan. As with air battle, the limited sea area of the Taiwan Strait theater is an asset to Taiwan's naval forces because it neutralizes the PLAN's numerical advantages. Taiwan defense planners calculate that thirty-six sufficiently armed surface combatants would be adequate to dominate the Strait.[104] Should battles extend to the East and South China Sea or the Pacific, Taiwan's destroyers and frigates are truly blue-water capable; the same cannot be said of the PLAN, which remains principally a coastal fleet. Taiwan's surface combatants are well equipped, but they would be vulnerable to the PLAN's much improved arsenal of ship-to-ship missiles, especially the Sunburns on the Sovremenny-class destroyers. Most of Taiwan's destroyers and frigates have modern integrated weapons control suites, fire-control systems, radars and sonars, optical tracking systems, and electronic countermeasures—all principally of U.S. origin. Most are outfitted with the Xiong Feng I and II, as well as Sea Chaparral and General Dynamics SM1-MR surface-to-surface antiship missiles.[105] In general,

---

104. Interview with Taiwan military expert, Taipei, July 9, 1995.
105. See Joris Janssen Lok, "Taiwan's Force Updates Revealed," *Jane's Defense Weekly*, January 16, 1993, p. 24; *Jane's Fighting Ships, 1995–96* (London: Jane's Information Group, 1995), pp. 690–700.

the entire fleet has either been upgraded or is newly built. The Perry and Kidd destroyers and Knox and Lafayette frigates are all fairly modern. Thus, one must assume that in any major naval engagement with the PLAN, Taiwan's oceangoing fleet would fare well.

Strategic Strikes

The fourth contingency for which Taiwan must prepare is a surgical strike by short-range ballistic missiles, or possibly bombers with air-launched cruise missiles, combined with debilitating electronic and information warfare. Such attacks could either come as a first wave of attack preceding a broader assault on the island, intended to suppress key command and infrastructure targets, or could be used alone as a punitive measure. Actually, strategic strikes by bombers are improbable, because the PLAAF's ancient fleet of H-5 and H-6 bombers is unlikely to be able to penetrate Taiwan's air defenses. Missiles are another story. As the "Taiwan crises" of 1995–96 proved, the PLA is prepared to use such weapons—one of the few comparative advantages it has. While the PLA has yet to develop and deploy ground-launched land attack cruise missiles, it does possess a large (and growing) stock of short-range ballistic missiles deployed against Taiwan (approximately 350 in 2002 and increasing by 50 a year). The M-9s are not very accurate at present (with a CEP of 300 meters) and hence are better suited to terrorize the local population than to take out specific targets (especially if those targets are hardened).

To counter this threat, Taiwan has taken delivery of at least four batteries of a modified version of the Patriot air defense (SAM) system built by the Raytheon Corporation (the so-called PAC-2 PLUS), although it does not yet possess the SAMs. Procurement of U.S. Aegis naval systems is also a high priority for Taipei, although Washington has deferred the sale. No doubt, all of these systems, if delivered and made operational, would have some effectiveness against incoming SRBMs, but significant "leakage" would overwhelm Taiwan's anti-missile defenses. Unless the United States were willing to share launch intelligence instantaneously with Taiwan, strategic targets on the island (particularly air bases) would remain completely vulnerable. The same applies to the use of Theater Missile Defense. Taiwan is interested in acquiring TMD, but Beijing has thrown down the gauntlet against its transfer, threatening a rupture in Sino-American relations. Taiwan's E-2T AWACs and the Changbai phased-array radar system would be of little use in detecting and targeting a ballistic missile attack. Taiwan does have an extensive series of SAM systems, but they are more effective against airplanes than missiles. Furthermore, Taiwan's air defenses are deployed to protect population centers rather than key military installations (the airbases at Hualian and Jiayi are particularly vulnerable). Even if Taiwan's air force fighters are protected in hardened bunkers at these bases, their runways are vulnerable to missile attacks.

Taiwan does have plans to develop its own medium-range surface-to-surface missiles. Thus far, the Xiongfeng II, which has a range of 170 kilometers, has reportedly been deployed on the offshore island of Tong Yin,[106] while the Jiandong II is deployed on Matzu.[107] However, some of its onboard naval surface-to-surface missiles (particularly the Harpoon) can reach targets in Fujian and Zhejiang provinces on the mainland. The air base at Wuhu, where the first squadron of Su-27s is deployed, is 300 nautical miles inland and thus out of range of Taiwan's naval missiles.

Any strategic strike by PLA missiles against Taiwan would no doubt be accompanied, or preceded, by a blitz of electronic warfare (EW) and computer network attacks. As discussed in chapter 6, development of EW and information warfare (IW) has been among the PLA's highest priorities— and it is highly likely that the PLA would undertake to blind Taiwan's missile and air defenses, intelligence, and command and control nodes in the earliest stages of a conflict. The intelligence and command facilities on Yangming Mountain north of Taipei and the underground base at Jiashan would likely be early priority targets. Others include Taiwan's Combat Air Command and Control Center in downtown Taipei (this center coordinates the island's multilayered air defenses), the Combined Operations Center at Yuanshan near Taipei, and the Communications Center at Longtan near Hsinchu.[108] With such critical sites neutralized or destroyed, Taiwan's retaliatory capabilities would be severely weakened, and the island would be open to air, naval, and amphibious assaults.

Amphibious Assault

Much of Taiwan's contingency planning is geared toward repelling an amphibious assault against the offshore islands (the first line of defense) and Taiwan proper. While some of the other, lower-intensity conflicts noted above are more likely possibilities than an all-out assault against Taiwan, it

---

106. Lu Chao-lung, "Missiles Secretly Deployed on Offshore Island," *Zhongguo shibao* (China Times), November 3, 1994, in FBIS–CHI, November 14,1994; "Hsiung Feng II Missile in Service," *Jane's Defense Weekly*, August 28, 1993, p. 7.

107. Interview with Taiwan military expert, July 9, 1995, Taipei.

108. See the discussion in John Zeng, "PLA Thinking about an Invasion of Taiwan in the Year 2000," in Peter Kien-hong Yu, ed., *The Chinese PLA's Perception of an Invasion of Taiwan* (New York: Contemporary U.S.-Asia Research Institute, 1996), pp. 145–47.

is a contingency that cannot be ruled out and one that Taiwan's forces have trained for.

It is also a contingency that PLA forces are increasingly training for. The PLA's annual Donghai (East Sea) exercises since 1994 have been joint air, naval, and ground force exercises, with amphibious maneuvers on the Dachen Islands off the coast of Zhejiang province. The 1996 exercises saw the deployment of a full complement of firepower, including Su-27s and new submarines and surface combatants. The Donghai No. 5 exercises during the summer of 1995 alerted Taiwan military intelligence to three new types of warfare *(denglu zhan)*: city warfare *(chengshi zhan)*, mountain warfare *(shandi zhan)*, and airdrop warfare *(kongtou zhan)*.[109] In each, Taiwan's military saw active exercises and contingency planning for an assault against, and attempted occupation of, the island. Taiwan is primarily mountainous (65 percent or 14,000 square miles), and hence not an easy target for parachuting.

At present, an amphibious landing and full invasion of Taiwan remain far beyond PLA sealift and airlift capabilities. The conventional wisdom is that, in such landings, a 5:1 numerical advantage is needed (irrespective of terrain): thus the PLA would have to land approximately 1.25 million troops on Taiwan within the first few days of the invasion. This is, of course, impossible. At present, it is believed that the PLAN only has the sealift capability to transport one or two divisions and about 300 tanks at a time, far short of the numbers necessary to establish a beachhead on the heavily fortified western approaches of the island.[110] It would take approximately 600 landing craft nearly two weeks to transport twenty infantry divisions to Taiwan.

Lack of landing craft is not the only reason that an amphibious assault against Taiwan would be extremely difficult for the PLA. There are also the critical factors of weather and geography. The 1996 "exercises" proved that the PLAAF and PLAN have a long way to go before they can operate in stormy conditions with limited visibility: once a modest typhoon developed, all aircraft were grounded, and ships returned to the mainland coast. Taiwan's best defenses may be its coastline, monsoons, tides, and mud. The western coastline of Taiwan consists of mud flats extending two to five miles out to sea, which present real problems for any landing force. The tides fluctuate considerably, but they average fifteen feet variance per day (leading to

---

109. Interviews with Taiwan defense and security officials, July 9–10, 1995.
110. Edward L. Dreyer and June T. Dreyer, "The Chinese People's Liberation Army's Perception of an Invasion of Taiwan," in Yu, ed., *Chinese PLA's Perception of an Invasion of Taiwan.*

a change of approximately one foot per hour). Low tide exposes miles of mud, an effective barrier to landing tanks and armored vehicles. Infantry crossing the mud on foot would likely become easy targets for Taiwan aerial bombardment and artillery emplacements ashore.

Even more daunting than tides and mud is the size of the Taiwan Strait and the effect of winds on the sea. At most points, the Strait is 90 to 100 miles wide, but the continental shelf makes the water relatively shallow, so that it is difficult for submarines to operate and hide. At the shortest distance, the Strait takes roughly ten hours to cross. More important, though, the seas are frequently very rough. Taiwan's two monsoon seasons (August–September and November–April) generate very high winds (often exceeding 45 knots), which cause twenty- to thirty-foot waves; even during calmer summer months six- to eight-foot swells are the average. The strong winds almost always blow from north to south, meaning that any landing craft attempting to traverse the Strait would be hit broadside (a "beam sea"). The "funnel effect" in the Strait also causes irregular and unpredictable currents near the coastline. Finally, during monsoon season, the rainfall in the area is torrential—260 inches annually in the north and 208 inches in the south (compared with Seattle's annual rainfall of 33 inches or the Amazon rain forest's 108 inches)—making visibility virtually nil. The wind and heavy rainfall would make a landing force's movement difficult on shore (presuming it got there), and approaching the mud flats and beach in an organized manner would be next to impossible. Any troops that made it ashore under such conditions would no doubt suffer from extreme seasickness and fatigue. Nor is the eastern shore of Taiwan open to amphibious invasion, given the transport distances involved and the fact that, in most areas, mountains abut the seacoast.

In brief, the lack of transport craft might be the least of the PLA's worries if it was ordered to invade Taiwan. Given that the population is concentrated in the central part of the island, PLA forces would probably be easily contained on the seaward side. Gaining the element of surprise would be almost impossible, because preparations for an amphibious assault would require large movements and massing of troops, easily detected by satellites. The Taiwan Strait is not the English Channel, and this would not be D-Day.

The Wild Card: U.S. Involvement

Of course, this and other scenarios are all subject to one significant intervening variable: the potential intervention of the United States on Taiwan's behalf. The dispatch of two aircraft carrier battle groups during the 1996 crisis signaled to Beijing, Taipei, and the world that U.S. involvement, under certain conditions, is a distinct possibility. The United States has made clear, and the Taiwan Relations Act (TRA) suggests, that an unprovoked attack or other coercive behavior toward the island (including blockades) would likely trigger an American military response, although the policy of "strategic ambiguity" has long dictated that exactly what kind of military response would depend on the circumstances. In an interview in April 2001, President George W. Bush went further by stating that the United States "would do whatever it takes to help Taiwan defend itself."

U.S. intervention would require substantial air and naval assets. U.S. Air Force AWACs would also need to coordinate an air interdiction campaign against the PLAAF or PLAN aircraft. It is doubtful that U.S. ground troops would be of much utility in such a conflict. Clearly, U.S. military involvement would primarily involve aircraft carrier battle groups (CVBGs). Consideration of such deployments and contingency planning remains, for good reason, hidden from public view. Suffice it to say, however, that CVBGs would encounter operating difficulties in the Taiwan theater that they have not experienced for many years. Chinese submarines pose a nascent but real threat. PLAN antiship missiles pose an even more serious threat, especially the SS-N-22 Sunburn fitted on the PLAN's new Sovremenny-class destroyers. These missiles may also pose some difficulties for U.S. Navy Aegis systems, which they were designed to counter. Chinese SLBMs, SRBMs, or MRBMs could also be fired against carriers (for which there is little precedent or suitable defense). Finally, rapidly improving PLA capabilities in electronic countermeasures and information warfare could seriously disrupt the CBVG's C^4I. In short, while PLA forces could not, at present, succeed in preventing U.S. naval and air forces from operating and carrying out their defensive missions ("area denial"), they could nonetheless make life complicated, difficult, and dangerous for U.S. commanders and forces.

8 Policy Implications
for the United States

How should the United States react to the range of reforms and progress in China's military modernization program outlined in this book? The United States should recognize that China has the legitimate right to modernize its military and protect its national security, if it does not threaten others. Generally speaking, the Clinton administration was less concerned about the pace or scope of PLA modernization than the current Bush administration. While there was concern over the PLA's buildup of short-, medium-, and intercontinental-range ballistic missiles and possible acquisition of cruise missiles, the prevailing view in the Defense Department during the tenures as secretary of defense of William Perry and William S. Cohen was that China's military remained at least twenty years out of date across the board. This view is shared by most independent analysts of the PLA.[1] Despite some important weapons acquisitions from Russia in recent years, and some new indigenous Chinese systems coming into the force structure, the Department of Defense during the Clinton administration believed that neither the United States nor its allies were threatened by the pace and scope of PLA modernization.[2] As is noted below, however, the Bush administration and DoD under Secretary of Defense Donald Rumsfeld take an entirely dif-

---

1. See James R. Lilley and David Shambaugh, eds., *China's Military Faces the Future* (Armonk, N.Y.: M. E. Sharpe; Washington, D.C.: AEI Press, 1999); David Shambaugh, ed., *China's Military in Transition* (Oxford: Clarendon Press, 1997); James Mulvenon and Richard H. Yang, eds., *The People's Liberation Army in the Information Age* (Washington, D.C.: RAND Corporation, 1999). See Zalmay M. Khalilzad et al., *The United States and a Rising China* (Santa Monica, Calif.: RAND Corporation, 1999).

2. See U.S. Secretary of Defense, *Select Military Capabilities of the People's Republic of China: Report to Congress Pursuant to Section 1305 of the FY97 National Defense Authorization Act.*

ferent view and are not so sanguine about the direction or strategic implications of PLA modernization.

To be sure, China's accelerated development and deployment of ballistic
missiles is a real source of concern. The PLA has embarked upon a comprehensive upgrading of its short-, medium- and intercontinental-range missiles. The entire force structure is moving from liquid to solid fuel and from
fixed to road-mobile launchers—which will improve their response time,
reliability, and survivability. It did not take the alarmist Cox Committee report of 1999 to convince skeptics that the PLA's Second Artillery was developing new generations of ballistic missiles with improved warheads,
deploying MIRVs, and developing cruise missile capabilities.[3] As described
in chapter 6, the PLA now has in service a full range of ballistic missile systems. The successful test of the DF-31 (8,000-kilometer range) in August
1999, and an assertive program to develop and deploy the JL-2 SLBM, all
are notable improvements for China's nuclear forces. The PLA is also hard
at work on developing land-attack cruise missiles.

As was described in chapter 3, great emphasis is also being placed on information warfare (IW) and other innovations associated with the revolution
in military affairs. China's ambitions in this arena, however, should not be
confused with capability. These are extremely complicated technologies to
master, test, produce, deploy, assimilate, and maintain. There exist numerous impediments—financial, human, technological—to China's ability to
build, deploy, and maintain such high-tech systems.

From the desire to develop sophisticated technologies and weapons systems, one might infer that China is preparing for asymmetrical military contingencies against opponents possessing state-of-the-art militaries (e.g.,
Japan or the United States), particularly in a potential conflict over Taiwan.
The purchase of aircraft, submarines, and destroyers from Russia all appear
to be contingency-driven. They seem to indicate preparations to present a
credible threat to Taiwan in the first decade of this century (probably
around 2005–7). Moreover, these purchases and the emphasis on improving electronic countermeasures and IW capabilities further suggest a readi-

---

3. See *Report of the Select Committee on U.S. National Security and Military/
Commercial Concerns with the People's Republic of China,* declassified version published by the U.S. Government Printing Office, May 25, 1999. For a thorough cri-
tique of the Cox Committee report, see M. M. May, ed., *The Cox Committee Report:
An Assessment* (Stanford, Calif.: Center for International Security and Cooperation,
1999). Also see Mark A. Stokes, *China's Strategic Modernization: Implications for
the United States* (Carlisle, Pa.: U.S. Army War College Strategic Studies Institute,
1999).

ness to engage and disrupt U.S. aircraft carriers and forces in a potential Taiwan conflict. The persistent attempts to acquire an airborne command and control capability and the development of fourth-generation fighters perhaps also indicate a desire to project air power into the South China Sea and beyond.

The conflicts in the former Yugoslavia (1999) and Afghanistan (2001–2) also added a greater sense of urgency to the PLA's modernization program. Lessons learned about U.S. strategy, tactics, and weapons are reshaping PLA allocative, doctrinal, and organizational priorities. While China cannot afford dramatically increased defense expenditure, and its access to Western defense technologies and weapons is severely limited, we may expect to see increased priority given to the PLA's ballistic missile and cruise missile programs, information and electronic warfare capabilities, C^{4}I networks, and anti-air defenses. These new priorities will supplement—but also will have to compete with—the existing emphasis on building up tactical air force, blue-water naval, and subsurface assets.

However, without access to equipment and technologies from the West, the PLA will have difficulties closing the conventional weaponry and defense technology gaps with Japan and the West. Indeed, these are steadily widening. Transfers from Russia are meeting certain "niche" needs of the PLA, but they are far from sufficient to provide the PLA with a power projection capability, much less the ability to carry out a successful attack against Taiwan. The PLA is also experiencing substantial difficulties integrating these new systems into its existing force structure.

THE EBB AND FLOW OF U.S.-CHINA MILITARY EXCHANGES

Exchanges between the U.S. and Chinese militaries take place in the context of the evolving strategic environment discussed above. Military ties are also conditioned by the overall state of the bilateral relationship. Historically, when the overall relationship is healthy, military exchanges have proceeded in a positive manner; conversely, when Sino-American relations sour, military exchanges always seem to be among the first casualties. Those who manage the relationship on the American side should keep in mind that military relations are only one component of the broader relationship and progress and regress in tandem with it. In other words, the Pentagon and Pacific Command should not run their own China policy.

Formal military exchanges between the United States and the PRC date from Secretary of Defense Harold Brown's visit to China in 1980, which initiated a series of exchanges between the services and academies of the two militaries (including defense intelligence exchanges), as well as the sale of nonlethal equipment and a loosening of export controls for dual-purpose technologies. With the visit of Secretary of Defense Caspar Weinberger to China in 1983, the United States agreed for the first time to sell military equipment and (defensive) weapons and technologies to China. The People's Republic became eligible for Foreign Military Sales (FMS) status in 1984, but the Reagan administration limited the weapons systems it made available to the PLA to four categories that were considered to meet the "defensive" criterion: artillery and ammunition; antitank missiles; air defense; and antisubmarine warfare. These criteria were soon expanded, because the PLA sought a wider range of equipment and technology, and the large American defense contractors began aggressively to lobby the White House and Pentagon for a piece of the China arms market. Among the projects approved during the second half of the 1980s were the $505 million "Peace Pearl" project, undertaken by the Grumman Corporation to upgrade the avionics in the PLAAF J-8 fighter, a $22 million program undertaken by Hamilton/ Bulova to upgrade the PLA's artillery shells and large-caliber ammunition, a $62 million project undertaken by the Hughes Corporation to build four counter-battery radars and train PLA personnel to use them, an $8 million sale of Honeywell antisubmarine torpedoes, and a $140 million agreement for Sikorsky Corporation (United Technologies) to sell China twenty-four UH-60A Blackhawk helicopters.[4]

After developing rapidly and extensively during the 1980s, Sino-American military relations had their ups and downs during the 1990s.[5] The decade began with their complete suspension following the People's Liberation Army's actions on June 4, 1989.[6] The United States and the European Union likewise embargoed the transfer of military equipment and technologies to China (embargoes that remain in effect to this day), aborting most of the projects noted above. The Sikorsky helicopters had been delivered and the ammunition project was close to completion, but only two of the four

4. For a discussion of these and other military exchange activities, see Thomas L. Wilborn, *Security Cooperation with China* (Carlisle Barracks, Pa.: U.S. Army War College Strategic Studies Institute, 1994).

5. See Jing-dong Yuan, "Sino-U.S. Military Relations, 1993–2001: Restoration, Achievements, and Pitfalls" (paper presented at the International Studies Association Convention, Hong Kong, July 2001).

6. Capstone delegations from the U.S. National Defense University, which were never formally suspended, resumed quarterly visits in 1991.

Hughes radars and none of the Honeywell torpedoes had been delivered. Production had not begun on the Peace Pearl program, and the cost over-runs had soured relations with the Grumman Corporation in any case, leading the PRC to terminate the project in 1990—even though two of its J-8 aircraft had already been delivered.[7]

As the freeze in bilateral relations began to thaw slightly in 1993, Assistant Secretary of Defense for International Security Affairs Chas W. Freeman Jr. was dispatched to Beijing in November to jump-start military exchanges. Freeman's initiative was successful and immediately bore fruit. It set in motion a series of exchanges during Secretary of Defense William Perry's tenure. While in office and subsequently, Perry himself displayed unusual commitment to the U.S.-China military relationship—although Perry's friendliness toward the PLA drew the attention of conservative critics in the United States.[8] Both sides wished to rebuild the defense relationship gradually, but it quickly (and quietly) picked up momentum. Initiatives to trace U.S. servicemen missing in action (MIAs) during World War II and a Joint Commission on Defense Conversion (a pet project of Perry's) were begun. Exchanges between the two National Defense Universities and some service staff colleges were resumed, and a series of high-level and service exchanges took place. Secretary Perry; Frank Wisner, undersecretary of defense for policy; Lieutenant General James Clapper, director of the Defense Intelligence Agency; Admiral Charles Larson and Admiral Richard Macke, commanders in chief of the Pacific Command; and General Merrill McPeak, chief of staff of the U.S. Air Force, all led delegations to China, and a port call was made by the USS *Bunker Hill*. General Xu Huizi and Xiong Guangkai, respectively deputy chief and assistant chief of the PLA's General Staff, and Lieutenant General Huai Guomo, vice-chairman of the Commission on Science, Technology, and Industry for National Defense (COSTIND), visited the United States.

Just as bilateral military exchanges were gaining momentum and some degree of mutual trust and confidence was being restored, the rapprochement was derailed by renewed tensions over Taiwan. In May 1995, the PLA aborted a visit by Air Force Commander General Yu Zhenwu and suspended other exchanges in response to the controversial visit to the United States of Taiwan's President Lee Teng-hui. Although the Chinese received the U.S. National Defense University Capstone delegation as planned in late May,

7. See Wilborn, *Security Cooperation with China.*
8. See Kenneth R. Timmerman, "The Peking Pentagon: China's Military Loves Bill Perry," *American Spectator,* April 1996, pp. 24–31.

no exchanges took place until July, when a U.S. Army Corps of Engineers delegation went to China. The tensions in the relationship during this period were palpable.

During the autumn and winter of 1995–96, tempers cooled, and it looked as though exchanges were back on track—including visits to China by the undersecretary of defense, two assistant secretaries, the chief of naval operations, and a series of NDU delegations, as well as a port call by the USS *Fort McHenry*. The PLA sent the Guangzhou military region commander to Hawaii for the fiftieth anniversary of the Japanese surrender and end of World War II in the Pacific, and a General Logistics Department delegation toured the United States. But then the PLA undertook its second round of provocative missile "tests" and live-fire exercises near Taiwan in March 1996 (the first round took place in July 1995). This round was meant to intimidate Taiwan citizens as they went to the polls for their first-ever direct presidential election. This time the United States reacted by curtailing defense exchanges. Secretary William Perry was incensed enough with the provocative Chinese behavior that, on instructions from the president, he ordered two aircraft carrier battle groups into the waters off Taiwan as a demonstration of U.S. resolve. For the United States, China's promise to "peacefully resolve" the Taiwan issue has always been a core condition for the joint management of the Taiwan question; the missile firings within thirty miles of Taiwan's two principal ports and large-scale air, naval, and amphibious exercises in the strait mandated a firm American response. Although there was no real threat of Chinese military action against the island, and the USS *Nimitz* and *Independence* operated well away from the Taiwan Strait, this crisis brought tensions to their highest level since the late 1950s.

Neither side wished to completely cease or suspend exchanges, but both decided to reduce their number and importance. Visits by defense educational delegations continued, but high-level exchanges were limited to DoD Undersecretary Walter Slocombe's visit in June 1996. Beginning in the fall of 1996, though, exchanges picked up again. The new CINCPAC, Admiral Joseph Prueher, paid an important visit to China in September, followed by the director of the Defense Intelligence Agency and other DoD officials.

New momentum was added in December 1996 with the long-postponed visit to the United States by Chinese Defense Minister Chi Haotian. General Chi and outgoing Secretary Perry held extensive talks, while counterpart talks were held with other members of Chi's delegation. Chi was given red-carpet treatment in Washington (including a meeting with the president) and a top-flight itinerary of military installations across the country, designed to impress him simultaneously with American strength and transparency.

Sino-American military exchanges expanded rapidly after General Chi's visit—until the mistaken bombing of the Chinese embassy in Belgrade in 1999, after which they were suspended again (by the Chinese side) for nearly a year. During the fourteen months from General Chi's visit to the suspension of exchanges in May 1999, a plethora of exchanges occurred. These tended to fall into four broad categories: high-level visits; functional exchanges; military educational exchanges; and confidence-building measures. A variety of important visits took place in each category, including visits to Beijing by Secretary of Defense William Cohen, Undersecretary of Defense for Policy Walter Slocombe, Assistant Secretary Franklin Kramer, and Deputy Assistant Secretary Kurt Campbell; visits by the CINCPAC and army and air force chiefs of staff; visits to the United States by PLA Chief of Staff Fu Quanyou and Logistics Chief Wang Ke; the inauguration of annual Defense Consultation Talks at the level of undersecretary and deputy chief of staff; observation by the PLA of the RIMPAC and Cope Thunder multinational exercises; the signing of a Maritime Military Consultative Agreement (MMCA) to avoid "incidents at sea"; a nuclear weapons nontargeting agreement; consultations on humanitarian relief; and the first-ever visit by PLA naval vessels to the continental United States.

The bombing of the Chinese embassy in Belgrade ruptured military exchanges for the fourth time in a decade. Following the resumption of military ties in February 2000 at the third round of the Defense Consultation Talks, a series of new exchange initiatives were advanced.[9] These included exchanges in five areas: defense policy; high-level strategic dialogue; functional visits; confidence-building measures; and meetings in multinational security forums.[10]

During the summer of 2000, Secretary Cohen visited Beijing for two days of talks. He signed a military environmental accord and secured a commitment to send PLA officers to the Asia-Pacific Center for Security Studies in Honolulu. He also invited China's minister of defense, General Chi Haotian, and the director of the General Political Department, General Yu Yongbo, to visit the United States. Cohen's trip was the highest-level and most important bilateral military interaction in several years. During his visit the secretary seemed to go out of his way to assure his PLA counterparts and the Western media that bilateral military exchanges would continue to grow and were an important component of Sino-U.S. relations. In a speech to the

9. See "DoD News Briefing: Mr. Walter Slocombe, Under Secretary for Defense for Policy," January 27, 2000.

10. Interview with DoD personnel, February 2000.

National Defense University, he described military exchanges as a "deliberately paced and balanced program that builds confidence and understanding."[11] The year, and the Clinton administration, concluded with another round of Defense Consultation Talks (DCT) between Undersecretary Slocombe and General Xiong Guangkai of the PLA General Staff Department in November 2000.[12] These talks covered a variety of global and regional strategic issues, but also agreed on a tentative plan for bilateral military exchanges in 2001. While Republican Party skeptics accused Slocombe and the Clinton administration of trying to tie the hands of the incoming Bush administration by agreeing in advance to such a set of exchanges, this plan was not binding on the new U.S. administration (in any event, the new Bush administration scuttled the plan after entering office).

In addition to these official exchanges, a variety of "Track II" exchanges between officials in their private capacities and security specialists in the NGO community took place;[13] representatives of weapons development and defense research laboratories (e.g., Sandia and Lawrence Livermore on the American side) met with their counterparts;[14] and American and Chinese officers began to meet more regularly at multilateral settings in third countries.

Military-to-Military Ties under the Bush Administration

The Bush administration entered office much less convinced than its predecessor of the value of engaging China. Leading members of the new administration's foreign policy and defense policy team were openly criti-

---

11. Address by Secretary of Defense William S. Cohen to the Chinese National Defense University, July 13, 2000.

12. See Slocombe's press briefing in Beijing on November 30, 2000.

13. Track II initiatives have included the Stanford-Harvard Preventive Defense Project; three delegations sponsored by the National Committee on U.S.-China Relations, each led by a former secretary of defense (Robert McNamara, James Schlesinger, and William Perry); the China Policy Program at George Washington University; the annual arms control dialogue sponsored by the Center for Nonproliferation Studies at the Monterey Institute of International Studies; and an officers' training program sponsored by the Kennedy School of Government at Harvard University. The Preventive Defense Project report is cited above, while the National Committee delegations have each published reports. See Robert S. McNamara et al., *Sino-American Military Relations: Mutual Responsibilities in the Post–Cold War Era* (1994); James Schlesinger et al., *Toward Strategic Understanding between America and China* (1996); and William J. Perry et al., *Security Studies Issues Delegation to the People's Republic of China, Hong Kong SAR, and Taiwan* (New York: National Committee on U.S.-China Relations, 1998).

14. For an excellent overview of these exchanges, see Nancy Prindle, "The U.S.-China Lab-to-Lab Technical Exchange Program," *Nonproliferation Review*, Spring–Summer 1998, pp. 111–18.

cal, and sometimes dismissive, of China and its strategic position in world affairs. During the election campaign, the president-elect often referred to China as a "strategic competitor," a phrase repeated by Secretary of State Colin Powell and other leading officials after entering office. The overall disposition of the new national security team toward Beijing was definitely more cautious and skeptical.

However, before the new Bush administration could review—much less put in place—their China strategy, the relationship was rocked by the EP-3 surveillance plane incident in April 2001, when the U.S. aircraft collided with a PLANAF J-8II fighter over the South China Sea and was forced to make an emergency landing at a PLA airbase on Hainan Island.[15] The Chinese detention of the American crew for eleven days and the escalating demands and counterdemands between the two governments cast a heavy pall over the relationship. The hardliners in the Bush administration believed that their critical views of Beijing were validated.

Even before the EP-3 incident, Donald Rumsfeld, the new secretary of defense, had suspended the schedule of planned military exchanges negotiated by the outgoing Clinton administration, pending a full review of the goals and purposes of such exchanges, as well as a careful review of the accomplishments of past exchanges. While this review was going on, proposed exchanges would take place on a case-by-case basis, and were to be personally approved by Secretary Rumsfeld.[16] Although he was clearly less enamored of U.S.-China military exchanges than his predecessors had been, when asked about the value of such exchanges with the PLA, Rumsfeld did not close the door to them, but rather cautioned that they needed to be more reciprocal in nature. "I don't think we ought to be so eager for military-to-military contact that we end up providing things to another country that they don't provide to us, or where the value is not roughly comparable," Rumsfeld said in a July 2001 interview.[17] The deputy secretary of defense, Paul Wolfowitz, went further than the reciprocity argument. In a letter to the chairman of the House Armed Services Committee, Wolfowitz stated: "The overriding objective in our military exchange program [with China]

---

15. For a firsthand account of the event, see Shane Osborn with Malcolm McConnell, *Born to Fly: The Untold Story of the Downed American Reconnaissance Plane* (New York: Broadway Books, 2001).

16. See Michael Gordon, "Rumsfeld Limiting Military Contact with the Chinese," *New York Times*, June 4, 2001.

17. Bill Gertz, "Rumsfeld Says U.S. Presence in Asia is Vital: Strength Key in China Strategy," *Washington Times*, July 25, 2001.

is to ensure that these exchanges benefit the United States. This is the principle by which future exchanges will be evaluated."[18]

The Pacific Command in Hawaii took a more positive view than the civilian officials during the early Bush administration. CINCPAC Admiral Dennis Blair went on public record several times endorsing military exchanges. Blair believes that direct military-to-military contact and communication are important elements in reducing misperception, enhancing security, and stabilizing relationships. He has personally pushed the idea of creating multinational "security communities" throughout the Asia-Pacific region, and he believes that the PLA must become an active member of such multinational dialogue and cooperation. In the wake of the EP-3 incident, Blair argued:

> Military-to-military relations with China are very important. It is important that we stay in communication with the PLA on a personal level, and it's more important that we try to involve them in multilateral activities where our interests run parallel. We stand toe-to-toe over Taiwan. That's no secret to anybody. I find that when I go to China that about 75 percent of the conversation is me giving lectures on Taiwan. But that's okay. You also don't want any misunderstandings on Taiwan. I tell them pretty clearly what our policy is and what would happen if it came to any military crisis. There are other things that we and the Chinese could and should cooperate on. Most of the things I am talking about are new missions, such as peacekeeping and non-combat evacuation of civilians from crisis areas.[19]

On another occasion, Admiral Blair observed:

> I think that our military to military relations with China need both objectives and criteria. The objectives are the elimination of misunderstandings. Military understandings are dangerous, I believe, when the fundamental military situation is as I've just described it to you and I think it's important for the Chinese armed forces, Chinese military officers to understand that personally, and for American military officers to understand that personally. I think a way to do that is to visit and talk. I've deepened my understanding of China by going there to visit and talk to them and I know that the Chinese officers who have visited us have also come away realizing what the United States can do. And they also come away realizing that not every military officer in the

18. Letter to Congressman Bob Stump (R.-Ariz.), June 8, 2001.

19. Gregory Beals, "Toe-to-Toe over Taiwan," *Newsweek*, June 18, 2001 (Internet edition).

United States is spending every waking minute trying to figure out how to thwart China. That's not what we do 90 percent of the time. So I think that understanding part of it is important.

On the criteria side I believe there has to be a rough reciprocity in these exchanges and it's no good if it's not.

A third area that I think is important is that although this Taiwan issue sits dead center in the middle of the U.S.-China military relationship, there are other areas in which the armed forces of the United States and the People's Liberation Army can and should be working together. We should be working together against terrorism. We should be working together against drugs. We should be working on international peacekeeping operations which are in both our interests. We should be working as I mentioned in response to an earlier question on this common problem of North Korea, whose missiles range China as well as they range U.S. forces in Korea. And we should be working on piracy and the free flow of oil out of the Persian Gulf to both China and to the United States and its allies.

So I think there are a number of areas in which the United States and China should actually be cooperating militarily, not just visiting and talking.[20]

Former Chairman of the Joint Chiefs of Staff Henry Shelton was also a proponent of Sino-American military exchanges. Shelton paid an official visit to China in November 2000, during which he argued, "The relationship between the U.S. and Chinese armies is an important component in [our] bilateral relations; and the development of friendship and cooperative relations between the two armies will promote mutual trust and understanding."[21]

It remains to be seen how the military exchange relationship between the United States and China will evolve during the course of the Bush administration. How it proceeds, if it proceeds, will depend on much more than the proclivities of officials in the Bush government. The conclusions drawn by the Pentagon from the review of past exchanges, as well as the redefinition of U.S. goals in the exchange program, will certainly have an impact. So too will the Congress, the media, and the public. Considerable skepticism exists in these quarters. To be sure, the Chinese government and the PLA also have their own reservations, as well as incentives, to pursue exchanges.

20. Admiral Dennis C. Blair, media briefing at the Council on Foreign Relations (New York), March 21, 2002, available at http://www.pacom.mil/speeches/sst2002/020321cfr.htm.

21. Li Shijia, "Zhang Wannian, Shelton Discuss Sino-U.S. Military Relations, Taiwan Issue," Xinhua Domestic Service, November 3, 2000, in FBIS–CHI, November 3, 2000.

OBJECTIVES OF SINO-AMERICAN MILITARY EXCHANGES

The U.S. and Chinese military establishments share a desire to enhance ties and to exploit complementary interests. But it is also evident that the two approach the military relationship with differing priorities and considerable baggage from the past, which impede the development of closer ties.

In recent years, the initiative to develop and expand military-to-military relations has largely come from Washington. For the most part, the PLA has been a passive and often reluctant partner in the exchanges. As former Deputy Assistant Secretary of Defense Kurt Campbell candidly stated, "The PLA wants 'shallow engagement' not 'deep engagement.' They are very ambivalent about moving too quickly with the U.S."[22] Chinese reluctance derives from a variety of factors:

· Continuing ill-will from the suspension of exchanges after 1989

· Continuing U.S. sanctions prohibiting weapons sales, defense and dual-use technology transfers, and spare parts for previously sold systems

· Concerns that the United States would not be a reliable supplier of military technology and would interrupt essential deliveries and support—as it did after June 1989

· Latent suspicions of an American "containment" policy that defines China as a strategic adversary

· Anger and frustration over escalating U.S. arms sales to Taiwan

· Opposition to U.S. alliances and forward-based forces in the Asia-Pacific region

· The redefinition of the U.S.-Japan Mutual Security Treaty and Defense Guidelines, and its potential application to Taiwan

· Inexperience in broad-gauged bilateral and multilateral defense relationships

· The insular and sometimes xenophobic "institutional culture" of the Chinese military establishment

In each of these categories, the PLA has substantial concerns and fears (which is not to say that they are justified). In particular, the PLA believes it has been unfairly singled out for punitive sanctions, while other sectors of Chinese government and society enjoy relatively unfettered access to Ameri-

22. Dr. Kurt Campbell, lecture at Center for Naval Analyses, October 23, 1998.

can trade, technology, and exchanges. PLA leaders are still angered over the termination of military assistance programs (notably the "Peace Pearl" program) and sanctions implemented after 1989. As one of the few published Chinese studies of Sino-U.S. military relations noted, "If sanctions do not end, the Sino-American relationship—and bilateral military relations in particular—can only be abnormal."[23] This and a study by former PLA Colonel Xia Liping both cite the "Taiwan issue" as the principal impediment to developing bilateral military relations.[24] Others in the PLA argue that these terminated programs and the refusal of the United States to relax sanctions (in particular to release spare parts for the Sikorsky Blackhawk helicopters and General Electric LM-2500 gas turbine engines) is proof positive of American attempts to "contain" China and impede its military modernization. Said one PLA senior colonel: "Your government says that you want China to be 'strong, secure, and prosperous'; but your policies suggest the opposite."[25] As an inducement to remove sanctions and develop military ties, some PLA interlocutors intimate that the PLA would be interested in buying helicopters, aircraft and ship engines, transport aircraft, AWAC aircraft, radars, avionics, and surface-to-air missiles.[26] Furthermore, the PLA bluntly warns that continued American sales of weaponry to Taiwan will inhibit the development of bilateral military ties.

The PLA's exchanges with the United States must also be seen as part of its overall "military diplomacy." As Ken Allen and Eric McVadon argue in their landmark study of this subject, China views its military exchanges with other nations as a component of broader diplomatic foreign policy, to advance China's national security interests, and not as a "stand alone" compo-

23. Shen Dingli, "Zhong-Mei Liang Jun Guanxi de Fazhan ji Lianguo Guanxi de Benzhi" (The Development of Sino-American Military Relations and the Essence of Bilateral Relations), in Xie Xide and Ni Shixiong, eds., *From Normalization to Renormalization: Twenty Years of Sino-U.S. Relations* (Shanghai: Fudan University Press, 1998), p. 55.

24. Xia Liping, "Zhong-Mei Anquan Hezuo yu Junshi Jiaoliu" (China-U.S. Security Cooperation and Military Exchanges), *Guoji Wenti Luntan*, no. 3 (1998): 54. Xia became a research fellow at the Shanghai Institute of International Studies after retiring from the PLA and Strategic Studies Institute at the National Defense University.

25. Interview with PLA personnel, May 12, 1998, Beijing. Since the Carter administration, the U.S. government had used the terms "strong" and "secure" either together or separately, in conjunction with other adjectives, when referring to the kind of China the United States desires, i.e., "An open, prosperous, stable, strong, and secure China." These terms have been quietly dropped from official U.S. lexicon in recent years.

26. Interviews with PLA personnel, May 12–15, 1998, Beijing.

nent of exchanges between military establishments.[27] As Allen and Mc-Vadon document, the quantity of the PLA's exchanges with foreign militaries has expanded greatly in recent years. The PLA has received between fifty and seventy-five high-level military visitors from abroad annually in recent years, and the PLA's most senior officers average at least one trip abroad every year. The visits to China are fairly pro forma and usually involve discussions and perhaps a visit to one or more showcase infantry or armored units. Russian and American military visitors seem to gain broader access to PLA institutions, albeit still limited.

The PLA also approaches exchanges with the United States with a distinct set of expectations of what it gains and what can be achieved from military exchanges with the United States. Based on extensive interviews with PLA personnel and many years of personal experience in U.S.-China military exchanges, David Finkelstein of the Center for Naval Analyses has authored the most thorough unclassified assessment of the PLA's expectations and perspectives.[28] Finkelstein notes that the PLA is "highly suspicious of U.S. motives in the military relationship," which he identifies as deterrence, intelligence, and influence. That is, the United States seeks to deter Chinese aggression against the United States, its allies in Asia, or Taiwan by revealing to PLA visitors the awesome strength of U.S. military capabilities (transparency enhances deterrence); to collect intelligence through visits to Chinese military installations and interactions with PLA interlocutors; and to influence PLA officers' perceptions of the United States in a positive direction. He also notes that the PLA views the Pentagon as fundamentally hostile to Chinese strategic concerns, because it is the government agency primarily charged with selling arms to Taiwan and strengthening the alliance with Japan.

Finkelstein also points to a radical difference in ideas about how cooperation in the military sphere should be achieved. For the Chinese, cooperation on specific issues should be the outcome of "mutual trust and understanding," which is the result of strategic understanding reached through dialogue and actions deemed by China to be "friendly" and nonhostile. For Americans, Finkelstein argues, the process is the opposite: agreement to cooperate on specific issues builds trust and understanding, which, in turn,

27. Kenneth Allen and Eric McVadon, *China's Foreign Military Relations* (Washington, D.C.: Henry Stimson Center, 1999).

28. David Finkelstein and John Unangst, *Engaging DoD: Chinese Perspectives on Military Relations with the United States*, Report No. CRM 99–0046.90 (Alexandria, Va.: CNA Corporation, 1999).

leads over time to strategic agreement. These differences result in "diametrically opposed" approaches to the phasing and pacing of military relations. The U.S. side wishes to construct a web of exchanges as quickly and as thoroughly as possible, whereas China pursues exchanges slowly and methodically. For the United States, military exchanges are seen more as a "stand-alone" component of bilateral relations, whereas Beijing views them as the result of strategic understanding between the two governments.

The identification of cultural and perceptual differences as a key element in misunderstanding between the Chinese and American militaries is a variable noted by just about every U.S. military attaché who has served in China in recent years. As one recent attaché observed, "We tend to underestimate the cultural gaps in the relationship. Cultural differences loom large and exacerbate the differences in substance and policy."[29] The Chinese side also places more emphasis on the symbolism than on the substance of high-level meetings and strategic dialogue: "What matters most to PLA visitors is who they see, not necessarily what they see."[30] Many U.S. officers involved in exchanges with the PLA over the years further note the PLA officers' preoccupation with hotels, tourism, shopping, and the social aspects of visiting the United States—what they derisively dub the "fruit basket approach."

What does the United States want out of the relationship? Officially, in 1997, the Department of Defense lists six "broad objectives" that guide its contacts with the Chinese military:

1. To engage the PLA, a critical actor in the PRC's national security community, on a range of global and Asia-Pacific regional security issues.

2. To increase Chinese defense transparency.

3. To establish confidence-building measures designed to reduce the possibility of accidents or miscalculations between U.S. and Chinese operational forces.

4. To conduct professional exchanges that are of mutual benefit.

5. To encourage PLA participation in appropriate multinational military activities.

---

29. Former U.S. Military Attaché to China, "Managing Sino-U.S. Military Relations" (off-the-record lecture at Sigur Center for Asian Studies, George Washington University, January 15, 1998).
30. Finkelstein and Unangst, *Engaging DoD*, p. vi.

6. To support the U.S. government's overall policy of engagement with China through selected functional programs.[31]

These are worthy and appropriate policy objectives and goals, but progress to date has been uneven.

Of particular concern to the American side is the continuing lack of PLA transparency and reciprocity in access to military facilities. Positive steps taken by the PLA have included an exchange of "transparency briefings" between General Xiong Guangkai and his DoD counterparts in April 1995;[32] the publication of a White Paper on Arms Control in 1996 and the Defense White Papers of 1998 and 2000; and permitting visits by some high-ranking U.S. military personnel to previously unseen PLA installations. For example, CINCPAC Admiral Prueher visited the PLAN South Sea Fleet in Zhanjiang, the 47th Group Army near Xian, and the PLA Air Force's 28th Air Division in Hangzhou; Secretary of Defense Cohen and Assistant Secretary Kramer were shown the Beijing Air Defense Command Center; former JCS Chairman John Shalikashvili was given a demonstration by rapid reaction units *(kuaisu fanying budui)* of the 15th Airborne Division in Wuhan; and former Air Force Chief of Staff (Gen.) Michael E. Ryan was permitted to visit several air bases, shown the F-8 II fighter, and allowed to pilot a training fighter. These steps do represent some progress, and the PLA should be so credited, but it is minimal and marginal when compared either with the levels of transparency among other Asia-Pacific militaries (to say nothing of U.S. military transparency) or with what the United States has asked to see. American requests for visits to bases and installations continue to be routinely rebuffed by the Chinese side. Even visits touted as "breakthroughs" are often to installations of modest value, such as the Beijing air defense command center shown to Secretary Cohen.[33] Cohen had two other requests refused by his PLA hosts, including a proposed visit to the PLA underground command center. The U.S. side reasoned that this was a reasonable request, because Cohen's counterpart had been shown the "tank" in the Pentagon, but the PLA rebuffed it by denying that any such facility existed. (The U.S. side refrained from showing the PLA satellite photos of the location.) During his July 2000 visit, Cohen was not shown a sin-

31. Office of the Assistant Secretary of Defense, *Report to Congress on Department of Defense Activities with China* (H.R. 104–563), February 28, 1997.

32. General Xiong presented very superficial, boilerplate explanations of PLA expenditure and activities.

33. John Pomfret, "China Shows Cohen Big Military Secret: Air Defense Center Opened to Pentagon Visitors," *International Herald Tribune*, January 20, 1998.

gle military base or facility aside from the new Ministry of Defense (where he had his meetings) and National Defense University (where he gave a speech).

Although such goals are probably unrealistic, the United States should seek increased transparency in the following areas:

· Defense expenditure

· Defense doctrine and military planning

· Assessments of regional and global security issues

· Various scenarios involving North Korea

· PLA force restructuring and modernization

· Ground force, air force, naval, nuclear, and command deployments and installations across China

In seeking such transparency, the United States proceeds from a simple premise: openness breeds trust, while secretiveness breeds distrust. Certainly, all militaries must safeguard their national security secrets, but this can be done while at the same time reducing misperceptions and suspicions through adhering to international norms of transparency. This includes, for example, full compliance with the UN Arms Register, publishing Defense White Papers based on the Defense White Paper template adopted by the ASEAN Regional Forum;[34] and the publication of annual strategic assessments modeled on the International Institute of Strategic Studies' *Military Balance* and *Strategic Survey*.[35]

Despite some progress on the Chinese side, DoD is not satisfied with the absence of candor and "depth" in the "strategic dialogue," and the Pentagon is growing increasingly frustrated with the lack of transparency and ac-

---

34. See CSCAP Working Group, *Promoting Regional Transparency: Defense Policy Papers and the UN Register of Conventional Arms* (Honolulu: Pacific Forum CSIS, 1996).

35. Indeed, the PLA National Defense University did so for the first time in 1998. See Pan Xiangting, ed., *Shijie Junshi Xingshi, 1997–1998* (World Military Situation, 1997–1998) (Beijing: Guofang Daxue Chubanshe, 1998). This volume also contains a brief discussion of China military expenditure, security environment, and defense policy (pp. 268–72), as well as a discussion of U.S.-China military exchanges (pp. 279–81). A follow-up volume was published in 1999: Pan Xiangting and Ku Guisheng, eds., *Guoji Zhanlüe Xingshi Fenxi, 1998–1999* (Beijing: Guofang Daxue Chubanshe, 1999). In 2000, the Academy of Military Sciences Strategy Department initiated its own annual strategic survey. See AMS Strategy Department, ed., *2000–2001 Nian Zhanlüe Pinggu* (Beijing: Junshi Kexue Chubanshe, 2000).

cess to Chinese military installations. As former JCS Chairman Shalikashvili noted in his 1997 speech at the PLA National Defense University:

> We should not fool ourselves. Improving military-to-military contacts will not be easy. And in order to earn big dividends, we must make a big investment. If we listen to the suspicious side of our military minds, if we do not pursue exchanges on a fair and equitable basis, if we lack openness, transparency, or reciprocity, or if we hold back even routine information on our military forces, then we will fail.[36]

While there is frustration among many on the American side, some closely involved in the exchanges believe that the United States has expected too much, too fast and has "set the bar too high" by unrealistically expecting the PLA to reciprocate at the same level of information openness and access to military facilities provided to Chinese (and other) foreign military visitors. This argument coincides with the PLA's explanations that because of the great disparity between American and Chinese forces, that the United States can afford to be more open; that the PLA has a different history and culture; and that transparency must be increased gradually, in tandem with the overall development of political and military relations.

There is some truth in these Chinese arguments, but they nonetheless mask a fundamental reluctance to open up the Chinese military establishment to foreign scrutiny. Such reluctance breeds suspicions. Sometimes this penchant reaches unreasonable and infuriating lengths, as when the PLA denies well-known facts and repeatedly rebuffs U.S. requests for visits to various installations. What the Chinese side does not realize is how much foreign analysts already know about Chinese military doctrine, capabilities, expenditure, and deployments—and this is the case in the private and scholarly sectors, to say nothing of U.S. government intelligence agencies. For example, the PLA would have a much clearer sense of the level of public knowledge abroad if studies recently published in the West were translated into Chinese.[37] Indeed, the issue of the translation into Chinese and open sale in China of the present volume offers an interesting test. Translation of such Western publications might make the PLA realize the futility of trying to hide well-known basic data.

36. General John M. Shalikashvili, "U.S.-China Engagement: The Role of Military-to-Military Contacts" (speech at PLA National Defense University, May 14, 1997).

37. When I broached the possibility of publishing Chinese translations of such studies with the Academy of Military Sciences Press, I was told that such translations would have to be restricted to "internal" channels and could not be made available to the general Chinese public.

A further problem in the area of transparency lies on the American side. That is, the PLA is actually quite transparent about a wide range of subjects in Chinese-language publications. Hundreds of books and dozens of periodicals published in China are routinely available to Americans (or any foreigner).[38] The primary sources used for this book are testimony to the range of materials and valuable information available in China. The problem lies in the fact that precious few American analysts and scholars of the PLA buy and use these materials in their research. Worse yet, the U.S. government makes little attempt to collect and translate these materials into English.[39]

PURSUING MILITARY EXCHANGES IN AN INCREASINGLY POLITICIZED ENVIRONMENT

Military exchanges in the period ahead will have to be very carefully managed on the American side, as the Pentagon's relationship with the PLA has come under increasing scrutiny (and criticism) from Congress and the media. Visits to Washington, D.C., by Defense Minister Chi Haotian, Deputy Chief of General Staff Xiong Guangkai, and CMC Vice-Chairman Zhang Wannian have all been sharply criticized in newspaper articles. General Chi was castigated for his role as chief of staff during the 1989 Tiananmen massacre, General Xiong for being the PLA's chief intelligence officer and for his alleged role in the 1996 Democratic Party fund-raising scandal (in which his deputy Major General Ji Shengde "donated" $300,000 to Democratic National Committee go-betweens), and General Zhang as a "butcher of Beijing."[40] One article counted "at least six PLA general officers with substantial responsibility for murdering their own young people, who have received full military honors here."[41] Some specialists in conservative Washington think tanks have also been openly critical of the military exchange relationship. For example, Richard D. Fisher, formerly of the Heritage Foundation and now with the Jamestown Foundation, is quoted as saying: "The ex-

38. To be sure, a number of publications are classified various levels of *neibu* (internal) circulation, but there are still a wealth of nonclassified publications available.
39. Only a miniscule portion of PLA periodicals and *Jiefangjun Bao* are routinely translated by the FBIS.
40. See Edward Timperlake and William C. Triplett II, "Mr. Clinton's Chinese Generals," *Washington Post*, February 12, 1999; Steven Mufson, "Dueling Invitations for Chinese Generals Visit," ibid., January 24, 2000. On General Ji's case, and his indictment in China, see John Pomfret, "Beijing to Indict Ex-Army Spy Chief," ibid., July 17, 2000.
41. Timperlake and Triplett, "Mr. Clinton's Chinese Generals."

perience thus far in our military-to-military exchange with China has been one in which the benefits have flowed largely one way, that is to China."[42] Fisher belongs to a loose alliance of members of Congress, congressional staff, think tank fellows, Republican Party political operatives, conservative journalistic pundits, Taiwan lobbyists, former intelligence officers, and some academics, who call themselves the "Blue Team"—euphemistically named for the enemy forces in PLA war games—which raises concern about Chinese military modernization in Congress and the public.[43]

Many of these concerns were expressed in the famous Cox Committee report of 1999, the study of a House of Representatives Select Committee on "U.S. National Security and Military/Commercial Concerns with the People's Republic of China."[44] Congressman Dana Rohrabacher (R.-Calif.) succinctly stated the view shared by many in Congress: "There is no country in the world that we are more likely to be at war with ten years from now than Communist China, and here we are modernizing their military. It is crazy to modernize a potential enemy's ability to fight a war, and that's what we're doing. It is insanity!"[45]

Similar views have been aired in the media, particularly the *Washington Times,* and some books with tantalizing titles like *Red Dragon Rising: Communist China's Military Threat to America* and *The China Threat: How the People's Republic Targets America* have been published.[46] These are influential in Congress and with the American public.

Bowing to these prevailing views, in 1998–1999 the U.S. Congress began to attach conditions to legislation that would constrain bilateral military exchanges, increase congressional oversight of the exchanges, and increase the Pentagon's reporting requirements to Congress. The most noteworthy of

42. Rowan Scarborough, "Experts Say U.S. Should Review Military Exchanges with China," *Washington Times,* May 27, 1999.

43. See Robert G. Kaiser and Steven Mufson, "Blue Team Draws a Hard Line on Beijing: Action on Hill Reflects Informal Group's Clout," *Washington Post,* February 22, 1999; J. Michael Waller, "Blue Team Takes on Red China," www.insight-mag.com, May 2001.

44. Part of the report was declassified and released to the public on May 25, 1999. See *Report of the Select Committee on U.S. National Security and Military/Commercial Concerns with the People's Republic of China* (declassified version, May 25, 1999) (Washington, D.C.: Government Printing Office, 1999).

45. Quoted in Bill Gertz, "Military Exchange with Beijing Raises Security Concerns," *Washington Times,* February 19, 1999.

46. Edward Timperlake and William C. Triplett II, *Red Dragon Rising: Communist China's Military Threat to America* (Washington, D.C.: Regnery Publishing, 1999); Bill Gertz, *The China Threat: How the People's Republic Targets America* (Washington, D.C.: Regnery Publishing, 2000).

these legislative "riders" was a lengthy section attached to the Fiscal Year 2000/2001 National Defense Authorization Act, which included (a) a "limitation on military-to-military exchanges and contacts with the Chinese People's Liberation Army" (Sec. 1201); (b) an annual report [by the Pentagon] on the "military power of the People's Republic of China" (Sec. 1202); and (c) the creation of a Center for the Study of Chinese Military Affairs (Sec. 914). This legislation established clear limits and extensive reporting requirements for the Department of Defense in its contacts with the PLA. The restrictions include forbidding any PLA personnel exposure to the following specified U.S. military capabilities:

- Force projection operations
- Nuclear operations
- Advanced combined-arms and joint combat operations
- Advanced logistical operations
- Chemical and biological defense and other capabilities related to weapons of mass destruction
- Surveillance and reconnaissance operations
- Joint war-fighting experiments and other activities related to a transformation in warfare
- Military space operations
- Arms sales or military-related technology transfers
- Access to a Department of Defense laboratory
- Release of classified or restricted information
- Other advanced capabilities of the armed forces

In addition, the act specified new conditions related to China's entry into the Missile Technology Control Regime, technology transfer, launch of U.S. satellites on Chinese rockets, export of high-performance computers and end-use verification for these, and Chinese espionage in the United States. Another concern of the Congress is that the U.S. military is inadvertently assisting PLA modernization through the provision of technical and operational manuals. While many are not classified, neither are they easily obtained—yet, as a means of "exchange," these manuals regularly find their way into PLA hands and are translated and published by the dozens every year by the Academy of Military Sciences Press and other military publishers in China. Many of these manuals are sent to the PLA as part of the reciprocal agreement for "exchange of materials" between the respective U.S. and PLA National Defense Universities, although knowledgeable sources claim that the PLA sends no materials in return.[47] Ironically, and unbeknown to either Congress or the Pentagon, many of these manuals also find their way to China via the Library of Congress's routine periodicals exchange with the National Library of China.[48] A substantial portion of the journals requested by China for exchange relate to U.S. military affairs.

Section 1201 of the FY 2000 National Defense Authorization Act also stipulated that the Department of Defense compile a report of visits by PLA general or flag-grade officers to the United States over the previous decade. This report was submitted to Congress in June 2001.[49] Several hundred pages in length, this report contains a substantial amount of information about PLA visits but virtually no qualitative assessment of the pros and cons of these past exchanges.

Many of the concerns raised by Congress are legitimate, and it is entirely appropriate that tighter scrutiny be exerted over exchanges with the PLA. While such exchanges can increase the clarity of each side's strategic viewpoints and reduce misperceptions, and to some extent deterrence is served by showing the PLA some of the strengths in America's arsenal, the exchanges must be more reciprocal.

What, then, should be the guidelines for the United States in pursuing exchanges with the PLA?[50] First, it *is* in American national security interests to have dialogue and interaction with the PLA. Having no channels of communication serves no constructive purpose and raises the real risk that a military confrontation (e.g., over Taiwan) could escalate dangerously. Second, military exchanges must reflect the status of overall Sino-American relations and should not be permitted either to be a "freestanding" element or to progress ahead of broader bilateral relations, particularly in the security realm. Implicit in this guideline is that the Department of Defense should coordinate closely with the White House and Department of State in formulating the package of exchanges each year, although DoD should administer them. Third, four levels of exchanges are appropriate: high-level strategic and defense policy dialogue; functional and educational exchanges (within the aforementioned parameters); confidence-building measures; and

47. Interview with Department of Defense personnel, February 10, 2000.
48. See David Shambaugh, "The Library of Congress' Contemporary China Collection (Social Science): An Assessment with Recommendations" (March 15, 1999).
49. Office of the Secretary of Defense, *Report to Congress of Past Military to Military Exchanges and Contacts between the U.S. and PRC* (2000).
50. The following represents personal views only.

joint participation in multinational security forums. Fourth, the United States should pursue a deliberate program that is keyed to clear benchmarks of progress, as well as to the limits established by Congress, and appropriate committees in Congress should be kept informed of exchanges in a timely fashion. Fifth, in general, expectations should be kept modest and any dissatisfaction clearly conveyed to the Chinese side. In addition to these broad considerations, several other recommendations are important:

- Exchanges should be bureaucratically anchored in the Office of the Secretary of Defense (OSD). In past years, PACOM tried to initiate and run its own set of exchanges with the PLA, and the PLA tried to manipulate these exchanges vis-à-vis OSD.[51]

- Establish a working group, chaired by the undersecretary of defense for international security affairs (ISA), that brings together all services, PACOM, and relevant offices to oversee and coordinate the exchanges.

- Do not expect equal access or precise reciprocal transparency with the PLA, but "pair" exchanges wherever possible.

- Broaden and deepen exchanges with PLA general headquarters, services, and military regions to the extent possible. Try all possible methods to have exchanges with real operators instead of intelligence (GSD Second Department) personnel.

- Know the history of exchanges and be familiar with the negotiating record prior to high-level exchanges.

- Brief all DoD delegations broadly on Chinese strategic culture, negotiating strategies, and the status of China's military modernization.

- Do not permit military exchanges to be a back door to meetings with high-ranking civilian officials, such as the secretary of state, vice president, or president (except under exceptional circumstances).

- Be mindful of the impression left, and real effects on, third parties in the Asia—particularly Japan and other American allies.

- Do nothing to augment the PLA's force projection capabilities.

- Devote increased financial resources for intelligence monitoring of the PLA—including a sustained effort to translate PLA publications.

51. See John Pomfret, "Even Up Close, China's Vision of U.S. Is Out of Focus, Defense Officials Indicate," *Washington Post*, February 15, 1998.

· Boost the China-related Foreign Area Officer (FAO) Program in the U.S. Army and Navy, and establish a similar program in the U.S. Air Force.

· Carefully monitor the lab-to-lab exchange programs.

· Establish funding for civilian "Track II" exchanges with the PLA via universities and research institutes.

Military exchanges should also become more value oriented. For example, the quality of exchanges can be improved in several potential areas:[52]

· Intensification of high-level strategic dialogue and expansion to different levels of the military and civilian national security bureaucracies.

· Expansion of regional security discussions to include Japanese, South Korean, and Russian armed forces.

· Initiation of functional exchanges in the areas of military medicine, environmental security, disaster, and humanitarian relief.

· Familiarization briefings to encourage mutual transparency, on topics such as doctrine, force structure, threat perception, national security decision making; defense expenditure, defense conversion, and civil-military relations.

· New confidence-building measures: more agreements to prevent accidental military confrontations, such as the Maritime Military Consultative Agreement, and to establish secure communications links and possibly provide notification of major weapons tests and exercises.

· Expansion of PLA participation in UN peacekeeping operations (PKO).[53]

· Dialogue and exchanges on nuclear weapons safety.

· Hosting PLA personnel at the Center for Asia-Pacific Security Studies in Honolulu, and arranging exchanges with PLA staff colleges as a means of becoming familiar with the next generation of PLA officers and with the ways the PLA's new doctrine is being operationalized.

52. This list draws from various discussions with U.S. military personnel involved in managing the exchanges and, in part, on Ashton B. Carter and William J. Perry, "The Content of U.S. Engagement with China" (Stanford-Harvard Preventive Defense Project, 1998).

53. See Bates Gill and James Reilly, "Sovereignty, Intervention and Peacekeeping: The View from Beijing," *Survival* 42, no. 3 (Autumn 2000): 41–59.

- Joint activity in combating nonconventional and transnational security threats, such as terrorism, organized crime, alien smuggling, and narcotics trafficking.

- Possible coordination of export control measures and closer consultation on implementing arms control accords.

This blueprint will be difficult to realize. The PLA will certainly have difficulty responding to requests for triangular meetings with Japanese Self-Defense Force (JSDF) personnel or multilateral meetings with Japanese, Russian, and South Korean military personnel; participation in joint exercises (the PLA has repeatedly refused to enter joint exercises as a matter of principle and policy since 1949); joint humanitarian relief (although there may be room for "parallel" action); accepting U.S. military personnel for training in Chinese military institutions; exchanges involving nuclear weapons; and expanded transparency. But they are areas that could potentially prove fruitful.

Clearly, as the U.S. government proceeds with its exchanges with the PLA, caution is required. Larry Wortzel of the Heritage Foundation, formerly a U.S. Army attaché in China, who has had substantial experience in bilateral exchanges with the PLA, argues for a "simple standard to govern future military cooperation [with the PLA]: [The United States] should do nothing to improve the PLA's capability to wage war against Taiwan or U.S. friends and allies, its ability to project force, or its ability to repress the Chinese people."[54] These are clear and sensible benchmarks and suggest a military exchange relationship limited essentially to dialogue and interchange, without any exchange of matériel or training. As long as the United States and China have divergent and sometimes conflicting strategic interests, it is not appropriate to enter into any kind of hardware or technology transfers with the PLA, nor to train PLA officers in U.S. military academies. Yet a robust program of dialogue can, and should, be pursued. This is warranted as a confidence-building measure (CBM) to reduce misperceptions and potential miscalculations. If and when Sino-American security interests and strategic perspectives begin to coincide, it will be appropriate to expand the range of interactions and visits to installations. Transfers of weapons and defense technology will remain inadvisable (certainly as long as post-Tiananmen sanctions remain in place).

The United States must carefully monitor the modernization of the PLA.

---

54. See Larry Wortzel, "Why Caution Is Needed in Military Contacts with China," *Heritage Foundation Backgrounder*, no. 1340 (December 2, 1999): 6.

At the same time, it should recognize that China has a sovereign right to develop its armed forces and that this process is protracted and complex. Currently, the PLA's conventional capabilities and weaponry are, at best, of early 1980s NATO vintage (notwithstanding ballistic missiles and nuclear weapons). As the revolution in military affairs advances militaries faster and further ahead along the technological curve, the PLA falls relatively further and further behind. While its gap with the state of the art may actually be widening, this does not mean that the PLA is unable to meet certain key niche needs in national defense and move ahead with reform of various aspects of military modernization, and potentially challenge its neighbors and American interests.[55]

A more modern, reformed PLA will be a fact of life for the United States and China's neighbors. Whether the PLA is modernizing, and will continue to do so, is not the operative question. Rather, the key questions are, to what ends will this more modern military be put, and will the United States and its allies in the Asia-Pacific region be able to coexist peacefully with a stronger China and a more modern Chinese military?

55. See Thomas Christensen, "Posing Problems without Catching Up: China's Rise and Challenges for U.S. Security Policy," *International Security* 25, no. 4 (Spring 2001): 5–40.

Name Index

Subject Index

AAM (air-to-air missile), 260, 263, 264

Academy of Military Sciences (AMS): administrative authority over, 120, 179–180; AMS Press and, 183, 294, 345n37, 348; Balkan war and, 6; concepts and, 57; during Cultural Revolution, 114; heliborne forces and, 100; research and, 180, 182; revolution in military affairs and, 74, 76, 80–81, 180; Taiwan and, 309–310, 311

accounting/auditing procedures, 185, 203. *See also* zero-based budgeting (ZBB) initiative

"active defense": as doctrine, 57, 68, 74; redefinition of, 62–66, 68

Afghanistan conflict, 6–7, 330

airborne warning and control (AWAC), 265

aircraft carrier, 270–271

air defense weapons: PLA arsenal, 256–258; Taiwanese capabilities, 323–324

air power: Afghan war and, 7; Gulf war and, 1; Yugoslav war and, 6, 85–87, 88

air-to-air missile (AAM), 260, 263, 264

All-Army Political Work Conference, 24, 28

amphibious capability, 270, 320–322, 324–326; exercises and, 102–103, 104

AMS. *See* Academy of Military Sciences (AMS)

annihilation, 58, 318–319

Anti-Chemical Corps, 89, 155

anti-ship missiles, 267, 281–282

anti-submarine warfare (ASW) capability, 269, 321

APC (armored personnel carrier), 255–256

Archive Office (GSD), 131

armed forces. *See* People's Armed Police (PAP); PLA (People's Liberation Army)

armed services. *See* force structure; PLA Air Force (PLAAF); PLA Ground Forces; PLA Navy (PLAN); PLA Second Artillery

armor construction, 254

armored personnel carrier (APC), 255–256

arms embargo, 21, 71, 99, 230, 260, 265–266, 331–332

arms purchases (by China): arms embargo (1989) and, 21, 71, 99, 230, 260, 265–266, 331–332; defense industries and, 70–71, 229–230; Israel and, 230, 257, 265; Russia and, 4, 70–71, 99, 218, 230, 257, 261, 262–264, 266–268, 270–271, 282–283, 330; United States and, 99, 230

Compositor:	Integrated Composition Systems, Inc.
Text:	10/13 Aldus
Display:	Aldus
Printer and Binder:	Thomson-Shore, Inc.
Indexer:	Marcia Carlson